Europe Reshaped 1848–1878

Blackwell Classic Histories of Europe

This series comprises new editions of seminal histories of Europe. Written by the leading scholars of their generation, the books represent both major works of historical analysis and interpretation and clear, authoritative overviews of the major periods of European history. All the volumes have been revised for inclusion in the series and contain updated material to aid further study. *Blackwell Classic Histories of Europe* provide a forum in which these key works can continue to be enjoyed by scholars, students and general readers alike.

Published

Reformation Europe 1517–1559
Second Edition
G. R. Elton

Europe Reshaped: 1848–1878
Second Edition
J. A. S. Grenville

Europe Transformed: 1878–1919
Second Edition
Norman Stone

Forthcoming

Europe Hierarchy and Revolt: 1320–1480
Second Edition
George Holmes

Renaissance Europe 1480–1520
Second Edition
John Hale

Europe Divided: 1559–1598
Second Edition
J. H. Elliott

Europe: Privilege and Protest 1730–1798
Second Edition
Olwen Hufton

Europe in Crisis: 1598–1648
Geoffrey Parker

Europe Unfolding: 1648–1688
John Stoye

EUROPE RESHAPED
1848–1878
Second Edition

J. A. S. Grenville

Copyright © J. A. S. Grenville 1976, 2000

The right of J. A. S. Grenville to be identified as author of this work has been asserted in accordance with the Copyright, Designs and Patents Act 1988.

First published in 1976 by Fontana Paperbacks
Second edition first published by Blackwell Publishers Ltd 2000

2 4 6 8 10 9 7 5 3 1

Blackwell Publishers Ltd
108 Cowley Road
Oxford OX4 1JF
UK

Blackwell Publishers Inc.
350 Main Street
Malden, Massachusetts 02148
USA

British Library Cataloguing in Publication Data

A CIP catalogue record for this book is available from the British Library.

Library of Congress Cataloging-in-Publication Data

Grenville, J. A. S. (John Ashley Soames), 1928–
    Europe reshaped, 1848–1878 / J. A. S. Grenville, — 2nd ed.
        p.   cm. — (Blackwell classic histories of Europe)
    ISBN 0–631–21914–5 (alk. paper). — ISBN 0–631–21915–3 (pbk.)
        1. Europe—Politics and government—1848–1871. 2. Europe—
    Politics and government—1871–1918. I. Title. II. Series.
    D389.G73   2000
    940.2'8—dc21   99–16617
                                                                        CIP

Typeset in 10.5 on 12pt Sabon
by Kolam Information Services Pvt. Ltd, Pondicherry, India
Printed in Great Britain by TJ International, Padstow, Cornwall

This book is printed on acid-free paper

Contents

Maps

Preface to the Second Edition

The first edition of *Europe Reshaped 1848–1878* has now been used by students for many years and gone through several printings. The readiness of the new publisher, Blackwell, to reset the text made a revision possible. My first consideration was whether I would have chosen the same structure today. For clarity, and to reflect the Europe I was writing about, the decision to organize the book around national divisions was then and is still, I believe, the best approach.

Second, should the historical account be widened to include more aspects of social history such as leisure or culture? *Europe Reshaped* can make no claim to be a 'total history'. Such an approach is of great value, but in a relatively short account to have included a much wider sweep of historical change would not have allowed sufficient detail and so led to mere generalizations of the important events discussed.

The decision to concentrate on the 'great powers' and to deal with smaller countries mainly in relation to them was explained in the preface of the first edition. In this edition I have at least briefly attempted to deal with the smaller nations from a perspective other than as mere pawns fought over by their bigger neighbours. The further reading now adds references to good national histories of countries not fully dealt with in this volume.

In two respects a substantial revision was required. In the 1970s when people in Britain spoke about Europe what they meant was continental Europe across the Channel. Today this is no longer true. During the later years of the Victorian age contemporaries including Gladstone thought that Britain was the model, with its sovereign parliamentary government, free trade and liberties, which, as the continentals advanced along the road of civilization, other nations would follow, some sooner, others later. What halted this progress and reversed it on the continent of Europe? How evident was the divergence between Britain and continental Europe already during the third quarter of the century? This theme in modern European history is hardly touched on in the first edition. In that edition Britain appeared only when briefly affecting the reshaping of continental Europe and usually in a secondary role except for the Crimea. In this edition I have added two chapters: 'Great Britain: Cautious Reform in the Authoritarian Decade', and '"Pax Britannica" at Home and Abroad'. They show that the growing differences between continental and British developments in the longer term were more significant than those that seemed similar.

In this new edition another change needs to be noted. In what was the 'Introduction' of the first edition I attempted an overview. The importance of fundamental underlying influences such as population growth was only briefly referred to. The impact of the industrial revolution and demographic trends, which were fundamental to the changes taking place, are in this edition more substantially analysed. The original short introduction has become a full chapter 1, 'Foundations: Europe 1848–78'.

Finally, in the light of more recent scholarship I have revised some of my views. In my own work as a historian I have written books based primarily on archival research which other historians were able to profit from in writing useful general syntheses. In *Europe Reshaped* the reverse is true and I am indebted to the many excellently researched works of my colleagues. The bibliography provides an indication of that indebtedness. It could have been greatly extended to include books I have not read in full or part. I am also grateful to Blackwell's publishing staff for their care in producing this new edition, and not least to Mrs Pauline Roberts who took such an interest and pains to type the substantial additions and alterations.

J. A. S. G.

The Institute for German Studies, The University of Birmingham,
March 1999

Preface to the First Edition

In writing this volume I have found no difficulty in accepting the general stated aim of the Fontana History of Europe. There is a place and a need for a narrative history of what used to be called 'political history'. Though social and economic history has now won for itself a more important place than when this series was first conceived, it seemed to me that no more was called for than a shift in emphasis. I have tried to clarify, on the basis of as much of the recent research as I could master, the great political and international changes of the years from 1848 to 1878. Such a revaluation has become especially necessary during the last twenty years when so much scholarship of the highest standard has been published. Any general history is overwhelmingly indebted to the patient research of many historians and in sifting through sometimes controversial interpretations, I have tried to steer a sensible, uncluttered course. One important aim of such a volume as this is to present a synthesis.

A criticism that has some force is that historians presenting what they claim to be 'European' history generally finish up writing the histories of the 'great powers' of Europe instead. What can be said in mitigation is that the great majority of the European peoples during the third quarter of the nineteenth century were subjects of one or other of the great powers. Further, that in analysing the forces of change the small states may be studied in their relations with the great powers. That is not to claim that the history of France should be investigated in preference to the history of Switzerland or of Spain.

My choice of subject matter was, therefore, not dictated by 'great power' chauvinism; rather by the practical consideration that it was better to deal with some major problems in depth rather than to spread the narrative encyclopedically over all regions of Europe. It also strikes me as undesirable, when considering this period of the nineteenth century, to attempt to force all problems into a 'European' mould. The divisive force of nationalism dominated the history of these years and social conflicts need to be studied in relation to the particular place or region where they occur. Where, on the other hand, a movement such as '1848 revolutions' can be considered from a European as well as a local standpoint I have tried to do so.

My thanks are due to the Librarians of the London Library, the British Museum, and the Library of Birmingham University, to numerous students over the last twenty years who, in tutorials and essays, have raised the questions that concern them, and to my colleagues who have discussed aspects of European history with me. Richard Ollard has not only been perspicacious in his editorial comments, but was unfailingly encouraging when personal circumstances made it more difficult to complete the book. In common with other authors in the series, I owe a debt to Professor J. H. Plumb who read the typescript. Miss Claire Lakin typed the difficult manuscript, whilst also coping with many other tasks. I am glad of this opportunity of expressing my gratitude for her help. Miss Gillian Briggs then retyped the heavily corrected typescripts with unfailing cheerfulness despite their frequently gruesome appearance!

Finally, I dedicate this book to Patricia, my wife, who ensured that the book was finished in serenity and happiness.

J. A. S. G.
Birmingham, July 1975

I

Foundations: Europe 1848–1878

For thirty years the monarchs and statesmen of Vienna had sought to give Europe peace and stability. Though the treaties of 1815 had been modified in detail, they had stood the test of time extraordinarily well. The problem of adapting policies at home successfully to the needs of changing society proved far more difficult. Social change was slowest in Russia and here repression could arouse less serious protest. In complete contrast, change was fastest in Britain, but the practical reforming policies of the Whigs and the Tories in the 1830s and 1840s contained social tensions and forestalled outbreaks of violence. Over the rest of the continent of Europe, during the year 1848, there occurred a massive breakdown of social coherence and government. The upheaval seemed all the greater because nothing so widespread had occurred so suddenly before. The forces of authority were eclipsed; yet as the wave of violence passed they were seen to be very much intact. So it becomes more difficult for the historian to explain why they had been eclipsed at all than to account for their eventual success.

The three decades that followed 1848 were a period of reform, authoritarian reform from above. Everywhere except in Russia the period closes with the transformation of government from the more or less autocratic to the constitutional. Before 1848, parliamentary assemblies worthy of the name were the exception rather than the rule. France and Britain were the leading constitutional European states. Not all these representative assemblies possessed equal powers to control the executive but by 1878 the participation of elected parliaments was recognized virtually everywhere except in Russia as an indispensable element of good government. In Vienna, Berlin, Budapest, Rome, Paris and London, the parliamentary assemblies were acquiring increasing power; some parliaments were already elected on the basis of universal manhood suffrage. Their progress was unstoppable, though it took defeat in war and revolution before

Russia would concede the inevitable in 1905/6. This increase of democratic influence did not necessarily, however, reflect the intentions of the rulers and their ministers on the continent or even in Great Britain. Bismarck's exercise in 'democracy', for example, was cynical opportunism. Important differences should therefore not be obscured especially the divergence of Britain and France on the one hand moving toward democracy and the other great powers in Europe. Nevertheless liberalism had made great progress.

The 'liberalism' of the mid-nineteenth century is not to be confused with our own contemporary definition. The liberals of the nineteenth century were searching for a just balance. They sought to avoid the tyranny of the masses which they regarded just as destructive as the tyranny of the monarchs. The possibility of a 'dictatorship of the proletariat' was far distant, but the liberals of the mid-nineteenth century understood its dangers. Liberals defeated the Chartist programme of 'one man, one vote' in Britain. In Prussia it was the conservatives such as Bismarck, and in France, Napoleon III, who wished to check the power of the liberals by offering manhood suffrage to the masses. Liberals fought for an effective parliament which should reflect the interests of all the people, but the poor and uneducated were not expected to understand their own interests; they would be represented by the enlightened, better educated and more prosperous members of society. On the question of the franchise the ideas of liberalism changed during the course of the nineteenth century but, in one respect, the tenets of liberalism stood for freedoms still defended in the twentieth century. These are the basic liberties of the individual, rich and poor, from monarch to the humblest citizen. They are now enshrined as aspirations in the United Nations' and the Council of Europe's Conventions for the protection of human rights, though in many parts of the world they are probably less observed today than they were a hundred years ago. Thus when the Frankfurt Parliament of 1848 debated the basic rights in the *Paulskirche* they were doing something of profound significance. They saw the importance of restating the rights of man and of establishing by constitutional means a code of standards so that abuses could be measured against this code and condemned.

The liberals have often been blamed either for deserting their 'working class' allies in 1848 once they, the liberals, had achieved their ends, or, alternatively, for failing to inspire them to complete the revolution against authoritarian rule. In fact the co-operation in the March days of 1848 was fortuitous and unplanned. On the barricades, in Vienna and Berlin, and in the countryside the desperation of the poor, their dissatisfactions and specific grievances, such as manorial dues or the oppressive behaviour of the king's troops, combined with liberal demands for civic freedom and participation in government to produce one heady and, to outward appearances, homogeneous movement which directed its force against the rulers, insisting on their bringing about radical change. But in France the French revolution of 1789 had given the peasants title to their land. This made them deeply conservative and they voted against the militants in Paris.

The poor and disadvantaged of Europe were not on the whole politically minded. The peasants in the German states were to win their freedom from manorial dependence and dues from the enlightened conservative ministers of the king. The liberals on the other hand felt misgivings at this breach of the rights of property, even if the owners were Junkers. Liberals did not hesitate to use troops to suppress peasant risings in the spring of 1848. But the peasants soon ceased to be a revolutionary force anyway. In France they rarely had been. In the towns the journeymen, craftsmen, small masters and artisans were threatened in their livelihood by the growth of industry. They came to look to the conservatives for protection and had little to hope for from the liberals. They had been the most revolutionary element in the towns because they had been hit the hardest by industrial expansion. But when they gathered in the workers' organizations in 1848 they were concerned with their welfare and with the protection of their livelihood, rather than with questions of political power. The measures of economic recovery undertaken by the liberal ministers of 1848 did not benefit them straight away but appeared contrary to their interests, for they strengthened the banks and industry. The best-off work people were generally those employed in the new industries. With a few notable exceptions, such as in some factories in Berlin, they were the least revolutionary.

The 'proletariat', as a class whose cohesion would depend on its consciousness that it was exploited by the bourgeoisie, Marx and Engels believed in 1848 was only just beginning to emerge. The poor were split in the towns and countryside into many differing groups of interests. Marx and the Communist League could count on only a few thousand, possibly only a few hundred, supporters. The organization *politically* of the 'worker' was a task for the future. The more far-seeing conservatives sought to outbid both the liberals and communists for support of the poor by seeking to bring about their economic improvement. Thus the clashes of interests in 1848 and 1849 cannot be reduced to a simple formula of the conflict of three classes, proletariat, bourgeoisie and princes, all motivated by economic self-interest. The progress of the revolution was much more confused. But at the time the propertied did believe that there existed a dangerous widespread communist conspiracy to deprive them of their possessions. Against this spectre they acted with, at times, ferocious violence, as in Paris in June 1848, in what they believed to be the defence of their possessions. For all their talk of the sovereignty of the people, the liberals mistrusted the people. With those leaders who advocated social revolution and resorted to violence they would not compromise; yet left without adequate popular support the liberals, in the end, were working in a vacuum and had to compromise with the crown. All the same they came out of 1848 far better than their weak position might have realistically warranted. In fact they lived to struggle again once more, not ever again in the streets and on barricades, but in parliamentary assemblies. The 1848 revolutions convinced the rulers that the liberals commanded a dynamic force in the state that could not be ignored and needed to be channelled into the safe paths of constitutional forms of government.

Just as reform was granted from above, and did not come about as the direct consequence of revolution, so the fashioning of 'nationalism' into an effective tool of war and diplomacy was also the achievement of those in authority rather than the working out of popular passions. Poets, historians, philologists, and a brilliant array of political philosophers, publicized nationalism and aroused enthusiasm for it. If any period of European history can be called the age when nationalism first triumphed it would have to be the decades of the mid-nineteenth century described in this volume. Europe was transformed when Italy and Germany were united. Simultaneously in Austria national consciousness sharpened internal conflicts and led to the Habsburg capitulation to Magyar demands. In the Ottoman Empire and in the Russian Empire also national risings occurred against established authorities. Yet we must be careful not to oversimplify. The passion of national fervour was generally only one element in a complex development. It served the interests of those who successfully used this weapon to exaggerate its importance. Patriotic history books attributed a degree of national hysteria to the masses in the third quarter of the nineteenth century that recent historical research does not support, whether we consider the history of German or Italian unification or even the insurrection of the Poles in 1863. When nationalism became rampant it did not, as the idealist Mazzini had prophesied, lead to the brotherhood of man, but brought in its train the unparalleled destruction of two world wars in the twentieth century. How differently Bismarck utilized national fervour! He believed he could turn it on and off like water from a tap. During his three wars of limited duration, 'nationalism' was for him no more than a useful ally. Then after 1871 Bismarck attempted to check nationalism again because it was in the nature of European nationalism, as President Wilson too was to discover, that there had to be superior nations which would get their way by force and, in turn, would suppress and partition the inferior. The triumph of

Hungarian nationalism in 1848 spelt the ruin of Slovak nationalism; the triumph of German nationalism in 1870–71, the suppression of Polish nationalism and so on.

The term 'transitional' is an overused historical phrase, yet it is apt when referring to the industrial development of continental Europe during the years covered in this volume. The full effects of the technological inventions and industrial expansion were not felt except in Britain until after 1878. Continental Europe remained overwhelmingly agricultural and the great majority of the people lived in the countryside. During the period covered by this book the vagaries of the weather still remained the single most important influence on the standard of living. Yet the trend of things to come was clear: the spread of the factory system, the railways, the movement from the countryside to the towns, the rising standards of living, though interrupted by cyclical depressions. New processes brought with them severe social tensions as valued old skills became redundant and industrial society began to rely on a smaller proportion of skilled as against unskilled workers. But progress was uneven throughout Europe, generally slowest in the east and the south and fastest in the west.

Britain led Europe and had set in motion the first industrial revolution. Technical inventions and the application of steam power since the late eighteenth century had created in England by mid-century the largest cotton industry in the world. Cotton was also the biggest industrial sector in Britain. By mid-century the groundbreaking phase of the industrial revolution had ended; the 1850s to the 1870s were years of steady growth. Britain relative to the other European countries had become the strongest economy in the world, her exports expanding rapidly dominated in value by textiles, coal and iron. Cotton was still king. Britain continued to rely on the industries established early on in the industrial revolution. A distinctive feature of the British economy first discernible during the third quarter of the nineteenth century was the significance of the income derived from foreign investment and the contribution of shipping, finance and insurance. British merchants were by far the largest world traders with a quarter of all the world trade being British. Britain already by the mid-century was an industrialized trading nation exporting manufactured goods and importing food and raw materials. One of the consequences was the mass migration of people from the countryside to towns. The greater the industrialization, the greater was the internal migration throughout Europe. This change had been most rapid in England and Wales where by 1871 only one-third of the population still lived in the countryside.

London had grown to 2,700,000 in mid-century, having more than doubled since the beginning of the century. By the 1880s London reached 5,000,000. No other European city could match such explos-ive growth in the nineteenth century. Paris was Europe's second most populous city with just over 1,000,000 people in 1850 and 2,300,000 in the 1880s. Berlin was under a 500,000 in 1850, as were Vienna and St Petersburg. What is even more striking is the extent of British urbanization; by mid-century, in addition to London's millions, three cities, Glasgow, Liverpool and Manchester, had populations of over 300,000 and Birmingham with 233,000, Bradford, Bristol and Shef-field were also growing fast. The impact on the social structure and politics of a large mass of factory workers and employees of all kinds was not lost on reformers and on the Whig and Tory governments of Victorian Britain, nor on Karl Marx labouring on *Das Kapital* in the library of the British Museum. In 1851 the majority of people were still working in agriculture, 1,750,000; domestic service overwhel-mingly employing women came second with more than 1,000,000 and the cotton industry employed 500,000. By 1871 domestic service had overtaken agricultural employment, by 1,700,000 to 1,400,000. Over the three decades from 1851 to 1881 the population of Britain had grown from 27,400,000 to almost 39,000,000. Industrialization made possible such growth without the doom laden prophesies of the Reverend Malthus coming true. Agricultural products could be imported from abroad to bridge the gap of British yields and paid from the income of manufacturing exports and trade. Even so an 'excess' of population of more than 8,000,000 emigrated overseas between 1850 and 1890.

The proportion of the population employed in agriculture in this period had in fact declined steadily from under a quarter in mid-century to no more than one in seven by 1880; those employed in manufacture, mining building and construction had reached some 50% in mid-century and remained around that level for the remain-der of the century.

The industrial revolution in Britain as elsewhere in Europe had been stimulated by the railway boom, which had begun much earlier in Britain in the 1830s than in the rest of Europe. By 1850 Britain, a smaller country had more length of lines than the German states, 7,000 miles as against 3,300 miles. British railway expansion con-tinued rapidly in the two decades from 1850 to 1870 doubling the length of lines.

Railway development was entirely financed by private enterprise unlike in the rest of Europe. In the last quarter of the century it had become evident that the British lead in manufacturing would not last and that Germany was poised to overtake her. This caused much anxiety. Yet estimates of the income per head of population put Britain still well ahead of all European countries before 1914. British income from trade and services, the returns on her overseas investments, her colonies and empire maintained her position overall as an economic power of the very first rank.

The industrial revolution in France during its earliest phase was mainly imported from Britain. Technological inventions were copied and British entrepreneurs, engineers and skilled mechanics came to France to set up machinery and to instruct. Early French industrial development was sheltered behind tariff walls of high protection until 1860. By mid-century France no longer relied on technology transfer from Britain but developed its own technological innovations. France was essentially a dual economy, rural and industrial with agriculture and industry contributing roughly an equal proportion of the gross national product.

France's industrialization was impeded by a lack of indigenous coal and competition was made difficult by the need to import it and to transport coal over long distances to the manufacturing centres. The leading export industry was silks, produced mostly in small mills around Lyons. A luxury product, it was made on hand looms and did not easily lend itself to large scale factory manufacture. Thus the 'domestic system' of work in the countryside continued to flourish for luxury goods and modifies a classification of 'rural' as 'identical' with agriculture. Cotton textiles were, however, produced mechanically and so in factories.

The cotton industry was the first to become mechanized in factories by 1815. Compared to Britain, however, the long years of war had pushed France further behind. Heavy industry with demand for iron was stimulated by railway construction and the iron industry grew rapidly in the 1850s and 1860s. Unlike most of the French industrial enterprises, family organized businesses of modest size, in the closing years of the Second Empire, Le Creusot became one of the world's largest industrial enterprises and large scale concerns in the iron and steel industry were organized in 1864 by the *Comité des Forges*. After the revolutionary upheavals from 1848 to 1851 and the economic slump, the 1850s under Napoleon III were the more dynamic period of expansion, golden years by comparison. One stimulant was the boom in the railway construction with the help of state subsidies. In 1850 less than 2,000 miles of railway lines had been constructed. Thirty years later 12,500 miles had been added. Locomotives were now built in France and of such good design that they were also exported.

Paris was transformed by the Prefect of the Seine under the emperor's orders. Baron Haussmann created the wonderful vistas of modern Paris, the great boulevards, cleared squalid slums and modernized the sanitation. It was not only beautiful but troops could easily pass through the city now. Though the revolutionary ardour of

the Parisians was not obliterated Paris had become Europe's spectacular heart of culture. Grand international exhibitions were held
in the city in 1855 and 1867. France in the 1860s was prosperous,
the second industrial power in the world after Great Britain. But
in the longer perspective of time France's golden years were short
lived.

Despite the undoubted rapid industrial progress of the mid-century
this was confined to the areas within the departments of north eastern
France bordering on northern Italy, Switzerland, the German states and
Belgium: coal, textiles and iron in the Nord-Pas-de-Calais, the silk
industry around Lyons, iron and coal in the Loire, cotton textiles in
Alsace and Paris with its diverse industry. The dazzle of Paris obscured
the realities of longer-term decline relative to her neighbours. France
remained a divided economy rural and industrial, in terms of employment predominantly rural. Less than a third of the manual labour force
worked in towns. That was not so different compared to Germany in
1870 but the gap between their respective industrialization would
widen enormously after 1871. French society was divided not only on
class lines but also as between town and country. The large land-own-
ing peasantry was conservative and traditional, workers in the towns
and cities volatile. The revolutionary outbursts in the major urban
centres Marseilles, Lyons and Paris created political upheavals which
did not impact on the other France to anything like the same degree.

During the last quarter of the century France as an industrial
power fell further behind Britain and the recently united German
Empire which had defeated her in 1870–71. More serious even than
the defeat on the battlefield in the longer term was the defeat in the
marriage bed. The French limited the size of their families. With the
exception of Russia, France in 1800 had been the most populous
nation in Europe; by 1910 France had been overtaken by Britain. A
comparison with Germany is even more striking:

	1850 millions	1910 millions		1800 millions	1910 millions
France	35.8	39.6	France	27.3	39.6
Germany	34.0	64.9	Britain*	10.5	40.8

To contemporaries in the 1850s and 1860s this extraordinary divergence, France's relative industrial stagnation after 1871 and Germany's spurt of growth and power was still hidden. The
consequences were profound for the history of Europe.

* Great Britain did not include Ireland; United Kingdom (with Ireland) 1800/1801,
15.9 millions.

Institutional and agrarian reforms in the first two decades of the nineteenth century releasing peasants from feudal obligations provided the necessary prior conditions of Prussian industrialization, but far from benefiting the small peasant farmers, their right to purchase their land enriched the Junker owners of great estates. Industrialization came relatively late to Prussia and the other 38 German states after 1815 divided by many currencies and external and internal customs barriers. The *Zollverein* gradually removed these obstacles until the wars of unification completed the process in 1871.

In Prussia the bulk of state expenditure went on the military. By mid-nineteenth century the relative backwardness of industrialization can be inferred from the little use of steam power in two of the more industrialized regions. In Saxony in 1840 only 50 steam engines were operating and in the Prussian Rhineland provinces 211. Thus the German states had to start from well behind. But then there came a spurt in railway construction and an improvement in communications with the building of canals and roads. Over 8,000 miles of railway line were constructed between 1850 and 1870 and provided the main push for economic growth. In the decade that followed the length of line almost doubled again. The changes that occurred are striking and foreshadowed Germany's future power as an industrial nation in the last quarter of the century. Deep mining developed in the Ruhr in 1850. Alfred Krupp, son of the founding ironmaster Friedrich, began manufacturing Prussian ordnance and the breachloading rifles in Essen. By the time of his death in 1887, Krupps had become under his leadership the largest steel and ordnance manufacturer in the world, employing 21,000. Also from small beginnings, August Borsig began by constructing steam engines in Berlin, and during the railway boom locomotives for the Prussian railways and also later for export abroad. Werner Siemens was a founder of the electrical engineering industry in Berlin and in 1866 invented the dynamo. These were just three of the industrialists who began building their pioneering and internationally renowned enterprises before unification. The expansion of textiles and mining was rapid. Production of pig iron increased from 500,000 tons in 1850 to 2,000,000 just 25 years later, easily overtaking France's 1,500,000.

Most of this industrial development in Berlin, the Ruhr and upper Silesia was taking place in Prussia, only Saxony was as industrialized. Constituting already before unification some two-thirds of Germany, industrialization gave Prussia an even greater preponderance of power.

German industry developed only fully after unification. Like France, up to 1871, Germany had remained predominantly agricultural with the proportion of the rural and town population little changed since early in the century; just over 70% of the population were rural. What had changed was the size of the population as a whole. Despite emigration of over 2,500,000 Germans overseas between 1851 and 1880 (another 1,300,000 emigrated in the following decade) the population of the German states had increased from 34,000,000 in 1851 to 45,200,000 by 1880. Significantly it was by 1871 that for the first time there were more Germans than French people in Europe and the gap rapidly widened to just short of 40,000,000 French men and women in 1910 and 65,000,000 Germans!

The Habsburg Monarchy was one of the four great powers of Europe in the mid-nineteenth century and despite her defeats in Italy and Germany and so her loss of influence in the heart of Europe, the Monarchy (after 1867 Dual Monarchy), remained a great power with a population in mid-century of over 30,000,000 and by 1880 of almost 38,000,000. Her political and economic development, however, differed from that of the other European powers, greatly affected as it was by the structure of a multi-national state. Industrial development was nationally centred in the Austrian dominated regions. The Czech and Austrian lands, Bohemia, Moravia and lower Austria followed the common trend of the initial phases of industrialization in the development of textile centres and engineering. In comparison with France and Germany, the Habsburg Empire's industrialization, however, followed a much slower pace and her agricultural sector was larger, her economy remaining predominantly agrarian and artisan.

As far as the peasantry was concerned their emancipation after the 1848 revolution on conditions not too onerous was a great gain in their lives and benefited agricultural progress. Rapid rail construction after the Austro-Prussian war resulted in 12,300 miles of track in the Austrian and Hungarian parts of the empire by 1880, one important indicator of modernization. A handicap was a lack of coal and coke in the empire except in the Czech lands. Industrialization was most rapid during the third quarter of the century, but lagged behind that of Germany, France and Britain thus widening the gap with them.

Small did not necessarily mean less developed. Belgium with good coal and iron deposits, ease of transport and a manufacturing tradition became industrialized early with Liège and Charleroi two major centres of the metal industry. Verviers north of Liège and Ghent became centres of a thriving modernized woollen and cotton industries. With its extensive railway network and free trade policies, Belgium by the mid-century had become one of the most industrialized countries in Europe with a population of less than 5,000,000 in 1866.

What was true of Belgium was even more true of Switzerland with its population of some 2,500,000 and which despite its linguistic divisions had rapidly outpaced England, Europe's leading industrial nation. A spirit of enterprise and the skill of its workforce, and the development of foreign trade and finance, established the country not only in the production of watches and clocks for the whole of Europe, but also in textiles and machinery.

In contrast, industrialization of the Italian states was mainly con-fined to Lombardy and Piedmont where mills produced silk ready for weaving in other countries particularly France. Progress was slow, much of the industrial processes carried on in small mills or at home. The pace did quicken after unification with railway con-struction but even by 1880 industrialization had made no great progress in a society overwhelmingly of peasants and craftsmen. That such industry as did develop was regionally concentrated mainly in the north-west was a pointer to the economic division of later decades. Her population had not increased dramatically from some 24,000,000 in mid-century to just over 28,000,000 in 1880.

Spain remained one of the poorest countries of Europe, its popula-tion increasing relatively slowly from 15,500,000 to 16,500,000 between 1860 and 1880. There are common characteristics of Eur-opean industrialization to be found in the Spain such as the rapid development of railways in the 1860s. Spain also enjoyed a boom in wine production for some three decades as the fungus phylloxera devastated French vineyards. Mining and metallurgical products rose rapidly in value after the 1860s, indeed for some 30 years after 1869 Spain became the leading exporter of pig lead, but Spain lacked sufficient indigenous coal to meet even her limited needs. Iron ore, later in the century a major export was only beginning to be mined before 1875. Factory production made real strides only in one region of Spain, Catalonia with its capital Barcelona, foreshadowing its working-class socialist future in the twentieth-century history of Spain. The region was the centre of cotton production which despite fluctuations in its fortunes grew rapidly from the 1840s to the 1870s. But looked at overall Spain in comparison with western Europe had not kept pace. Three-quarters of its people depended on agriculture, on her exports of wines and minerals and agricultural products. Her claim to be counted once again as a great European power was irretrievably lost.

Russian industrialization had made little impact before 1860. The great growth of population was taking place in the countryside. Russia was the least urbanized country in Europe. The political and social problems of this rapidly expanding population was the key question which would also determine the growth of agricultural production to feed the people, to provide earnings from exports and create the capital needed for industrialization. The emancipation of the peasantry in the reform of 1861 and its results were crucial to Russia's industrialization which did not expand rapidly until the 1880s. The reforms in Russia are considered in more detail in chapter 15; the burdens imposed on the peasantry in making annual redemption payments for land they did not own but mostly was held by the *mir*, the village commune, did nothing to encourage the more productive use of land. The steady growth of agricultural products was the result of the new cultivation of land by more and more peasants. Their conditions of life and income improved little and created a cauldron of disturbance and unrest. As elsewhere in Europe the first significant stimulus for industrialization in the vast country was the construction of railways. In 1852 the earliest important link was constructed between St Petersburg and Moscow. Little further progress was made in the 1850s. But when railway construction passed from the state into private hands expansion was rapid in the succeeding decades. Besides introducing technical innovations to a backward economy the opening of the country made possible greatly increased export of grain of crucial importance to the Russian economy. The two decades saw some beginnings of industrialization later to become of real significance. For example, the output of oil was just 8,000 metric tonnes in 1863 and rose to 2,673,000 in 1885. By then Russia's oil wells were the only significant producers in Europe. In 1904 Russia produced 10,794,000 metric tonnes of oil. Between 1850 and 1870 Russia's production of pig iron remained at the low levels of Austria before increasing significantly with more rapid industrialization in the early twentieth century. Russia's peasants grew the most grain in Europe with increases of 5% every decade between 1845 and 1865, and 7½% between 1865 and 1875. When the 1840s are compared with the end of the century Russia's grain production had expanded by 26% though her population had more than doubled. Russia remained the poorest country in Europe behind Italy and Spain and far behind the developed western European nations, Britain, Germany and France and the wealthy small countries Belgium, Switzerland and Denmark.

Some important economic and demographic changes in Europe can be illustrated by statistical comparisons (as shown in tables 1–6) which provide a snapshot of the changing national relationships that underlie the historical developments during the third quarter of the century.

Table 1 Population in millions (with changing frontiers where applicable)*

	1800/1	1850/1	1870/1	1890/1
France	27.3	35.8	36.1 (1872)	38.3
Great Britain	10.7	20.9	26.2	33.1
Ireland	5.2	6.5	5.4	4.7
German states		34.0	40.8	49.4
Austria		17.5	20.4 (1869)	24.0
Hungary		13.2	15.4 (1869)	17.5
Italian states	17.2	24.4 (1852)	26.8	30.3
Russia	36.0	68.5	84.5	117.8

Table 2 Grain crops output, annual averages (in million quintals)*

	Austria	Hungary	France	Germany	Italy	Russia	Britain	Ireland
1845–54	50.4	50.2	146.6	122.6		363.3	64.0	23.4
1855–64	60.0	68.1	158.5	153.7	57.2	381.2	68.0	16.7
1865–74	56.5		160.1	204.8	73.1	410.1	70.0	13.5

Table 3 Output of coal and lignite, annual averages (in million metric tonnes)*

	Austria	Hungary	France	Germany	Italy	Russia	United Kingdom
1845–49	0.8	0.02	4.4	6.1			46.6
1855–59	2.2	0.3	7.6	14.7			67.8
1865–69	5.3	0.7	12.7	31.0	0.05	0.5	104.7
1875–79	12.3		17.0	49.9	0.1	2.2	135.7

Table 4 Output of pig iron, annual averages (in thousand metric tonnes)*

	Austria	Hungary	France	Germany	Italy	Russia	United Kingdom
1845–9	146.0	36.0	488.0	184.0		200.0	1,784
1855–9	226.0	80.0	900.0	422.0		254.0	3,583
1865–9	227.0	98.0	1,262.0	1,012.0	20	310.0	4,984
1875–9	283.0	135.0	1,462.0	1,770.0	19	424.0	6,484

Table 5 Raw cotton consumption, annual averages (in thousand metric tonnes)*

	Austria, Hungary	France	Germany	Italy	Russia	Britain
1845–54	26.5	65.0	21.1		21.5	290.0
1855–64	32.7	74.1	42.0	1.8	34.3	369.4
1865–74	40.8	85.9	85.6	11.2	53.1	475.8

Table 6 Length of railway lines, 1914, frontiers in miles (approximate)*

	Great Britain,	France	Germany	Austria, Hungary	Italy	Russia
1840	1,590	270	310	100	13	18
1850	6,500	1,900	3,900	1,100	410	334
1860	9,700	6,100	7,400	3,000	1,200	1,100
1870	14,400	10,400	12,600	6,400	4,300	7,200
1880	18,700	15,400	22,600	12,300	6,200	15,200

* The above figures are based on the statistical appendix compiled by B. R. Mitchell for the Fontana Economic History of Europe, General Editor C. M. Cipolla, vol. 4, Part Two (Collins, 1973). For further details regarding these and other statistics, pp. 738–820. Also for British statistics, Peter Mathias, *The First Industrial Nation: An Economic History of Britain 1700–1914* (Methuen, 1983).

Statistics clearly show the underlying fundamental transformation of Europe during the nineteenth century. The demographic change is one of the most striking. The growth of population not only was a major factor transforming Europe, the excess of the poorest and the persecuted changed the wider world. Their impact on the development of the United States and South America the 'white' Dominions, Canada, Australia and New Zealand, and emigration to the Cape of South Africa all became part of their integral history. Of the estimated 13,000,000 who left Europe to go overseas between 1850 and 1890 more than half were from Great Britain and Ireland. Parallel to this transoceanic migration was Russia's expansion on land to Central Asia and beyond the Urals. The middle period of the century marks the beginnings of an age of mass migration mainly from Europe but also within Europe. The Irish who moved to Britain and the Poles who moved to the Ruhr are examples of this economic migration. The repressions after 1848 on the continent and tsarist persecution of the Jews added a further dimension to European migration.

The statistics of these tables also reveal the acceleration of the pace of change after the mid-century especially on the continent of Europe.

But the people living through these turbulent decades did not have the advantage of hindsight or knowledge of clear patterns. These would show that Germany was on the threshold of powering away and that the gap between the more advanced industrial nations and the less advanced would continue to widen. What concerned contemporaries was whether traditional values would survive? How should policies change to meet the new conditions brought about by the industrial revolution? For rulers the mid-century was an age of uncertainty, of optimism mixed with apprehension. Could peace and order be maintained? The emergent strata of society roughly labelled 'middle class', though this description obscures many differences, now played a significant role in society, and in the economy, and demanded to be listened to and participate in government. Social tensions were increasing. The 'labouring class' brought into close contact in factories and towns could now begin to organize to press their claims and concerns. Conditions of poverty and destitution were no longer accepted as the blind hand of providence. In 1848 the revolutions on the continent of Europe were the clear signal that a wide spectrum of discontent was challenging the existing order.

After the relatively peaceful years from 1815 to 1848, the succeeding three decades, by way of contrast, were punctuated by the wars of the great powers in 1854–56, 1859, 1864, 1866, 1870–71, and in 1877–78. But except for the Crimean War never more than two great powers (not counting Italy in 1866 as a 'great power') were simultaneously at war. Thus warfare during these years never assumed the European dimensions of the Revolutionary and Napoleonic eras or of the two world wars of the twentieth century. The wars of the 1850s, 1860s and 1870s, moreover, were fought, not to attain 'supremacy in Europe' but with well-defined and strictly limited aims; they could, therefore, be ended when these limited aims had been achieved and did not need to be pursued to the complete destruction and 'unconditional surrender' of the enemy.

Looking back on the political, social and international upheavals of these years, the period, seen in the wider setting of what followed, was, nevertheless, comparatively civilized. Despite all the tensions, actual bloodshed, the result of war or civil strife, was confined. Those who ruled were not tyrants oblivious of considerations of human decency and feeling, but, on the whole, they strove for the fulfilment of 'reasonable' national objectives and for the betterment of the people whom they believed they were best equipped to govern. Inevitably personal ambitions also counted for much and, as the succeeding pages show, the developments of the 30 years from 1848 were not just the outcome of inevitable and impersonal forces.

Part One

Revolutionary Europe 1848

2

France and Europe 1848

What the opposition wanted in France in 1848 was to change the government. What the opposition sparked off instead was a revolution. At least it was a half-revolution which swept away the king. But the politicians were not swept away and within a few weeks they tamed the revolution.

From 1789 to 1871 no form of state achieved stability in France in place of the traditional authority of the monarchy. The fall of the monarchy in France and the foundation of the first republic in 1792 was an event of enormous importance; it was a challenge to the old Europe; the dynasty that had ruled France for centuries was overthrown and with it the society and beliefs it stood for. When Charles X in 1830, and Louis Philippe in 1848 were sent into exile, not dynasties were overthrown, or even monarchies as they had existed in France before 1789, and still existed in Europe, but individuals who had served as heads of state. We employ the same word, 'revolution', to describe the fall of Louis XVI,* Charles X,* Louis Philippe and Napoleon III, but a gulf separates the transformation of 1789, from the constitutional changes in France during the era following the Congress of Vienna when heads of state, who took the titles of 'King' or even 'Emperor' and who claimed to rule for life and hereafter through their descendants, were driven from power for failure in war (1815 and 1870) or for having identified themselves in government too closely with an unpopular party (1830, 1848). In Louis Philippe the role of head of the government and head of the state had become so closely bound up with each other that the fall of the former brought inevitably in its train the fall of the latter.

---

* Of course Charles X was a 'legitimist' Bourbon king, but the 'restored' Bourbons, their divine right to rule shattered, proved to be in no stronger a position in nineteenth-century France than rival claimants, royal and republican.

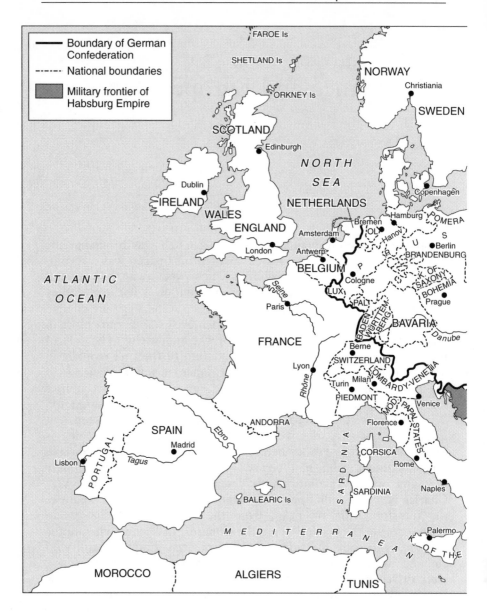

Map 1   Europe in 1848

Rival contestants for power, all of them now lacking unquestioned traditional rights to rule, sought some substitute by appealing to the particular historical tradition most appropriate to their claim. And so they assumed the mantle of one of the great protagonists of the French historical drama, when France during the period from 1789 to 1804 passed from constitutional monarchy, to republic, consulate and empire. Every change after 1830 could be justified by an appeal to the past. The same was true of the opponents of the revolution. Metternich, Tsar Nicholas and Frederick William IV pretended, or believed, the spectre of the great French Revolution was upon Europe once again. Pretended, because it suited their domestic absolutist policies to believe in the French revolutionary bogy as a weapon against European liberalism with its demands for a widening of the basis of power and constitutional government. Possibly they pretended so hard that they really persuaded themselves that what they conjured up was true. After the great French Revolution with its repercussions which plunged Europe into turmoil for a generation, *any* revolution which occurred in France was exaggeratedly hailed as an event of European significance.

The King of the Belgians, directly in the line of revolutionary fire, spoke for the monarchs in general when he expressed his feelings writing to Queen Victoria on 26 February 1848, 'I am very unwell in consequence of the *awful* events at Paris...What will soon become of us God alone knows; great efforts will be made to revolutionize this country; as there are poor and wicked people in all countries it may succeed.'*

The more liberal rulers appreciated that the poor had aspirations which could not easily be satisfied by the preservation of the political status quo. Actually there was no revolution in Belgium, only a fiasco which led to the temporary arrest of Karl Marx. More royal letters followed. On 27 February the King of Prussia called on St George, God, and Old England, the queen and Lord Palmerston to 'proclaim that our forces are united'; this alone would earn Queen Victoria the blessings of millions. But Frederick William IV only wanted a united 'word', no united deeds. A more restrained letter from Tsar Nicholas spoke of the intimate union between Russia and Britain which he thought perhaps existed for the purpose of saving the world.

The continental monarchs were play-acting too. There was to be no conservative coalition of princes as in 1792/3 which would crusade against republican France. There was indeed to be no intervention in 1848 against *revolution* at all. What confused this issue was the attitude the powers should take up on *national* questions entailing shifts in the balance of power. Prussian aggrandizement in

---

* *The Letters of Queen Victoria*, vol. I (London, 1908) p. 149.

the Baltic at the expense of Denmark raised problems of European importance since they affected both Russian and British national interests. That the plight of the Duchies of Schleswig-Holstein became intimately bound up with the German revolutionary fervour of 1848 was seen by the great powers as a further complication. Similarly with Italy, what concerned Britain and France was not the revolutionary fervour of northern Italy or even Italian unification, but the effect of the conflict between Piedmont and Austria on the balance of power.

Palmerston wished to see Austria preserved as a great power in Europe and believed her stronger without her Italian possessions, but he also wanted to contain France and keep her out of northern Italy. The French hoped for a success in Italy for the republic and an increase of territory. With the desires of Italians, none of the foreign ministers of the great powers was primarily interested.

British and Russian pressure in the end helped to induce Prussia to withdraw from the Duchies in the summer of 1848 (p. oo). The diplomacy of the 'Italian question' was equally tortuous and complex. Would the French Republic intervene? Would Britain intervene? Neither did so; the conflict was resolved by the force of arms between Austria and Piedmont (p. ooo).

This leads the historian to an important general conclusion about the revolutions of 1848. Despite considerable diplomatic activity, none of the great powers actually intervened anywhere in Europe in 1848 or affected in any significant way by international action, the course of events. The political forces struggling for predominance during the 1848 revolutions in Europe, in spite of stirring French manifestoes, private monarchical protestations of solidarity, and international socialist manifestations operated locally, each within their national contexts. There was little effective co-operation between any of the political groupings that transcended national frontiers, whether it is socialists, liberals or conservatives we are considering. The lack of co-operation between the 'nationalities', German, Czech, Hungarian, French, Polish, 'Italian', and so on, is an equally striking general feature of the revolutions of 1848.

By the spring of 1849 the revolutionary movements had practically ended everywhere. There was only one important bastion of 1848 left – Hungary. With all international revolutionary dangers past, Russia now intervened in Hungary to help the Habsburg Monarchy. But this 'exception' to non- intervention in the revolutions of 1848 occurred in an already different phase of European history.

How different the politics of Paris in 1848 and 1792 were is illustrated by the departure of the king. Louis Philippe left in panic, but no guillotine awaited him, Guizot or the aristocracy. The flight to England was planned by Featherstonhaugh, the British Consul in Le

Havre. Louis Philippe had abdicated on 24 February 1848 but did not leave France until a week later on 2 March. The king and queen had lived concealed in a gardener's cottage at Honfleur. Guizot hid in Trouville. The royal pair were brought to Le Havre, where the consul passed them off as his uncle and aunt. Consul Featherstonhaugh has provided posterity with an account of the adventure; 'At last came the King, disguised, his whiskers shaved off, a sort of casquette on his head, and a coarse overcoat, and immense goggles over his eyes. Not being able to see well, he stumbled when I advanced, took his hand and said, "Ah, dear Uncle, I am delighted to see you." Upon which he answered, "My dear George, I am glad you are here." The English about me now opened the crowd for their Consul, and I moved off to a quiet and shaded part of the quay. But my dear Uncle talked so loud and so much that I had the greatest difficulty to make him keep silent.'*

The king and queen were at length safely escorted on board the boat for England, where they were among the earliest arrivals in 1848 of that strange assortment of refugees, first royal personages, including the brother of the King of Prussia, also Metternich, then later, with the change of fortunes, the revolutionaries, Kossuth, Marx and others who all claimed asylum. They were all thought quite harmless. All but one of them really was.

Palmerston was ready to accept the provisional government set up in Paris even though formal recognition was delayed. This was in line with the pragmatic attitude which he revealed when he wrote only a few days after the events in Paris, 'We must deal with things as they are, and not as we would wish to have them.' He did not actually welcome the revolution; he believed a republic to be more inclined to endanger peace than a monarchy; he recognized the danger arising from the instability of France and Europe, but Palmerston also rejected any 'ideological' response to revolution. There was no haste. Events would show how British interests were affected. Meantime Britain would avoid taking a harsh line with the new government as that would most likely provoke French aggression.

Alphonse de Lamartine, the new French foreign minister, as a gesture to past revolutionary tradition (he himself was a poet and historian), and to appease the contemporary revolutionary stance, issued a *Manifesto to Europe* on 4 March. Its style was noble. The treaties of 1815 were repudiated *de jure*, but at the same time the frontiers of 1815 and 1830 were recognized and acknowledged in practice. France had no designs on Belgium – this to reassure Britain. There was to be no revolutionary war. France wanted all the world to know that 'we want to go forward in fraternity and

* *The Letters of Queen Victoria*, II, pp. 156–7.

peace'; France would only fight if 'constrained or threatened'. Republican ideals would be spread by words, not by deeds, not by war, but by example.

In the spring and summer of 1848 the French hoped to profit from the conflict between Piedmont and Austria to acquire for themselves Savoy. They offered help to the Piedmontese but Piedmont was not willing to purchase France's alliance in 1848 or 1849 with territorial cession. So the Second Republic held to the peaceful policy laid down by Lamartine on 4 March, notwithstanding the many emigré clubs of Germans, Italians, Iberians, Poles, Belgians, Greeks, Magyars, Rumanians and Swiss who were agitating France to intervene in their national cause. Armed bands actually crossed from France into Savoy and southwest Germany later on in March and early April. Lamartine could not prevent this; he in any case welcomed the departure of the radicals; they posed no real threat to the countries they invaded, lacking the support of French troops. They were a greater threat to a conservative provisional government in Paris. The revolution in France had not made the French political leaders more adventurous at home and abroad, but less.

Yet the mere spread of the 'word' of revolution in France proved no empty phrase. The immediate impact of the news of the fall of Louis Philippe was great; in the little capitals of southern and southwest Germany, in Vienna, in Prague, in Pesth, in Berlin, in the Polish provinces, in Milan, in many parts of Europe it appeared as if something momentous had occurred once again as in 1789. The 'sovereignty of the people' had been proclaimed in Paris which called in question all established authority in Europe. It was now up to the nations of Europe to set themselves free. Opposition to authority, which already here and there had resulted in clashes of arms before February 1848, now drew new strength and inspiration from France. No one knew anything about the nature of this revolution in France. What influenced Europe was not so much the course of events in the France of 1848 as the imagined historical parallel, the revival of the ideas of 1789–95. The restoration had not buried them; in 1848 political leaders and thinkers had to grapple once again with questions about the rights of man, the limits of authority, social, economic and political justice, and the fraternity of nations. What is more, for some exhilarating months, these politicians and thinkers thought that they had an opportunity to put their ideas into practice. In this sense the ideas associated in 1848 with the folklore of the French Revolution of 1789 provided a sort of muddled but common ideology for all the revolutionary movements. Yet each 'revolution' was different. There was no common conspiracy that explains their simultaneous outbreak. The spread of revolution was spontaneous.

The history of the revolution in France in 1848 clearly illustrated the distinction between the struggle for power of rival contesting governing élites (which had led to the revolution in the first place) and the attempt to bring about changes in society and in the lot of the common man which was to lead to bloodshed in June. The revolution in its initial stage was decided in Paris. The conservatism of the peasantry and the countryside as a whole could only make its weight felt later and could not affect the outcome in February 1848. The poor of Paris, the unemployed craftsmen and the workers in their numerous small places of employment still suffering from the depression, attempted to achieve better conditions through political change much as the Chartists hoped to do in Britain. But the parallel with Chartism here ceases. Chartism was a conscious political mass movement attempting by constitutional means to change the political framework. In France by 1848 the impulse was violent, revolutionary and unorganized. The beginnings of what might have become a more conscious political mass movement of ordinary people had been crushed during the early years of Orleanist rule, at Lyon in 1831 and 1834 and in Paris in 1832 and 1834. The parallel here is perhaps with the revolutionary British trade union movement in the 1830s. 'Moderate' Chartism grew though, in strength after the revolutionary failures. No such moderate movement of protest developed in France and, if it had, would not have been tolerated as it was in contemporary England. However conditions of poverty remained whilst a growing consciousness of poverty and rising expectations provided the seed bed for violence in Paris and the urban centres in the 1840s. When authority was shaken in 1848, (as it could not be in the 1830s), a revolutionary force would spring to life, not because the political leaders cynically intended to make use of the masses to succeed in their own efforts for change, but because the conditions were right.

The historian Alfred Cobban has written that '1848 in France was a revolution by accident'.* The revolution was an accident in the sense that the disputes of the governing élites weakened the authority of the whole establishment of the state and created the conditions for a spontaneous revolution not anticipated by the political leaders. In their bitter struggles with each other for power the privileged overlooked the 'politics' of the unprivileged altogether and then found it difficult to control the popular demands for fundamental change voiced by the Parisian poor. But the accidental theory of this revolution does not satisfy, for the long and bitter quarrel between the well-to-do politicians of the Orleanist monarchy was not accidental, nor their selfish disregard for the poor. It cannot be regarded as accidental

---

* A. Cobban, *A History of Modern France*, II (1965), p. 133.

that bad social and economic conditions can move the poor to violence for short periods, even though the poor tend to be the most quiescent section of society viewed from broader historical perspectives.

Louis Philippe had grown old and stubborn. He was seventy-five and survived his overthrow by only two years. He relied for support on the *bourgeoisie*, who had ousted the landed aristocracy from power in the 1830 revolution. However this *bourgeoisie* was no homogeneous 'middle class'. They were not accepted by the aristocracy, born to the ermine, and also separated from the large majority of the people, by reason of wealth or professional position, and by an acute sense of their own importance which in their eyes raised them above the common people. As a privileged group they were as keen on the social differences between them as on those which separated them from 'below'. The wealthy *bourgeoisie* derived their position from the land, finance or industry, and also included in its ranks the men who had reached the top of the professions, and the leading positions in the service of the state. This group jealously guarded its identity and political power from the 'middle' *bourgeoisie*, of the less prosperous and less distinguished professionals and the *petite bourgeoisie* who were excluded from the franchise. Divisiveness went even further. Those who shared a high degree of wealth and status took different sides on the issues of legitimacy and clericalism. The politicians of the *haute bourgeoisie* grasped for power and were locked in bitter rivalry, a state of affairs encouraged by Louis Philippe. He wished to rule himself. His ministers were more civil servants than members of an independent government; the king played them off against each other. So in reality Louis Philippe was both king and 'first minister'. The stratifications and divisions of French society made it possible for Louis Philippe to rule personally, but this later left him without any broad support in the troubles that overwhelmed king and government in February 1848.

The revolution, never intended by the politicians of the *haute bourgeoisie*, was nevertheless started by their rivalry. Guizot dominated the governments of the 1840s as the king's loyal ally. He governed in strict parliamentary fashion, but corrupted parliamentary rule by influencing the electoral process through control of the prefects and *maires* and the deputies by offering various inducements. With the onset of the decline in European prosperity after 1846 the main appeal of Guizot's political programme, which rested on the promise of increasing wealth rather than on widening the franchise, ran into increasing discontent. The rivalry of politicians now coincided with economic distress.

The political 'left' after its disastrous insurrectionary experience of the 1830s disintegrated; the hard core revolutionaries not in prison were driven underground. Military discontent had also been dissipated. During the 1840s demands for reform and attacks on the Guizot government were propagated by two Parisian journals, *Le National* the more moderate, and *La Réforme*, more openly radical. Within the system, the main complaint of the opposition led by Odilon Barrot and Adolphe Thiers was their exclusion from office. Guizot's position in the 1840s appeared virtually impregnable. The parliamentary opposition believed their only hope of gaining office was to make common cause with groups outside parliament who wished to limit royal power and to widen the franchise. It was a dangerous game. Who would be the rider and who would be the tiger?

The organization by the parliamentary opposition of political banquets began in July 1847 in Paris and then spread to the country. These were affairs for the pretty well-to-do. Orator after orator denounced corruption and demanded franchise reform. Thiers in the chamber meantime bitterly attacked Guizot. This was an attack by the privileged on those among them who selfishly sought to monopolize power. The aim was a change of power among the privileged, not a sharing of power with the less privileged. The leaders of this campaign wanted no real change of system, least of all a revolution.

On 14 January 1848 Guizot forbade the holding of the seventy-first banquet in Paris. It had been planned by the elected officers of the National Guard from the XII, the most revolutionary 'arrondissement' of Paris; they had invited the politicians of the opposition to attend and the republicans accepted. Now the politicians were uncertain what to do; they intended to proceed with the banquet, but by prior arrangement with the authorities, to disperse quietly at the request of the police; they thought they had achieved a neat compromise between defiance and acquiescence, but the schemes of the 'privileged' opposition in and out of parliament to put pressure on the king and to secure the dismissal of Guizot no longer influenced the course of events after the opposition paper *Le National* published on 21 February 1848 a detailed plan for a demonstration calling on the people of Paris to support the deputies in a procession to the banquet. That evening, the 21 February, the banquet was cancelled. *Le National* on 22 February counselled calm; only a handful of deputies, led by the eloquent Lamartine, wished to proceed. The parliamentary opposition had taken fright and wished no bloody confrontation in Paris. That evening, on 22 February, a crowd assembled in the Place de la Madeleine, unaware the banquet had been cancelled; a procession of students attracted attention, but a detachment of the tough Parisian police, the Municipal Guard, a force which altogether was some 3,500 strong, was able to clear the crowds.

The 'revolution' occurred during the following two days, on 23 and 24 February. The historian is still inadequately equipped to explain precisely how a crowd of demonstrators was transformed into a force strong enough to carry through a revolution, topple the king and the forces at the command of the established authority which, on the eve of the revolution, seemed overwhelmingly strong. Besides the 3,500 'toughs' of the Municipal Guard, there were 30,000 garrison troops scattered in various barracks and 80,000 members of the National Guard; the Municipal Guard remained loyal to Louis Philippe; the troops were not really tested, the National Guard was, at best, of doubtful value to the dynasty. From all but the wealthiest parts of Paris, this citizen militia with their elected officers, once the mainstay of the July monarchy, had become disenchanted with a régime that so selfishly manipulated the narrow base of administrative and electoral power and denied a vote to all but the rich among them. They would not fight and perhaps die for Guizot and Louis Philippe. Although they did not *make* the revolution, they did nothing to suppress it; some even went over to the 'crowd' and many fraternized with the rioters.

But who organized the revolutionary 'crowd'? Were the barricades and fighting entirely spontaneous? How important were leaders in the crowd? Were they incidental to it or did they play a planned and crucial role in focusing the anger of the crowd? To these questions we unfortunately have no satisfying answers. One thing is clear: there was plenty of inflammable human resentment in Paris where many thousands lived in poverty, misery and desperation, mocked by the fine manners and dress of the better-off.

All day on 23 February the excitement and tension continued in Paris; more people congregated in crowds than before. That afternoon Louis Philippe decided to drop Guizot to appease the parliamentary opposition and the National Guard. An old Orleanist politician, Molé, was appointed to head a new government and Thiers, at first overjoyed, joined the ministry. Now Louis Philippe thought the crisis was over and expected everyone to go home. The parliamentary opposition certainly took that view and many National Guardsmen did go home. There was a lessening of tension, yet obscure leaders gave the situation a further twist. The barricades, which had been hastily thrown up, were not dismantled. In the evening a procession of some two hundred men formed and marched down the Boulevard des Capucines. When they came level with the Ministry of Foreign Affairs, they clashed with troops who would not let them pass. This was the flashpoint. Just as later in Vienna and Berlin, whenever the civilian crowds met troops who were totally inexperienced in such a situation and generally outnumbered, a fatal gunshot was heard – no one could ever discover from which side it was fired – followed by the soldiers discharging a volley into the crowd.

In Paris, the many dead and wounded caused by indiscriminate firing into a crowd sealed the fate of the Orleanist monarchy. The dead were laid in an open cart which was drawn around Paris to inflame the populace. The message was spread that it was better to fight than to wait to be massacred. The situation now slipped out of the control of the privileged would-be banqueters, the aspiring politicians locked in a struggle of 'ins' and 'outs' all of whom had been ready to work within the framework of the July monarchy. It is believed that as many as 100,000 Parisians poured into the streets and they erected hundreds of barricades all over the city. This was a professional job; paving stones, upturned omnibuses, some four thousand trees, lamp posts and railings were all used to create formidable barriers, some of which were ten feet high. Louis Philippe responded by appointing Marshal Bugeaud to command both troops and the National Guard. This was a provocative gesture as Bugeaud had already 'distinguished' himself by 'massacring' the workers of Paris in 1834. Intending to strengthen his hand, Louis Philippe also called on Thiers to head a new ministry. Thiers first insisted on bringing in an outspoken parliamentary opposition leader, Barrot; then Thiers demanded that Bugeaud be relieved of his command. It ended with Bugeaud and the troops being withdrawn from the city. If Thiers believed that he enjoyed general popularity and would be able to exercise authority, he was soon disabused. There was some fighting on 24 February. The revolutionaries were not to be pacified with a mere change of government, the new gang replacing the old. Everywhere the *Marseillaise* could be heard; the spirit of 1789 was alive once more.

The lack of support from the National Guard, the small size of the Municipal Guard and the withdrawal of most of the troops from Paris, left the king and his ministers completely defenceless. Louis Philippe had no stomach for civil war and bloodshed. He might have appealed to the country for support against 'radical' Paris, but he never considered this course of action. He was really too old, had lost all hope of recovery and abdicated in favour of his grandson. So the Parisian crowd had made their revolution; would they now be able to organize a truly revolutionary government that would make a clean sweep of the privileged Orleanist politicians? It was a revolution of a large militant section of the common people of Paris; would power really fall into their hands?

With the abdication of Louis Philippe the focal point of power shifted from the Tuileries to the Chambers. Here the Orleanist deputies tried to maintain their privileges by agreeing to a Regency; but just at this moment when they were trying to manipulate the political pawns to their own advantage, rioters broke in and brought the meeting of the chamber to a chaotic end. Most of the deputies fled; but not every deputy lost his head. There were those who saw an opportunity to make a quick change from being Orleanists to becoming enthusiastic Republicans; they were determined to provide the body of the revolution with a conservative head. The trouble was that for a few hours it seemed there would be two self-appointed heads. That the Orleanist dynasty would end with its first incumbent was clear to the realists. Only the magic of proclaiming a 'Republic' could restore law and order. The politicians remaining in the chamber hastily drew up a list of members of a new government; modesty played little part in their proceedings since they nominated themselves; all belonged to the era of the July monarchy; they were moderate reformers, republicans of expediency rather than conviction. On the list was the poet and historian, Lamartine; probably the cleverest of the group of politicians, he enjoyed great popular prestige. François Arago was a famous astronomer reputed to be a republican, but, in fact, had little sympathy for the workers of Paris; Crémieux and Marie were moderates and opposed to revolutionary demands; Ledru-Rollin, in reputation the most radical and revolutionary, was more of a demagogue than a socialist leader of the people. They hurried to the Hôtel de Ville to be popularly acclaimed by the people. Here they were later joined by four men who had been chosen as members of the government by the newspaper, the *Réforme*: the journalist Marrast; another journalist, Flocon; Louis Blanc, famous for his treatise on the Organization of Labour and a mechanic, Alexandre Martin, who, known as 'Albert', symbolized the representation of the people. The politicians from the chamber were faced with a tricky problem. Wisely they realized they could not appeal to constitutional niceties, so they admitted the men chosen by the newspapers. All these self-appointed leaders of the revolutionary government were received good-humouredly by the crowd. The remarkable fact about 24 February and the days which followed in Paris was that there was much chaos and a cessation of business; police and troops had disappeared, yet there was a total absence of violence or vindictiveness. Political and 'class' opponents were not harmed, shops were not looted and property was respected. Karl Marx called it, with heavy irony, the 'beautiful revolution'. These were the days of hope and romanticism. A new world was being founded by the people. When a few weeks later, in May and in June, disillusion set in, the beautiful revolution turned into bitterness and bloodshed.

During the first days of the revolution the 'Provisional Government' established its authority by responding promptly to the demands of the militant crowds surrounding their hastily commandeered offices in the Hôtel de Ville. On the 24th, Lamartine, standing on the balcony, personally proclaimed the 'Republic'. On the following day Louis Blanc's decree was read to the crowds, 'The Provisional Government engage themselves to guarantee...labour to every citizen. They take it to be necessary for the workmen to associate with one another, in order to reap the legitimate reward of their toil'. On the 28th the 'National Workshops' were instituted. To reassure the working people, a 'permanent commission for the workers' was immediately installed at the Luxembourg Palace under the presidency of Louis Blanc to propose practical measures of help. It began by recommending the abolition of competitive wage bargaining and fixed maximum hours of work. It made no more progress as the members of the commission lost themselves in a cloud of dispute and discussion. This may well be what the conservative members of the provisional government wanted. Louis Blanc was fobbed off with a high-sounding task that diverted his energy from the essential decisions of central government.

The 'socialist' republic appeared established. The next step taken by the provisional government marked a further swing to the conservative republic. This can now be seen with the benefit of hindsight. The provisional government carried on its shaky mandate by turning decisively away from the politics of privilege to democracy. But democracy transformed the socialists from the 'voice' of the people into something less, a minority party of the people. Ledru-Rollin, as Minister of the Interior, was the most radical of the members of the provisional government. Too late did the radicals and socialists realize that democracy, that is universal male suffrage, would lead to the victory of reaction. The peasantry was not only the largest section of voters, but also easily influenced by local notables, and by the clergy. They were suspicious of towns, and fearful for their patches of land. Largely illiterate and beyond the propagandist efforts of left wing political leaders in the urban centres, the majority of the peasantry voted against socialism and the republic. They became the mainstay of the party of order.

On 5 March the provisional government decreed that elections, on the basis of universal manhood suffrage, were to be held on Sunday, 9 April. After radical demonstrations against so early an election which, it was realized, would have the effect of taking away the decision from Paris, the election was postponed until 23 April. The orthodox financial management of the economy by the provisional government meantime polarized politics, while it reassured the owners of property and financiers. All government debts were honoured and interest was scrupulously paid; to balance the budget an extra direct tax, falling heaviest on the peasantry, was decided on. Louis Blanc's scheme of 'National Workshops', which would have involved large-scale government credits to expand industry and thus create employment, was emasculated and only the famous name retained. 'National Workshops', in the sense of places of employment or public works, scarcely existed. Instead, administrative machinery was set up to register the unemployed and pay them a small dole. Only 12,000 men, out of the 120,000 unemployed in Paris, were actually set to work levelling a small hill. The peasantry and unemployed workers, the poor of the country and the poor of the city were set against each other. The peasantry provided constitutional support for the conservative republicans, the party of order, who stood for the inviolability of property. Those who had a stake in property, large or very small, were prepared to defend it by force against the propertyless with their 'anarchist' and 'communist' ideas. To call yourself a 'republican' could, in the France of 1848, mean entirely different things. De Tocqueville described the Paris scene: 'I saw society split in two: those who possessed nothing united in a common greed; those who possessed something in a common fear. No bonds, no sympathies existed between these two great classes, everywhere was the idea of an inevitable and approaching struggle.' Yet the great majority would have accepted the label, 'republican'. The 'defence' of property was to entail in June 1848 the repression of a desperate minority by the government of the republic representing the majority.

The 'defence' was now in April, May and June of 1848, in the hands of the newly constituted National Guard of Paris whose membership had been opened to all and whose strength had reached 100,000 men. They elected moderate and conservative officers early in April. A new police force, the *Garde Mobile*, was formed which was tough and dependable, and five regiments of the regular army were stationed in the city. The National Guard in the provinces and the army outside Paris remained as a potential reserve. A conservative provisional republic could rely on all the force it needed to preserve law and order against any attempt of further social revolution provided its leaders were united and determined to use it. The handling and containment of a huge radical demonstration of 40,000, by the National Guard, was on 16 April already a peaceful curtain-raiser of how the militant crowd had lost the power to influence events.

The elections were a grave but not altogether unexpected disappointment for the left wing in Paris. Ledru-Rollin had done all he could to combat the conservatism of the countryside. As Minister of the Interior he had manipulated the electoral administration, but the alliance of the clergy, the notables, and the propertied, together with the majority of the peasantry who resented the increase of taxation to pay for the Parisian unemployed, proved overwhelmingly strong. The electorate, increased from the 250,000 of the July monarchy to 9

million, turned up at the polls in astonishing numbers; some 84% of
the electorate voted. The result all over France, including Paris, was
to return conservative and moderate members, not socialists or radicals. Alfred Cobban has estimated that of the 900 deputies, half were
monarchists divided in their allegiance between Orleanists 300 and
Bourbon Legitimists 150; about 350 supported the clerical cause for
freedom of education, i.e. the right of the church to control its own
schools; there were only a few 'red' republicans or socialists. Only
one radical leader, Armand Barbès, was elected in Paris together with
twelve socialists.

The newly elected assembly now began its task of constitution
making. It paid much attention to political and legal matters, but
social problems it equated with the danger of social revolution. The
assembly was more concerned to show a firm hand in face of the
demands than to find any equitable or humane solution to the related
evils of unemployment and destitution. Politically the principle of the
'division of power' was enshrined and carried to a degree of absurd-
ity. The provisional government was replaced by an executive commission of five which discussed policy, whilst ministers individually
carried it out; both executive commission and the ministers were
responsible to the assembly.

Rightly despairing that any social change could be expected from
this assembly, diverse left wing political agitators on 15 May 1848
attempted to overthrow the assembly by force. A demonstration by
an unarmed crowd succeeded in entering the chamber but was soon
after easily dispersed by the National Guard. The only result was the
removal and arrest of all the well-known left wing political leaders.
The more radical politicians disappeared from the life of the Second
Republic; Louis Blanc, once a member of the provisional government, was the most notable casualty. The February Revolution had
by June 1848 led to the conservative republic.

However the conservative republic of May 1848 was still *provisional*. Many of its supporters were far more concerned with the
survival of conservatism socially than the republic politically; but
for the time being they recognized that, like body and mind, they
could only survive together. One more desperate challenge of the
Parisian poor had to be faced, the June days. The poor had no chance
of success against the authority of the state united against violence
and social revolution.

With the savage repression of the June insurrection, the politicians
of the republic faced the future with more confidence. Their rule was
no longer provisional. The people could not wrest it from them.
What the conservative politicians discovered in 1848 was that the
majority of the people did not want to do so. The surest way to
maintain the social order was to ask for its sanction by the majority

through the electoral process. The unaccepting minority could then be repressed with all the vigour of the state. The liberal era, used in its nineteenth-century sense, began in France in 1848 and from then on survived through various constitutions and forms of state. Its hallmarks were moderate reform, an emphasis on material prosperity, the sanctity of property, and a fair judicial system, except to the opponents of the social and economic basis of the state. Actual political power was entrusted to the few who could deliver this programme. So France passed from revolution to the conservative Republic, then to the authoritarian Empire, and after that to the liberal Empire, and finally to another conservative Republic, without much concern to the majority of Frenchmen who turned their backs on revolution by the urban poor and on the idea of government by the socialists.

3

The Habsburg Empire and the Revolutions of 1848

On 26 and 27 February 1848 rumours reached Vienna of dramatic events in Paris. Not until the 29th was it known for certain that a revolution had overthrown Louis Philippe. What worried the good citizens of Vienna was what Metternich might do in response. He had met previous revolutionary outbreaks by trying to concert internationally a conservative reaction and if need be intervention to prevent the spread of the liberal disease. But intervention in France and in the German states meant war, a major upheaval, likely to ruin the trade and finance of the monarchy. The very possibility caused a panic in Vienna and in other large cities of the monarchy; the run on banks everywhere forced some of them to close. Events in Vienna during the following month of March illustrate once again how vague in meaning the very word 'revolution' is. The liberals and constitutionalists pressed demands more or less common to liberals throughout Europe, for freedom of thought, of the press, and an end to censorship, freedom of religion and more representative government. There was no socialist revolutionary ardour for a fundamental change of society. Far from it – the early reactions of the Viennese to the upheavals elsewhere in Europe can be seen as the kind of enlightened conservatism which existed in England after the Reform Bill of 1832. The Viennese wished to assure themselves of growing prosperity for which the maintenance of peace and some mild reforms were necessary prerequisites. Metternich symbolized the danger of reaction.

In Hungary the revolutionary movement proved in the end more dangerous for the cohesion of the monarchy than the disturbances in Vienna. Lajos Kossuth on 3 March delivered a speech in the lower house of the Diet that marked the real beginnings of the revolutionary movement there. He proposed that the Diet present an address to the crown and laid a draft before the House. He demanded not reform but a total change of system of government for Hungary; a ministry responsible to a Hungarian parliament and not to Vienna.

Kossuth did not attack the Pragmatic Sanction as such, but the union with Austria's other lands was henceforth to be personal to the monarch; in Hungary, for the enactment of laws, the monarch would be dependent on the ministry and parliament. But Kossuth went even further. He warned that constitutional government could not be safely secured unless absolutism was replaced by general constitutional institutions for the different nationalities. Without these the monarchy would not remain united. In expressing this need for co-operation among the constitutional supporters of the empire, Kossuth failed to envisage how disruptive national aspiration would turn out to be.

News of Kossuth's fiery speech, when it reached Vienna, encouraged the liberal opposition to formulate constitutional aims and to insist on the dismissal of Metternich who would never have genuinely accepted such demands. It was widely believed that the State Council advising the Emperor Ferdinand was not unanimous and that two of the Archdukes, John and Ludwig, favoured concessions; above all it was rumoured that the Archduchess Sophie, wife of Ludwig, was on the side of the opposition. Metternich's position was no longer impregnable as it had been in the reign of Francis I, now that a weaker monarch occupied the throne. No doubt this belief that there existed sympathy in high places was largely misplaced – but the records of the deliberations of the State Council during March 1848, despite some hesitations and inconsistencies, do reveal a real aversion to causing bloodshed in Vienna and a growing conviction that the crown's interests were more endangered by Metternich's inflexible attitude than by concessions to demonstrators. In this respect Frederick William IV of Prussia and Ferdinand and his advisers thought much alike and behaved according to a broadly similar pattern. They lacked the single-minded ruthlessness which would have inclined them to use force regardless of cost. The Habsburgs and Hohenzollerns of the nineteenth century believed in an autocracy divinely ordained; they were convinced that they had been uniquely chosen by God to rule their people and that they were responsible for the administration of just and good laws and the inculcation of popular obedience to the throne and the altar whose clergy owed obedience to the monarch also. But they were not despots, whose actions were arbitrary. They regarded power as a responsibility and not as a licence to fulfil personal ambitions. That is why despite their severe limitations and outdated outlook on a changing society, they continued to enjoy wide and genuine respect in the nineteenth century.

Metternich was behind the negative imperial response on 10 March to the presentation of liberal grievances. On 12 March 1848 the students of Vienna met to formulate a petition with the usual requests for popular representation, freedom of the press, instruction and religion – nothing very radical, especially in the manner of its delivery by two professors of the university. On 13 March the estates of Lower Austria met in Vienna in the Landhaus in the Herrenstrasse. That day and those that immediately followed were decisive for the revolution in Vienna. What happened in the way of expression of popular feeling was more like a threatening demonstration, or perhaps to put it more strongly a civil disturbance, than an armed uprising, which in fact never occurred. The meeting on 13 March of the estates, for the most part conservatives, was put under pressure by a large crowd of students and others in the courtyard. They wanted their demands for constitutional government to be presented to the emperor in the Hofburg. Revolution was not on their mind; they trusted the emperor to put everything right.

The assemblies of this kind were not always orderly. Disorder attracted the disorderly. A further element of possible trouble was caused by the influx of workers, who frequently took Mondays off and left the factory areas of the outer suburbs for the centre of the city.

The Council of State acted as might be expected; some troops were placed under the command of the 30-year-old Archduke Albrecht. To restore order among an excited stone-throwing and cat-calling crowd requires experience and tact which the young soldiers – a detachment from Italy – and their commander lacked. The troops were under pressure and outnumbered. There was no deliberate premeditated attempt to fire on the crowd, but as in Paris, some shots rang out and four people in the crowd fell dead and more were wounded. The crowd was dispersed; groups engaged in more fighting throughout the inner city; in the suburban working-class areas machines were smashed, shops looted and factories wrecked. Here among the factory workers the unrest had become mainly economic and social. Thus from the outset in Vienna the disturbances revealed two really antagonistic roots: the liberal constitutionalists supported by the better-off in the inner city and the workers outside, who were blindly and violently expressing their protest at the inadequacy of wages, at unemployment and the conditions in which they lived. Then there were the ragged beggars and violent criminals present in any large city, viewed without charity by anyone, the better-off, the authorities or the socialists; they were referred to by the authorities disdainfully and harshly as the criminal poor. The very large number of active students, for the most part as badly-off as the workers, formed something of a link between professional men, radical politicians and workers, and as time went on voiced more violent and radical demands. Despite the heterogeneous make-up of the 1848 revolutionaries joint hatred of the army and police was a common enemy during the early days of 1848.

The hours of the afternoon and evening of the 13 March were crucial. The citizens of Vienna were keen to maintain order and respect for the persons and property endangered by workers and radicals. They demanded that the city should be entrusted to them and that the National Guard and the students, who had formed an Academic Legion, should be armed while the hated soldiers were to be withdrawn. Metternich was to be dismissed and an answer was required by 9 p.m. The advisers of Ferdinand were undecided. Prince Windischgraetz was in the city ready to restore order with troops. But in the end the archdukes in the Council of State advised capitulation to all the demands. Metternich, loquacious to the end, the most celebrated figure of European conservatism, was forced unceremoniously to flee from the city. The Habsburgs spared his future little thought. It was Baron Rothschild who supplied him with the financial means to leave Vienna, but the Baron reinsured himself by providing free meals for the student patrols in the city.

There is no need to follow in close detail the concessions that were wrung from the Council of State from every part of the monarchy during the remainder of March, April and May of 1848. When the emperor did not give way at the first time of asking, further threats sufficed to persuade him and his advisers. The demands crowded in almost day by day from all directions of the compass. On the morning of 15 March the promise of calling by 3 July 'representatives of the Estates of Our German-Austrian and Slavonic Realms and of the Central Congregations of our Lombardo-Venetian Kingdom', who would then be asked for advice, was not enough to satisfy demands for a 'Constitution'. By the same afternoon, abolition of censorship and the calling of representatives to advise on a constitution which 'We have decided to grant' was publicly proclaimed outside the Hofburg. The Viennese burghers did not doubt that with the promise of a constitution victory had been won. Two days later the Hungarian delegation which had arrived in Vienna was granted a 'responsible Ministry', but 'subject to the preservation intact of the unity of the Crown and of the link with the Monarchy'. Once started on an appeasing role the Council of State gave the appearance of following it without more prompting. A 'responsible Ministry' was set up in the western lands of Austria on 20 March with Count Franz Anton von Kolowrat as Minister President and Baron Franz Pillersdorf as Minister of the Interior. But in the absence of any sort of parliament, the ministers – all old loyal servants of the crown – of course remained responsible to the monarch and the Council of State. The Ministry tried loyally to carry on the thankless task of government with little support and less thanks from the court.

In Hungary Count Lajos Batthyány, a moderate reformer, was entrusted with the formation of a ministry which included the respected Ferencz Deák and also Kossuth. This ministry and the Diet adopted the 'April Laws' which transformed the government of Hungary; all dues and servitudes the peasants owed their landlords were ended, proportionate taxation was extended to all inhabitants of Hungary and thereby the traditional tax privileges of the nobility abolished; religious freedom (except for Jews), freedom of the press, a National Guard, were among the more important reforms enacted. In Hungary, the monarchy became constitutional and limited by the Diet and the ministry and no law became valid unless signed by both the king, or his representative in Hungary, the Palatine and the responsible minister. Joint ministers for the empire as a whole residing in Vienna henceforth had no say in Hungary; the union between Hungary and Austria was a personal monarchical one. But the crucial question as to who was to control the Hungarian troops was side-stepped by a compromise. The Diet accepted the monarch's prerogative for the use of these troops outside Hungary and the monarch's right to make military appointments, but a Hungarian ministerial counter-signature was required.

In Vienna, April was a peaceful month and the ministry seemed to have the situation under control. There had been no need for severe repression of the workers who had returned to the suburbs. On 25 April a draft constitution was published by imperial patent. It had been drawn up by Pillersdorf and had received the approval of the ministry and the apparent approval of the archdukes. Judged by the standards of its day, the provisions were liberal, but they satisfied no one. For the Poles and Czechs the constitution was too centralist, denying them sufficient autonomy; the students and more radical supporters objected to the proposed upper and lower house and the imperial right of veto. The ministry in Vienna was now losing power to a committee of students and representatives of the National Guard. In May there were new disorders culminating in the demonstrations of 15 May. The ministry gave way again and Ferdinand agreed to the calling of a single chamber constituent assembly on a popular franchise.

The question one is bound to ask is why the emperor and the State Council in the spring of 1848 gave way with so little resistance. The detailed records of the time can tell us what happened, but to penetrate the motives and the actual responsibility for the final decisions is far more difficult and historians can do little more than express opinions. It is evident that the advisers of the emperor were divided. Count Anton Kolowrat, a Bohemian magnate, with a long record of loyal service to the monarchy had, by 1830, in the reign of Francis I, become the principal counsellor on internal affairs, as Metternich was on international affairs. More flexible than

Metternich, Kolowrat behaved and acted as the great Bohemian magnate he was; he was ready through better financial management and a few concessions to try to release the pent-up feelings of opposition and frustration produced by Francis' and Metternich's attempts to keep everything exactly as it was. Kolowrat's ruling passion was not reform as much as opposition to Metternich. He welcomed demands for the dismissal of Metternich from whatever quarter as an opportunity to bring about the fall of his rival. But Archduke Ludwig and Ferdinand's younger brother, Archduke Franz Karl, both supported Metternich. The same is true of Franz Karl's wife, a Wittelsbach, Archduchess Sophie, who was credited with liberal sympathies she did not possess. Nevertheless the first loyalty of the family was not to Metternich but to the Emperor Ferdinand, whose mental helplessness only emphasized the need to protect the institution of the monarchy. The decision to give way and grant constitutions was primarily a family decision. As far as Ferdinand possessed influence it was employed to avert violence and bloodshed.

The reasons for conciliation were complex. The decisions to give way were certainly taken quickly and reluctantly, pointing to a loss of nerve. According to a diarist in the Hofburg, where the Council of State was assembled, the angry mob was frightening. Yet it is not a satisfying explanation. News from many parts of the monarchy showed that the troubles were not isolated in Vienna and that physical force was lacking to master the situation everywhere simultaneously. It therefore made tactical good sense to give way. But there were also more positive attitudes. Some members of the Habsburgs, as for instance the elderly Archduke John, were ready to adapt to the new spirit of the age, and believed that Metternich's ideas now belonged more to the past than the present and future. But in the last analysis it would be mistaken to overlook the sense of paternalism felt by the Habsburgs. After decades of overwhelmingly peaceable relations in the capital and in the Hereditary Lands, they could not straight away adjust themselves to use force on the people. The personal popularity of the monarchy seemed never to have stood higher and the Habsburg family was anxious at least during the early months of 1848 to avoid the odium of bloody repression. On the other hand they were certainly not above deceit and could close their eyes to brutal repression by their generals, whose success later gave them an ascendency in the imperial family council.

1848 marks a watershed in the relationship of the monarch, the people and the nationalities. After the bloody repressions in Vienna, Prague and in Hungary, the simple picture of the benevolent monarch and the trust placed in the mere words of princes was gone for as long the live memories of 1848 and 1849 survived. Only Francis-Joseph's longevity outlasted these bitter memories.

The 15 May 1848 marked a real turning-point in the Austrian revolution of 1848. It was no longer a question whether the monarchy could get by with a so-called 'responsible Ministry' making unwelcome liberal concessions. Government was exposed to popular clamour. The imperial court no doubt exaggerated personal danger to themselves – there was none, but the fate of the royal family during the great revolution in France was never far from their mind. Flight was decided on and the emperor and archdukes with their families departed in great secrecy for Innsbruck on 17 May, leaving the ministry behind in Vienna to cope as best it could. Ferdinand noted in his diary, 'We were told that the people and the students meant to storm the Palace, set it alight, and murder us; that was the reason that forced us to leave Vienna.' Elsewhere in the empire the pendulum of reaction was now gaining the ascendant. The high points of radical and constitutional success in Vienna also marked the beginnings of its failure.

Once having given way in Vienna, the family council of archdukes for a time seemed to lose their grip on power. At Innsbruck they were reduced to temporizing and manoeuvring among the national demands brought to the court. They followed no higher principle than expediency and nothing they did carried much conviction. They were not convinced themselves and secretly opposed any limitation of monarchical rights and powers. Their consent was sought by all sorts of delegations to provide a stamp of legitimacy to various and different movements within the empire. But the fact that they were asked at all, also reveals the underlying attachment of these disparate rival groups to the monarchy. In fact only one national group, the Italians of Lombardy-Venetia, rose in actual rebellion against the crown during the early months of 1848.

Northern Italy was the crucial battleground for the monarchy during the spring and summer of '1848'. Unrest and demonstrations against Austrian rule had spread from the countryside to Milan in mid-March. The Austrian forces in Milan, well trained, armed and some 10,000 strong were unable to cope with a civil insurrection. A third of them, moreover, were Italian soldiers many of whom deserted. What made the military situation even worse was that throughout northern Italy the Austrian troops, numbering perhaps 100,000, were scattered in various garrison towns. Marshal Radetzky, an outstanding military leader though now 81 years old, saved his army from disaster by withdrawing on 22 March the troops remaining loyal to the famous military stronghold formed by the Quadrilateral – the fortresses of Peschiera, Mantua, Verona and Legnago. But in Venice the Austrian troops surrendered and a republic was proclaimed.

These events took Charles Albert, king of neighbouring Piedmont-Sardinia by surprise. His record of 'reform' had been meagre. Nor had he shown much interest in the unity of Italy. He was in outlook one of the more old fashioned backward rulers. Lombardy-Venetia under Austrian rule could indeed boast more genuine progress and good government than the kingdom of Piedmont. What motivated Charles Albert was the chance of territorial aggrandizement. He wished to make Piedmont the most powerful state in Italy, a state to be reckoned with also in Europe. But for Charles Albert, Piedmont-Sardinia was a state of its own, not to be submerged in a union or confederation of other Italian states great and small. At most he would consider leading a federation of Italian states dominated by Piedmont rather as Austria dominated the German Federation. Before 1848 Charles Albert had been more concerned to fight liberalism with Metternich as an ally than to free 'Italy' from Austrian domination. But Metternich's fall, and the collapse of Austrian power in Milan in March 1848, proved too much of a temptation to a king whose view of absolute monarchy rigidly held to eighteenth-century concepts of 'benevolent despotism'. Furthermore Cavour warned him that not to support the uprising in Milan could cost him his throne at home. Although ill-prepared for the military venture, he crossed from Piedmont to Lombardy on 23 March with a numerically superior force of 60,000 men. He occupied Milan but failed to catch Radetzky's army. Radetzky meantime waited for reinforcements with his multi-national force which included Hungarians, Croats and Germans. During April, May and June of 1848 he built up his army with troops raised in Moravia and Silesia. The nationalities of the Austrian Empire rallied to the imperial cause Radetzky represented; in the suppression of Italian nationalism they found a common purpose, which did not, however, diminish in the slightest their continual mutual conflict and rivalry with each other or their national chauvinism as far as their own people in the empire were concerned!

The 'revolution' in Bohemia was a frail intellectual plant enjoying neither the determined support of the Czech nobility nor of the mass of peasantry or industrial workers. It is indeed hard to speak of 'revolution' at all in Bohemia during the spring and summer of 1848. In the decades preceding 1848, there had been a great cultural Czech revival concentrating on philology, literature and history. This new-found pride in their cultural past had been encouraged by the imperial administrators. Czech journals were published, some continuously from 1830 through 1848 until a renewed censorship closed them. Františeck Palacký, a Protestant from Moravia, historian, and the most distinguished among the Czech cultural nationalists, had founded the Czech Museum and thus 'institutionalized' the Czech cultural revival of the 1830s and 1840s. None of this activity was 'revolutionary': it received both imperial patronage and the patronage of the Czech nobility. Nor was there any revolutionary motivation behind the increasing exchanges and cultural contacts between the various branches of the Slav family of nations. They culminated in June 1848 in the gathering of the first Slav Congress in Prague, a congress which made Europe aware of the existence of the Slavs.

But the stirring events elsewhere in Europe, in Paris, Frankfurt, Vienna and Pesth were bound to involve the politically conscious in Prague to consider the future of the Czech nation in the Habsburg Monarchy and in the Europe of 1848. The Slavonic Congress exposed to the influences of Prague meantime revealed political differences as well as a common feeling of Slav solidarity. The congress did formulate a stirring response to the pretensions of the German Frankfurt parliament which supported Prussia in its retention of Polish territories and regarded Bohemia, Moravia and Silesia as part of the new Germany. Palacký, in his celebrated reply to the invitation to join the deliberations of the Frankfurt parliament (11 April) had rejected the German claims. He declared he was Czech and not German. He saw especial danger in the nationalist claim for a German state embracing all Germans for it undermined the existence of the Habsburg monarchy. The Habsburg monarchy for Palacký, and for the Czechs who thought like him, was the best guarantee of national Slav identities threatened by two powerful neighbours, Russia and Germany. The Slav support for a monarchy, reorganized to be sure to allow for national federation, was expressed in a well-known passage of Palacký's letter to Frankfurt, 'Assuredly, if the Austrian state had not existed for ages, it would have been a behest for us in the interests of Europe and indeed of humanity to endeavour to create it as soon as possible...'. The Slav nationalities of the Danube Basin were not strong enough to survive alone among the great powers; they thought they could best find safety and freedom as part of the Austrian state. But their combination in the empire as a unified Slav entity was impossible to realize. Divided linguistically, culturally and religiously as Czech Orthodox, Catholics and Uniates, their actual co-operation was limited against the Magyars and the Austrian Germans. Mutual rivalries and fears of domination by the stronger over the weaker divided Czechs and Slovaks, Poles and Ruthenians and the mass of the peasantry was little stirred by the nationalism of the intellectuals. They looked to the monarchy for emancipation from the feudal exaction of the landed nobility.

The imperial court made paper concession to popular demands in Prague during March and April of 1848. The leadership of the Czech national and liberal cause had been taken over by a national committee appointed in mid-March at a popular meeting of radicals and intellectuals which had gathered at a wine-house in Prague. They petitioned the emperor for autonomy from the Germans in Vienna. With the Germans in Bohemia, Moravia and Silesia they had no quarrel. They petitioned also for the maintenance of the 'constitutional link between the lands of the Bohemian Crown' (thus emphasizing the unity of Bohemia, Moravia and Silesia), for complete equality of Czechs and Germans in Czech lands, for a reformed Diet and a central administration, for a civil service of natives of the lands knowing both Czech and German, together with the usual liberal demands made everywhere – freedom of the press, an end of censorship, and the creation of a National Guard. By 8 April 1848 successive imperial edicts had accepted many of the points but sidestepped the question of the administrative unity of Bohemia, Moravia and Silesia.

The Silesian and Moravian Diets could be relied upon to reject Czech claims, which they did later in April 1848. The German minority in Bohemia too had by now become alarmed, preferring the link with Austria to remain as strong as possible. The Czech national leaders were increasingly determined to free Bohemia from the control of radical Vienna and the disorders in Vienna in May and June enabled the Czech leaders to represent themselves as favouring legality; they offered loyally to back the emperor against his recalcitrant German subjects. But the hopes of the Czechs were dashed by Prince Windischgraetz.

Unable to obtain imperial permission to occupy Vienna, he turned on Prague instead. In Prague on 12 June unemployed artisans and textile workers had in their desperation taken to the streets. The provocative response of the troops led to some barricades and to violence predominantly by students from the Polytechnic (College of Engineering); this served Windischgraetz in turn as an excuse to refer to 'revolution'. He withdrew his troops from the city; he next threatened to bombard Prague and called for its 'surrender'. Some shots were actually fired; the city surrendered and Windischgraetz occupied Prague and extinguished a 'revolution' that in a real sense never was. Of the 100,000 inhabitants of Prague not more than 1,200 fought at the barricades and 800 of these were inexperienced students. But it was enough for Windischgraetz whose wife had been killed by a random shot perhaps meant for the prince. Every expression of Bohemian political opinion was now suppressed, and the more radical students and political leaders in Prague arrested and imprisoned for having fomented the 'May conspiracy' against the state. But no general unrest followed in Bohemia; the peasants were not affected and the professors, including Palacký, returned to their studies. But 1848 nevertheless represented a gain for the Czechs. It brought them equality with the Germans; they also became a political force in the monarchy.

The Hungarians, like the Czechs, were no willing rebels against the authority of the monarch. Unlike the Czechs, the Hungarians had traditionally enjoyed separate and special rights. They had greatly extended these by the April laws of 1848, but the Magyars were royalists to the core. They were also 'centralists', not of course as far as the government of the Habsburg Empire as a whole was concerned, but for the government of the lands of the Kingdom of St Stephen. Their attitude in 1848 to the nationalities within Hungary, to the Slovaks, Ruthenians, Rumanians, Germans, Serbs and Croats, as for instance exemplified by Kossuth was one of cultural tolerance, which, combined with social reform, especially in improving the status of the peasantry, was expected to reconcile the nationalities to centralist control of a parliament and government in Pesth which was predominantly Magyar. This was the common illusion of the dominant nationality in multi-national states. Their own strong national feelings blinded them to the strength of the nationalism of other peoples. At best, as in Hungary and in the Habsburg Empire, some safety-valve in the form of a measure of cultural and local autonomy was at times provided, but it rarely sufficed to contain national aspirations for independence propagated by a minority and in the end tacitly accepted by the majority.

During the spring and summer months the problem facing the Magyar government was not a question of their *theoretical* rights of independence under the crown. They had gained an acceptable solution in the April laws. But practical difficulties multiplied over finance, and the control of the Hungarian army. Just as serious, and in the long run disastrous, proved the struggle over the extent of Hungarian jurisdiction. Especially important from the point of view of who controlled the army was the question of the control of the military frontier and Fiume which had no self-governing institutions and over which the monarch asserted 'reserved rights'. On this issue the Hungarians gave way except that they insisted that Fiume was essential as Hungary's outlet to the sea. The Magyar majority in Transylvania pushed union with Hungary through the Transylvanian Diet unanimously on 30 May.

It is a mistake to regard the minorities of the Hungarian kingdom as entirely opposed to Magyar rule. The smaller national groups were in fact not solidly hostile to the Magyars. Some Slovak nationalists desired a separate Slovak nation within a Hungarian 'federation of states'. While certainly many Rumanians were hostile to incorporation in Hungary, some Slovak peasants, most of the Ruthenians, the Swabians and Catholic southern Slavs sided with the Magyars. It is very difficult to quantify; one has to be cautious of sweeping generalizations in speaking about the attitudes of the minorities. There were many followers in rival armies fighting each other during the course of 1848 and 1849 for no particular cause or for a cause misrepresented to them. They followed the promises of leaders or were simply prejudiced and ignorant. In '1848' there frequently existed a wide gulf between the romanticism and noble cause espoused by the leaders of revolutions and the mindless brutality and violence of soldiers and peoples driven to vent their frustration on those whom they looked on as the 'enemy'. Thus the Jews in central Europe frequently were made scapegoats for the distress and suffered from violence and general anti-Semitism.

The Hungarians faced their most serious trouble in Croatia. The Croats and Serbs had traditionally opposed the efforts of Hungary to absorb them. The Croats succeeded in securing and maintaining their own autonomous institution, the Diet in Zagreb. The Serbs, with no institutions of their own in the monarchy, were traditionally used by the monarch to help keep the Hungarians in check. In 1848, Croats and Serbs once more gladly allowed themselves to act in the name of the emperor to free themselves from Hungarian control.

In March 1848 Josip Jelačić, a colonel of one of the frontier regiments, had been appointed Ban of Croatia. He had become a fanatical Croatian patriot, believing in the establishment of an 'Illyrian' state, swearing loyalty to the crown and driven by hatred of Magyar 'tyranny'. During the spring and early summer of 1848 the imperial court at Innsbruck played a weak game of expediency backing in turn Hungarian government deputations who protested at the pretensions of Jelačić, and backing Jelačić who protested against the Magyars and assured the emperor of his own complete loyalty. The monarchy had need of both Hungarians and Croatians before Radetzky's armies, with the help of all the nationalities including Hungarians and Croats, had removed the Italian danger.

Not until July and August 1848 did the monarchy feel strong enough to seek to undo all the constitutional concessions made in the name of Ferdinand since March. The Austrian armies under Windischgraetz moved forward against the various national groups and constitutional governments whose existence had been sanctioned by the emperor and each of which individually continued to express its loyalty to the monarchy and accepted in different forms the Pragmatic Sanction and the concept of a Habsburg Empire.

The activities and purposes of the many centres of revolutionary and national activities in the empire in the summer of 1848 reveal no general and settled pattern. They tended to cancel each other out. Imperial neglect had proved the fastest route to a general dissipation of the strength of the warring groups and nationalities.

In some places, such as Vienna, there were three or more rival centres of power at one and the same time. A divided Reichstag; the ministers who formed the government of Austria, loyal to the crown, with little power in the city though making claims of central control over the other nationalities; this centralizing policy provoked resistance from the minorities in Austria. For the majority, participating in the various Diets, parliaments, governmental and national committees, the rivalry of nationalities cut across the liberal and constitutional demands common to all. The great failure of the liberals and constitutionalists in the monarchy lay in their total inability to make common cause. Thus Austrian German liberals could join hands with the reactionary forces in the empire to thwart the Hungarians. Czech Slavs offered their services to crush the Germans; Czech Orthodox Slavs and Serbs to crush the Magyars and the Catholic Slavs and the Ruthenians fought for Hungary. The nationalities were also divided among themselves. On the political left, among the minority who gained some representation in national committees and parliaments, a sense of common cause in the end emerged, but it was too late and they were too weak. The peasants for the most part were concerned with their own status and looked to the monarchy as their best defence against exacting nobles. The artisans and factory workers were moved to sporadic violence and demonstration by economic conditions made worse by the disruptions of 1848. They had no long-term plans or aims, and for the most part, had never heard of their would-be leaders or of theories of class revolution. They acted instinctively and were pacified by economic concession or repressed by force. Amid all this chaos, the manœuvrings and duplicity of the court, principally the council of Archdukes, stands out. Their contradictory orders only increased the general chaos, but paradoxically the general feebleness of the monarchy in 1848 made the task of ultimate monarchical restoration the more easy in 1849.

The multiplicity of social and national divisions which produced the chaos, left the monarchy in the end as the only possible solution for the restoration of general peace and order. There also were many liberal revolutionaries who, within six months of the beginning of the unrest, turned gladly to the court and the Austrian armies as providing the only way out of disorder and chaos. For those who remained true to what they looked upon as the spirit of 1848 a bitter end awaited at the hands of the imperial armies, whose cohesion throughout the turbulent months had never seriously wavered. They suppressed a 'revolution' that had been defined as such by the imperial family and the most conservative supporters of the state crown. But the revolution was largely of their own making because they chose to call revolutionaries all those who demanded national autonomy, and liberal, constitutional institutions. Many of the 'revolutionaries' retained a personal faith and loyalty in the monarchy and displayed what, in the circumstances, proved a misguided and excessive respect for legality. They wanted and actually seemed to secure imperial consent for their 'revolution'.

The social or radical revolution in the towns enjoyed little support. But everyone, except some territorial magnates, was agreed on the need to complete the emancipation of the peasantry. Who can say what the course of Habsburg history would have been had the monarchy been both stronger and more enlightened in 1848/9? Was a great opportunity for a modernized imperial federation lost? More probably the monarchy, not by deliberate choice but through general weakness, had followed the best course of just muddling through. It survived through the nineteenth century and well into the twentieth. As an effective form of government, rather than as a representative symbol, monarchy lasted as long in the Habsburg domains as elsewhere in Europe and as an 'empire' the Habsburg through many changes and vicissitudes, had survived longer than any other in modern times.

4

German Unity and the Frankfurt Parliament

Germany already existed in 1848 but not in the sense of Britain or France. Germany possessed federal institutions, the most important being the Diet which met in Frankfurt; there were federal frontiers, a common language and national feelings, but despite these attributes of the modern state, 'Germany' did not really exist in 1848. There was no German government, administration, or German army. The Germany of 1848 was a loose alliance of rulers, but there were curious anomalies. The two most important states in the German Confederation also possessed territory that did not form a part of it. Thus Prussia's Polish territory and the Habsburgs' Hungarian domains did not fall within the confines of the mid-nineteenth-century German Confederation. Then there was the case of Denmark, a non-German state, only a small part of whose territory was within the German federal frontier. These were not considered serious problems as long as there was not German national unity. And even when there was much talk by the people's representatives sitting in the Frankfurt parliament to found a nation they did not at first realize how serious an obstacle the Habsburg lands, where German and non-German territories were linked in one monarchy, would prove to be. Even if the Prussians would agree to be absorbed in the new Germany, how could the Habsburgs? To the rulers of the Habsburg Monarchy, German unity would mean either exclusion or the break-up of their empire. The creation of a German nation in 1848 necessitated a re-ordering of allegiances and precedences: Germany first and Prussia and the German states second; for the 'Germans' of the Habsburg Empire it also meant placing Germany before the Habsburg Empire. How many Prussians and Austrians when it came to it were really prepared to embrace new allegiances?

In 1848 the impetus for a German national revolution came not from Prussia or Austria, but from the political leaders of the small south-western German states. One such state, composed of diverse pieces of land, was the Grand Duchy of Baden, which, though ruled by a totally undistinguished family, with the help of a French-style administrative bureaucracy, played a role in 1848 out of all proportion to its size and power. This was because of its constitution. The Baden parliament was elected on a franchise wider than elsewhere in Germany and it became the cradle of the German constitutional movement. There is a strong link between the leading politicians of the Baden assembly and the later Frankfurt parliament. Moderate liberals, such as Adam von Itzstein, Karl Welcker, Friedrich Bassermann and Karl Mathy made appeals for a more unified Germany in the place of so many small sovereign states.

From Baden too emerged the more radical and even revolutionary politics of 1848; its leaders were Gustav von Struve and Friedrich Hecker. The division between constitutional liberals and the revolutionary republican radicals, which became sharply delineated in April 1848 and whose consequences were to be tragic, were not so clear to begin with. There were no political parties as such but the different viewpoints came to the fore clearly enough in the autumn of 1847 when the more extreme Baden opposition dominated a meeting at Offenburg. The programme adopted there contained not only the usual liberal demands but also social demands which, in the context of the time, were socialist and revolutionary: just (that is graduated) taxation, a people's army, access to education for all, and the resolution of the conflict between labour and capital. There was still some vagueness in these aims. In fact the radicals coming together at Offenburg soon sub-divided into two groups. There were those who interpreted the programme as leading to a republic; they intended a complete break with the princes and established society, and in 1848 led a people's uprising and proclaimed a republic. Then there were the radicals who wished to unite Germany through a people's parliament, not in collaboration with the princes. This group did not resort to force.

In Heppenheim the viewpoint of the most prominent conservative or moderate liberals was expressed and made known throughout Germany by the *Deutsche Zeitung*. The liberals who met in Heppenheim also came from Baden, and the south-western German states. They consciously spoke for 'German' liberalism. These assemblies of liberals and radicals in the autumn of 1847 regarded themselves as representing Germany; the moribund Diet of the German Confederation they believed represented merely the old-established particularist interests of the princes.

After the revolution in Paris in February 1848, the liberals and radicals agreed to meet in Heidelberg to bring about a transformation of German institutions. On 5 March 1848, 51 prominent liberals and radicals gathered there; some came from other German states, but most from the south-west. It needs to be noted that they actually began this self-appointed political work for German unity *before* the revolutions had succeeded in their own states. Working in the opposite direction, the King of Prussia was talking about an international conservative alliance with Russia and Austria to crush the revolutions in Europe. At the time of the Heidelberg meeting Metternich was still Chancellor and Austria presided over the Federal German Diet. Thus the 'German' revolution preceded the revolutions in the individual German states. These opposition leaders looked directly to the German people for support. Their move was audacious and unexpectedly successful. Their business: the creation of a *German* parliament. The radicals and liberals could agree so far; but for the moderate liberals the 'revolution' was strictly 'tactical'. They did not wish to overthrow thrones or to endanger property, and they were opposed to social revolution.

Soon radicals and liberals parted company, but not before joint plans were agreed for the summons of a preparatory parliament (*Vorparliament*).* This assembly, like the earlier meeting of the 51 reformers, had no constitutional or elective basis. It was, however, a much more imposing body. 574 representatives gathered in the Paulskirche in Frankfurt on the last day of March and deliberated for five days. The Paulskirche in years to come was looked on as the cradle of German democracy. Frankfurt had been chosen as it was the seat of the German Confederation. The trouble was that now there were two assemblies in Frankfurt, the old Diet of the German Confederation and the new *Vorparliament* both claiming to speak for the whole of Germany. Fortunately the men who represented their rulers in the Diet of the German Confederation had largely been replaced as a result of the successful revolutions which, by then, had occurred in most of the German states in the latter part of March. New representatives were despatched by freshly installed liberal governments. There was thus some political sympathy between the members of the German Confederation and the *Vorparliament*; but at first there was also rivalry between the two bodies. Who was to be responsible for German unification? The German people or the German states? There were now too many parliamentary assemblies in Germany when a few months earlier there had been too few. In fact both the old Diet and the new *Vorparliament* played a role in the calling of a German parliament.

The day before the *Vorparliament* met, the Federal Diet in haste called for speedy national elections in the individual states, but it was

---

* *Vorparliament* is usually translated as 'preliminary parliament', or, pre-parliament; this does not convey the actual meaning of '*vor*', which is here better rendered as 'preparatory'.

the *Vorparliament* that spelt out the franchise. A serious struggle between the radical and liberal politicians on this issue had developed in the *Vorparliament*. In the end a vague compromise was reached. Every citizen of majority age who was 'independent' was entitled to vote in their state in constituencies theoretically of about 50,000. The actual size of constituencies varied considerably. Although not expressly stated, only men were allowed to vote; but this was not the manhood suffrage it appeared to be. It was left to the more or less liberal governments in the states to define 'independence'; domestic servants, for example, were excluded in Austria. The elections, moreover, were usually indirect; the voters elected 'electors' who decided on the members to be sent to Frankfurt. However, no one was excluded from voting on grounds of religion, class of property; thus the rights of citizens was strengthened. The Federal Diet endorsed these decisions of the *Vorparliament* on 7 April 1848 and then gave up the ghost. It could not hope to become the focal point of a new Germany. It designated the German national parliament which would meet after the elections its legal successor. The *Vorparliament* also dispersed but appointed a committee of 50 to act as a watchdog until the German national parliament should meet. The means by which the German national parliament, known as the Frankfurt parliament was brought into being was thus complex and involved – but it proved practicable. Despite administrative overlaps and rivalries, a clear course was decided on, evidence that the need for an elected German parliament was regarded as the overwhelming issue. This was the road to a peaceful and constitutional German revolution.

In view of the uncertainties in Germany and the novelty of what the politicians were attempting to conjure up, a united Germany by means of national elections, the actual organization of such elections was an achievement; but the extreme radicals despaired of bringing about the political and social changes they thought essential through parliamentary and electoral processes. Hecker and Struve returned to Baden where they attempted to lead a peasant and worker rising. They proclaimed a republic on 12 April 1848. They were supported by a 'German legion' which crossed from French Alsace and which was led by a well-intentioned poet, Georg Herwegh. The revolutionaries found little support and faced determined liberal leaders; a combined force of rather unreliable troops from Baden, stiffened by troops from Hessen and other German states defeated Hecker's republican supporters. By the end of April it was all over. If Germany were to be unified it would not be done by a republican uprising sweeping away the princes and their states. This first test of power between liberal evolution hoping to work with the princes and the republican revolutionaries intent on creating a new society was a decisive and a correct indication of the balance of power between them throughout the revolutionary year. The continuing importance of the powers of the individual states in suppressing the rising was also emphasized.

The idea of a national parliament aroused great German enthusiasm, but in the Austrian half of the Habsburg Monarchy the Czechs and Slovaks refused to vote. It has been estimated that about half of all those who were theoretically entitled to vote actually did so. Despite all the various state interpretations and restrictions – in Prussia incidentally there were not many – the 596 members of the Frankfurt parliament were elected by a very wide franchise, giving more people the right to vote than did 'liberal' Britain at the time.

Frank Eyck, historian of the Frankfurt parliament, has described it as, above all, a lawyer's parliament. It certainly was the most educated assembly of any parliament then in being and quite probably more academic than any that has existed since; eight out of ten of its members had received a university education, the majority in law. These men were well qualified to hammer out the niceties of constitution-making, though their legal training did not guarantee the endowment of wisdom or a wider practical view of the world. It is interesting to look more closely at the composition of the Frankfurt parliament.

In many ways the kind of men sent to Frankfurt by a popular vote were not what might have been expected. Not a single working man was elected and only one peasant. By way of contrast, two political censors of the old régime also managed to reach Frankfurt. The majority of the members came from the influential social minority of professional men: teachers, civil servants and lawyers. There were relatively few landowners or businessmen. Though the representatives were drawn from a narrow band of society, there were many able men in the Frankfurt parliament. Quite a number of them had not been born to influence but had risen on their merit.

The Frankfurt parliament began its labours on 18 May 1848, that is only three months after the tentative proposals had first been made for a national German parliament. Elections had been successfully organized for the first time throughout the lands of the German Confederation. The whole thing seemed like something akin to a miracle. Whatever opinion may be expressed about the subsequent lack of success of the German political leaders of '1848', they had not spent the ten weeks before the parliament met in idle visions. The gathering of a German parliament in the Paulskirche was a *practical* success.

Unhappily the Frankfurt parliament possessed no power, except what it could create for itself out of nothing or persuade the individual states of the confederation to give it. Its strength was moral.

The cardinal fact of the revolutions of 1848 is that the separate German states continued to exist, to be sure under different governments after March 1848, but separate and guarding their separate status. Here lay an essential paradox and contradiction in the Germany of 1848. There was pride and attachment to the idea of a unified Germany, especially in dealings with Germany's neighbours, but the majority of Germans who lived in the larger states, especially in Prussia and Bavaria, also wished to preserve the identity and independence of their own state. Only the revolutionaries of the left, and they were everywhere a minority, had no strong feelings about state loyalties; their prime aim was social revolution and the foundation of one or several republics. For different reasons, the revolutionary 'left', and the liberals of Frankfurt striving for unity, both underestimated the German form of the 'nationalities' problem, the strength of the German states. Without great popular support, which was not forthcoming, the states could not be swept away or reduced to provinces (Länder). It is this which made the efforts of the Frankfurt parliament to build up a unified Germany around the nucleus of the assembly so unreal.

The parliamentarians in Frankfurt cannot really be condemned for both trying to build up centralized power and for living in 'cloud cuckoo land'. Did they have a slim chance which they lost by their mismanagement? Like all hypothetical questions an answer can only express an opinion. It must be remembered that membership of state and national parliaments was based on the same electoral roots. It is evident that the Prussian liberals remained loyal Prussians. Had they exercised a clear choice in favour of German unity it is improbable that in 1848 any more than in 1849 they could have persuaded Frederick William IV and his army to submerge Prussian policy in a wider German sovereignty of the people. What was thus required of the Prussian liberal was both a denial of Prussia and of the Hohenzollerns – quite unthinkable! And even if the liberals had called on revolutionary support from the people, the repression in Prussia would have come sooner and would have been as violent and bloody as in Paris. The answer therefore is that little could be done in the Frankfurt German parliament, though this was not evident at the time. The decisive course in 1848 was being shaped in the Habsburg Empire and in Berlin, not in the free city of Frankfurt.

The Frankfurt parliament got down to important business straight away. Heinrich von Gagern was elected the first President of the assembly, a distinguished, sincerely liberal man with considerable political experience but with none of the genius or force of personality which outstanding leaders possess. He was virtuous and not ruthless, full of good qualities but lacking in those that can fashion success from adversity; like the Frankfurt parliament judged as a whole, he was altogether too noble of character for the task in hand but reflected the ideal of the majority of the parliamentarians of the time.

Next the parliamentarians tackled the basic question of the relationship of the Frankfurt national German parliament to all the parliaments which were assembling and passing legislation in their own states which required the signature of their prince. They solved it speedily by declaring that the constitution they would frame was to be sovereign; they tactfully did not deny the right of state parliaments and princes to promulgate state legislation but declared that this legislation would only be valid as long as it did not run counter to the constitution which would be drawn up by the national assembly which was based 'on the will and election of the German people, to found the unity and political liberty of Germany'.

So now by the end of May 1848 the Frankfurt parliament had declared itself sovereign over princes and state parliaments though it possessed neither an army nor a government. The assembly next created its own government for Germany and decided on the election of a temporary head of state. They avoided a Prussian. John, an Austrian Archduke, was found and duly elected on 29 June 1848 by the assembly. He was an unusual Archduke with a reputation for liberal and national German ideas, unostentatious and married to the daughter of a village postmaster. He was also rather elderly (66 in 1848), lacked the strong personality to match his ambition and had to divide his attention between Frankfurt and Vienna. Could this Habsburg be the head of a Germany which also included Austria, thus entailing the possible break-up of the Habsburg Empire? Or would he work for a German Empire excluding his own people, the Austrian Germans? The riddle never had to be solved. He was given the title of Imperial Regent (*Reichsverweser*).* He was vested with the 'provisional central power' and it was his responsibility to appoint ministers. The first minister-president was Charles Prince Leiningen, Queen Victoria's half-brother and a confirmed liberal. A number of other ministers were appointed, including Schmerling as Minister of the Interior. But there were no ministries or bureaucracy to carry out their decisions. Crucial was the question of the army, or rather armies, each hitherto regarding its own ruler as sole commander-in-chief. Without an army loyal to the central government there could be no real authority. The one army capable of filling the bill in 1848 was the Prussian, engaged in fighting the Danes. A Prussian general, Eduard von Peucker, was appointed 'Minister of War' but

---

* In the Holy Roman Empire after the death of an Emperor an Imperial Regent was appointed until a new Emperor could be elected. The title chosen in 1848 emphasized both continuity and the caretaker nature of the office.

only accepted on condition that the Prussian army would continue separately and that he would not have to act in any way contrary to the command of the King of Prussia. Peucker's attempts as Imperial Minister of War to gain control in 'exceptional circumstances' of the armies of the separate states found no support in Prussia, Bavaria or Austria whose rulers commanded the only armies that mattered. The central *power* of Frankfurt was non-existent in reality despite the successful creation of Federal institutions. The power depended on the willing co-operation of the individual states or rather of their rulers. These were biding their time and had no intention of fulfilling the minor constitutional role the liberals were designing for them.

The Frankfurt parliamentarians have also been condemned for exhibiting chauvinism in regard to the Poles, and of denying rights to other nationalities which they demanded for Germans. But a policy of freedom for all Poles would have been totally impractical as it would have set the Prussian state against Frankfurt and probably led to immediate Russian intervention. Poland was partitioned; it could not be reconstituted without the simultaneous defeat of Russia, Austria and Prussia which did not occur until 1917–18. The altruism required to free Poland, moreover, as a gesture of national brotherhood would have been virtually unique in history.

The nationalism of Frankfurt manifested itself in particular in relation to the predominantly ethnic German provinces of Schleswig-Holstein which the King of Denmark tried to bind more closely to his kingdom; but it must be noted that the climate of general liberal opinion throughout Europe did not consider that minorities possessed the right of self-determination; had such a view existed it would have benefited the Danes in northern Schleswig. On the other hand, the Frankfurt parliament did not seriously consider that the non-German territories of the Habsburg Empire should be forced into a united unified Germany. There was no general agitation against Palacký or the Slavs. Thus it does not seem appropriate to look upon the moderate liberals of Frankfurt as the forerunners of the Nazis or to accuse them of excessive nationalism when their primary aim was to make a reality of a German nation.

There were no actual modern parties as such in the Frankfurt parliament but there were distinct groupings ranging from the conservative right to the republican left as well as a large number of uncommitted members. The division which was revealed by the debates of the Frankfurt parliament from May to August 1848 was basically between two groups. There were those who were opposed to a social revolution and who believed German unity could only be built federally with the co-operation of state parliaments and princes. They were the great majority; but a minority did not wish to make existing institutions work. Their real aim was revolution; they were less concerned with the form of German unity than intent on removing all power from the princes, and if possible the princes themselves. At best they were genuinely democratic, believing that an elected German parliament could supersede the governments and the authority of the princes. Their influence was greater than their number as they manœuvred, cleverly aligning themselves tactically with other groups on the issues which cut across ideological differences between the Centre and the Right in order to further their own aims. None of this was to have much influence on the course of events in 1848–9. By the time the Frankfurt parliament turned to their main task of framing a constitution for Germany, the King of Prussia and the Habsburg Emperor were making ready to put an end to the aspirations of 1848 in their own dominions. Despite the early successes of the 1848 revolutions in Prussia and the German states there probably never was a genuine chance of creating a unified German nation at Frankfurt ruled by a German government in the name of a German monarch. The foundation of a German republic in 1848 based on the votes of the people was an even more remote possibility. This has to be borne in mind before easy and hasty judgments are made on the words and actions of the German liberals of 1848.

5

Prussia and the Constitutional Cause in Germany in 1848

What happened in Prussia in 1848 was decisive for the cause of constitutionalism and for German unity, since the other 'German' great power, the Habsburg Monarchy, was immobilized internationally. Threatened in Italy and Hungary, the rulers of the Habsburg Empire could only act as onlookers in the German troubles of the revolutionary year. This gave Prussia a unique chance to play a dominant role in German affairs. But Prussia did not grasp this opportunity. It was a failure, not only on the part of the king and his conservative advisers, but also of the Prussian liberal ministry whose feelings towards German unification were ambivalent. They failed in 'Germany' because in the last resort they were not all that anxious to succeed.

Prussia was a reality and Germany was not. Prussia had become a large and powerful state in its own right with its own traditions, many of which, in the fields of education, administration and law, were progressive. Even in 1871, at the pinnacle of Prussian success, William I was loath to submerge the reality of being 'King of Prussia' for the shadow of 'German Emperor' – at least that is how he viewed it at the time. To the more prosperous and solid Rhinelanders and the growing population of Berlin it looked, in the spring of 1848, as if Prussia was heading in the right direction; good government would go hand in hand with prosperity. Another obstacle to unification was that although Germany did not exist the smaller German states did, and how could the princes of the separate states be coerced into giving up their powers? A third obstacle is sometimes put forward by historians. They argue that Germany's neighbours, especially Russia, would not have permitted German unification but wished to keep Germany weak and divided. In fact the contrary is true. With Austria paralysed, Germany's neighbours were too preoccupied with their own internal troubles, real or imaginary, to risk war over the future of Germany. If there was one year in the nineteenth century when Germany could have been unified without a European war it was 1848. Instead Germany was to be unified by three wars. These 'wars of unification' left a legacy of military glorification and a belief that what Germany had gained by the sword she would only be able to keep by the sword. From this mentality there developed the myth of malevolent neighbours and the phobia of the danger of becoming the victim of a hostile encirclement. Its counterpart was the often outwardly aggressive style of German foreign policy with its emphasis on 'blood and iron'.

In 1848 the disorders in Prussia were nothing like as widespread as in the small south-western German states with their many poor peasant smallholders. The prospect of giving up being a Prussian in order to become a German did not, after all, prove so very enticing. How would this new untried Germany be governed? There was not any theoretical objection to a united Germany on the part of the liberals – quite the contrary – but rather a general feeling that the priority had to be Prussia first, then Germany. After all, in territorial extent, if the Habsburg dominions are excluded, Prussia comprised two-thirds of Germany in 1848! So what seemed important to the liberals in Prussia, and the youngest and most energetic of them sat in the parliament in Berlin and not in the assembly at Frankfurt, was to consolidate their political position in Prussia. When that was achieved, the German question too would somehow be solved. The constitutional and liberal ministry in Berlin, led by the Rhinelanders Camphausen and Hansemann, thus was more concerned with strengthening its own power in Prussia against the Right and the Left than to hand over its power and play a subservient role to the national parliament in Frankfurt. They simply did not see themselves as a 'caretaker' administration until such a time as a government for all Germany had been formed.

There was no class-conscious 'proletariat' (or a large 'middle class') in Prussia; it is possible to identify groups which had common problems, such as apprentices, unemployed factory workers, beggars, shop assistants, domestic servants and so on, some of whom for a period of time co-operated together bound in an immediate common purpose; but how they each saw the future differed widely nevertheless. As for the peasants of Prussia, although they were not everywhere as quiescent in 1848 as Bismarck pictured them in his *Reminiscences*, they made no joint effort with the townspeople. There was no revolutionary conspiracy, very little organization or planning, and consequently, no co-ordination. There was also widespread reverence for the Hohenzollern dynasty of Prussian kings and faith in its intentions and benevolence. There was practically no desire in Prussia for a republic; specific reforms were demanded, though there was no clear recognition in March 1848 that while some meant constitutional reform, others were struggling for social reform. It is even doubtful whether national sentiments played a significant role among the poorer sections of the community.

In this situation much depended on the character and attitude of the monarch. It is a curious coincidence that four thrones in Europe were simultaneously in the hands of monarchs who all showed signs of mental incapacity in 1848. Ludwig I of Bavaria's infatuation for Lola Montez clouded his judgment; Louis Philippe, intellectually ossified, gave up his throne in despair; Ferdinand of Austria was physically handicapped and mentally weak, and Frederick William IV, on whom so much hope had been placed by liberals, already in 1848 exhibited the symptoms of the mental incapacity that overtook him ten years later.

Frederick William IV was a gifted man, he was artistic and a patron of the arts. In moments of elation, Frederick William was given to the grandiose. He was struck with awe by St Peter's in Rome. He romanticized the Middle Ages, a common intellectual trend of the 1820s and 1830s, and saw himself as part of the divine scheme, a prince responsible to God, the father of his people. His view of society was hierarchical, a pyramid with himself at the apex. He believed that the people could not rule themselves or demand rights; the different 'orders' of the provinces of his kingdom should be represented by councils, nobles, burghers, craftsmen and so on, who would petition the king to make known their needs. He admired the organization of the Catholic Church and eased the position of catholics in Prussia. He revered what he looked upon as the centuries-old tradition of the Holy Roman Empire and saw in Metternich a friend and ally. Consequently he was disinclined to assert Prussia in rivalry to Austria for supremacy in 'Germany', whose very existence would be a break with tradition. The new-fangled ideas of a modern German nation which would sweep away the Holy Roman order, the rights of princes, their states and institutions, were entirely alien to his outlook. For him the empire really was 'Holy', an almost mystical union of princes linked with the Habsburgs and a hallowed past. He regarded a constitution as a piece of paper which republics produced. Constitutions were foreign French inventions, the product of an era that had produced the Terror in 1793 and the guillotine. Frederick William's personality was split, half modern and the other half out of tune with his day. He was the first Prussian king to summon a sort of parliamentary assembly. Representatives from the separate provincial estates were called together in one assembly known, not as the Prussian parliament, but merely as the United Diet; they gathered in Berlin in 1847. Frederick William addressed them not as parliamentarians but as obedient subjects completely subservient to the throne. 'I am moved to declare solemnly that no power on earth will ever succeed in prevailing on me to transform the natural relationship between prince and people, the relationship which by its inward truth has made us so powerful, into a contractual constitutional one. Never will I permit a written sheet of paper to come between our God in heaven and this land...to rule us with its paragraphs and supplant the old, sacred loyalty.'

Even in an age when monarchs still believed in the virtues of absolutism, Frederick William's ideas seemed decidedly odd. He could be generous and tolerant, allowing some academic freedom – for instance he reinstated the venerable cultural patriot, Ernst Moritz Arndt, in his professorship at Bonn – all this was mistaken for 'liberal tendencies'; with a swing in mood he could be petty, spiteful and vindictive. At times, when he wished, he could exercise great charm and was a gifted speaker and writer; he would equally lose himself in foolishness. His one consistent virtue, unusual for a Prussian prince, was his lack of interest in the army and lack of desire for territorial aggrandizement. On manœuvres, the guns could not be fired too near his person for fear of injuring his sensitive nerves. This was the strange man who ruled over the old Prussia, a state powerful and in some ways progressive, but dedicated in the 1840s to order and not military expansion or international rivalry. For the liberal Germans to pin their hopes on him to provide the leadership necessary to create a constitutional modern Germany was a pathetic illusion.

When the news of the revolution in France reached him, Frederick William IV's first reaction early in March was to try to form a conservative front of states and he sent appeals to Russia and Britain. His overtures were coolly received in London and St Petersburg. At home Frederick William was ready to make some tactical concessions to appease the opposition. Presumably to remove one focus of opposition, Frederick William decided to adjourn the meeting of the United Diet but promised that the Diet would henceforth be called regularly, a concession for which this parliamentary assembly had hitherto striven in vain. The United Diet's dispersal at this critical juncture, however, was not a wise move from the king's point of view. The debate about the constitution could now no longer be contained in the council chamber at a time when political tensions were beginning to make themselves felt in the streets of Berlin.

On 13 March 1848 the first clashes occurred between the royal troops and the Berliners. Three days later the news of the revolution in Vienna greatly affected the mood in Berlin. Feeling ran high against the large numbers of troops the king had called into his capital from garrisons outside the city. Prince William of Prussia,

Frederick William's younger brother, who later reigned quietly and decently as William I, in 1848 led the military party at the palace, which stridently argued that no concessions should be made to popular demands. The prince soon had to place himself beyond the anger of the population and like many other failures of 1848, socialist and conservative, sought refuge in England. After much hesitation, Frederick William IV decided on further concessions to avoid conflict. He promised to recall the United Diet soon and to end censorship. These concessions were made on Saturday, 18 March, that is *before* the fighting flared up in Berlin.

The populace now pressed their still unsatisfied demands. They were more of a local character than matters of ideological or constitutional principle. The troops were to leave Berlin and to be sent outside the boundaries of the city. The king was assured that he would be safe among his subjects. Unhappily as the crowds, mostly of better-dressed citizens, gathered that afternoon outside the palace, the king gave the order to clear the palace square – typically he had taken two steps forward and now was taking one step backwards. When troops and citizens confronted each other at such close quarters, with tension running high between them, the order to clear the crowds from the palace square was likely to lead to violence and brutality. Two shots, probably fired by some grenadier in panic, an occurrence in 1848 so characteristic of these urban confrontations between citizens and soldiers, turned a peaceful demonstration into a full-blooded riot. The people cried 'Betrayed!' and took to the barricades; but the king's troops won control of the centre of the city. The king could easily have mastered the situation in Berlin by force. The army was efficient, ruthless and completely loyal. In fact, the army was more ruthless than the king. He spent an anguished night of indecision in the palace; he abhorred bloodshed and decided to address a personal appeal *To my dear Berliners* which, on the following morning, was pinned to the trees of the city. The king promised to discuss all issues and to withdraw the troops from Berlin (meaning gradually). On Sunday, 19 March, complete confusion reigned in the palace; instead of partially withdrawing to the inner city as the king expected, the troops, due to a misunderstanding never fully explained, departed from Berlin altogether and the king, who even before the violence had considered retiring to Potsdam, was left behind in the palace guarded only by the citizens of Berlin. Spontaneously they required the king to honour their dead just as he would honour the dead grenadiers who had fallen in battle. It was a gesture of deep symbolic significance. The king felt he had no choice though he was appalled at siding with his people against the army which served him. On the balcony of the palace, he saluted the bodies of the victims drawn up in carts before him in the palace square.

Frederick William's heart was not in this role of 'citizen-king.' His complete safety in Berlin pointed to the possibilities of transforming the dynasty into a 'popular' monarchy; but he hated such notions as much as bloodshed. This the Berliners did not know. They deluded themselves into thinking that a new bond had been forged between the people and the Hohenzollern rulers. They believed that they had beaten the army and that Frederick William was on their side.

Once safely back in Potsdam, Frederick William expressed his true feelings. He looked back on the days he had spent alone in Berlin with his subjects not with pride, but with humiliation. He accused the Berliners of having usurped the divine order in forcing the hand of the king. He had all the same made important concessions. He had accepted in principle constitutional government, the appointment of ministers from the liberal opposition of the United Diet, and the calling of a new parliament whose main task it would be to come to an agreement with the crown on a constitution for Prussia. He planned no revenge. He allowed the making of policy to remain with the newly appointed Prussian government of liberal 'March ministers', but his letters from Potsdam written at this time show how much he disapproved of their policy, although he contemplated no active steps against Berlin or the ministry. He regarded the ministers personally as loyal and worthy subjects though following policies that seemed to him to be misguided.

The new Camphausen ministry in Berlin was composed of liberals completely loyal to the crown and as determined to oppose social revolution as the king and the Junkers. They envisaged a constitution in which the monarch and ministers would share power only consulting parliament. The ministry supervised the elections to a Prussian parliament, or national assembly as it was called, on the basis of a franchise of manhood suffrage, a franchise far in advance of the British at that time. Manhood suffrage was a common aim of liberals in 1848. In France, as has been seen, it proved a weapon that supported the conservative social stand of the French liberals. It may be that the Prussian liberals too recognized that the conservative countryside would hold the militants in check in the towns. In any case, there was another safeguard; the elections of members of parliament were to be indirect, the people electing electors who would choose the members of the parliament, a device intended to ensure that extremists would be excluded.

In questions of foreign policy, the new minister responsible, Heinrich von Arnim-Suckow wished to follow a vigorous German policy. He believed that the revolutionary situation should be utilized to unify Germany without the Habsburg dominions by placing the King of Prussia in the forefront of a German movement. This was later Bismarck's 'solution'; it was a unification from above and not by the people. What Arnim wanted was to stultify the efforts for unity by democratic means through a German parliament.

Arnim also vigorously pushed forward the Polish question; he was at first ready to abandon the Duchy of Posen (Prussian since 1815 again) and to recreate a Polish nation in order to roll Russia back eastward. Arnim even welcomed the prospect of war with Russia as creating the fervour necessary for a Prussian solution of German unity. There was talk of an alliance with revolutionary France in April 1848, but the government in Paris was not prepared to go beyond moral support. Nothing came of Arnim's Polish plans. When Poles and Prussians clashed in Posen it soon cured the Prussians of espousing Polish nationalism. Anyway, to champion Germans who were suppressed, rather than Poles, was far more likely to gain Prussia the applause of 'Germany' So Arnim was determined to espouse the claims of Germans in the Duchies of Schleswig-Holstein, dragging the King of Prussia into a war against Denmark (see p. 75).

Frederick William IV was deeply opposed to all these policies. He would not 'usurp' the imperial crown which belonged to Austria. In his private letters he condemned a 'German' unity that would have excluded a third of the 'imperial' lands; nor would he accept a crown from any but the hands of princes. Similar contradictions beset him when he followed Arnim's policy of war with Denmark on behalf of the Duchies of Schleswig-Holstein. The Prussian conquest of the duchies quite appealed to him, but acting on behalf of, or even in parallel with, the parliamentarians of Frankfurt against the wishes of real monarchs, like the Tsar of Russia, filled him with shame. His insistence on concluding an armistice with the Danes, known as the Armistice of Malmö, on 26 August 1848, marks the resumption by the king of control over Prussian foreign policy and the repudiation of Arnim's ideas. Similarly, by the summer of 1848 there was little left of the Prussian liberal policy in Poland. Those Poles in Prussian Poland, who had come into conflict with Germans living there, had been supressed by the army in the spring; a little later the greater portion of Posen was admitted to the German Confederation and only a small part was left for a future Polish nation, of which less and less was heard. The most likely explanation of Prussian foreign policy in the summer of 1848 is that the king, having taken charge of policy again, was determined to dissociate Prussia from the causes championed by the 'usurpers' of the divine powers of princes and so from the 'Executive' for Germany at Frankfurt. This rather than fear of Russia or Britain explains his policy sufficiently. What seemed like a Prussian retreat was in fact a reassertion of the royal prerogative. He wanted to discredit all self-styled popular rule, especially that of the parliamentarians of Frankfurt.

Internally the Camphausen Ministry did not succeed in transforming Prussia despite elections and the meeting of the new Prussian national assembly in May. Drafts for a constitution were laid before the national assembly but the ministers could not gain parliamentary approval for a constitution which would have permitted parliament no effective control over the king. The constitutional settlement remained in dispute up to the moment when the king dismissed the parliamentarians in December 1848 (p.75). Meantime the army remained loyal to the crown. Indeed the whole administration was still absolutist in sentiment and so the liberals in the towns, and especially in Berlin, became isolated from the countryside. They also isolated themselves from the poor whose expectations they could not fulfil. For liberalism in Prussia, as elsewhere in Europe, was not a licence for social revolution or intended to pave the way for handing over control to the populace and their militant leaders in the towns. The liberal ministry filled the power vacuum created by the departure of the king and the army to Potsdam by forming a Civic Guard in Berlin. The better-off were prepared to fight for law and order and to preserve their way of life. The Civic Guard was composed mainly of those with a financial stake in stability. The Prussian liberal ministry was discomfited by the radicalism of the left in the Prussian parliament they had created. The frustrated left wing opposition, excluded from a share of power, began to organize democratic and socialist clubs. Numerous meetings were held and petitions sent. The lack of improvement of economic conditions and general dissatisfaction and disappointment at the lack of tangible benefit from the victories of March led to a renewal of tension in the city. Although nothing as widespread and serious as the 'June Days' occurred in Berlin, there was a serious clash between the Civic Guard and the populace on 14 June 1848, when a mob invaded and seized arms from the Arsenal and Military Museum (Zeughaus). The underlying issue at stake for the few militants was whether the March 'revolution' should now be completed and the sovereignty of the people should be seen to be established or whether Prussia, with the king's approval, should move along the path of constitutionalism which he could claim had begun before the events of March in Berlin. Were the 'March days' the beginning of a new era or irrelevant? Continuity and legality or revolution? There was no doubt where the majority and Camphausen stood. They opposed violence and disorder. The militants in Berlin were easily brought under control but the task of trying to defend a legal order on behalf of a king who, in Potsdam, was unreliable in his support, was too much for Camphausen.

In Potsdam, meantime, the king was surrounded by a court camarilla of advisers, a kind of alternative ministry, urging him to act.

Frederick William IV indecisively waited on events which, as it turned out proved to be his best policy. During the summer of 1848 the question still appeared to remain open whether the 'March' days would lead to a broadly-based constitutional government, or whether the conservative Prussian order would be restored. What had become clear was that the liberal ministry of Camphausen stood hopelessly in the middle, and that no stability could be found in this middle position of compromise between the enlightened political absolutism of the pre-1848 years under the Prussian crown on the one hand, or to a form of popularly-based government on the other, which would reduce the position of the crown to only symbolic significance. Faced with this unpalatable choice, the old liberals in the end preferred to throw in their lot with the crown, rather than with the revolution. Already in June 1848, soon after the clash at the *Zeughaus*, Camphausen had resigned. Similarly, on the wider question of Germany, the Germany the Frankfurt parliament tried to create could neither gain the acceptance of the Prussian crown, nor the sustained support of Prussian liberals, whose personal loyalty to the Prussian king took precedence over any national or constitutional cause.

The truth is that the 'revolution' in Prussia had never amounted to much more than a serious riot in Berlin and industrial unrest in Silesia and the Rhineland. It had been given the semblance of success by the king's readiness for a time to allow the making of decisions to pass from his hands to that of the liberal ministry; but so fundamentally strong was his position, so unsuccessful the revolution in terms of force, that from the moment the king decided to resume control of Prussia's officers and to select his ministers, that power was his for the asking. And this is the unexpected development: blind reaction did not follow when the force of the revolutions of 1848 had spent itself. The Prussian conservatives were not reactionaries but in many ways they too looked forward to a reformed, modernized Prussia. The astonishing rise of Prussia during the third quarter of the nineteenth century would not otherwise have been possible. Prussia could never have become the vigorous leading German and continental European power if the king's ministers had merely wished to turn the clock back. They undoubtedly opposed with all their strength the notion of 'parliamentary sovereignty'. In its place the conservatives of the 1850s and Bismarck in the 1860s sought to create a novel constitutional structure. It contained concessions to liberal ideas of representative government; it theoretically also confirmed the monarch's divine right to rule whilst limiting his freedom to act in practice. It was intended to allow the authority of the state to be exercised by the conservative elements of Prussia in the interests of the state. Theoretically the concept was full of contradictions but the constitutions functioned for half a century during which period Prussia became a world power. The King of Prussia lacked the strength of will to make himself an absolute ruler in 1848, and listened to his advisers, whose loyalty to the institution of the crown could not be doubted. By character, Frederick William was inclined to temporize and so he consented eventually in December 1848 to the plans of his ministers to impose a political compromise, not at the behest of politicians, but by the Grace of God in conformity with the Prussian crown motto, taken by him quite literally, *Gott mit uns* (God with us). (See p. 113.)

6

Britain and Russia in 1848 and the Diplomacy of the Powers

Two great powers Britain and Russia, both belonging to Europe, yet geographically flanking the continental land mass, remained virtually untouched by the tide of revolution; but here the similarity between their experiences ended. To a Europe in turmoil, the historical evolution and the institutions of these two states seemed to polarize the conflict of the mid-nineteenth century: liberalism versus autocracy. Britain had won for herself an image as the champion of liberalism; Russia was denounced and hated by all reformers from the moderate to the extreme as the leading representative of autocracy. Since the days of the 'Holy Alliance' the tsars of Russia were credited with the desire to use their huge armies to crush individual liberties at home and abroad, to act in other words as the 'gendarmes of Europe'. Although such crude national characterizations do not stand up to a close examination, powerful images, even when far removed from the truth, do influence contemporary society.

It might be supposed that the struggle in 1848 on the continent of Europe, where issues of social change, individual and political rights and national feeling all played so large a part, would form a testing battleground between Britain and Russia, between liberalism and autocracy. The diplomacy of the previous quarter of a century, dominated in Britain by Canning and Palmerston, was concerned, in part, with the success or failure of the constitutional cause in western Europe. Now in 1848 the conflict had spread, and Palmerston was once more foreign secretary. He popularly personified John Bull and liberalism as Nicholas I, Tsar of Russia, was the symbol of arch-reaction. Would their intervention and influence on the events of 1848 prove decisive for the revolutionary cause? It might have done so had they intervened. But nothing is more striking than the contrast between their words and their deeds. Britain and Russia played a waiting game, more concerned to keep out of war and to insulate themselves from unrest and extremism than with furthering ideological causes on the continent. The impact of Russian and British policies was at best marginal and measured by their effect it is difficult to credit either country with having brought about any decisive change in Europe during 1848. Even the claim that they kept each other in check is doubtful since in 1848 there was more co-operation than antagonism between them.

If we were to judge the situation by the royal correspondence of 1848 we would reach a very different and mistaken conclusion. The crowned heads of Europe wrote to each other letters of doom-laden prophecy. If the revolutions succeeded then none of them would be safe. The spectre of 1792 seemed to haunt them all. From the complete safety and happy domesticity of Buckingham Palace Queen Victoria wrote to her Uncle Leopold, the King of the Belgians; 'Since 24th February I feel an uncertainty in everything existing, which...one never felt before. When one thinks of one's children, their education, their future – and prays for them – I always think and say to myself, "Let them grow up fit for *whatever station* they may be placed in – *high or low.*" This one never thought of before, but I *do* always now. Altogether one's whole disposition is so changed – *bores* and trifles...one looks upon as good things and quite a blessing – provided one can *keep one's position in quiet!*'* It was of course absurd for Queen Victoria to fear for the safety of the royal family in July 1848, especially when months earlier the Chartist demonstration of 10 April had passed off in so orderly and constitutional a manner. There was no possibility of revolution in Britain, not even in Ireland as it turned out.

Few of the Chartists sought revolution or violent confrontation. At heart the vast majority respected and trusted Britain's institution and especially parliament. They wished to reform and strengthen parliament not to replace it. And to the House of Commons the Chartists sent their petitions. The hey-day of Chartism had long passed in 1848, for the movement was at its most formidable during the depressed years from 1838 to 1841. Renewed economic crisis in 1847 and 1848 and the events on the continent gave Chartism one last lease of life. The British working people were not in the least revolutionary and the 'middle class' landowners, traders and shop-keepers backed the government's formidable precautionary efforts to preserve law and order. The monster meeting on Kennington Common organized by the Chartists for 10 April 1848, turned out a mild affair and the smaller than expected crowd quietly dispersed when refused permission to cross the bridges of the Thames to Westminster. In some provincial towns Chartism proved more riotous but nowhere

* *The Letters of Queen Victoria*, II, pp. 183–4.

was it a serious threat. More surprisingly the 'Sister Isle', Ireland, remained quiescent, stunned by its economic misfortunes. In 1847 and 1848 Irishmen had been prominent in the leadership of Chartism, but in Ireland itself a much more revolutionary conspiracy was planned by 'Young Ireland'. The government was well prepared here too to suppress the conspiracy. The only practical outcome was a vain attempt to capture Kilkenny. Practically no one in Ireland heeded 'Young Ireland's' call to revolution and the planned rising was a fiasco, and its leaders were marched to jail or fled into exile.

The repercussions of 1848 in Britain reflected the enlightened sense of self-preservation and confidence of the broad British middle and ruling classes. Typical of the enlightened viewpoint was the advice Prince Albert sent to Lord John Russell, the Prime Minister, on the very day, 10 April 1848, the Chartists met on Kennington Common. He hoped there would be no repression or bloodshed as it was unnecessary. 'I don't feel doubtful for a moment who will be found the stronger, but should be exceedingly mortified if anything like a commotion was to take place', he wrote, and went on to urge that positive steps should be taken to help the unemployed; 'I find, to my great regret, that the number of workmen of all trades out of employment is *very* large, and that it has been increased by the reduction of all the works under government, owing to the clamour for economy in the House of Commons... Surely this is not the moment for the taxpayers to economize upon the working classes!'* Avoiding extremes, a sufficient number of those who were privileged politically and economically in Britain recognized that they must continue to ameliorate bad working conditions, permit trade union associations, allow working people an opportunity of sharing in greater prosperity and offer gradual political enfranchisement. The lack of violence in England convinced most Whigs and Tories that in following policies of reform since 1832 and in not being panicked into measures of violent repression they were on the right road.

The same attitude of avoiding extremes also motivated Britain's policy abroad. In the House of Commons Palmerston declared in March 1848, 'I hold that the real policy of England – apart from questions which involve her own particular interests, political or commercial – is to be the champion of justice and right; pursuing that course with moderation and prudence, not becoming the Quixote of the world, but giving the weight of her moral sanction and support wherever she thinks that justice is...' The qualification 'apart from'... is vital to an understanding of Palmerston's policy

---

* *Letters of Queen Victoria*, II, p. 168.

of 'Britain first'. Later on in the same address to the Commons Palmerston emphasized his pragmatism in judging each situation on the merits of how it affected Britain, 'We have no eternal allies, and we have no perpetual enemies. Our interests are eternal and perpetual, and those interests it is our duty to follow'.*

The need for timely reform and adaptation was the unwelcome counsel Palmerston had showered on the continental rulers large and small before the outbreak of the revolution. He preferred the 'unreformed' rulers to uncertain revolutionary leaders. Palmerston genuinely believed in constitutional principles but not to the point where he would contemplate encouraging revolution, whose consequences could endanger peace and British interests. For all Palmerston's diplomatic activity before and during the revolution of 1848, it is doubtful that it accomplished much. The King of Prussia did not listen to his advice and the Queen of Spain sent home the British ambassador. But the most extraordinary aspect of Palmerston's attempt to tutor Europe had been the decision in September 1847 to send Lord Minto, a Cabinet Minister, to the Italian courts, 'to teach politics in the country in which Machiavelli was born', as Disraeli later scathingly put it. Minto was received politely but judged by results his mission was not a success. In January 1848 Italy passed from general ferment to revolution when Sicily rose against the rule of the King of Naples (p. 209).

Once the revolutions had broken out, Palmerston urged the traditional British policy of 'non-intervention' on neighbouring states. He created an impression that Britain would oppose intervention, but this was bluff. And so he warned Metternich against intervention in Naples. He followed in February and March 1848 a similar policy in regard to the newly proclaimed Republic in France. On 26 February 1848 he instructed Lord Normanby, the British ambassador in Paris, 'to acknowledge whatever rule may be established with apparent prospect of permanency, but none other. We desire friendship and extended commercial intercourse with France, and peace between France and the rest of Europe. We will engage to prevent the rest of Europe from meddling with France ... The French rulers must engage to prevent France from assailing any part of the rest of Europe.' To this policy Palmerston held firm and in so doing gave some slight moral support to Lamartine and the conservatives who precariously dominated the provisional government. Palmerston made it clear that Britain had no quarrel with the republic as such, or with any particular form of government in France, and that good relations would depend entirely on the foreign policy pursued by the provisional

* K. Bourne, *The Foreign Policy of Victorian England 1830–1902*, (Oxford, 1970), p. 291.

government. If France did not behave aggressively toward her neighbours then, wrote Palmerston, 'our relations with France may be
placed on a footing more friendly than they have been or were likely
to be with Louis Philippe and Guizot.' Lamartine's famous manifesto
of 4 March 1848 denouncing the Vienna settlement did not unduly
alarm Palmerston for the provisional government in the same breath
had promised to respect the frontiers of 1815 and 1830. Palmerston's
policy of realism designed to strengthen moderate French opinion,
whilst restraining France from intervening in Belgium, in Germany
and northern Italy, was in great contrast to Queen Victoria's sentimental attachment to the French Orleanist family. But though the
queen wrote indignant letters to Lord John Russell, the Prime Minister, complaining of Palmerston's lack of principles, as she viewed it,
her own influence on British foreign policy at this time was, fortunately, negligible. (Later in her reign, the queen's instincts on questions of foreign policy were to prove sounder.)

Soon no power was in a position to intervene in France. The
Austrian Empire was in turmoil. Prussian and German interests
barred the path of Russian troops moving west, which in 1848 was
unthinkable anyway. The French provisional government until the
summer of 1848 needed only to concern itself with Britain. When
Palmerston declared he would prevent Europe intervening against
France provided France did not intervene in Europe the threat he
implied was that if France did intervene outside her frontiers, she
might find Britain arraigned against her. But Palmerston was probably doing no more than restating limited traditional British interests
in defence of Belgium and the Channel coast.

Palmerston actually thought that the most important threat to British
interests lay in the diplomatic consequences of revolution and war in
northern Italy. So he advised the Austrians what to do. They should
leave Italy. Not surprisingly his advice went unheeded. The Austrians
would not accept the view that their traditional role as the predominant power in Italy had become a source of weakness rather than
strength. The early reverses the Austrians suffered in northern Italy in
March 1848 seemed to confirm Palmerston's judgement. What Palmerston feared above all was a revival of French intervention such as
had occurred during the Revolutionary and Napoleonic Wars. When
Piedmont went to war with Austria in March 1848 (see p. 210),
Palmerston's diplomatic intervention was designed to bring about a
compromise; to save Austria, to establish a compact northern Italian
state and to keep out France. France did not intervene in 1848. The
provisional government had enough problems at home and was in no
mood to engage in any risky adventures abroad. In any case Austria
was not vanquished. After Radetzky's recovery and victory at

Custozza (24 July 1848) had forced an armistice on Charles Albert there was much Anglo-French diplomatic activity in Turin and Vienna. Palmerston continued to work for a compromise peace settlement and co-operated with France not because he desired French help but to prevent France from taking unilateral action. This Anglo-French alignment was not built on a community of interests or on common feelings of sympathy for Italian nationalism but on suspicion. It was all futile. Charles Albert put an end to speculations when in March 1849 he denounced the armistice he had concluded with Austria the previous year. Radetzky made further diplomacy pointless by decisively defeating the army of Charles Albert once again at the battle of Novara (23 March 1849). Radetzky's victories enabled Austria to dictate the peace of Milan (6 August 1849) to the vanquished Piedmontese. There is no evidence that in deciding to be moderate the Austrians were influenced by pressure from Palmerston or Louis Napoleon. The credit for this belongs to the Austrians.

The situation was now in the summer of 1849 completely changed. In France the provisional government had been replaced by the conservative clerical republic with Louis Napoleon firmly installed as President. When the French finally did intervene in Italy Palmerston did nothing to stop them. In the summer of 1849 the French landed in the Papal States, occupied Rome, ended the Roman Republic and so drove Garibaldi and Mazzini into exile. Both the revolution and 'national cause' – to the extent that it existed – had been crushed by Austria and France. Austria had played a decisive role; France a very secondary part (p. 75). Palmerston's contribution looks best in Blue Books and the columns of Hansard.

France in 1848-9 did not repeat the role she had played in Europe in 1796-7 when the launching of the Italian campaign was the prelude to the Napoleonic conquest of the continent. History proved no reliable guide to the statesmen of the mid-nineteenth century though they seemed forever to be looking backward. The great issue which was to affect the history of Europe for the next hundred years was not the danger of French aggression but the consolidation of German power. This may seem obvious to historians now. It may seem strange that so few contemporaries during the 1850s and 1860s recognized how momentous the German 'question' was becoming for the future of Europe. Indeed this was not appreciated until the overwhelming power of Germany on the continent had become an established fact during the last quarter of the nineteenth century.

Successive British foreign secretaries before 1870 could not have been expected to regard an aggrandized Prussia or, if it came about, a united Germany as a danger to the peace of Europe, developments more than thirty years later. That would pass judgement with the hindsight of history. Their eyes, from Pitt and Castlereagh to Palmerston, were almost exclusively fixed on the dangers of French and Russian expansion to the peace of Europe. Despite the German connexions of Queen Victoria and Prince Albert, despite or perhaps because of the Hanover link, 'Germany' was seen as a geographical expression; the German states were expected to arrange their affairs to contribute to the 'balance of power' and thus to act as a barrier to Russia in the east and France in the west. This view of 'Germany' presupposed a good Austro-Prussian relationship and an internal 'balance of power' between them with Prussia the weaker and junior partner. A consolidation of German power that excluded Austria, or which would be based on some liberal federation of states, such as might have emerged from the Frankfurt parliament, won little sympathy from Palmerston. The British ministers could not imagine that a unified Germany was even a possibility; particularism, the division of Germany into many small states and territories, was somehow regarded as a law of nature. In 1848 Palmerston referred to German unity as a 'phantom' and a 'plaything'. He believed that to the extent that its realization would weaken Austria's position as a great power it did not serve British interests.

The attitude of France, even whilst Napoleon III was championing nationalism elsewhere, was not very different. France's leaders, whoever they were, did not regard it in France's interests to encourage the emergence of strong independent neighbours, such as unified Italy and unified Germany might one day become. But neither British nor French misgivings produced any consistent policies. British policy was largely a matter of words not deeds. France's policy of indecision in the end meant she got the worst of both worlds and a republic.

The great Powers felt a lack of sympathy for the cause of German unity and concluded that the German troubles were in any case not worth a war. This explains why their diplomacy on the Schleswig-Holstein question during 1848–9 was so ambiguous and confused. The two duchies of Schleswig-Holstein came to play a crucial role in the affairs of Europe for two decades, not because of the intrinsic importance of the dispute over them but because German nationalism was inextricably bound up with their fate. It is a paradox that the dispute about the duchies provided Prussia with both the means of discrediting the German nationalism of Frankfurt in 1848 and 1849 and the means for promoting German nationalism of the Prussian variety in 1864 and 1866. The duchies were really pawns in a much bigger game.

The essentials of the Schleswig-Holstein question are not as complicated as popular legend has made them out to be. The Duchies of Schleswig and Holstein were supposed to be indissolubly linked; their sovereign was duke of *both* duchies, and he was also the King of

Denmark. Four hundred years earlier, in 1460, a sovereign lost in the mists of history had sworn an oath to maintain the indissoluble link between the duchies in perpetuity; but perpetuity is a long time. In fact what is actually forgotten is that the two duchies *were* divided. They only became 'indivisible' once more in 1773. The second aspect of the question is that the Duchy of Holstein, but not Schleswig, had also formed a part of the Holy Roman Empire since the sixteenth century. However, Napoleon solved that by not including Holstein in his Rhine Confederation. The statesmen of Vienna should have left well alone; after all they had accepted many of Napoleon's changes in Germany and paid little regard to national feelings as far as any could be discerned in 1815; but in 1815 it was decided to make Holstein, but not Schleswig, a part of the new German Confederation and the Danish King-Duke a member. So now the duchies were at one and the same time indissolubly linked and treated differently! The Schleswig-Holstein question was thus created to plague the nineteenth century. The third important ingredient involved arose from the different laws of succession in the duchies and Denmark. In Denmark, in the absence of a male heir, the throne could be inherited through the female line; in the duchies, however, the Salic law applied, according to which only the closest male line could succeed to the dukedoms (a situation similar to the succession laws in Britain and Hanover, so that in 1837 Victoria became the heir to the British throne but could not succeed William IV as sovereign of Hanover). These three elements together make up the Schleswig-Holstein question in its legal aspects. More important was the development of German nationalism in the duchies and the Danish nationalist response.

The certainty of conflict over the succession laws had become evident in the 1840s. Christian VIII's eldest son, the later Frederick VII, was childless. On his death (which occurred in 1863), the Danish crown would then pass to Christian IX who traced his descent through his great-aunt Louisa; but the closest male descendant of the Danish royal house was Christian, Duke of Augustenburg, who would, according to the Salic Law, be entitled to succeed to the duchies. In a famous 'open letter' Christian VIII in July 1846 declared that the Danish succession law would apply to the Duchy of Schleswig, of which he was undisputed sovereign, but conceded that its application to Holstein, member of the German Confederation, was doubtful; but he also declared that it would be his aim to maintain the integrity of Denmark and the union of Schleswig and Holstein. This hardly clarified the future and was met with a storm of national protest in Germany. The great majority of the inhabitants of the duchies were ethnic German with a relatively small proportion of Danes in northern Schleswig.

The next stage of crisis occurred two years later on Christian's death on 20 January 1848. Frederick VII who succeeded to the throne of Denmark and the dukedom of the duchies, a week after his accession, announced a new constitution which provided for one parliament for the duchies and the Danish kingdom. In this he was supported by the Danish liberals. The new constitution did not actually set aside any of the existing institutions in the duchies, but the provincial representatives of Schleswig-Holstein probably rightly looked on this single greater Danish parliament as a stepping stone to a single greater Danish state; they demanded a new and separate constitution for the two duchies and the admission of *both* duchies into the German Confederation. This the king and his ministers rejected. On 24 March 1848 the Germans in the two duchies thereupon proclaimed a provisional government at Kiel independent of Denmark basing the revolt on the fiction that their sovereign Duke and King of Denmark was 'no longer free' and declaring 'We will not tolerate the sacrifice of German territory as a prey to the Danes!' For many German patriots the 'defence' of the Germans in the duchies became linked in their minds with the simultaneous efforts to create a unified Germany.

As the revolution broke out in the duchies, the Duke of Augustenburg in Berlin opportunistically prepared to take the lead as a German prince and appealed to the King of Prussia for aid against the Danes who were preparing to occupy the duchies. The new Prussian Foreign Minister, von Arnim, saw this as an opportunity of substituting Prussian leadership in the national question for social revolution at home. Early in April Prussia went to war with Denmark, ostensibly in support of the claims of the Duke of Augustenburg. The German Federal Diet recognized the provisional government of Kiel, and the Prussian Ministers, the German Diet and the liberals and radicals throughout the German state, all divergent elements in the weeks of upheaval and revolution, vied with each other in calling for the defence of the Fatherland. The King of Prussia conducted the war on behalf of the German Confederation with the help of troops from some of the northern and central German states, but already by mid-May 1848 Frederick William IV was having second thoughts about siding with the German revolution against the wishes of established monarchs, the Queen of England and the Tsar of Russia. There had been, moreover, no enthusiasm among the monarchs of the German states for war. The Danes could not do much on land but their navy blockaded the coastline and hurt trade; Prussia and the German states could do nothing on sea as they had not a single warship between them. So began a veritable German naval fever, which in the time available could lead to no results but marks the emotional origins of the German naval fever in the reign of the last Hohenzollern,

William II, early in the twentieth century. The Schleswig-Holstein conflict, it should not be overlooked, also aroused Scandinavian national fervour and a liberal '1848' Swedish Ministry promised help. In June some 4,500 Swedish-Norwegian troops actually landed in Denmark. The Germans, therefore, did not have things all their own way.

The tortuous path of peace negotiations, which within a few weeks separated Prussia from the cause of nationalist and liberal Germany as represented by Federal institutions in Frankfurt, began in May 1848 and fighting ended when Prussia and Denmark signed the armistice of Malmö on 26 August 1848 to the general indignation of German liberal patriots (p. 65). The liberals and radicals in Frankfurt accused the Prussians of betraying the national cause but they could do nothing about it. The Frankfurt parliament had begun its great labours three months earlier but the writing was already on the wall. The independent course taken by the King of Prussia showed the real distribution of power, both in Prussia and in Germany.

By the summer of 1848 the diplomacy of 'revolutionary' Europe was drawing to a close. Prussia and Austria were reverting to their traditional forms of government. In the smaller German states and at Frankfurt the men of 1848 were allowed to play out their roles a few months longer until Austria and Prussia found it expedient to put an end to their work. The tsar was reassured by the return to order and, in 1849, did his bit to hasten the restoration of Habsburg rule in Hungary (p. 108). Palmerston, despite his rhetoric about liberalism, was also reassured by the restoration to power of the continental monarchs, and welcomed the conservative turn of events in France. In the two questions in which he actively intervened in 1848 and 1849, northern Italy and Schleswig-Holstein, he achieved little in the former and to the extent that British pressure, together with Russian and French, had persuaded Frederick William IV to withdraw from the duchies – and as has been seen it is doubtful whether international pressure had been the primary reason for Frederick William's decision – Palmerston helped to injure the efforts of the Frankfurt liberals. As the new men of 1848 were losing their grip in Europe, the diplomacy of the powers marginally hastened that process; certainly no single state in Europe materially had helped their cause, neither 'revolutionary' France nor 'liberal' Britain.

Tsar Nicholas' first consideration in 1848 was the preservation of stability in Russia. He was more concerned to prevent the poison of liberalism from infecting his own dominions than filled with zeal to stamp out revolution elsewhere. Thus, as has been seen throughout 1848, he held to a cautious and conservative line of policy.

Nicholas had been successful according to his own lights. He believed the danger to Russian society came from without, from foreign doctrines and foreign influences. He had ascended the throne in 1825 when the *Decembrists* had attempted their insurrection and applied the lessons he had learnt from that secret conspiracy throughout the remainder of his reign. With the help of the secret police and of censorship he attempted to stamp out disaffection and to defeat the international conspiracy which he thought threatened the fabric of Russian society. He isolated Russian thought as much as possible from western influences. After December, 1825 his rule was seriously threatened again only once in 1830 and 1831 when the nationalism of the Poles led to a widespread rising. With brutality and ruthlessness the Poles were crushed and placed under martial law for the next twenty-four years. Organized opposition to the tsar's autocracy was confined to a few educated noblemen and writers. They were, however, powerless when faced with the organization of the imperial chancellery, whose 'Third Section' not only watched over all foreigners in Russia but arrested and exiled anyone who aroused the slightest suspicion. It has been estimated that during Nicholas' reign some 10,000 people a year were exiled for indetermined periods of time to Siberia. Any unorganized unrest, such as peasants resorting in desperation to violence, was put down ruthlessly by Nicholas' large disciplined army which blindly followed the tsar's wishes and into whose ranks the mass of the peasantry and dissidents were forced. However, the huge Russian Empire, lacking modern communication, was difficult to rule from the centre. Despite the tsar's frequent travels and interventions, a corrupt bureaucracy flourished as never before.

Censorship and persecution of the intelligentsia aroused the vocal enmity of the small minority of educated Russians, whose capacity for attacking the intellectual narrow-mindedness of the tsar was disproportionately effective. Judged by Russian standards, the era of Nicholas I, for all its undeniably repressive aspects, was not totally negative and barren. Censorship was not equally severe at all times. Indeed a brilliant circle of writers brought international renown to Russian literature during Nicholas' reign.

The role of the writer in Russia was, in the nineteenth century, and has remained in the twentieth, quite different to his role in Britain. In Britain a few writers, such as Dickens, fictionalized contemporary social problems, but in mass movements of protest the part played by writers was marginal. In Russia only the writers were able to express new ideas openly and so they have often been the only visible form of protest. Other activities which opposed the state in any form had to be conducted secretly and conspiratorially. Their impact only became evident sporadically in some violent outburst, whose origins remain frequently obscure for lack of surviving evidence. Though harassed, these literary opponents of the tsar's bureaucracy were able to continue and even to hold office as servants of the state. Alexander Pushkin, for instance, was tolerated for a time in the Russian government service after writing the *Ode to Liberty* (1820). Although involved with the *Decembrists* he had escaped punishment, and later in 1832, despite his liberal views, was restored to the staff of the Ministry of Foreign Affairs. Nicholas Gogol left Russia in 1836 to live in exile and greater freedom; his famous play *The Inspector General* lampooned the provincial bureaucracy and, with persuasive humour, revealed the corruption and stupidity of the tsar's administration. Yet it was not banned. Nicholas wished very cautiously to bring about reforms and so regarded Gogol's work as salutary, aware as he was of the truth of the portrayal. Mikhail Lermontov wrote verses in praise of Pushkin in *The Death of a Poet*. Judged as subversive, Lermontov, then a young Guards officer, was reduced to the ranks and exiled to the Caucasus. But he was allowed to return in due course to St Petersburg where he was lionized by society. Lermontov lived recklessly and, like Pushkin, was killed in a duel. Despite the vigilance of the censors, Peter Chaadaev in the *Philosophical Letters*, the first of which was written in 1829 and published in 1836, deplored Russian isolation from the West and Russia's backwardness and he advocated that Russia learn from the West in order to pass through the necessary same phases of development. The notion that Russia should learn from the West shocked and angered Nicholas. Chaadaev was declared insane and confined to his own home.

Chaadaev's characterization of Russia as bankrupt intellectually, belonging neither to the East nor to the West, led to debate and argument between two groups of intellectuals, the Westernizers and the Slavophiles. The revolutionary failures of 1848 for decades gave an ascendancy to the Slavophiles; but all ideas were regarded by Nicholas as being potentially dangerous and during the last stifling years of his reign the Slavophiles were under constant police surveillance.

For Alexander Herzen, Chaadaev's *Philosophical Letters* were an inspiration. Herzen, influenced by the ideas of Saint-Simon, became Russia's most celebrated and influential critic and was eventually exiled. Unmasked by the secret police as 'dangerous to society' he was banished from Moscow and employed as a minor official in a remote provincial town. However he was allowed to return to Moscow where he formulated ideas of an entirely new social order. In 1847, with official permission, Herzen was permitted to travel abroad. Michael Bakunin too belonged to these radical reformist Moscow circles of the 1830s and 1840s. They posed no serious threat to Nicholas I. The tsar punished the writers, sometimes harshly, but despite his absolute powers, he respected their life. Those in government employment were frequently restored to office after a suitable period of time. Once returned from exile or prison, discrimination against the individual concerned ceased and such 'ex-enemies' of the state were more magnanimously treated than would have been conceivable almost anywhere else in Europe. Nicholas' aim was correction, to make an example of those who deviated from his line of thought, but not extermination, the only solution Stalin thought possible, a century later.

Nicholas modelled himself on Peter the Great and the rulers of the era of enlightened despotism. He regarded himself as a father of his people, certain of his divine right and superior judgement but acting, so he believed, for the good of all his subjects. His life was organized on military lines and he felt at his ease in later life only in the company of the officers of his army. Nicholas was an austere, bleak man, driven by a sense of duty to God and his people. He constantly travelled through his empire in a vain effort to correct the abuses of his state and to see justice done. The disastrous Crimean War was all but lost when in 1855 Nicholas died. But to see his reign as a particularly dark period of Russian history when repression and militarism became dominant would be a mistake. The thirty years of his rule are also notable for the genuine attempts of the tsar to introduce reforms, a fact sometimes forgotten by judgements based on the post-1848 period only.

Army officers no longer ran the administration. Merit, as measured by educational standards, was at least intended to become the criterion for determining the grade of civil service appointment. Of course there was a wide gap between intention and reality. Whilst it is true that in the reign of Nicholas surveillance by the police and the encouragement of informers rapidly spread, the treatment of offenders, or suspected offenders, was relatively lenient. To the tsar's surprise his policies succeeded sufficiently for the revolutionary years of 1848–9 to pass Russia by. But Nicholas' outlook was in certain aspects positive. His attempts to reform the bureaucracy may have had little practical effect, but his effort to diminish the grievances of the poor led him to recognize the root problem of Russian society: serfdom. The tsar shied away from the difficulty of freeing the serfs and providing them with land at the expense of the rights enjoyed by the nobility who owned most of the land. He therefore concentrated his efforts on reforming the lot of state serfs and of the serfs on crown lands. These reforms, carried through during the 1830s and 1840s, although small in themselves, pointed the way to the emancipation of the serfs by his son, Alexander II in 1861.

Nicholas' reign also marked the beginnings of Russia's railway development. The first line between St Petersburg and Moscow was completed in 1852 three years before his death. Nicholas' reign was not notable in achieving much industrial progress. The pace of Russian industrialization had slowed down since the tremendous impetus given by Peter the Great during the first quarter of the eighteenth century. It was to intensify again during the last quarter of the nineteenth century. But the industrial revolution had some effect on mid-nineteenth-century Russia. In the spinning mills around St Petersburg and Moscow, a small group of industrial workers had begun to emerge. Russian industry, based on the new technology, was very small in relation to rural Russia as a whole and its products were designed to meet domestic demand. Yet it provided the base for a remarkably steady and high industrial growth rate during the latter part of the nineteenth century. But there was another side to the coin of Russia's progress.

The rapid increase of Russia's population, and the size of the tsar's armies, created in the minds of Western liberals before the Crimean War a sense of menace. The Polish cause owed much of its appeal to this fact. How little Russia actually was to be feared was demonstrated by the tsar's behaviour during the revolutionary outbreaks. He acted solely within the narrow confines of national interests. He needed his armies to crush any threat to the Russian Empire from without and within and had no force to spare against revolutionary German states, let alone France, even if his troops could have been organized to fight away from home, which was more than doubtful. The image of Nicholas I as the 'Gendarme of Europe' was nothing but a mirage. His offers of help to German princes could hardly be taken seriously and, in any case, who wanted to quarter Russian troops in their towns and countryside?

Poland was the most sensitive region of the empire. If Prussia supported Polish nationalism, and this seemed possible in March 1848 when Arnim's star was in the ascendant and Prussia promised a national reorganization of their portions of partitioned Poland, then a war between Russia and Prussia would ensue. The tsar stood firm and the King of Prussia reasserted Prussia's traditional policies. The cause of Poland was abandoned by the summer of 1848 in Berlin and in Frankfurt; German nationalism buried any prospect of a reconstitution of a Polish nation from the territories acquired by Austria, Prussia and Russia during the partitions.

The only intervention ordered by the tsar outside the borders of the Russian Empire in 1848 was against 'Rumanian' nationalism in the still – Turkish principalities of Moldavia and Wallachia. The influx of Western ideas through the young noblemen educated in Paris, who returned to Wallachia, was highly unwelcome to the tsar. It was intervention outside Russia, however, only in a technical sense. Although the two principalities had remained under Turkish suzerainty formally, they were practically protectorates of Russia. The tsar obviously would not tolerate a national revolution in Bucharest and the spread of notions of democracy and socialism to a region so close to his own empire. Only the fear of international complications, especially Austrian and British opposition, had earlier on made the tsar draw back from annexing the principalities outright. His anxiety not to raise the 'Eastern Question' still made the tsar cautious after the outbreak of the revolution in Bucharest in June 1848. To observe the proprieties, the tsar attempted to persuade the Turks to join Russia in a joint occupation. Failing to achieve this the Russians finally crossed into Moldavia at the end of July 1848. The Turks countered by occupying Wallachia. By October both Turkey and Russia were in occupation of the principalities and agreed to exercise joint responsibilities for the supervision of government in them; and what did the British and French do to support the Rumanian cause against Russia and Turkey? Nothing. Characteristically Palmerston looked at the situation from the point of view of British interests which were identified with the maintenance of the Ottoman Empire. The British Ambassador in Constantinople therefore counselled the Turks to crush the national risings against them. Nationalism and liberalism were forces that could be used to aid British interests in the west; nationalism or constitutionalism could be invoked in Belgium, Spain and Portugal in order to check France, but in the Balkans they were dangerous forces undermining Turkish stability and thereby exposing the Mediterranean flank to Russian penetration. Polish nationalism, on the other hand, was a useful lever to keep the Russians busy at home. If this seems a cynical interpretation of British foreign policy it has to be remembered that Palmerston, as did Nicholas, placed British interests as he saw them before my other consideration. As for the French, whilst sympathetic to Rumanian nationalism, the Second Republic neither could, nor dared, to do anything to help revolutionary causes elsewhere and thereby provoke British and Russian hostility.

Besides Moldavia and Wallachia on Russia's southern border, and Poland in the west, the tsar faced a third sensitive area, the Baltic. Whichever state controlled Denmark would control the narrow straits from the Baltic to the North Sea. Although no longer as important strategically and economically as in the eighteenth century, the tsar wanted to maintain traditional Russian interests. To the tsar it seemed that Prussia after the March days was playing a dangerous role of exploiting nationalism to serve its own desire for aggrandizement. Nicholas' sensitivity to Prussia's Polish plans has already been noted. Prussia's apparent siding with the German nationalist agitation in Schleswig-Holstein seemed to Nicholas the height of irresponsibility (see p. 77). Once more Palmerston and Tsar Nicholas worked along parallel lines against Prussia with the object of protecting Danish independence and the king's sovereignty over the duchies. Possibly the motivation of their diplomacy is of greater significance than its effectiveness. But beyond acting cautiously when specific Russian national interests were involved, the tsar confined himself to merely sending advice to his fellow monarchs. They in turn mastered the revolutionary forces with their own resources (for an account of Russia's intervention in Hungary in 1849 see p. 108).

In the face of all the rhetoric of revolutionary as well as monarchical pledges of solidarity, the Europe of 1848 still strikingly illustrated the conservative predominance of the great powers of the Vienna settlement of 1815, namely Russia, Austria, Prussia and Britain, whose nationalist interests in the end prevailed over all other considerations. On the other side of the fence, the 'workers' and 'peasants' were simply not conscious of any ideological identity of interest and they scarcely knew about the few intellectuals who espoused this particular cause. Marx's theories about the conflict of classes and his call for fraternal working class solidarity bears little resemblance to the actual events of 1848. The influence of his teaching became profound only later in the century. The strongest force in Europe during the decades that followed was not the resultant movement of European society through class conflict but nationalism.

Part Two

Authoritarian Europe

7

The Aftermath of Revolution: France 1848–1851

In February 1848 France had blazed the trail of a new revolutionary era in Europe or so it seemed to contemporaries. Only five months later, in June, Paris became the scene of the bloodiest reaction witnessed anywhere on the continent during the revolutionary year – a precursor of a different kind. The 'June Days' marked the violent failure of the social revolution that had formed an inseparable part of the social and political revolutions of the previous February and March. After June, the social revolution was dead and was to remain so for more than a generation.

The Second Republic since April 1848 in the hands of the propertied, the conservative and moderate politicians, was partly to blame for provoking the insurrection it feared. The assembly thought it would nip a socialist conspiracy in the bud by taking preventive measures although there was no such conspiracy. The assembly decided the best way to curb the growth of unruly elements in the capital was to limit the paying of outdoor relief which masqueraded under the title of the 'National Workshops'. The payment of this dole attracted the destitute in large number from the provinces to Paris. It seemed prudent to the politicians to disperse them. But to do so without causing an eruption required cunning, skill and patience. Instead, fear and contempt drove the assembly into ill-advised repression. On 22 June the assembly decreed that all unmarried workers in the 'National Workshops', that is those on relief, should join the army; the married men were told to go to the provinces where public works would be provided; alternatively if they refused they would lose all relief payments; no more destitute men would be admitted to the 'National Workshops'. In short the Paris unemployed were asked to choose between the army, the provinces, or starvation.

The assembly anticipated trouble and entrusted to General Eugène Cavaignac, an experienced soldier with a record of campaigning in Algeria, the overall command of the Garde Mobile, the army and the

National Guard. With such force at his command a haphazard rising had no chance of success.

The outbreak of violence appears to have been a spontaneous rising of the poorer people of Paris goaded to the barricades by a republic that had betrayed all their hopes of work and dignity without which political reform becomes an empty formula. The economic conditions which were bad in Paris in February 1848 had become even worse in June. The new harvest had not been gathered and the unemployed lived at subsistence level. The socialist leaders had been removed from any active participation by the repressive countermeasures which had followed the demonstration of 15 May. This was a rising not of a single indentifiable group of 'proletarians' or 'workers' but of the disappointed poor. There were few factories in Paris and industry was essentially on a small scale, each workshop employing an average of five workers. Those who manned the barricades were building workers, metal workers and mechanics, workers in leather and textiles, unskilled labourers, and domestic servants, but they were also joined by a significant number of clerical workers, small shopkeepers and owners of small workshops. The refusal of the assembly to meet their primary needs, rather than political consciousness or an understanding of socialism, was why these men turned to violence.

Fighting began on 23 June 1848. Barricades had been thrown up in the poorer sections of Paris and some 50,000 starved and armed men faced General Cavaignac. The majority of the National Guard had stayed at home. Some even fought on the barricades. Those who rallied to Cavaignac, however, together with the Garde Mobile were merciless opponents of the 'rabble' they faced. The fighting lasted four days and on 26 June organized resistance ceased. The loss of life had been surprisingly moderate; some 500 insurgents and perhaps a thousand of the government forces had been killed in the struggle. But a most horrible massacre followed. Many insurgents were shot out of hand, hunted through the streets, and altogether anywhere between 1500 and 3000 were cut down or shot by Cavaignac's guardsmen, police and troops. Of the 12,000 imprisoned, more than 10,000 were sentenced to long terms and thousands were deported.

This savage repression was responsible for the subsequent ideological significance of the June days. The slain and persecuted became the first martyrs of the class struggle. For Karl Marx the 'June days' were an event of seminal importance in the struggle of the proletariat against the bourgeoisie. On 11 June Marx's friend and collaborator Engels had already denounced the French Assembly as an 'Assembly of capitalists'. Marx and Engels interpreted the June insurrection as the forerunner of an immense and decisive struggle between the proletariat and the bourgeoisie. According to Marx, in the bitterness following on the bloody repression by the bourgeoisie of the 'workers' revolt', lay the seeds of the future defeat of the bourgeoisie, for it would remove the illusion from the workers' eyes that compromise was possible. The illusions of the February revolution had been destroyed. Now France, Marx pointed out, was split into the nation of the property owners and the nation of the workers. Thus the defeat of the workers in June came to be shown as really a victory, for it doomed the bourgeoisie. Marx's 'class' analysis of the nature of the insurrection coincided in many ways with the views of the 'moderates' and also of such astute observers as de Toqueville.

The importance of the June insurrection lies not in what it really was but what people believed it to be. A powerful myth was born. Marx saw his historical evolution through class struggle substantiated. But 'class' is a blunt and often nebulous concept. Roger Price has clearly shown that the revolutionary participants could not even be described as 'workers', for there were few factories and factory workers in Paris at that time; the label 'proletariat' does not fit them well. The June insurrection was a heterogeneous movement of the lower groups of Parisian society and included many Marx would have described as *petite bourgeoisie*. There was no clear-cut programme. If anything united the revolutionaries it was anger with the assembly which was attempting to undo the success of the February revolution. Now in power, the new rulers seemed no different from the old. The June insurrection was a violent protest at the course the revolution had taken; it was negative in opposing the establishment rather than positive in advocating any socialist programme. With memories of the virtually bloodless revolution in February those who manned the barricades hoped, perhaps even expected, to repeat their success of a few months earlier, not anticipating the bloodshed that was to follow on the defeat of their efforts.

General Cavaignac was hailed by the assembly as the saviour of the republic after his bloody successes in the streets of Paris, and the assembly appointed him virtually to be the military dictator of France. Yet surprisingly the assembly survived under his protection and settled down to the work of framing a constitution for the republic. Cavaignac did not abuse his immense powers. He rejected the Napoleonic example and remained true to the republic giving its supporters the opportunity to work out permanent institutions in order to provide political and social stability. This became the programme of the majority of the assembly, the party of order. The draft of the constitution was prepared by a small committee and then debated in the chamber during September and October, before being finally adopted on 4 November 1848.

A single chamber of 750 members was created; they were to be elected every three years by universal male suffrage; the party of order had learned an important lesson in France in 1848; universal male suffrage would best insure stability and conservatism by allowing preponderance to rural France over the unruly capital. The constitution, however, made a fetish of the principle of the division of power with the avowed intention of preventing dictatorial power from falling into the hands of an executive or dictator with perhaps the return of another terror. In the single chamber was vested the power to make laws. The executive power was substantially in the hands of a president. The great issue which was debated was whether the president should be elected by the assembly or by a direct popular vote. There were arguments both ways. In the end the assembly decided that the president should be elected for four years by universal manhood suffrage; that he would not be allowed to stand for a second term; and if none of the candidates who put themselves forward as candidates received two million votes then the choice would become the responsibility of the assembly. What the constitution did not provide for was what should happen if the popularly elected assembly and the popularly elected president were at loggerheads. The danger a popular president recalling past dynastic glories presented to the survival of the republic was not overlooked. That this danger was a present one and not hypothetical was already clear since Louis Napoleon and a revival of Bonapartism had by the autumn of 1848 become a political force to be reckoned with. The assembly did not consider one other important aspect; it would be easier for one man, the president, to project himself as standing for stability and order than it would be for an assembly with its diversely expressed opinions to do so. Perhaps they were misled by Cavaignac, a soldier without the guile of the politician, and one of those rare men who could abandon power when it was within his grasp. Cavaignac respected the written constitution; for Louis Napoleon it was a scrap of paper. Cavaignac earned the hatred of many Parisians for doing what many wished him to do as long as they believed their property in danger. Louis Napoleon, who given the chance would probably not have acted differently, arrived on the political arena without a stain.

The rise of Louis Napoleon is an improbable tale of a man and his times acting on each other to create a second emperor and a second empire; the historical sequence of events was consciously borrowed from an illustrious past. Myth and reality had combined in a strange way to rescue Louis Napoleon from the failures of his early ambitions. As the nephew of the great emperor he bore the most famous name in nineteenth-century France: that, and confidence in his 'destiny', as well as determination and ability, were his personal assets. Yet with his German accent, short-legged stature and undistinguished 'bourgeois' appearance he appeared an unlikely heir to the Napoleonic heritage. But those who voted for him, voted for what he was believed to stand for, a symbol rather than a live man; few people in 1848 could have actually even glimpsed him, let alone heard him speak.

The Napoleonic cult had been vigorously pushed during the July monarchy so that, it was hoped, the Orleanist dynasty might profit from the reflected glory. Historians, artists, writers and poets all contributed to the cult and so did leading Orleanist politicians. Napoleon I's great achievements were enhanced by the shimmering halo of romanticism. The greys and the blacks, so much a part of the picture of the Napoleonic epoch, were made to disappear. The contrast with the lacklustre Bourbon restoration was a pointed one. Napoleon I's name was coupled with that of Caesar and Alexander and Charlemagne. He had made France great and given it an empire. He was the protector of nations struggling to free themselves. He had brought to France order, freedom of religion and liberty. He had reconciled the conflicts of society. Napoleon I himself had deliberately originated many of these legends. What appealed to the majority of Frenchmen in the mid-nineteenth century was the Napoleon I who was credited with having brought peace and prosperity, security and orderly government. Of course this was an extraordinary perversion of history. But in mid-nineteenth-century France there was no lust for glory or for war, whether of the revolutionary or Napoleonic variety. Frenchmen were content to bolster their national pride by recalling the military achievements of the past. The 'glory' of the present would have to be cheaply won without risk. Prince Louis Napoleon understood this mood when he later proclaimed that he stood for peace, *l'empire c'est la paix*.

Louis Napoleon timed his rise to power shrewdly after 1848 and with a sure political instinct which he had hitherto lacked. At the time of the revolution of 1848 he was forty years old; he put behind him the role of needy adventurer who had already gambled and lost three times. Expelled from the Papal States in 1830, he and his brother joined the Carbonari in Florence; sentenced to death by the Austrians, he returned to France and from there sought refuge in Switzerland and England in 1831. He next plotted revolt in Strasbourg in 1836 and having failed had to leave France; then he conspired again in Boulogne in 1840; this time he was caught. It was difficult to take him seriously. There seemed no link between the revival of Bonapartism and the escapades of this young man. He was condemned to life imprisonment in the fortress of Ham but was humanely treated. He did not lack ordinary comforts or even a mistress and made good use of his time writing papers on social and military matters. In 1846 he escaped from the fortress dressed as a workman and reached England with a young actress, Elizabeth

Ann Haryett, known to historians as Miss Howard. In February 1848 he sensed that the revolution in Paris might provide him with opportunities and so he returned to France. When no one paid attention to him he left again for England in time to enrol as a special constable to help control the Chartists – an eccentric gesture on his part.

There was something very durable about Louis Napoleon despite his early record of political failure. As a writer and propagandist he had already won considerable success. His best known work *Des Idées napoléoniennes* was first published in 1839 and many editions later had sold half a million copies before 1848. The message of the book was that the 'Napoleonic idea' was as relevant to the present and future of France as it had been in the past. The cult of Napoleon was not just homage to the past, but its force lay in the claim that Napoleon's ideas pointed the way to the future. Louis Napoleon had fashioned what were supposedly Napoleon's ideas to suit mid-nineteenth-century France; thus he claimed that Napoleon's ideas were not for war, but that his aims and policies had been directed to social, industrial, commercial progress and were based on humanitarian values. They could thus be made the basis of a whole forward-looking programme. Among Louis Napoleon's writings when in the prison in Ham was a small brochure, *L'Extinction du paupérisme*, which showed his concern for social problems and earned him a reputation as the patron of the oppressed.

From April 1848 onwards, and especially after June, with the help of financial backers, Louis Napoleon and his supporters embarked on a publicity campaign in France with great professional skill. Pictures, medals, matchboxes, and flags were widely distributed among those who read little. Louis Napoleon set out to woo the masses whom he intended both to lead, guide and manipulate whilst basing his power on their support. It was this bid to become a leader of the people through the direct link of universal suffrage and plebiscite that has led historians to study him as a forerunner of the dictators of the twentieth century. There are some theoretical parallels of methods, similarities in how one man's drive for power was translated into the reality of leadership, also in the way in which the rule of one man could be strengthened by periodic direct appeals to the people, circumventing representative assemblies and party politics. But it is foolish to press these parallels too far. Judged by their personalities, ideas and actions there is no similarity between the humane and on the whole judicious Napoleon III who led France for twenty-one years until old age, and the maniacal destructive Adolf Hitler, who ravaged Europe and was responsible for the deaths of millions.

After the June insurrection Louis Napoleon's opportunities had enormously increased. The republic was discredited in the eyes of the great majority of French people although paradoxically this majority embraced many rival political and social groups. Orleanist and Legitimist politicians contemplated an eventual 'restoration', meantime they would be content to wield power under the banner of the 'republic'. The minority of genuine republicans in the assembly and outside it saw in the newly converted republicans their old opponents. Then, as has been noted, there had developed strong bonds among those men of property large and small who feared they had much to lose by a 'red' republican revolution. At the same time one of the most popular names on the June barricades was that of Louis Napoleon. His concern for the poor had successfully been spread about; he was also naïvely reputed to be very rich and willing to use his riches to expunge poverty. Louis Napoleon had managed to assure the Catholic Church that he supported their claim to have a right to provide education side by side with state education. (In France 'freedom of education' in the nineteenth century was an issue between state and church; in England in the twentieth century its meaning is quite different; 'freedom of education' is more a social question.) The socialists also despised the sham republic and placed the blame for the bloody June days on Cavaignac. They would shed no tears if these parliamentarians were swept away. At the other extreme the conservatives of many different hues – sometimes described as the 'party of order' which implies more cohesion than these groups possessed – despite the success of Cavaignac, took serious fright and wanted to see the republic strengthened by a firm executive. Consequently Louis Napoleon by promising everyone something however contradictory was able to attract overwhelming support.

When on 26 September 1848 Louis Napoleon finally took his seat in the assembly to which he had been elected in Paris and four other départements he did not cut much of a figure as a parliamentarian. His lack of oratory and his uninspiring appearance paradoxically turned out to be essential ingredients for his success. Many of the leading politicians of the assembly, including Thiers and Toqueville, in their unbounded conceit, and with an eye solely on their own advancement, misjudged Louis Napoleon's personality and ability. They thought of him as a harmless, even stupid man, whose loose moral life reflected a general superficial approach. About Louis Napoleon's absence of moral scruple they were right. For the rest, they soon discovered their mistake.

Louis Napoleon's growing popularity in Paris and the countryside gave the prominent Orleanists the idea that he might serve as a useful figurehead on whose appeal they would come to power. The bar against any member of the family of a former ruling dynasty had been removed by vote of the assembly. Louis Napoleon cleverly lined up essential political conservative support for his candidacy for the presidency in December 1848. The conservative monarchist forces, divided between Orleanists and Legitimists, responded to these overtures as offering them also the best chance of defeating the republicans who actually believed in a republic. Guizot, Thiers, Barrot and Molé, all leading politicians of the July monarchy decided to back his candidacy and so did the catholic hierarchy, with few exceptions, and prominent journalists; Dumas and Victor Hugo also joined the Napoleonic bandwagon; the writers did so from romantic conviction; for the rest it was a question of political calculation.

The election of 10 December 1848 was a triumph for Louis Napoleon. He secured close to $5\frac{1}{2}$ million votes against his nearest rival, Cavaignac, who obtained $1\frac{1}{2}$ million votes. Of the four other candidates, Ledru-Rollin collected just over 370,000, and Raspail, Lamartine and Changarnier secured in electoral terms only negligible support. What is noteworthy about these candidatures is the political demise of Lamartine, who had been in all but name the leader of the provisional government before the June days. This marked the country's total rejection of the men identified with the February revolution of 1848. They were now blamed for the excesses of June, for broken promises and for the continued economic distress. Another interesting aspect of this election is that in Paris, Louis Napoleon carried everyone of the twelve *arrondissements*, both the most legitimist Faubourg Saint-Germain (the 10th) as well as the poorest quarters. Louis Napoleon was the most popular choice even of the workers in the towns. A minority of politically conscious workers voted for Ledru-Rollin in Paris, Nantes, Toulouse and in the Midi and Nord.

Once elected on so popular a vote it was obvious that despite all the constitutional guarantees intended to perpetuate the republic, a conscious Bonaparte would not be content to serve merely one four-year term of office. To do so would have been to contradict all Louis Napoleon had written about or stood for – the restoration of a new Napoleonic epoch of progress. This vision could not be reconciled with a genuine parliamentary system, elections, political parties and changing leaders. From the first it was therefore logical that the president should present himself as above party and faction which were characterized by him as weakening France and responsible for all social evils.

The years 1849 to 1851 mark the period of unequal struggle between the president and the assembly; on paper they were evenly matched, their power divided, with the assembly ultimately responsible for the republican constitution and empowered to remove any president who broke it. But the fundamental weakness of the assembly lay in the circumstance that the majority of Frenchmen and even the majority of the deputies did not see any positive virtues in the republic as established by the constitution. Louis Napoleon controlled the administration, which throughout the constitutional changes since February 1848 had remained centralized. Through the prefects, dependent for their appointment on the executive, and their local patronage, Louis Napoleon possessed an effective bureaucracy to govern France, which could exert influence over elections and provide a direct link between rulers and governed. As long as Louis Napoleon could retain the loyalty of these props of power, and overwhelming popular personal support, the assembly and the republic would become irrelevancies in the state.

He was the prince-president now. He was not an absolute head of state; the constitution Louis Napoleon had sworn to uphold ensured the separation of power on the American model. But 'President Napoleon' was a contradiction in terms; 'Napoleon' was not just a past ruler but embodied a whole concept of the state, of France and of empire which Napoleon's heir was determined to revive. Napoleon I's programme for the French nation would be resumed after an interval of thirty-five years. And it was this continuity Louis Napoleon deliberately sought to emphasize when on 1 December 1852 he assumed the title of Emperor Napoleon III, not the Second. By implying that Napoleon's son, the Duke of Reichstadt, was rightfully Napoleon II, he denied the legitimacy of the Bourbon restoration of 1814.

The years of preparation were nearly over. As president in 1848 his term of office would be for four years. At first he was content to consolidate his own popularity. He wanted Frenchmen to think of him as standing above political parties and social conflict, as the natural head of state, who represented the will of the French people as a whole. He emphasized constantly that he was the choice of the people, whilst doing his best to depict the parliamentary constitutional conflicts as unpatriotic, and as the squabbles of lesser men, who placed their own interests before those of France. He profited from their mistakes and made it appear that he championed the cause of the people against the politicians who were seeking to deprive the people of their rights. Sophistication was necessary to recognize in Louis Napoleon himself an unscrupulous and manipulating politician second to none and such sophistication was lacking. Nor was its lack made up by a vigorous opposition. The political opposition was enfeebled by adhering to worn-out monarchist solutions, Orleanist or Bourbon, which enjoyed little popular support after the failures of Charles X and Louis Phillipe. The social opposition lacked leadership, and when violent was easily suppressed.

Nothing went right for the politicians of the Second Republic, the men of the Orleanist era and of February 1848. Apart from a small but committed political following which each of them commanded, the majority of Frenchmen abstained from politics or voted against the squabbling politicians and for Louis Napoleon, the man who projected himself as the strong, enlightened leader. Louis Napoleon recognized and exploited this general mood of disillusionment with politics, with strife and with violence when he embarked on tours through the country. Even the people who had once supported direct action in the streets did not forget the days of June and the hopelessness of fighting against the organized police forces and the army. The political leadership of all shades of opinion was regarded as having failed the people and as having caused their suffering. When the constituent assembly was finally dissolved and elections were held in May 1849 for the new legislative assembly a third of the electorate did not bother to vote.

Thus the assembly was dangerously isolated from the start as well as deeply divided within itself between Legitimists, Orleanists, Catholics and Republicans of the right on the one hand who formed the majority, and a radical socialist minority on the other. The monarchists and Catholics favoured the Second Republic as paving the way for a restoration of the monarchy, but the stubbornness of 'Henry V', the legitimist pretender, precluded any 'sensible' arrangement with the Orleanist dynasty. After all if the Legitimists had all abandoned the principle of 'legitimacy' there would be nothing left for them to stand for and that proved to be the case although plans for a restoration were dusted down after each and every traumatic experience in the nineteenth-century history of France.

The prince-president bided his time. During the first nine months he left the government of the country to a ministry led by the Orleanist Odilon Barrot which commanded majority support in the assembly. This government made it its main concern to make the country secure from socialism. In January 1849 the country-wide organization of the so-called 'red republicans' was suppressed. When nevertheless in spite of all the government could do the 'red republicans' made a good showing in the elections of May 1849 and obtained 180 seats, the huge conservative majority, the supporters of order, who had secured two-thirds of the total 750 members, took fright and decided the time had come for firm measures. There were two enactments passed intended to strengthen the existing social fabric; an education law, the Falloux law, and a measure designed to reduce the electorate by a third and thereby to deprive the most unstable and poorest section from exercising political influence.

The Falloux law was a retrograde step. The provisional government set up in February 1848 had tried to enact legislation extending free and compulsory education to all children up to the age of 14. The schools were to be secular and religion was not to be taught in them. To the Legitimist and Catholic Frédéric de Falloux, Minister of Education in the Barrot government, this education plan was anathema. Free compulsory education without benefit of religion would, he believed, only promote socialism and anarchy. Many formerly anti-clerical republicans, such as Thiers, echoed these views after the June days. So the education law actually passed in March 1850 permitted the church to organize private primary and secondary schools and though it provided for some state supervision greatly increased the power of the church. The schools were neither free nor compulsory and where a church school existed, the establishment of a secular school was not encouraged; religious education was obligatory. No wonder that Marxist and socialist writers identified the church with the cause of political reaction.

In June 1849 Ledru-Rollin attempted to rally the 'red republicans' calling on the people to defend the constitution which Louis Napoleon and his allies were attempting to destroy by extinguishing the liberties of the Roman sister republic. Louis Napoleon had indeed sent an expedition to Rome with the purpose of restoring a once liberal pope to his dominions (p. 213). He earned neither the applause of Italian patriots, nor the gratitude of the pope who long since had repented his liberal leanings. But the Italian expedition was the occasion not the true cause of Ledru-Rollin's half-hearted challenge. There was no insurrection worthy of the name although protest was widespread. Some 7000 demonstrators gathered in Paris but only in Lyons was there widespread violence. The demonstrators were brutally dispersed. The assembly now had an excuse to pass further repressive measures designed to eliminate the loose alliance of the left. De Tocqueville, an acute observer of the scene, scathingly compared the June days of 1848 and 1849, writing, 'In June 1848, the leaders failed the army; in June 1849, the army the leaders.' Socialist propaganda had become much more widespread throughout France in 1849, but the militancy of the masses had declined. The republic was not in serious danger from the left, but from the right, and it was the prince-president who successfully undermined it. The key to success was the attitude of the *gendarmerie* and the army which Louis Napoleon assiduously flattered with his attention.

In October 1849 Louis Napoleon took advantage of criticisms and high-handedly dismissed the Barrot Ministry even though a majority of the assembly supported it. At a stroke the power of the assembly was thereby diminished. His stated reason for doing so was openly condemnatory of the politicians. The republic he claimed was threatened by anarchy; what France required was 'strong rule' and a 'clearly formulated policy'. He left no doubt as to who was capable of providing strong rule. France, so Louis Napoleon declared, was groping for the guiding 'hand and will of the man elected on

December 10'. At a time of continued economic distress many turned to Louis Napoleon for leadership and resolution and away from the debates and compromises of parliamentary government.

Nevertheless the cause of the red republicans was not dead as was shown by the results of the elections in March 1850 when the 30 expelled members of the assembly were replaced. The left succeeded in winning 20 of the 30 seats despite the repressive measures of the government. A new electoral law was passed which reduced the electorate by a third and meant in practice the abandonment of universal suffrage. This new electoral law required that all voters had to provide evidence of three years' residence in the same *canton*. This eliminated the itinerant poor. In some départements and especially, in the industrial and urban regions as many as half the electorate were disenfranchised. Overall it has been calculated that the electorate was reduced from 9½ million to 6 million. To make sure that the militant left would be excluded, the electoral law, moreover, disenfranchised everyone who had been found guilty by the courts. The prime minister countersigned all these laws, though later he was to claim that he had opposed the assembly's efforts to deprive the people of their rights.

In January 1851 Louis Napoleon felt strong enough to dismiss the commander of the Paris garrison and National Guard, General Changarnier who was openly contemptuous of the prince-president and supported the cause of an Orleanist restoration. Predictably the year of 1851 would see the constitutional crisis reach a climax.

The new presidential elections were due in the spring of 1852 and, as matters stood, Louis Napoleon could not seek office then again. Louis Napoleon organized a campaign throughout the country to change the constitution. He would have preferred a peaceful, even constitutional, change to make his position secure. A majority of the assembly was prepared to go along with his wishes, but the fathers of this constitution had done their work well. A two-thirds majority in favour of change could not be mustered on one occasion, let alone on three separate occasions as was required. There was, therefore, by the autumn of 1851, no other choice left to him but to surrender the presidency in 1852 or to overthrow the constitution itself and to seize power. Could anyone seriously have doubted which of these alternatives he would adopt?

The Second Republic, which could count on only a small number of genuine supporters among the members of the assembly, was doomed. The assembly which did not believe in the republic could hardly effectively organize its defence. Once more Louis Napoleon perfectly exploited the assembly's ambiguous position in a speech in November, 1851 which contained this typically lofty appeal: 'How great France could be, if she were permitted to attend to her real business, and reform her institutions instead of being incessantly troubled either by demagogic ideas or by monarchist hallucinations!' The 'reform' to which he was referring was to allow him absolute power; the only 'demagogy' or monarchist 'hallucination' permissible was the Napoleonic.

Louis Napoleon was adopting the modern techniques of propaganda. Their main point was to hide the central issue: Louis Napoleon's bid for power. This was achieved by omission and by relying on the people to regard the obvious as being too obvious to be true. The people were invited to identify Louis Napoleon not with one political force among several in the state, not even as an important political leader with a following of his own, but with 'France'. If the French people desired order with freedom, prosperity and progress, unity and patriotism social peace and the maintenance of the church, or any of these things, in fact all that was best in France, then they should entrust their future to Louis Napoleon, the one man who would selflessly strive to achieve them. They must rid themselves of the squalid contentious parliamentary assembly. Parliament had won so little esteem in the eyes of the French people that there were not many ready to defend the parliamentary form of government. It had filled a temporary need and few mourned its passing. Why, in contrast, were parliamentary institutions in Britain held in such high regard? Certainly the difference between the two parliaments widened in this period. In Britain during the third quarter of the nineteenth century the modern two-party system emerged; in France party politics became more personal and divisive. In Britain the need for a government dependent on a parliamentary majority was firmly established, in France it did not survive long. The unquestioned supremacy of parliament in Britain never found acceptance in France. A *coup d'état* in Britain would have been resisted violently and if the opponents of parliament were strong enough, would have led to civil war. In France in December 1851, Louis Napoleon's seizure of power produced only localized but widespread disturbance and protest.

Louis Napoleon had assured himself of the support of the highly centralized French administration by appointing prefects, judges and officials loyal to himself. The church was almost totally on the side of Louis Napoleon. It regarded as its great enemy socialism and atheism, and saw in the prince-president a saviour from socialist revolution. The clergy gladly offered *Te Deums* for the president and for the mission confided to him by the French people. Legitimists and Orleanists were predictably less enthusiastic. Still they too had feared a socialist insurrection in the spring of 1852. For them Louis Napoleon was very much the lesser of two evils.

The day chosen for the *coup* was 2 December, 1851, the anniversary of the victory of Austerlitz. With the co-operation of the *gendarmerie* and key personnel in the administration and the army, the carefully laid plans were carried out virtually without a hitch. The Palais Bourbon, where the parliament was in session, was occupied. A number of prominent deputies were arrested and the efforts of deputies to meet later on were easily foiled. As the Parisians woke up that morning of 2 December they found the streets placarded with proclamations announcing the dissolution of the assembly; no one but the politicians involved regretted that. 'Democracy', however, was not to be abolished; on the contrary, by implication the blame for the reduction of the suffrage was placed on the assembly; now ostentatiously Louis Napoleon proclaimed that universal suffrage would be restored and that the people would be asked to vote on a new constitution. In this way the president stood the events upside down. He claimed that he had not destroyed the Second Republic but was its saviour from the machinations of the assembly determined to destroy it. The establishment of a dictatorship was justified by an appeal to popular sovereignty; 'the solemn judgement of the people', Louis Napoleon declared, was 'the sole sovereign I recognize in France'. The army, on whom the success of the *coup* depended, was solidly loyal to the new Napoleon.

Among civilians there was popular support for Louis Napoleon, even more widespread apathy, but also determined resistance. In Paris along the Boulevard de la Poissonière on 4 December there was a demonstration of the politically more aware and militant, some 1200 people in all. But the mass of the Parisian poor held aloof from insurrection. The indiscriminate firing of the troops killed many innocent onlookers and overcame a few traditional barricades; fighting civilians, the casualties among the troops were light. All over the country many potential leaders who might have organized resistance were arrested. In the Seine area nearly 3000 were placed in custody and it has been estimated that 25,500 arrests were made throughout France at the time of the *coup*. The new industrial centres such as Lille, Mulhouse, where prosperity at last was reviving, remained undisturbed. More serious was the spontaneous wave of protest and insurgency in some of the regions, though easily suppressed. The unexpected bloodshed was to haunt Louis Napoleon, but was also grist to the propaganda that his *coup* had forestalled a general socialist insurrection. The widespread fear of such insurrection now assured him of the grudging support of the monarchist conservatives, both Legitimist and Orleanist. Louis Napoleon could count on the support of all those who wished to preserve the social status quo, a broad mass of Frenchmen. They had received a fright in 1848. Henceforth a majority could always be found to oppose social revolution even if the price to be paid was personal rule.

8

The Aftermath of Revolution: Austria, Prussia and 'Germany'

Liberal nationalism triumphed nowhere in 1848–9. Nationality remained submerged in the three great dynastic states of continental Europe, Prussia, Austria and Russia. The three monarchs and their ministers demanded that a man's loyalty was to his prince; it did not matter whether he was 'Italian', Serbian or a Pole. This view regarded nationality as being essentially secondary; at best it was to be culturally encouraged but where by becoming political it threatened the cohesion of the state it would be ruthlessly suppressed. The liberals of 1848 took a different view of nationalism. It took a more significant place in their thinking. Equally important, they actually behaved more in the way Georg Wilhelm Friedrich Hegel would have approved than according to the ideals of Giuseppe Mazzini, though few of them consciously modelled themselves on the largely unread doctrines of the philosophers.

If we consider Hegel and Mazzini from the point of view of their understanding of history and their own times rather than from the point of view of their influence, the contrast between them helps to clarify our ideas about 1848.

For Hegel the nation was the highest authority; he believed that a divine force moved through nations, and a nation's supremacy revealed its purpose. Nations were destined to struggle for supremacy. The past had belonged in turn to the Oriental world, the Greek world and the Roman world. His own times, Hegel believed, would witness the German era, the highest development so far. History was the process of struggle until in the end all conflicts would be resolved. Nationality would inevitably struggle with nationality and through the pursuit of power the national mission would be fulfilled. The divine purpose was bound to triumph so that the vanquished were not to be pitied for they fulfilled their purpose. Only the state that was right would win, thus might became right, a historical right that Hegel regarded more important than any other right.

For Mazzini liberalism and nationalism were reconcilable, the one supporting the other; both the individual and the nation were to him sacred. He called for a religious spirit working together with democratic principles as the best means of achieving human progress. Religion enobled a society where the individual would enjoy two freedoms: personal and the freedom of national association. All peoples who wished for nationality, so Mazzini taught, had a sacred right to have their wishes fulfilled for it was God's purpose. He thought that when the peoples were permitted their will unfettered they would live in harmony. Nation would not fight nation. Each would make its distinctive contribution to the broad progress of humanity. Thus Mazzini not only believed in the divine destiny of the Italian nation but also preached the national causes of the Slavs, the Hungarians, the Poles, and indeed of every group that expressed a desire for national identification. Like Hegel he saw a divine purpose. God had divided mankind into distinct groups, nations each different, but each with equal rights. The nation expressed the will of the individual. Thus democracy and nationalism were harmonized. Mazzini's ideals belonged not only to Italy but to Europe and beyond. Whilst having faith in the ultimate unity of humanity Mazzini correctly recognized that nationalism was the great motivating force of nineteenth-century history. But Hegel was closer to the mark with a philosophy of national conflict and struggle than Mazzini with his vision of the brotherhood of free nations. Yet Mazzini's idealism remained a powerful stimulus in the twentieth century to those national leaders, from President Wilson on, who since 1919 have attempted to find a way of replacing national conflicts by some form of international order. But it would be difficult to deny that even in the twentieth century national conflict has remained the predominant theme of international relations.

In 1848 liberals could applaud the victory of the princes over fellow liberals espousing another national cause. German liberals could rejoice with Radetzky that he had defeated the Italians. In 1859 they sided with Austria rather than Piedmont. The princes were thus enabled to defeat liberalism in part by turning the weapon of nationalism against each liberal group in turn. And nowhere can this be seen more clearly than the way the struggling nationalities of the multi-national Austrian Empire threw away the possibility of success in their attempt to achieve national supremacy at each other's expense.

During the summer months of 1848 the social revolution was in the process of defeat and rejection throughout Europe. Outside of Vienna, the impetus for revolution had all along been more national in spirit than social. The social revolutionaries of Vienna almost immediately after the fall of Metternich aroused the fears of those Viennese with property or a stake in the professions. The departure of the emperor and his court in May 1848 was felt as an almost personal blow by the loyal Viennese. As the moderates and conservatives among the Viennese gradually recovered their nerve, the radicals in Vienna became increasingly isolated whilst the population in the countryside payed homage to the emperor at Innsbruck. The tension and suspicion between the town and country was indeed one common feature of the 1848 upheavals in continental Europe. Since Europe was still overwhelmingly agricultural, and the rank and file of the armies reflected the conservative countryside, this helps to explain why it was that imperial authority could recover from the collapse of the spring of 1848. Towards Vienna the imperial court at first temporized and sought to strengthen the moderates. Under pressure, the Pillersdorf ministry was dismissed in July 1848 and a new ministry, under Wessenberg, installed with some members in it satisfactory to the reformers. But the ministries responsible for control of finance and of troop reinforcements remained in the hands of men entirely loyal to the emperor.

The *Reichstag*, whose convocation had been promised the previous March, (p. 39) actually assembled in Vienna during the month of July. This first constituent parliament of the empire (though there were no representatives from the Hungarian half of the empire), accentuated the differences of the nationalities. The elected representatives could find no common purpose. There were groups of the left and right among the nationalities but they could not work together because overriding all other questions was that of the future of the empire. The Czechs opposed revolutionary Vienna because it was German. They worked for a strong unitary empire predominantly Slav. They could thus co-operate with those Austrian-Germans of the right who supported the court. The majority of the deputies took their seats not according to their political feelings, but in national blocks. But one great reform was passed in 1848. The emancipation of the peasantry was one of the major achievements of '1848' and the imperial court and government had less to fear from the peasantry though the problem of the landless peasant was not solved by the abolition of serfdom. Nevertheless the reforms of the liberals later immensely strengthened absolutism in the Habsburg Monarchy.

Between Vienna, the court, the ministry and the *Reichstag* there was an apparent reconciliation in the summer months of 1848. The Emperor Ferdinand and the court had returned to the capital; the workers and the radical 'left' groups seemed to be under control when workers' demonstrations were bloodily suppressed on 23 August 1848 in the 'Battle of the Prater'. There was an outward air of normalcy. Was the Habsburg Empire about to become a constitutional state? All these appearances were false. The archdukes remained conservative in the extreme. The compromised Emperor Ferdinand would be removed and replaced by a successor free of the constitutional promises made by Ferdinand. The *Reichstag* could solve nothing. Real power lay with the armies loyal to the emperor. Windischgraetz had mastered the unrest in Bohemia, having made a brutal example of the student demonstrators in Prague in June. He was anxious to reduce the 'rebels' in Vienna and could scarcely be held back. By the end of August 1848, moreover, Radetzky's victories in northern Italy immeasurably strengthened the imperial prospects of recovery. There was less need for troops and for money. The armies of Radetzky and Windischgraetz, no longer tied down in Bohemia and Italy, were now available for service in whatever lands of the Habsburgs imperial authority needed to be upheld. They were soon employed.

By the autumn of 1848 Hungary was reluctantly driven into open conflict by the shifty policy of the court who found in Bach, the Minister of Justice in the ministry in Vienna, a strong supporter of centralism. The Hungarians were denied the right to a separate Hungarian army. Deák, who came to Vienna to work out a settlement, found that concessions and promises previously made by Ferdinand were simply withdrawn. The 'April laws' on which Hungary's separate institutions had been based, were repudiated, and the Hungarians were faced with demands to subordinate their government to the 'Austrian government' in Vienna. The historic rights of the Hungarians were fast being eroded. The means of driving the Hungarians to a military confrontation was found in the Croat-Hungarian conflict.

Jelačić was reinstated in all his offices as Ban of Croatia and with the emperor's support in mid-September invaded Hungary from Croatia. He was given the task of restoring order in Hungary on the emperor's behalf. The Serbs meantime were attacking southern Hungary. Whilst all this was going on the Batthyány government in Budapest was still attempting to avoid an irrevocable breach with the emperor and so offered no resistance at first to these military moves. But the moderates in Hungary were rapidly losing ground to Kossuth who passionately called for national resistance. When at the end of September 1848 Count Lamberg, a highly respected Hungarian, arrived in the Hungarian capital as imperial plenipotentiary, he was murdered by an angry mob. This savage act was interpreted back in Vienna as the final challenge to imperial authority. Early in October Jelačić was appointed, in the emperor's name, commander-in-chief of all Hungarian forces and of the National Guard. This step in turn convinced even the moderates in Budapest that the emperor and the 'Germans' would settle for nothing less than the abandonment by the

Hungarians of all historic rights to a separate national life. To appoint a Croat commander-in-chief of Hungarian troops and militia was regarded as an intended national insult. And so it was. The Hungarian Diet in this dire emergency turned to Kossuth as the only man capable of saving Hungary and appointed him president of a committee of national defence with practically dictatorial powers.

Jelačić had at first advanced rapidly and unopposed but he was easily checked by a smaller Hungarian force before reaching Budapest. Just two weeks after entering Hungary Jelačić was in headlong retreat towards the Austrian frontier pursued by the Hungarians. As a military factor he had counted for little in Hungary; once on the borders of Austria his soldiers, however, acted as a barrier between the Hungarians and Vienna where the conflict in Hungary sparked off new violence and open resistance to the emperor's ministers.

In Vienna the Wessenberg government and the court, backed by the more prosperous citizens, had continued to repress the poor. In the city, despite the repression, a militant radical leadership had remained intact. Its most prominent members tried to preserve the gains made the previous spring, which were now rapidly slipping away. They found little support in the *Reichstag*. The *Reichstag* majority, caught up in endless nationality conflicts of their own, was more anxious to prove its imperial loyalty and to stay within the law than to fight for social progress. Hungarians, and the delegates they sent in September to plead the cause of Hungary in Vienna, were rejected by the *Reichstag* where opposition to them was led by the right, and by the Czechs. The radicals in Vienna saw the link between Hungary's success and their own. If Hungary were crushed by the imperial armies so would they be. But the radicals were in a minority in the *Reichstag*. Jelačić's appointment as commander-in-chief of Hungary on 3 October 1848 and the likelihood of open war between the emperor and the Hungarians for the first time thus forged an alliance between two groups in the empire of different nationality, the Hungarians who backed Kossuth and the German radicals in Vienna. The consequence was a rising in Vienna and its subsequent reduction by imperial troops, one of the most disastrous episodes in the whole history of the modern Habsburg Empire.

On 6 October a mob in Vienna had been stirred up to prevent the War Minister in the Wessenberg ministry, Count Latour, from despatching troop reinforcements to Jelačić intended for use against the Hungarians. Crowds surrounded the railway station. The German-Austrian troops refused to board the train. More troops were despatched and indiscriminately began firing on the crowd. This incensed the workers and students who formed the main part of the crowd and they seized control of the inner city. At the war ministry the government was meeting surrounded by a howling mob. Count Latour was the particular object of their hatred. The crowd took the law into their own hands and broke into the building. All the ministers escaped. Only Latour unfortunately rather than risk leaving hid himself in the building. He was found, hauled out, brutally murdered and hung naked from a lamp post. This was the counterpart of Count Lamberg's murder on the bridge between Buda and Pesth. The psychological impact of this particular violence, the assassination of one of the emperor's ministers was of great importance: it created a breach that nothing but further violence could close. The emperor's court and principal advisers regarded the Hungarians and Viennese as rebels, with whom negotiations were impossible. The emperor and court left the city once again and followed the more prosperous citizens who had been leaving Vienna all summer long. The court settled in Olmütz in Bohemia well protected by Windischgraetz and most of the ministers accompanied the court. The Czech members of the *Reichstag* departed en bloc as did many other deputies.

But nothing is clear-cut in the Habsburg Dominions. The *Reichstag*, or what was left of it, continued to function in the city, its constitutional right unchallenged. Indeed one member of the government courageously remained behind in Vienna. The *Reichstag* even voted the budget for 1849. The railway line remained open between Olmütz and Vienna and the minister preserved a theoretical legal continuity of government. But Windischgraetz was only waiting to beat the Viennese into unconditional surrender. At Olmütz the more liberalminded ministers, led by Count Stadion, tried to preserve constitutional rights and to restrain Windischgraetz. But this time the Field-Marshal could not be stopped. The *Reichstag* was prorogued and told to reassemble outside Vienna the following month of November at Kremsier close to Olmütz. The city meantime was entirely surrounded by Windischgraetz and Jelačić. Inside Vienna fortifications were hastily improvised. An ex-subaltern, Wenzel Messenhauser, was put in command of the heterogeneous armed men that could be collected to defend the city. Appeals were sent for help. From the Frankfurt parliament some radical deputies arrived on their own account to encourage the Viennese; and one of them, Robert Blum, was shot after the fall of Vienna. But there was no official encouragement from Frankfurt and of course no supplies or troops. Instead two official commissioners were sent by the 'Central Power', the government set up by the Frankfurt parliament, on a perfectly pointless mission of mediation. The Frankfurt parliament refused to back either Hungarian nationalism or radical Vienna. Whether they did so or not would in any case have had no practical effect on the course of events in the Habsburg Empire. A few volunteers had trickled into Vienna from other parts of Austria, but the Viennese placed their reliance on the recently victorious Hungarians.

The Hungarian troops unhappily were in two minds what to do. Their position on the frontier was not strong. More importantly the Hungarian commander and many of his officers felt scruples about taking up arms against the emperor's armies outside the Hungarian kingdom. Their strong sense of loyalty to the emperor made them half-hearted rebels. Kossuth was more of a realist. He expected no settlement with the emperor. For him it was a fight to the death for Hungarian independence. With tremendous energy he sought to awaken his fellow Hungarians to the need for an uncompromising struggle. He urged at the Hungarian headquarters that a junction with rebellious Vienna provided Hungary with an opportunity of military victory. It is doubtful whether anything could have been done. Even the fiery new commander of the Hungarian troops, Arthur Görgey, when he crossed the Hungarian frontier, was unable to break through the armies encircling Vienna. He was easily defeated by Jelačić. Unhappily the appearance of Hungarian cavalry on the outskirts of Vienna on 30 October encouraged the Viennese to resist. Windischgraetz now had the opportunity he wanted to smash Viennese resistance without mercy. Despite a determined fight Viennese citizens who believed they were upholding the constitutional legality of the spring of 1848, were beaten. No quarter was shown. Two thousand Viennese were killed in the speedy reduction of the city by Windischgraetz's troops. It was the bloodiest repression of 1848 in Europe, exceeding in brutality even the June days in Paris.

Now only Hungary remained as a serious centre of resistance. The men of 1848 in the western (Austria) half of the monarchy were imprisoned or forced into the army; many changed sides; nevertheless relatively few were condemned to death, though among them were Messenhauser and the Frankfurt radical Robert Blum. The breach with the constitutional promises of the spring of 1848 to Hungary and the empire was emphasized by the abdication of Emperor Ferdinand, and the succession of his young 18-year-old nephew, Francis Joseph, in December 1848.

The new Schwarzenberg ministry was determined to crush all Hungarian resistance. Under Kossuth's influence the Hungarians refused to accept the change of throne as far as the Kingdom of Hungary was concerned. At the beginning of the year, 1849, the military brilliance of Görgey saved Hungary from disaster. Windischgraetz had attacked and easily enough occupied Buda-Pesth on 5 January but Görgey had withdrawn the Hungarian forces intact. Hungary remained unconquered and an admiring western world applauded Kossuth and Magyar bravery without, however, sending help. The Austrian armies seemed to be incapable of extinguishing all Hungarian resistance in the field and Kossuth's armies won some victories against the Slovaks and Saxons in Transylvania, who since February had been aided by Russian troops. In April 1849 Kossuth proclaimed Hungarian independence. Windischgraetz was defeated and Kossuth reentered Buda-Pesth in triumph as Regent. But the successes of April were ephemeral. On 1 May 1849, Schwarzenberg officially requested Russian help. Tsar Nicholas readily obliged and in mid-June Russian and imperial armies began a concerted invasion of territory under Hungarian control which drove the Hungarians back. Despite all Kossuth and his generals could do, defeat was inevitable. The Hungarian defence was heroic but useless since neither England nor France had any intention of intervening. In August 1849 Görgey replaced Kossuth to negotiate a surrender to the Russians. Kossuth and some of his followers fled to Turkey. Görgey, judging all further resistance as merely uselessly shedding blood, unconditionally surrendered to the Russian commander-in-chief at Világos on 13 August rather than to the Austrian general.

After the surrender the Austrian General Haynau took vengeance on leading Hungarians. Görgey's life was spared because the tsar chivalrously had given his word and Francis Joseph's instincts were decent enough, but Schwarzenberg advised that Haynau be allowed to establish courts and to try and to execute Hungarians judged as rebels. On 6 October 1849, a day that was to become important in Hungarian history, thirteen imperial officers who had served as generals in the Hungarian armies were executed. The moderate Batthyány was shot as well. During the month of October the courts martial organized by Haynau pronounced death sentences and executed more than a hundred people. Once again the emperor, possibly on the advice of his ministers, intervened and refused Haynau authority to carry out some four hundred death sentences already pronounced by the special courts. In the repressions besides those executed some two thousand Hungarians received long terms of imprisonment. Haynau's name became a byword throughout Europe for brutality and Francis Joseph and Schwarzenberg shared in the odium. Yet these events need to be seen in perspective. A whole nation had been in arms against the emperor and judged by the standards of the day only a small proportion of the rebels were actually executed after the battles, though many were maltreated. Haynau's unlimited powers, moreover, were revoked after less than a month. The cold-blooded general no doubt believed he was doing his duty. The emperor and Schwarzenberg, though less narrow in vision, thought it necessary to make an example of traitors, especially leading officers who had taken up arms against the emperor. Imperial authority rested on the army and rebellion could not go unpunished.

That Haynau's executions should have aroused such emotions, and should have been stopped comparatively soon on orders from Vienna, says much for the moral standard of mid-nineteenth-century Europe. Neither Francis Joseph nor Schwarzenberg wished to shed blood needlessly. By the standards of the twentieth century they would have been judged positively humane.

There was a curious diplomatic sequel; the Near Eastern crisis of October 1849. Kossuth was a refugee in Turkey and so were a number of prominent Polish officers who had fought for the Hungarians. The Russians called for the extradition of the Poles, who were Russian subjects, and the Austrians then demanded the extradition of Kossuth and other subjects of the emperor. The Turks saw this as an opportunity to play off the great powers against each other. Palmerston and Louis Napoleon ordered the British fleet and French fleet to the vicinity of the Dardanelles to support the Turks or to persuade them not to extradite the Hungarian patriots. Meantime the Russians decided not to pursue their claims and the Austrians had to abandon their efforts also. What is of interest is that this short-lived alliance of France and Britain in Turkish affairs proved a precursor of the Crimean alliance just four years later. The episode belongs to the history of the Eastern question rather than to 1848. In support of liberalism, the actions of Palmerston and Louis Napoleon were no more than a gesture. Kossuth was interned in Turkey and then allowed to leave. After a tumultuous welcome in the United States Kossuth eventually came to London where he was equally rapturously received and decided to settle in England with the other exiles of 1848.

The legend was born that Kossuth represented the people in their fight against the eastern autocrats, the constitutional cause against despotism. All this is far from reality except that the majority of Magyars had fought bravely. The general conflicts of 1848–9 affected the Habsburg Empire in different ways: there were social conflicts and conflict among the nationalities. The Hungarian struggle was a quarrel about the separate historic rights of the kingdom of the crown of St Stephen, rights which had been extended during the spring of 1848; the court and the government in Vienna sought just as determinedly to extinguish during the months of reaction. In their attitude to other nationalities there was little difference between the government of the western domains and of the empire (Austria) and the government of Hungary. In Hungary the Magyars insisted on political primacy; other national groups were permitted rights of language and custom, in short only national rights that made no claims to political self-government. Haynau's behaviour in Hungary after the war may be compared with Kossuth's brutal repression of earlier Slovak attempts to free themselves from Magyar control. The Magyars also summarily killed many hapless Slovaks who had been defeated by them. In this respect there was little to choose between 'Kossuth's gallows' and 'Butcher Haynau'; only the cheering crowds in Britain and America knew nothing of all this.

Within the Habsburg Empire, the Schwarzenberg ministry not only brought the resistance of national movements to an end – the last to fall was the Republic of Venice in August 1849 – but also the promised people's constitution. The *Reichstag* at Kremsier actually worked out a far-reaching constitution which sought to come to grips with both the problem of the nationalities and absolute powers of the emperor. The projected Kremsier constitution would have turned the emperor into a constitutional monarch and allowed parliament a share of power in government; it would have abolished all titles and abolished the privileged position of the Catholic Church. The emperor would no longer have been ruler by 'Grace of God' for the constitution actually stated 'sovereignty proceeds from the people'. All this was anathema to Francis Joseph, the ministers and the military. Instead of the *Reichstag*'s constitution, the Schwarzenberg ministry on 6 March 1849 announced the emperor would proclaim a constitution and had no further need of the *Reichstag* which had wasted its time. The new royal constitution left to the monarchy unfettered control of the army and foreign policy. Parliament, though it was to be called every year, could be dismissed by the emperor who also preserved a veto over all legislation. The emperor was to be assisted by an imperial council whose members he would choose. In practice the elected parliamentary body was little more than two debating chambers, an upper and lower house. The constitution confirmed the monarchy in all its essential powers. At the same time there were some progressive elements. At the local level of districts and communities a good deal of autonomy and popular representation was supposed to be encouraged. This was the work of Count Stadion. The nationalities enjoyed non-political rights of linguistic equality and every subject equality before the law; all forms of serfdom were abolished. One of the most important aspects of the constitution was that it abolished all Hungarian and other national political rights though lip service was paid to the Hungarian constitution. There was to be only one parliament, one citizenship, one legal and customs system throughout the empire. What Schwarzenberg attempted was to create a strongly unitary governed state which would allow the nationalities only equal cultural rights and the people some representative institutions at the level of the community and district. Only the Italians in Lombardy-Venetia were to be permitted a separate status for a short while longer.

Jelačić, who had fought for the emperor in hopes of receiving rewards was disappointed. Croatia was permitted no separate political existence. What was intended as a permanent solution lasted only a decade. Defeated in two wars in 1859 and in 1866 the monarchy was forced to make concessions to the strongest nationality in the empire once again. The will of the Magyars for self-government had not been broken by defeat in 1849 as the history of the monarchy was to show during the succeeding decades. Their attachment to the crown of St Stephen strangely outlasted even the fall of the house of Habsburg and persisted to the close of the Second World War. History has shown the Magyars to be a stubborn and tenacious people unwilling to accept the apparent logic of events.

Within the space of a few months the majority of Prussians, even the Berliners, seemed to lose their ardour for the 'March revolution' and for German unity. Popular feelings are often extraordinarily short-lived; yesterday's martyrs cease to arouse any feelings; the politicians and ideologies once apparently on the crest of a wave are later forgotten and left in isolation. So it was in Prussia. The election of the Austrian Archduke John as provisional head of the empire by the Frankfurt parliament offended Prussian national pride; in the summer of 1848 there was a quite remarkable revival of patriotic fervour for the King of Prussia. The clashes at the arsenal in June 1848 (p. 66) had induced a feeling among the law-abiding Berliners that more force was needed to guarantee law and order than the liberal parliamentary ministry could provide. There were many who hoped to see a substantial increase of seasoned troops in Berlin to reinforce the handful stationed there after the king's departure. In the royalist camp at Potsdam, on the other hand, the victory of the Habsburg armies and especially the conquest of Vienna in October encouraged visions of putting an end to the parliamentarians and ministers in Berlin by force if necessary. So by the autumn of 1848 the course of events in Prussia and in Germany combined to undermine the constitutional experiment which the king had acquiesced in since the previous March.

Frederick William was changeable and two-faced; uncertain as to what he should do next; how to judge when the moment would be right to reappear as the ruler of his people. The reactionary entourage surrounding him in Potsdam tried to stiffen the monarch's resolution. Frederick William now lived in Sans Souci, the delightful small palace Frederick the Great had built for himself. Frederick William had inherited his most famous ancestor's artistic sensibilities, but none of his ruthlessness, good judgement and determination. So periodically Frederick William travelled to Berlin to receive his bourgeois ministers led by Auerswald and Hansemann, the capable Minister of Finance in the previous Camphausen administration. In Berlin, Frederick William acted as a law-abiding constitutional monarch. In Potsdam, he derided the efforts of the ministry. The Auerswald/Hansemann ministry lasted until the summer, when attacked by the Prussian National Assembly on the one hand and lacking support from the king on the other, it too resigned. How could any ministry succeed that believed in the maintenance of the Prussian monarchy but as a constitutional monarchy, when the king would not accept limitations of power imposed by any of his subjects and a majority of the Prussian National Assembly looked for some sort of partnership between king and parliament. No administration could govern for long given the prevailing royal and parliamentary attitudes. Prussian liberals admired but misunderstood British constitutional practice believing it provided for a balance between sovereign, parliament and people. By the autumn of 1848, Frederick William IV had appointed a general, von Pfuel, to head a new ministry. Troops in the streets of Berlin now were much more in evidence. Surprisingly General Pfuel did his constitutional best in the circumstances. He genuinely attempted to reconcile the preservation of all executive power in the hands of the monarch with the demands of the parliament for some measure of control and supervision. There is no need to follow here these political efforts in detail. The hard-working ministers and the politicians of the assembly were allowed to play their parts only just as long as Frederick William remained in a state of indecision.

In Berlin during October there was some unrest. Workers fearful for their jobs clashed with the citizen militia of the more prosperous citizens. It was in the interests of the counter-revolution to exaggerate the seriousness of the occasional turmoil in the streets. The great majority of the members of the Prussian National Assembly and the ministry had no difficulty in mastering the situation. When Pfuel resigned soon after taking office it was not because he could not govern but because he would not act as the agent of a royalist *coup* to overthrow the constitutional arrangements. Frederick William was finally dropping the mantle of constitutionalism. Into Pfuel's place stepped Count Brandenburg, uncle of the king, a general without Pfuel's constitutional scruples a soldier accustomed to giving orders to troops, unimaginative, and a Junker ready to serve the crown; a leading conservative administrator, Otto von Manteuffel joined the ministry, and early in November 1848 Brandenburg announced a royal order proroguing the Prussian National Assembly; it was to reassemble not in Berlin but in the small provincial town of Brandenburg. Berlin, quite unnecessarily, was placed under military siege. But the king continued to waver. Certainly the constitutional disorders produced by a few workers in Berlin served only as an excuse for making an end of the March concessions. The Prussian National Assembly offered passive resistance to the king's unconstitutional behaviour. The response of the king and Count Brandenburg was to try to intimidate Berlin by occupying the city with thousands of troops. From the splintered political opposition no further effective resistance was possible. The occupation of Berlin was virtually bloodless. In some provincial towns especially in the Rhineland and Silesia, wherever stagnating crafts and industry made workers desperate, there was violence and bloodshed in November. The Prussian soldiers made short work of industrial unrest and the socialist clubs. Meantime the emissaries from the Frankfurt parliament were politely received in Berlin. They demanded a return to constitutionalism. But there was no chance that the King of Prussia would accede to the resolutions of the Frankfurt parliamentarians. The impotence of Frankfurt in November 1848 foreshadowed the rejection by Frederick William five months later of Frankfurt's proffered crown.

To the last Frederick William hesitated. When the Prussian National Assembly attempted to reassemble late in November in Brandenburg it was so hopelessly divided between the majority of the left and a more conservative minority which tried to exclude the left that the dissolution of the discredited national assembly by the king now mattered little. Though the parliamentarians had behaved in a personally courageous manner in resisting the king's authority, insisting on their constitutional rights internal political divisions had prevented them from agreeing on any realistic programme. The king had consented to their being summoned as proposed by the original United Diet (p. 61) and they had supposedly worked since May 1848 with the crown in order to agree on a constitution for Prussia. Various drafts had been debated until abruptly on 5 December 1848 by royal decree the national assembly was dissolved.

That same day, 5 December 1848, by another royal decree, the king granted his subjects a constitution of his own free and unfettered will. As he had not much will of his own this document really represented the views of his conservative and reforming ministers.

It is tempting to dismiss these conservative efforts as mere window-dressing intended to cloak reaction in an acceptable garb. But this would be a misleading oversimplification. Since the times of Frederick the Great and the foundations of Prussia, certainly since the days of Stein, Hardenberg and Scharnhorst, support for the power of the monarch and his divine right had been complemented by a reforming modernizing spirit which sought to ensure the happiness and rights of the individual subject and his protection against the arbitrary power of the state. What these conservative Prussians aimed at was not parliamentary government and the sovereignty of the people, but a compact between people and monarch, leaving to the monarch the exercise of all ultimate executive power but ensuring the basic freedom of his subjects from illegal acts on the part of the state. The December 1848 constitution added the feature of consultation through representative assemblies such as had been promised since the Congress of Vienna. The most novel aspect of all was that henceforth Prussia would always possess a written constitution and would set an example later to Germany; it was a constitution capable of modification and change. A representative, not entirely subservient, voice was henceforth able to speak, to debate and at times to engage in conflict with authority and to force modifications on the ruler and government. At the same time it proved never strong enough, neither originally nor in later forms, to tilt the balance of power away from the monarch or the authority of the state. Consequently the Prussian and imperial German parliaments, in contrast to the British, did not become the ultimate source of power. One reason why this was so can be seen in the balance of benefits and limitations bestowed by the first Prussian Constitution of December 1848.

The liberal aspects of the constitution astounded contemporaries. It seemed a Prussian king in the moment of victory had enshrined the principle of democracy. Two chambers were created. The second lower chamber would be elected by manhood suffrage; every adult (male) Prussian could exercise his right to vote more than thirty years before every Englishman did so. The first chamber, however, was weighted by age (males over thirty were given the vote) and by high property qualifications in favour of the wealthier. Nowhere was the privilege of birth, being a member of the aristocracy, a criterion of the *right* to vote. But the liberal aspects of the constitution were weakened by other articles. The ministers hoped to prevent militant representatives from sitting in parliament by not allowing any payment to members of either of the chambers. The two chambers were granted the right of participation in legislation, and especially to vote for the budget (article 99). But what was granted could be taken away since the monarch reserved to himself extensive emergency powers to rule without the consent of the chambers, to suspend civil rights, and to collect taxes without annual parliamentary consent. The financial independence of the monarch was also guaranteed. All executive power, the appointment and dismissal of ministers, and control over the administration, was reserved to the monarch. There lies the essential difference with the evolving parliamentary democracy in Britain. Furthermore the monarch could revise the Prussian constitution whenever he wished. Thus the constitution and working of the parliamentary chambers was given a provisional character. The constitution, however, also guaranteed the king's subjects civil rights, freedom of person, of movement, of religion, of assembly and of association, and provided for an independent judiciary. To be sure these rights could be set aside. Extensive police surveillance, political trials and so on did allow arbitrary abuse of power in Prussia during the years before the First World War. At the same time the Prussian judges built up a reputation for incorruptibility and independence. A legal norm, in all but exceptional cases of pressure, upheld by the courts, did give the subjects of the King of Prussia the reassurance that they lived in a state where the rule of law was constitutionally intended to prevail.

The Prussian constitution brought the Prussian state to the forefront of well-governed continental European states. It was intended to outshine the more restricted constitutions of the smaller German states, and anticipated the constitution being debated at Frankfurt. The Prussian ministers intended the constitution not only to satisfy the aspiration of all but an irreconcilable minority of Prussians but also to serve as a possible monarchical model for a German nation – an alternative to the Frankfurt parliamentarianism. It was as well received in Prussia by the king's subjects as it perturbed the smaller German courts and the Frankfurt national parliament who saw themselves in danger of being outbid. Prussia's reconciliation of people and crown was in striking contrast to the Habsburgs' suppression and wars in their dominions. Nor were the Prussian reforms merely paper ones. The Brandenburg-Manteuffel government followed them up with a whole series of measures emancipating the Prussian peasantry (see p. 134).

It is also true that the new Prussian parliaments were generally subservient to the crown until the end of the 1850s. The democratic franchise was soon modified when in May 1849 the 'three class suffrage' was introduced. Theoretically every adult Prussian male retained the right to vote for the lower second chamber. Voting for the actual deputies was indirect (unlike Britain). The votes were cast for members of an electoral body who in turn chose the actual deputies to sit in the parliamentary assembly. The Prussian voters now were divided into three classes, the smallest group of high taxpayers elected one third of the 'electors', the larger middle group of taxpayers the second third, and the last, by far the largest group of small taxpayers or non-taxpayers, the third group of electors. These 'electors' then acted as one body to choose the deputies sitting in the second chamber. This system based on wealth produced for a decade an overwhelmingly conservative parliamentary chamber. Soon the first chamber too was changed in composition into something akin to the British House of Lords. The rights of the two chambers over voting an annual budget remained vague. The monarchy thus retained the means of exerting absolutist power. In practice, Prussian absolutism had come to an end. The monarchy continued to be authoritarian, but the monarch's power fell short of absolutism. For all its shortcomings the Prussian constitution in its final form (31 January 1850) though imposed from above created a genuine parliament which later strove with some success (though it also had to accept failures) to widen its rights and powers at the expense of the monarch and the ministries who wielded power in his name. Over the army, the monarch's crucial weapon to support him at home and Prussia's policies abroad, the king meant to and succeeded in retaining absolute control. On this crucial question the first great conflict between monarch and parliament was to develop before the decade of the 1850s had drawn to its close.

At no time did the rulers of the German states accept the authority of the Frankfurt parliament to speak for 'Germany'. As Frederick William IV unambiguously pointed out the gentlemen at Frankfurt had appointed themselves to this task and had no legal rights which only the German princes could have authorized. The Habsburgs and Hohenzollerns were united on the point of opposition to the idea of a popular 'German' sovereignty being exercised through the elected representatives of the German people. But for many months it served Prussia's and Austria's domestic and international policies to tolerate and have polite dealings with this 'German' parliament and the 'Central Authority' and 'Imperial Regent' this assembly had created in the months of May and June of 1848 (see chapter 4). Polite words were cheap as long as the Prussian and Habsburg armies remained under the sole command of their monarchs. The Frankfurt parliament and imperial government could exercise no executive authority except in so far it seemed good to Prussia and the major German states.

The Frankfurt parliament was also deeply divided within itself between shades of the radical left, the liberal centre and the right. The representatives of the left preferred a republican form but were less concerned with the details of constitution-making than with ending the oppression of the rulers. They wished the 'revolution' to end in the sovereignty and victory of all the people and the overthrow of the princes. Once this was achieved, it was a matter of no great moment to them whether 'Germany' should consist of a unitary state or of several smaller republics or what precise role was to be assigned to minorities. They overlooked the problems posed by the nationalities of Polish, south Slav, Italian, Dutch, Danish and French minorities who would have been included in a wide Germany whose frontiers they hoped would extend at least as far as those of the Holy Roman Empire. Once the people were free, nationalism as a divisive force they believed with Mazzini would simply disappear. At the same time they were amongst the most ardent nationalists when it came to the test case of Schleswig-Holstein. The left in its various groupings formed a substantial minority in the Frankfurt parliament. On the right sat the defenders of the rights of the states who wished to limit the role of the Frankfurt parliament and the development of any form of central authority responsible to a German parliament. The majority, who were moderate liberals, attempted to achieve a practical compromise between state rights and central authority; they worked for a constitutional monarchy where the rights of a parliament and the rights of the people would be guaranteed by a written constitution accepted by the monarch.

It was this liberal majority which guided the way in which the Frankfurt parliament tackled its most important task: the framing of a German constitution. And what they did was at first sight surprising and even foolish, no more than was to be expected of a group of academics, so those who derided the parliamentarians write. For months they debated the fundamental rights of the German people. In fact there were good reasons for dealing with the basic rights of each citizen before tackling the problems involved in framing a German constitution. The one was dependent on the other. Once the civic rights for every 'German' citizen had been agreed by the Frankfurt parliament, no constitution in any individual state would be valid that set any of these rights aside. This was the most effective way the Frankfurt parliament could devise of influencing the constitutional struggles in the states. The ruler of a state could not then grant less than what had been agreed for 'Germany' by Frankfurt. That was the intention. There were two further reasons why those responsible for framing a constitution turned first to 'basic rights'. The basic rights were an issue on which the various factions in the Frankfurt parliament were most likely to agree. The moderate liberals wished to get the parliamentarians used to working with each other before tackling more contentious issues. In this way the question of the 'sovereignty of the people' was side-stepped. Another grave problem was deliberately postponed: the relationship between Frankfurt, Berlin and Vienna was not finally settled. The Frankfurt parliament had no alternative to postponement. Prussia could not be coerced by Frankfurt and the future of the Habsburg Empire was uncertain in the summer of 1848.

The liberal majority of Frankfurt had no realization that time was running out for constitutional experiment. That has only been clear to historians with hindsight. The liberals of 1848 had confidence in the future and believed that the constitutional changes brought about by the March revolutions would be consolidated and deepened in the German states. So great a task as the creation of the new German nation could not be hastened; to do so might jeopardize the cohesion of the Frankfurt parliament and damage the relationships with the individual states, with their ministers and their rulers. It was a reasonable way of looking at the contemporary German scene. Revolution by force, such as the most extreme radicals had advocated, had no chance of success and would create social chaos. With hindsight we can see that already by the summer of 1848 a transformation of Germany by a national parliamentary assembly had become an impossibility. Had the Frankfurt parliament acted more decisively and quickly as historical critics would have had them act, they would have been dispersed far earlier than they were. The Frankfurt liberals' only chance lay in working out an agreement with the King of Prussia, who had avoided an open break with the liberals in Prussia and seemed favourably disposed to the German national cause.

The 50 articles of the fundamental rights of every German were debated and approved by the Frankfurt parliament in December 1848. They became 'German' law. These rights included equality before the law and the abrogation of privileges of class; freedom of religion, of association, of assembly, and freedom from censorship and arbitrary arrest. They could only be guaranteed on paper, for all these basic rights remained inoperative unless individual states chose to accept the law. For all that they were not valueless, but just like today's 30 articles of the United Nations' Universal Declaration of Human Rights, they set a standard of civilized behaviour; goals and ideals acquire a moral force which can be shown to have a perceptible influence on governments except the most extreme. The German rulers of the mid-nineteenth century certainly the King of Prussia, accepted such rights even when they believed that for reasons of state they could exceptionally be set aside.

In mid-October 1848 the Frankfurt parliament began its work on the constitution. Before the debates in Frankfurt had got very far, Vienna had fallen to the army of Windischgraetz; Berlin was occupied by royal troops; the Prussian liberal ministers were no longer in power and the Prussian National Assembly had been prorogued to a small provincial town – the usual device for depriving the assembly of power and prestige. The possibility of revolution, or even of constitutional change from below was at an end in both Prussia and Austria. It is this fact which made so many of the debates at Frankfurt in the autumn and winter of 1848 a matter of purely academic interest. As the historian Golo Mann has so well put it: 'the difficulty was that whenever the Assembly wanted to achieve something real its own unreality became apparent'. Frederick William IV and the conservatives might for tactical reasons appear to negotiate and discuss with Frankfurt but they would never have accepted from the German parliamentarians conditions for co-operation which they would not accept from the Prussian parliament. They would never agree to the notion of the king and ministers being responsible to parliament. For the Habsburg conservatives such as Schwarzenberg exactly the same was true: parliamentary sovereignty was anathema to them. The

Habsburgs had an added reason for implacable hostility to Frankfurt: German unity could not take precedence over the unity and centralization of the multi-national Habsburg Empire which included German speaking Austria. The Habsburgs wished to dominate German affairs, Italy, and Slav eastern Europe as they had for centuries before 1848, not to unify Germany.

There is no need to follow in detail the party manœuvres of the Frankfurt parliament on the constitution during the winter of 1848 and the spring of 1849. It soon became evident that it was not realistic to think in terms of recreating territorially the old 'Holy Roman Empire'. The most difficult problem to solve was the future of the German-speaking portions of the Habsburg Empire. The smaller German states tended to favour a so-called *Kleindeutsch* (smaller German) solution which would have excluded the Habsburg Empire altogether and left the predominant power to Prussia. The larger German states were opposed to Prussian predominance and so wished to bring the Habsburgs in as a counterweight. The Austrian-Germans at Frankfurt also favoured the larger German concept of *Grossdeutsch* (greater Germany). Schwarzenberg would have no truck with either party but saw as the Habsburgs' natural sphere a multi-national middle European domain extending Habsburg dominance well beyond the actual frontiers of the empire in 1848. This meant the practical abandonment of German unity for Schwarzenberg despised weak and divided neighbours. Even the *Grossdeutsch* party at Frankfurt had to admit this truth in the end. But if by the spring of 1849 the *Grossdeutsch* groups prepared to accept Prussian leadership, they wished to limit its power as far as possible and won concessions from the *Kleindeutsch* liberals. The groups of the left meantime were prepared to make a deal. They would make possible a majority vote in the Frankfurt parliament for a hereditary Prussian emperor of Germany – though they had always opposed the rule of all princes – they would support the *Kleindeutsch* solution, but in return they demanded the strengthening of parliament and a democratic franchise.

The outcome of all these debates and deals was the constitution for the German Empire adopted by the Frankfurt parliament in March 1849. The 'left', the democratics, had won two major concessions: (1) the emperor would only be able to delay the passage of legislation not veto it permanently if the parliament passed the law three times in successive sessions; (2) the lower house of the parliament was to be elected in practice by direct male suffrage and secret ballot, every German male at least 25 years old of 'good repute' being granted the vote. The rights of parliament (the *Reichstag*) were extensive. The consent of the upper and lower house was required for legislation; annual budgets were to be voted on and the *Reichstag* would be able to control closely the expenditure of money. The hereditary emperor's powers also were extensive and the constitution as a whole did not allow parliament undisputed control over the monarch and over the government as in Britain. But it was a constitution whose franchise was more democratic than in Britain at that time and tilted the balance of ultimate power firmly in the direction of parliament away from the monarch. The constitution allowed for some separation of powers on the American model, but would have enabled parliament to exert strong influence and supervision over the imperial government. Frederick William IV was elected emperor on 28 March 1849 without great enthusiasm. About half the members of the Frankfurt parliament voted for him, the other half abstained.

When the president of the Frankfurt parliament, Eduard Simson, and a deputation of members set off for Berlin and offered the crown to Frederick William IV on 3 April 1849 they must have hoped for some chance of success. Frederick William had openly stated his attachment to the German cause and the King of Prussia had himself after all granted the vote to every Prussian male only a few weeks earlier. But Frederick William's dislike of the 'gentlemen' at Frankfurt and all they stood for was deep-rooted and had been strengthened by the events of the past year. He would never have consented to limit the powers of the monarchy to such a parliamentary assembly, or to any parliamentary assembly, nor would he consent to entrust the future of Prussia to a Germany whose fate would have been controlled by a German parliament of doubtful composition. All these were hard-headed and sufficient reasons for his refusal. Emotionally he was bound to the concept of 'divine right' and could not accept a crown voted by the people's representatives; he later referred to it as the 'crown by the grace of bakers and butchers', the 'dog collar' which would turn him into 'a serf of the revolution of 1848'. At the time, however, he seemed to prevaricate as usual. Twenty German governments lent their approval to his election and to the constitution, but the four largest states, the kingdoms of Hanover, Saxony, Württemberg and Bavaria, said nothing. There could never really be any doubt about the outcome. Frederick William refused the crown without formally saying yes or no by informing the parliamentarians that the crown was not theirs to offer. The Prussian government meanwhile rejected the constitution of Frankfurt in the form presented and so took the formal breach between Prussia and the German parliament of Frankfurt upon itself. Bavaria, Saxony and Hanover thereupon speedily joined Prussia in the rejection of the Frankfurt constitution.

What remained now, in the spring of 1849, of the Frankfurt parliament and its central power? The Austrian and Prussian members, loyal to their monarchs, departed from the assembly. In a pathetic show of strength the 'rump' of the Frankfurt parliament, mainly south German democrats, decided to go on and to speak for the German nation. The end of all the high hopes of the German parliament was at hand. The city government of Frankfurt would no longer harbour what now seemed more like a revolutionary assembly. The 130 members of the Frankfurt parliament who were left decided on the sort of bold move that had worked in the spring of 1848 but was doomed to failure a year later; they called for the election of a constituent German *Reichstag* in August. They themselves moved to Stuttgart the capital of Württemberg but were not able to function there for long. In June 1849 they were dispersed by the King of Württemberg's soldiers. But the end of all their hopes did not pass unnoticed in Germany. Support for the ideals of a democratic national Germany and bitter disappointment with the outcome of the revolutionary year did lead to some popular uprisings in May and June 1849. The King of Saxony had to flee from Dresden; there was also unrest in some Rhineland towns and in the Bavarian palatinate. The most serious and organized resistance occurred in Baden. Prussian bayonets put an end to the disorders; by mid-July the last spark of the Baden rising had been extinguished; the Prussians remained in occupation of Baden for more than two years. The 'counter revolution' not only crushed the aspirations of the democrats: it also demonstrated the power of the King of Prussia in Germany. It encouraged the King of Prussia to work for some union of Germany under his auspices now that the 'representatives of the German people' had been got rid of. The king was spectacularly unsuccessful.

Prussia's military and diplomatic weakness in the face of Austrian opposition to a Prussian-dominated German union was demonstrated for all to see in 1849 and 1850. Frederick William IV's romantic imagination dreamt of leading a reconstituted Holy Roman Empire in harmony with the Habsburg Emperor. He never came to practical grips with the fundamental problem of how the western lands of the Habsburgs could become a part of the reconstituted German Empire under Prussian leadership. Yet he could not altogether relinquish the national cause; in a proclamation to the German people in 1851, he declared that he did not wish to stand accused of having 'ceased to care for the cause of German unity', or of having 'grown unfaithful to my earlier conviction and my assurances'. But by 1851 the king's pose as a champion of the German nation had worn thin. Two years earlier, in the spring of 1849, there were still liberal supporters of German nationalism who placed their hopes in the King of Prussia despite his rejection of the imperial crown. One of these was the Prussian, Joseph Maria von Radowitz, who had spent much of his life attempting to strengthen the institutions of the German Confederation.

Radowitz had served Prussia long and faithfully. He had been Frederick William IV's friend for many years. He held the rank of a general in the Prussian army and had been entrusted before 1848 with diplomatic missions designed to reform the German Confederation. In the Frankfurt parliament he led the Prussian faction of the right. Radowitz, in common with a few enlightened conservatives, also recognized the need for social reform, the need to reconcile the people with the crown. He was a pious convert to Catholicism, an ardent champion of German nationalism, and a believer in the divine right of kings. Faithful to the Prussian crown, Radowitz, essentially a clever and able man, attempted to solve the German question in conformity with the beliefs of the King of Prussia. In the period immediately after 1848, Radowitz was the minister who had the greatest influence over Frederick William IV. His efforts all failed though they were certainly ingenious.

The 'Prussian Union Plan' for which Radowitz won Frederick William's support in 1849 conceived of a narrower German union led by Prussia, with a unified system of law, and a strong central government, and with the King of Prussia in control of the army. This smaller German federal *Reich* would borrow the Frankfurt constitution suitably amended to strengthen royal authority. Austria would be excluded from it. But the German Federal *Reich* would also be in permanent alliance or 'union' with the Habsburg Empire. This larger federation, or *Bund*, would be similar to the old Diet; there would be no parliament or central government for the larger union and Austria and Prussia would share the primacy of the wider *Bund*. Thus apparently the *Grossdeutsch, Mitteleuropaisch* (i.e. mid-European, consisting of all of Germany as well as all Habsburg territories) and *Kleindeutsch* solutions of the German question in Europe would be reconciled. Schwarzenberg was implacably hostile. He saw in this plan a way of removing Austrian influence in Germany. But faced still with revolutionary problems in the Austrian Empire, he could do no more than bide his time before attempting to destroy the Prussian plan. Thus Prussia was able at first to pursue it with some success. A. 'Three King's Alliance' between Prussia, Saxony and Hanover was formed in May 1849, but its continuation would depend on winning the support of two south German states, Württemberg and Bavaria, which did not wish to be drawn into the Prussian net. The smaller German states saw no alternative but to accept the Prussian proposals. Radowitz next called an assembly of all the German states to Erfurt to found the German *Reich* as conceived by him. But Bavaria and Württemberg refused to come. The 'Erfurt Parliament' in March 1850 was thus something of a fiasco since only Prussia and the smaller German states attended. Schwarzenberg, after the suppression of Hungary, was now ready to resume Austria's policy of seeking predominance in Germany. He summoned the Diet of the German Confederation to Frankfurt in May 1850 and the following September declared that the Confederation of Germany and the Diet had been re-established. Now there were two assemblies claiming to speak for Germany, the Diet at Frankfurt dominated by Austria, and the 'Erfurt Parliament' dominated by Prussia. A showdown between them soon occurred.

The Elector of Hesse-Cassel was locked in constitutional dispute with his parliament. The elector appealed to the Frankfurt Diet for support. But the 'Erfurt Parliament' claimed the matter should be decided by Prussia and its allies at Erfurt. They supported the parliament! Hesse-Cassel was of vital strategic importance to Prussia, since this little territory separated Prussia from the Rhineland; thus the military communications ran through this territory. Besides the conflict there now represented a test of strength between Prussia's German union and Austria's determination to re-establish the state of German affairs as if 1848 had never occurred. Austria mobilized and so did Prussia, or attempted to since the Prussian mobilization revealed serious military shortcomings. For all the outward show of strength Frederick William and the ultra-Prussian conservatives were not ready to take on Austria militarily. The will to win was lacking; possibly the military strength to do so also. Radowitz had to go. In his place Otto von Manteuffel was appointed and at Olmütz on 29 November 1850 he yielded to Austria. The subsequent conference at Dresden from December 1850 to spring of 1851 merely served to formally re-establish the Diet of the German Confederation and to lay to rest all further schemes of reform. This political 'humiliation' has been seen as marking the nadir of Prussia's struggle for primacy in Germany. Recent research, however, has shown that this view is an oversimplification. In the struggle for economic predominance, Prussia made great strides in the 1850s through the *Zollverein* even while giving way militarily to Austria for the time being.

9

The 1850s: The Authoritarian Decade in Austria and Prussia

The decade of the 1850s presents an extraordinary contrast to the turmoil of the 'hungry forties'. The peoples of Europe were politically quiescent. There were no more fights on the barricades; perhaps the lesson that it was useless to fight the trained army of the state had been learned. On the continent of Europe a more enlightened brand of conservatism, recognizing the need for reform and change, took the place of the more stagnant political conservatism of the 1840s. The state was paternalist and authoritarian. Exaggerated hopes were placed in the ability of the rulers to provide prosperity and banish poverty.

Below the political surface there are also aspects of continuity between the 1840s and 1850s. The two decades saw a remarkable continuing population growth, especially in Russia, Britain and 'Germany' and to a much smaller degree in France. Despite the development of industry, which absorbed some of the increasing rural populations in the towns, land could no longer provide a living for all those wishing to live by it during these years. The new world became the 'safety valve'. This was well recognized and in those countries where the increase of population outstripped agricultural and industrial expansion in Britain when we include Ireland, southwest Germany, Prussia and Scandinavia, no hindrance was placed in the way of the migrants. On the contrary, in Prussia for example efforts were made to ensure that the migrants were properly treated by the shipping companies. In the decade of the 1850s more than 2 million people left the British Isles alone; from the German states, especially south-west Germany, another million emigrated during the same decade and they were joined by Scandinavians in large numbers. But this human tide of migration, mainly to the United States, was not a new phenomenon of the 1850s but a continuation of the migration of the 1840s. It is a myth that the '1848' revolution was the cause of the migration from Europe. At best it was a small additional factor. For every famous exile of '1848', a Karl Marx, Kossuth or Carl Schurz, there were tens of thousands who left to gain a better living. When the migrants of the 1850s and 1860s reached their destination overseas they sought to maintain the cultural traditions and links with their European 'home'. Whilst many people were better off in the 1850s and 1860s and the numbers of those who could be said to belong to the 'middle class' increased, so did poverty and destitution for others. It was not people with adequate standards of living who emigrated in their millions to the United States. To speak of a general growth of prosperity during the third quarter of the nineteenth century whilst correct according to the law of averages is a rather misleading generalization. There were great variations of wealth between one group of workers and others, between one country or region of a country and another – one only has to think of Ireland in this connection. Variations also between a good year and a bad year, between the effects of a good harvest and a bad one. Fluctuations in levels of real income could be violent. The 1830s and 1840s were a period so appalling for the majority of the poor with real wages often falling, that it is only by comparison with these bleak decades that the 1850s and 1860s seemed an improvement for the majority. In Britain, the country where industrialization had made the greatest progress, one Englishman out of every seven was a pauper and the first volume of Henry Mayhew's *London Labour and the London Poor*, with the grim picture of destitution it depicts, was first published in 1851 as 'a cyclopaedia of the condition and earnings of those that will work, those that cannot work, and those that will not work.' All this has to be set against the cult of progress exemplified by the Crystal Palace.

Politically it was a quiet decade in Europe. There was no revolutionary challenge from below. It was a decade of patriotism and of general popular support for all varieties of nationalist movements, whether Polish, Hungarian or Italian, though none of the complex issues involved could be grasped by ordinary people. The Tsar of Russia was seen as the archenemy of social and national progress by liberals and radicals alike. The Crimean War was welcomed as a fight against autocracy and the causes of Hungary, Turkey and Poland enjoyed a brief period of popularity.

Another aspect of the 1850s is the growth of government administration and bureaucracy. Everywhere on the continent governments were authoritarian. In France, Louis Napoleon's constitution for the Second Empire made the centralized administration the chief instrument of the government; the legislature enjoyed little real power. The Habsburg Empire became a byword for centralized bureaucracy during the 1850s; the representative features of the constitution of 1849, the work of Count Stadion, the Minister of the Interior, were not put into effect except at the local level of the communes. Even these modest reforms did not outlive Stadion. Prussia was scarcely less authoritarian, though in comparison with France and Austria, the Prussian parliament possessed some genuine residual powers. In the 1850s, the Prussian ministers' chief aim was to re-establish royal power and to enlarge the state's role in social and economic questions. Politically it was a period of reaction; a system of spies and of police surveillance watched over the lives of every suspicious subject to prevent any disturbance of domestic tranquillity. It was also a period of reform imposed in the name of the monarch, reform from above.

In the Russia of Nicholas I the bureaucracy was being given an increasingly greater role in the state, though the vastness of the empire defeated attempts at effective centralized administration. During the last years of the tsar's reign Russia stagnated and all initiative was stifled.

Britain presents a contrast to the picture of continental Europe. Political leaders recognized the need to base their influence on the broader issues; the political privilege of the better-off was diminishing. The reformed parliament grew in strength and stature, so did the development of representative local government; centralization, however, was also a significant trend. Centralized inspectorates were created to ensure that legislation in matters of health, factory conditions, education and local administration was observed. The British solution to the government of the modern state was thus a unique blend of centralization, local representative institutions and a representative parliamentary legislature. The growth and reforms of the civil service was one complementary aspect of the increasing importance of central administration.

Central state authority made possible some reforms in the 1850s and generally took upon itself the protection of the rights of individuals. On the continent of Europe the decade of authoritarian rule thus was not entirely negative in its effects. The 1850s were also the decade which saw the passing of one spectacular reform: the legal emancipation of the peasantry throughout central and eastern Europe. Without strong central authority this reform could scarcely have been pushed through effectively, but it should be noted that the economic emancipation of the peasantry was very much more gradual. The new means of communication by electric telegraph, it is worth remembering, aided centralization and made control over all regions of a state more feasible.

Another important aspect of the decade after 1848 was the continued industrial expansion which brought increasing prosperity to some. However, the degree to which the state deliberately encouraged industrial growth in the 1850s, and so should receive the credit, has been generally exaggerated. The state's contribution to industrial growth in France of the Second Empire, in the Habsburg Monarchy and in Prussia, tended to be indirect. Much emphasis was given to the rapid development of railways. Though Russia remained industrially stagnant in the 1850s and expansion was to occur only later in the nineteenth century the state here too had made a significant contribution initiating the construction of railway lines.

The optimism of the rulers and of the industrial 'pace setters' and their self-confidence in material progress, was symbolized by the Great Exhibition of 1851 at the Crystal Palace where new technological marvels from all over Europe were shown and patronized by royalty. Napoleon III was not to be outdone. Crystal Palace was followed by the Paris Exhibition of 1855, the most splendid and opulent yet seen; but we must not be carried away by these 'spectaculars' into generalizations about the new prosperity of the age. The great exhibitions have to be assessed for what they were, technological 'circuses'. No doubt 'people of quality' saw them as great wonders of wealth but the majority of people were not affected as they toiled on the land or in a factory. If they symbolized anything it was the contrast between wealth and poverty in mid-nineteenth-century Europe.

Yet surrounded by so much poverty, the rulers and the more affluent minority were not threatened anywhere seriously on the continent after 1848–9. One reason is that everywhere on the continent, except in Hungary the armies had proved themselves as the reliable instruments of the established order. (Louis Philippe never tested the army's loyalty which later served the 'Republic' and the emperor). The soldiers proved their blind loyalty again in 1854 and 1855, whether they fought in the Crimea for the tsar emperor or for queen and parliament. Obedience to the command of the monarch was the one thing regarded by the rulers as essential for the preservation of the modern state; they at any rate could not forget the traumatic experiences of 1848 when the 'people' had challenged their authority. There was thus on the continent of Europe an extreme sensitivity on the part of the rulers towards any attempt by a parliamentary legislature to gain influence over the command of the army or over the revenue necessary to maintain it. Britain again provides a striking contrast. The army was firmly under the control of the cabinet of civilians and so ultimately was dependent on parliament. In reality parliament was sovereign not the monarch. This divergence between Britain and the continent is of great significance. The army (or navy) could never play in Britain the role it continued to fulfil in Austria, Prussia and Russia as the personal instrument of the sovereign. That does not mean parliament was not prepared to use the army if necessary against 'the people'; extreme precautions were taken during the Chartist demonstrations. The one thing all the armies had in common was obedience to whoever represented the ultimate authority of the state.

As the decade drew to a close the authoritarian rule was modified on the continent. Two wars in different ways fundamentally affected the policies of the rulers: the Crimean and the Italian. Napoleon III felt strong enough to allow more political liberty and discussion in France. In the Habsburg Empire for the opposite reason; the result of failure in war forced Francis Joseph to make some concessions to the critics of the centralized authoritarian monarchy. In Russia, a new tsar, Alexander II in the aftermath of defeat, emancipated the serfs and cautiously pursued a number of important reforms (see chapter 15).

The decade of the 1850s may seem to lack glamour, lying between the spectacular revolutionary year of 1848 and the 1860s when the map of Europe was transformed; but both domestic and international developments in the 1850s had a lasting and important influence on the years that followed, for the fundamental shift in the balance of power in Europe, evident after the victories of Prussia, had its origins in the 1850s. Russia's Crimean humiliation, Britain's growing isolationism from continental power conflicts, the financial and the military weakness of the Habsburgs, the increasing strength of Prussia, all these changes occurred in the 1850s and they paved the way for the spectacular realignment of European power in the following decade.

Schwarzenberg and Bach, the two ministers who in succession dominated the empire's policy, believed the weakness of the Habsburg Empire lay in excessive nationalism and the divisiveness this created. It was an odd conclusion coming after 1848–9 when these very national rivalries had aided the recovery of imperial authority. Schwarzenberg's and Bach's solution was to try to create a unified monarchy. But before the work of reconstruction could begin, Habsburg authority had first to be re-established throughout the empire.

In the western lands of the monarchy military reaction won the upper hand in November 1848, but in the eastern half of the monarchy Hungary's bid for independence still threatened the very existence of the Habsburg Empire as a great power. Beset by so many troubles at home, the Habsburgs could exert little control abroad especially over German affairs except to reject any notion of permitting Austria to be incorporated in a German union (p. 122).

The loyal Habsburg armies, on whom the future of the empire depended, were led by Marshal Windischgraetz, an extreme conservative of narrow outlook and little vision. Windischgraetz had no time for the *Reichstag* reassembled at Kremsier and even less for the constitutional work on which the deputies there were engaged. At the apex of power, the Emperor Ferdinand was weak and indecisive, but waiting in the wings was Francis Joseph his nephew, a young man of eighteen with little experience. He was available to take on the burdens of the throne as soon as the court and army thought the right moment had come (see p. 104). Despite the military successes already won in northern Italy and the subjugation of Vienna and Prague, the future of the monarchy internally and internationally remained full of uncertainty in the winter of 1848–9. The fundamental questions of how the empire would be governed, and by what manner of constitution, remained to be clarified. Nor was there any agreement as to how the nationality problem should be tackled so that peace and order would prevail in the many lands of the Habsburgs. What forces would emerge as predominant; the emperor, the ministry or the army? What, if any, share in government would the people be permitted through representative institutions? How could the economic welfare of the country best be furthered?

A little more than two years later, by April 1852, the outlook of the Habsburg Empire had been transformed. There was general tranquillity. In Hungary, however, the sense of nationalism remained strong. But the Schwarzenberg-Bach period saw the successful establishment of a centralized government and a centralized administration throughout the monarchy. There was little open dissent. The Habsburg Empire was now called the *Gesammt Monarchie*, thus emphasizing its 'wholeness'; it was not to be mistaken for a federal amalgamation of the various nations under one monarch.

Almost the whole of the history that remained to the Habsburg Empire was presided over by the emperor who had been brought to the throne as a young man in the revolutionary year of 1848. Francis Joseph spiritually lived in a past age and just like Nicholas I modelled himself on the enlightened despots of the eighteenth century. He had some solid virtues, especially a sense of moderation and decency; he was personally incorruptible; he believed it to be his duty to serve his people; he was able to suppress his prejudices and succeeded in winning a genuine loyalty from his many subjects so varied in religion and nationality; he lived modestly and frugally in the Hofburg, the great pile of a palace in the centre of Vienna. He was rather bleak and cheerless and shared with Queen Victoria a total lack of good taste in the arts. He married for love the beautiful Elizabeth, a Wittelsbach (Bavarian) princess in 1854, but his family life became notoriously unhappy as the somewhat unstable Elizabeth, to escape the stifling etiquette of the Vienna Court, travelled restlessly through Europe. A decent but rigid and unimaginative man, Francis Joseph despite his youth and inexperience possessed complete faith in his divine mission to rule his people and desired to do so without benefit of their participation. He was an absolutist at heart and in later years it was only defeat in war that forced him to accept the role of a constitutional monarch. The two pillars of his throne were the army and the church; his relationship to both were very special to him. Although in no way intellectually out of the ordinary he was painstaking and thorough, his memory was said to be extraordinary as was his gift for speaking the many languages of the empire. He was not bigoted nor did he identify himself with German Austria, but rather saw himself as the father and ruler of all his people, above any one nationality or even social class. The sheer longevity of his reign, his virtues, and the stoicism with which he bore family misfortunes, in the end won him a measure of love and respect.

Prince Felix zu Schwarzenberg was his first minister president during the early critical years of his reign. Every contemporary observer remarks on Schwarzenberg's haughtiness and arrogance. The prince looked on his fellow noblemen as belonging to an incompetent class. He gave the impression that government was an unwelcome burden to him. Elegant, cynical and unscrupulous, to outward appearance Schwarzenberg seemed to lack the qualities of statesmanship. Yet how much of this was a pose? His political instincts were sound: his sense of timing excellent. He realized he could not master all the monarchy's problems at home and abroad simultaneously and so he energetically tackled each crisis in turn; meanwhile he would take a conciliatory course on other issues and so kept open all possible options. What was crucial for success was to recognize the right order of priority, what had to be dealt with at once and what could wait.

The subjugation of Hungary was the most immediate and urgent task. Elsewhere in the monarchy he could afford to temporize. When appearing before the *Reichstag* at Kremsier in November 1848, Schwarzenberg declared that it was his ministry's intention to place itself at the head of the movement to provide the monarchy with 'liberal and popular institutions'; he gave the parliamentarians the assurance that he too wanted a 'constitutional Monarchy, sincerely and unreservedly'. Of course he was temporizing. But Schwarzenberg was no simple reactionary either. He recognized that the government and administration of the monarchy needed a thorough reform if it was to survive. The *Reichstag* in Vienna and later in Kremsier seemed to him incapable of government, hopelessly bogged down as it was in national conflicts. The Hungarian parliamentarians had even rebelled against the emperor. The greatest threat to the monarchy, Schwarzenberg diagnosed, was nationalism in its political manifestations. Elections and representative institutions only appeared to strengthen nationalist movements to the detriment of the cohesion of the empire. And so when Schwarzenberg thought of reform, he was not thinking in terms of strengthening parliaments or allowing the particularist desires of the national groupings effective expression. It would be reform from above; the establishment of a centralized government and administration that would bring benefits and prosperity because it would act with fairness and competence. That was his intention. At the centre of power, the ministers would be responsible to the emperor and not to any *Reichstag*. A measure of popular representation and autonomy was to be allowed an outlet by creating communal, district and regional elected councils.

The Kremsier *Reichstag* was prorogued in March 1849; no other *Reichstag* ever assembled again to debate and participate in the government of the whole empire. The absolutist period lasted until the defeat of the Habsburg Monarchy in the Italian wars of 1859–60.

The Schwarzenberg ministry assembled an able team of administrators; Count Philipp von Stadion was minister of the interior until 1850, Alexander von Bach, minister of justice, Philipp von Krausz, minister of finance, and Karl von Bruck, minister of commerce. Schwarzenberg speedily restored the military fortunes of the monarchy. Hungary was conquered in the summer of 1849, and peace was concluded at Milan on 6 August 1849 with a defeated Piedmont. After that Schwarzenberg faced Prussia's ambitions in Germany. Here too Schwarzenberg soon gained the upper hand. The traditional ascendency of the Habsburgs in Germany and Italy appeared to be re-established by the close of 1850. It was not evident that the monarchy's position was not as strong as it seemed.

At home too success was more precarious than was outwardly apparent. The centralized administration did restore order and brought about an expansion of commerce. But the non-German peoples resented the predominance of German-speaking administrators throughout the empire. The German liberals of 1848, on the other hand, disliked the new government for its hostility to liberal constitutionalism. The Hungarians offered no further open resistance but wanted to win back their historic independence. They had lost it completely (politically and economically). Bruck abolished their separate customs and tax rights. Hungary was incorporated in the centralized monarchy. Former 'allies' were treated no better than former 'enemies'. The Croats had to abandon all ideas of autonomy despite their faithful support of the emperor in 1848. By 1852, Schwarzenberg could claim that he had largely fulfilled the programme he had set himself of bringing about 'the unification of the lands and races of the Monarchy in one great body politic'.

National autonomy and parliamentary constitutions were the two legacies of 1848 Schwarzenberg was determined to destroy. He first succeeded in ridding the monarchy of those independent councils and assemblies the national groups within the empire still possessed. Next it was the turn of representative rights. On 31 December 1851 Francis Joseph issued the rescripts known as the 'Sylvester (New Year) Patents'. They went perhaps even further than Schwarzenberg desired. The imperial declaration corresponded very much to Francis Joseph's own absolutist ideas. All the reforming aspects of Schwarzenberg's ministers in the fields of law, local representation, linguistic and national equality were wiped out at a stroke. The only considerable gains of 1848 that the emperor still promised to respect were the emancipation of the peasants, the equality of all the emperor's subjects before the law, and freedom of worship.

It was left to Alexander von Bach, who succeeded Schwarzenberg as minister-president when the latter died in 1852, to carry through the emperor's wishes. Bach was a devout Catholic and wished to restore the church to a position it had not enjoyed for decades. The conclusion of a Concordat with the Holy See in 1855 re-established and conferred considerable rights and special privileges on the Catholic Church. The Concordat represents the climax of Francis Joseph's reaction.

Yet, just as in Prussia, conservative centralized control did not mean that no reforms were carried through. The unification of the empire, the development of railways and communication, the liberalization of the tariff which brought the monarchy closer to free trade, and the new and on the whole improved administration despite its tendency to excessive bureaucratization, did bring benefits. Industrialization expanded and there was a spectacular, nearly four-fold, increase of exports by 1854. Until the slump of 1857, which affected the whole of Europe, the authoritarian decade was also one of economic development in the Austrian Empire; the freeing of the peasants was an immense achievement in the long run and though it caused difficulty, contributed to the rising prosperity of the monarchy.

There were, however, two serious weaknesses: state finance and the army. The taxes which were collected provided insufficient income to meet the administrative and military expenditure of the empire. The army, kept short of funds, was notoriously inefficient. For this sad state of affairs Francis Joseph was in large measure responsible; he placed the wrong men in charge of the army. Military efficiency deteriorated as the uniforms became more splendid; officers were selected on the basis of their social standing. The decline of the Habsburg army was soon to be demonstrated on the battlefields of northern Italy and Bohemia. Defeat in war in the last resort made it impossible for the empire to gain the increasing measure of stability for which Schwarzenberg and Bach had laboured in the 1850s.

The 1850s have been judged as a humiliating and unsuccessful period of Prussian history. It is a superficial judgement. Certainly on the international front Prussia did not cut a great figure avoiding military conflict with Austria in Germany in 1850, and with Russia in 1854 during the Crimean War. Prussia appeared to have slipped irrevocably to the second rank of European powers.

As it turned out this reputation of weakness proved an important asset to Bismarck during the years from 1862 to 1866; he was able to achieve Prussian supremacy in Germany without arousing the hostility of Prussia's neighbours. They believed mistakenly that all that happened was that a better balance of power had been achieved when in fact a totally new constellation of power was in the making. It took the defeat of France in 1870 to shake contemporaries out of their preconceived judgements about Prussia's role in Europe. But Bismarck alone did not create Prussia's strength. His success was in part based on the work of his predecessors during the previous decade.

The conservative ministers of the 1850s who led Prussia were not opposed to all change and reform but only to the growth of parliamentary influence. There were men among them who served the Prussian state with vision and ability. They had to overcome the opposition of the king's personal friends, like the brothers Leopold and Ernst von Gerlach, deeply religious and ultra-conservative men, who were known collectively as the Court Camarilla. The sentiments of this group were those expressed by Alexander I in the 'Holy Alliance' of 1815. They detested nationalism and false patriotism and believed in a universal Christian moral order. But Frederick William left the ministers to govern and carry through commercial and social reform. The Prussian parliaments during Frederick William IV's reign as sovereign (he became totally mentally incapacitated in the autumn of 1857), were ready to accept the demands of the royal government dominated by Otto von Manteuffel, minister of the interior from 1848 to 1850 and minister-president and foreign minister from 1850 to 1858.

Manteuffel was a conservative reformer. He believed the best way to strengthen the crown and the social hierarchy was to introduce genuine economic and social reforms for the welfare of the Prussian peasantry and of working men. The crown, he believed, could rely for support on the broad mass of the peasantry. 'The sound elements of the nation, and we still have those, thank God,' he wrote, 'are to be found in the rural folk, but they make little noise and are therefore rarely noticed.' The enemy to Prussian tradition, Manteuffel believed, was the bourgeoisie which was ready to support revolution and desired power for itself. For the 'so called educated class', he wrote, he felt nothing but contempt adding 'one characteristic of this class is a combination of arrogance and cowardice, both spring from Godlessness.'

The most notable social reforms of the king's conservative ministers benefited the peasantry. In 1849 Manteuffel persuaded Frederick William IV to approve decrees (finally passed in March 1850) which freed all small tenant farmers, in whatever form they held their tenure, of all feudal obligations. These obligations could be changed into money payments and the state provided low interest loans enabling the peasants to hold their land as free proprietors. More than 600,000 peasants took advantage of these measures. Two systems of agriculture now prevailed side by side in Prussia. East of the River Elbe lay the vast Junker estates farmed by landless labourers; west of the Elbe the small peasant farmers tilling the soil in holdings which unfortunately became too small. Rural reform could not overcome the basic economic problem of overpopulation on the land. The state could only establish social freedom not economic freedom and prosperity. The Prussian government aided overpopulated regions as best as it could by supervising the companies which encouraged emigration and by placing no obstacles in the way of population movement. Certainly emigration up to 1858 was largely from the overpopulated regions, due more to economic hardships than political protest.

The Manteuffel ministry also vigorously intervened on behalf of the worker in industry. Uniform wage rates were encouraged; employers were no longer permitted to supply goods (usually at inflated prices) in lieu of money wage payments; financial help was given to those industries which were depressed; inspectors were appointed to ensure reasonable factory conditions; there were even courts established to arbitrate and help to settle industrial disputes; holidays on religious days were enforced; stiff legislation was enacted to prohibit the employment of children under 12 and to regulate the conditions of work for young people. Authoritarian Prussia, with its rapidly expanding bureaucracy had a clear advantage over Britain in enforcing factory safety, health and education legislation. Inspectors supervised regulations and teachers were civil servants. Britain with its commitment to minimal government and local control with few bureaucrats and inspectors could not check abuses and inadequacies as effectively.

Manteuffel sought to reconcile the poor with the crown. The ruler and his ministers he thought should make themselves responsible for solving the new social problems of the industrial age. Manteuffel believed that the rulers of the modern age ought to concern themselves not only with military affairs, and law and order, but also with agriculture the arts and sciences, and with industry and commerce. The ideal before Manteuffel was that Prussia would become a well governed state, governed in the interests of all the people. In that way the monarchical society would justify itself in ever-changing conditions and undermine any hold the liberals and socialists might gain over society, for Manteuffel regarded them as false prophets who sought to act in their selfish class interest with sedition in their hearts. Manteuffel's policy of bringing the king into alliance with the lower classes in order to defeat the liberal middle class became a basic tenet of much of the Prussian conservative thought, from Manteuffel in the 1850s to von Roon and Bismarck. It explains why manhood suffrage held no terrors for the progressive *conservatives* but was at first at least regarded with misgivings by the liberals. These conservative assumptions also help to explain how social democracy was able to develop so strongly in Germany during the last quarter of the nineteenth century, an outcome totally unexpected by the conservatives.

It is a common error to think that the conservative ministers acted in close alliance with the Junkers. They no more wished for the Junkers to exert political power than that the liberals should enjoy any. The Junkers had not been permitted to show any signs of political independence since the days of the Great Elector. The ministries of the 1850s as has been seen, promoted rural reform and the emancipation of the peasantry, overruling the interest of the Junker landowners. The ministry also sought to protect, and where possible to re-train, the artisans whose livelihood was threatened by industry. New factories were encouraged to provide employment for them. But nothing could hold up the inexorable industrial tide and with it the gradual destruction and destitution of the guilds and craftsmen.

The Manteuffel ministry also encouraged the growth of trade and industry. The years from 1848 to 1859 saw a great expansion. Production and foreign trade more than doubled during the decade of the 1850s. Prices also rose and the benefits brought by this expansion were uneven; nevertheless, overall, there was a rise in the standard of living. The best known and most striking way in which the state sought to promote the economic development of Prussia was through the *Zollverein*. The Prussian ministries moved steadily towards free trade and through an expansionist policy enlarged the area through which goods could travel freely. Free trade encouraged the export of agricultural produce, and despite the misgivings of industrialists, also of manufactured goods. Some industries, such as the textile industry did suffer, but the expansion of industry as a whole is evidence that a free trade policy made sound economic sense. There was more, however, to the *Zollverein* than that. The *Zollverein* was an economic weapon in Prussia's political struggle for primacy in Germany. Prussia might be too weak to take on Austria militarily, as Olmütz had demonstrated, but economically Prussia with every year that passed grew stronger and could force the smaller German states to her side and away from the more protectionist Habsburg Empire. For the German states trade with Prussia was crucial economically; they could not afford to stay outside the system and in trade rivalry with the *Zollverein* states. Schwarzenberg saw the political implications of Prussia's economic policies and he tried to counter them by proposing a wider customs union embracing the Austrian Empire and the German states; a moderate protective trade barrier would safeguard the less developed economic regions. His motive was not mainly economic. Schwarzenberg was concerned for Austria's position in Germany. He wrote to Francis Joseph in November 1851 that 'the most effective means available to Your Majesty's Government towards the assertion and permanent increase of its influence throughout Germany, must be reckoned its active participation in fostering her common economic interests'.* It was politics by other means. But Schwarzenberg and his successors failed to create an Austrian Customs Union with the German states. Bavaria, Württemberg, Saxony, the two Hessen states and Hanover, faced in 1852 with the choice of deciding for or against Prussia's *Zollverein* could not afford to alienate Prussia economically despite their desire to use Austria politically to check Prussia's power. What Prussia had lost by diplomacy and a vain show of force in 1850 she compensated for by her growing economic power in Germany.

With the Prussian parliaments the Manteuffel ministry had no trouble during the years of Frederick William IV's reign. Manteuffel often by-passed parliament altogether. Policy was conducted by 'administrative means'. The other side of the coin of Manteuffel's administration was political reaction. Political freedoms, the freedom of the press and association were all repressed. Politically, the last years of Frederick William IV's reign, before mental incapacity forced his withdrawal from ruling, were stagnant. But expectations of constitutional progress were not high among the liberals when Frederick William's brother became regent.

Prince William, who on his brother's death in 1861 succeeded to the throne as William I, was at first believed to have more reactionary views than his brother. In 1848 he had fled to London to escape possible danger from the anger of the Berlin populace, though he probably never was in any danger. William, as Prince of Prussia, had devoted all his life to the Prussian army; he deeply felt the humiliation Prussia had suffered at Olmütz in 1850. Then the Prussian army had been found wanting; not surprisingly army reform for the sake of Prussia's future greatness became his first priority. He understood the needs of the army well and masterminded the reforms which were to prove of such significance to Prussia's constitutional development and

* H. Böhme, *The Foundations of the German Empire* (Oxford, 1971) p. 69.

international position in the 1860s. William I's character and personality strongly contrasted with that of his elder brother. He possessed none of his brother's romanticism, flexibility and artistic temperament. William I was a practical, military man of the 'old school', with a sense of honour; he could also nevertheless be persuaded by more clever men, like Bismarck, to follow a course he had initially disapproved of.

His first political instincts were generous. He wished to end the political intrigues of the court camarilla and the dubious methods of suppression of the Manteuffel years, the spies and the whole system of censorship. He accepted the constitution of 1850 because it had been granted by a King of Prussia; but he interpreted it strictly; he would rule constitutionally but according to 'rigid limits set by me'. By this he meant that parliament could debate and advise, but that the King of Prussia was above party and ultimately responsible only to God. William I was a devout Protestant, a man of his word. A rather stiff soldier but not unattractive judged by his 'type', William I was an absolutist at heart but believed in the rule of law. His outlook reflected the simple nationalist values of the second half of the nineteenth century. Already 60 years old when he became regent, he rather surprisingly ruled for another 28 years, though during the last fifteen years or so the tough old gentleman, who even survived the bullets of assassins, left everything to Bismarck's judgement.

On becoming regent (1858), William dismissed Manteuffel and put in his place a group of ministers with conservative and liberal leanings. The atmosphere of comparative freedom led people to talk of a 'new era'. The parliamentary elections of 1858 gave the moderate liberals for the first time a small majority. They were hoping for a significant parliamentary role in the making of policy which the prince regent never had any intention of conceding. The new parliament first made use of its freedom of discussion to debate passionately the Italian War of 1859. The Prussian liberals too longed to unite a free Germany; they wanted Prussia to play in Germany the role Piedmont was playing in Italy. But the Prince Regent of Prussia would have none of that. Not for him the path of revolution. Nevertheless he could not prevent a radical political 'grassroots' movement from springing to life. This was the National Union (*Nationalverein*) founded in September 1859. The opposition parties of the defunct Frankfurt parliament joined hands to work for German unity to be led by Prussia on the basis of the constitution for Germany drafted by the Frankfurt parliament in 1849. This was just as unacceptable to William in 1860 as it had been to Frederick William IV in 1849. There is no need for the historian to analyse in detail the differences between the National Union and the regent. The gulf was created by

William's view that the question of Germany unity could only be solved by the princes, not the people. The National Union was not a success and was not permitted to function in Prussia or indeed in any other of the larger German states.

Although the obstacle to German unity was Austria, and national self-interest pointed to the support of Piedmont and France against Austria in the Italian War of 1859, popular feeling in Prussia and the German states veered in exactly the opposite direction demanding help for the German-Austrian cause. There revived a veritable hysterical patriotic outburst against the France of Napoleon III – reminiscent of 1840 – and the prince regent was tempted to gain Prussia's advantage in the most obvious way open to him. He offered Austria help at the price of Austria conceding to Prussia primacy in Germany; to back his demands he mobilized part of the Prussian army. Everything went wrong. The Austrians were defeated in northern Italy and preferred to conclude a rapid peace with Napoleon III (p. 224). Then the Prussian mobilization of 1859, far from showing that Prussia was ready to fight, revealed the serious organizational shortcomings of the Prussian army. The only conclusion to be drawn from the prince regent's clumsy diplomacy during 1859 was that Prussia had not yet entered the era of *Realpolitik*.

The failure of Prussian foreign policy on the German question dismayed the liberals who were patriotic Prussians to a man. The growth of the *Zollverein* was for them no compensation. They had no confidence that economic policies, however successful, would overcome the particularism of the German states. They could not imagine a military solution: the Prussian army existed to defeat malevolent foreign nations, especially the French, not to coerce fellow Germans. Prince William too had spoken of making 'moral conquests' in Germany. For the liberals this meant that a constitutional and liberal Prussia should lead Germany by its example. But it was just at this time when it was most essential to maintain harmony between the Prussian parliament and the king and his ministers of the 'new era' that there developed an open breach between them on the issue of military reforms.

The Prussian constitutional conflict from 1860 to 1862 is remarkable from several points of view. It would have been difficult to foretell that after the quiescent 1850s, the Prussian franchise would produce a parliament dominated by liberals who were determined to struggle for a liberal constitutional state. The question of army reform brought into the open the very different concepts of the king and the liberal politicians on the future of a modernized Prussia. Behind the complex technical issues of how many years a Prussian should serve in the regiments of the line and how many in the reserve, and how many new regiments should be raised, was the fundamental question of whether parliament should retain financial control over army expenditure and so in effect control over the budget. Without such a right parliament could not effectively share decisions with the king's ministers. The king insisted on three years' service with the regiment of the line to instil discipline and blind obedience in his subjects. The army, William considered to be the main prop of the monarch in time of danger, and he thought the liberal parties were determined to undermine the loyalty it owed the king alone. In General Albrecht von Roon his Minister of War, the king found an enthusiastic supporter of the Prussian army and of royal power. Roon warned the king that if he gave way to the lower chamber of parliament which insisted on two years' service, it would gravely effect 'that part of the nation which leads Your Majesty's armed forces and which the All Highest himself has always found to be the staunchest pillar of his throne'; 'that I would never survive!' minuted William. The liberals in the lower chamber resisted royal autocracy and the military entourage surrounding the throne; they too wished to see Prussia powerful, but not through an army blindly obedient to the monarch. The liberals and radicals set great store by the militia (*Landwehr*) formed during the 'War of Liberation' against Napoleon; they wished to base Prussian power on the reforming spirit of Scharnhorst, Gneisenau, Hardenberg and Stein and on an army 'rooted in the people'. Theirs was also a Prussian tradition; but for the king, the *Landwehr* was not only inefficient militarily – in this he was right – but also imbued with the bourgeois spirit; he was adamant that the regular army must be free from the mischief of constitutional ideology. William believed that three years' service turned a man into a loyal soldier, whereas but two years left him a citizen with ideas of his own uneradicated, which was bad.

In February 1860 Roon introduced the army bill to the Prussian parliament. It contained a reform of the old *Landwehr* also the requirement that Prussians serve not two but three years with the regiment of the line, and an increase in the army establishment, all of which William regarded as indispensable for the efficiency and loyalty of the army. The lower chamber would not accept these changes, especially not the virtual destruction of the *Landwehr*, but agreed on the need for military reform. The government withdrew the army bill and the liberals compromised. Without conceding that they could consent to the actual method of reform the regent desired, the lower chamber voted the necessary funds *provisionally* for one year as the government now requested in order to maintain the Prussian army. William's response to the failure of the army bill was to disregard the parliament; he denied the right of the parliamentarians to have any say in 'his' army. The army was reorganized simply on his orders. The liberals in the following year now had to face the challenge.

Should they accept the *fait accompli* or resist and defend constitutional principles? Georg von Vincke, who led the liberals, when the question came before parliament again in the spring of 1861, induced a majority of the lower chamber to vote the necessary funds for the army provisionally for one further year. However this proved too much for the more stout-hearted defenders of constitutional principles who accused the majority of liberals of giving way under the subterfuge of granting the money provisionally. The liberal party split and a new party was formed in 1861 the German Progressive Party (*Deutsche Fortschritts Partei*).

The Progressive Party was patriotic, Prussian nationalist, loyal to the monarch, but insisted on the full implementation of the Prussian constitution. In the elections of December 1861 the Progressive Party won many seats though not an outright majority in the lower house; the 'old liberals' were divided into a more aggressive and a more conservative faction; the conservatives were almost eliminated. In March 1862 the conflict came to a head. The lower house would not pass the money bill for the army; the king would not accept two years' military service. The king dissolved parliament and replaced his liberal ministers with conservatives among whom Roon was the dominant figure. He hoped that during the new elections he would be vindicated. But the elections of April-May 1862 were a disaster for the king and a triumph for the Progressive Party and their allies in the new parliament. In September 1862 the majority of the lower house once again would not pass money bills for the army. William I, who was an honourable man and so shrank from unconstitutional measures, could see no way out but abdication. German history might have developed differently had William acted as he first intended. His abdication would have been a great victory for parliamentary constitutional government. But the 'liberal' crown prince, Frederick William, married to Victoria, Queen Victoria's eldest daughter, counselled his father against abdication. He was more of a 'Prussian' crown prince than many historians suppose. William I therefore more out of a sense of duty than anything else, decided to carry on. In the dire circumstances Roon advised the king to turn to the wild Junker, Otto von Bismarck, the defender of royal supremacy, the man very confident that he could master the crisis. With Bismarck's appointment as minister president on 23 September 1862, Prussia and Germany really entered on a 'new era'. France had done so ten years earlier.

10

Napoleon III and the Authoritarian Decade of the Second Empire

Fearing upheaval and social revolution, the majority of Frenchmen did not mourn the passing of the republic in December 1851. The republic had disappointed everyone except the politicians who directly benefited from it. It had become a republic only in constitutional form. Although there were few genuine supporters of this republic, the politicians were deeply divided on the issue of what should follow it. This gave Louis Napoleon his opportunity. The influence of conflicting historical traditions divided the French into more than one kind of republican, into Legitimists and Orleanists, pre-1789, 1789, 1815, 1830 and now the Orleanists Bonapartists' turn had come again. Louis Napoleon's rising star was confirmed by two plebiscites, the first approving the *coup* of December 1851, and the second held a few months later in November 1852 approving the restoration of the empire; both Louis Napoleon had won with a resounding majority of more than seven and a half million out of the total of some eight million votes cast. Even making allowances for official pressures, and for the fact that some one and a half million Frenchmen had abstained from voting, it is clear that Napoleon III now undoubtedly enjoyed the support and confidence of the great majority of Frenchmen despite, or perhaps, rather, because of the severe repression of the radical opposition to the *coup*.

They were first and foremost against social revolution and never overcame the fright of '1848'; they wished to see their property secure and protected from the 'urban red mob'. They despised the self-seeking politicians in Paris, if they gave any thought to them at all. French parliamentary assemblies did not fulfil the role of the British parliament in the nineteenth century French parliaments enjoyed little popular support, nor did people look to parliament for a guarantee of their personal liberties or for their fair share of the nation's prosperity. In Britain political and social progress was achieved through parliamentary legislation; parliament was the focus of debate and the source of executive power. Simultaneously through the nineteenth century, the development of modern political parties and an ever-widening franchise permitted in Britain greater popular representation without the loss of effective government. And so the history of Britain over the centuries came to be regarded as revealing a purpose, an inevitable civilizing progression from early kingship in the ninth to parliamentary democracy in the twentieth century. Here was a model for the rest of the world to follow and a standard by which the progress of other countries could be measured. The influence of the British 'example' was indeed great in the nineteenth and twentieth centuries. But to judge the history of every European country by reference to a British 'norm' would lead to a lack of understanding of essentially different processes at work. In rural France the peasants were still dependent on the nobility and the privileged group known collectively as 'notables'. Napoleon III's centralized state freed the peasants from their control where the parliamentary republic had failed. Napoleon III was a conservative in the sense that he believed in reform from above, but could be radical in devising solutions to the problems besetting France.

The first three months of Louis Napoleon's rule after the *coup*, were personal and dictatorial. Arrests throughout France, it is estimated some 25,500, followed on the *coup*. Louis Napoleon intended to stifle any opposition from the start; widespread arrests also added plausibility to Louis Napoleon's claim that he had forestalled an imminent socialist revolution. His arrests were arbitrary and in sending 9000 men to Algeria and expelling another 1500 from France, he at first acted harshly. However, as soon as he felt secure he set up a judicial commission to review the sentences passed: more than 3000 prisoners were quickly freed and during the course of the decade most if not quite all, of the political prisoners were set free. By 1859 only some 1800 men, including Ledru-Rollin, were excluded from a general amnesty. Napoleon III was essentially a humane man. There were to be no forgotten political prisoners during the years of the Second Empire or widespread repression and loss of liberty. His rule contrasts strikingly with dictatorship in the twentieth century though he has been called the first modern dictator. His rule was authoritarian but he did not attempt to create a loyal Bonapartist party. Twentieth-century dictatorships are built on the foundation of a 'one-Party' system and terror; the party establishes the only correct lines of thought, and the police and prison camps ensure that dissent does not spread or go unpunished. There was no such terror in the Second Empire and political debate and even opposition became increasingly prominent. The twentieth-century dictators increased their grip and progressively destroyed the last vestiges of individual liberty the longer they ruled. Napoleon III took the opposite course; after an authoritarian early period he gradually reduced the authoritarian aspects of his régime.

Napoleon III was described by Marx as a fool and by some historians as an adventurer and an opportunist. Contemporaries after 1852 found it difficult to fathom his motives and called him a sphinx. His contribution to French history was a unique one. The Second Empire was no slavish imitation of the First. The First Empire, so Napoleon III believed, was incomplete; military defeat had prevented its full development. He was convinced it was his destiny to build on the foundations of the First Empire and to adapt its institutions and policies. From the start he seemed to accept change as necessary and constructive, not to be resisted blindly. That had been the fault of Metternich and the men of the restoration in France. Napoleon III admired Britain precisely for the way in which the institutions of government were constantly adapted to new needs. One characteristic of the Second Empire was thus the deliberate series of changes initiated by the emperor. After the *coup*, he believed France needed a period of firm authoritarian rule. The new constitution which he presented to France in January 1852, all ready-made a few days after the *coup*, allowed him immense powers.

The constitution was modelled on that of the year VIII, (1800) and extolled Napoleon I's institutions in its preamble. The power of parliament was drastically reduced. The senate acted as the guardian of the constitution and its members were, to all intents and purposes, Napoleon III's nominees. The lower house of 260 members could meet for only three months in the year. The members could merely discuss legislation placed before them by the Council of State dominated by Napoleon III's nominees; the discussions of the lower chamber were not even to be reported in the press. Ministers could not be asked questions in the chamber. They were not dependent on the majority of the lower chamber elected by manhood suffrage but served Napoleon III in a subordinate capacity. Everything was done to strengthen the executive and to reverse the principle of the separation of powers that underlay the constitution of the Second Republic. The executive was made supreme and Napoleon III was its head, assured of office for ten years. Emperor in everything but name, he remedied this defect in December 1852 with the overwhelming approval of another plebiscite.

Napoleon III's new system relied on a centralized administration, just as Napoleon I's had done. Under the guidance of the minister of the interior, the prefects in the départements exercised greater powers than ever before and enjoyed more prestige and higher salaries. They acted to carry out the will of the central government, but also as the guardians of the communes and municipalities into which France was divided. The central administration numbering during the Second Empire about 250,000 loyal men dependent on Napoleon developed an *esprit de corps* and a degree of efficiency that avoided the worst dangers of bureaucratization to which the system might otherwise have led. The country was thoroughly controlled even to the extent of returning only members to the lower chambers at times of elections who unquestionably would support Napoleon III and the policies of his ministers. From 1852 to 1854 and 1860 to 1863, the Duc de Persigny, a man devoted personally to Napoleon III and a fellow conspirator, presided over the administration as minister of the interior until his excessive zeal in permitting no dissident opinion to be heard made him an embarrassment to Napoleon III who by the 1860s wished to give his régime a more liberal outlook. Strict censorship of the press throughout France was effectively established by requiring that no newspaper in Paris or the provinces could be published without government authority and that any newspaper could be suspended or suppressed after three warnings had been given to it by the prefects in the province or the minister of the interior in Paris for publishing news or comment regarded as unsuitable. The prefects were supported in the provinces by the police whose number, power and functions were extended.

On the army, mindful of the glories of Napoleon I, his nephew bestowed many indications of his esteem. He increased the army's social status and pay and inaugurated ceremonials and military reviews to raise morale. Above all, he fought two foreign wars in the Crimea and northern Italy which gave the armies of France new marshals and fresh battle honours – Sevastopol, Magenta and Solferino. In the Church Napoleon III recognized another important ally for his régime. During his most authoritarian phase he carefully cultivated the Church, increased its wealth and influence and in return the curés guided many of their peasant flock to the polls to support the emperor and to accept his benevolent rule.

But repression and personal power were for Napoleon III only a means and not an end itself. It is this which earns him a claim to be regarded as much more than an adventurer and opportunist. He sincerely believed that he could bring to an end the cycle of revolution and 'restoration' and renewed revolution. He wished to set France on an evolutionary course of changing institutions which would bring, as its benefit, order and prosperity. He had no precise plan or blueprint how this might be achieved. For all his appeals to the Napoleonic past, Bonapartism was no consistent doctrine. In a speech soon after the *coup d'état* he declared that his present régime did not close the door in any way to improvement and that his aim was to lay the foundations 'of the only structure capable later of supporting a wise and beneficent liberty'. Power is addictive. How far Napoleon III was actually ready to concede power is an open question. He only felt the time was right when he had to do so under domestic pressure and failures abroad. Even then he continued to preserve as much power for himself as possible. Napoleon III had no set ideology, he was not afraid of contradictions and felt free to change his policies as occasion required. To the great majority of Frenchmen, Napoleon III offered what they wished and they gave him their support for two decades. His authority meant a guarantee of property and wealth, political and economic security from law and order. But he was also seen as the guarantor of the gains of the French revolution: the equality of all citizens, and the opening of careers to talent. Finally, fundamental to Napoleon III's outlook, was his view that a leader must work with and not against the fundamental forces of his age. He saw nationalism as one of these. Nationalism was transforming Europe; he would ally himself with it. Another was that the mass of the people were making their weight felt in the state, that they were going to count and could not be treated as mere subjects of the ruler owing him blind obedience. He would work with these popular desires and seek to satisfy rising expectations by improving the well-being of the peasantry and of the urban workers. Through the use of plebiscites, and manhood suffrage at times of the elections to the lower chamber, the masses could be given a sense of participation by being asked for their consent for what had been done in their name without actually allowing them any share in the making of policy.

Having spent years diagnosing the social political ills of France, how successful was Napoleon III when it came to practical measures and politics? Politically his authoritarian rule won general approval during the decade of the 1850s. The leadership of the opposition was silenced and enjoyed little popular support, whether Legitimist or Socialist; many Orleanists entered Napoleon's service. The elections for the lower chamber in 1857 once again returned an overwhelming number of government supporters as it had done in 1852. Everywhere Napoleon III was enthusiastically acclaimed, whilst his centralized administration retained a firm grip on the country.

Political stability and order was the most important need the French people felt. Napoleon III fulfilled that need. But he sought to do more, to heal the wounds and class conflicts of French society. He shared the views of enlightened conservatives of the age that the state must concern itself with the welfare of the poor. France was still an overwhelmingly rural society and industrialization and the growth of towns was slower in nineteenth-century France than in Britain, part of Germany and Belgium. Some three-quarters of the population lived in the countryside when Napoleon came to power; that proportion had gradually declined to only about two-thirds when the empire came to an end. Rural society was backward and well protected from competition; the land was largely divided between small peasant landowners whose feudal obligations had been abolished by the French revolution. The peasants tenaciously clung to their land and supported conservative traditions, submitted to the authority of the state and to the Catholic Church and were opposed to radicalism and socialism in the towns.

Research has thrown doubts on Napoleon III having followed any consistent economic programme to modernize and industrialize France. He probably had not studied the teaching of Comte de Saint-Simon, who died in 1825 and who stressed the overwhelming importance of providing for increasing material welfare of the masses in preference to the barren political conflict of the past. Napoleon III had independently reached similar conclusions; prosperity was more important to the masses than the possession of abstract political rights. Napoleon III's economic ideas were fairly rudimentary, seeking through public works and other means to help the peasant in the countryside and the worker in the towns. He wished to create conditions of full employment, but he was not an apostle of industrialization. He was more concerned that the majority of Frenchmen, and that meant the peasantry, should be content. A decade of low interest rates and plentiful credit helped the peasant landowners to meet their debts. But as far as industrialization was concerned there was no sudden fast expansion during the Second Empire made possible by ample credit as so many historians have supposed.

In encouraging the growth of communications, the Second Empire was not inaugurating a new policy but rather continuing the policies followed since the restoration of 1815. The work of opening up France through a system of canals and rivers, begun soon after 1815, was completed during the Second Empire. But railway development had been slow in France; during the 1840s the state intervened to quicken the pace. Napoleon III continued the efforts of the July monarchy and helped to promote a fast period of railway expansion during the 1850s and 1860s. By 1848 only 1800 kilometres of railway lines had been laid; when the Second Empire came to a close a network of 17,500 kilometres existed. It was a significant economic achievement, which not only encouraged the metallurgy industry engaged in actual construction, but also created towards the close of the Second Empire a larger, more unified, French market stimulating increases in production.

The pace of industrial growth was comparatively slow and gradual in nineteenth-century France. The early years of the Second Empire witnessed only a marginal quickening of pace. Whilst statistics must be treated with considerable caution, the growth rate each year varied from about 2.5% to 1.8% for the greater part of the nineteenth century. The development of communications, the adoption of new techniques, such as the Bessemer process in the iron and steel industry (discovered in 1855), together with some state help and encouragement to industry, and after 1860 more foreign competition (see p. 9), stimulated the spread of industrialization. But seen against the general perspective of the nineteenth century, the Second Empire was not an exceptional period of rapid industrial growth.

The financiers and bankers were the one group whose success was spectacularly evident during the Second Empire. The conservative private bankers of the Orleanist period, such as the Rothschilds, were now joined by new enterprising bankers and merchants; they founded the Crédit Foncier and Crédit Mobilier in 1852. In 1863 the Crédit Lyonnais was established as a deposit bank. Napoleon III and his close associates were attracted to these more speculative financiers and they were involved in some of their ventures. Much capital was sent abroad. The role of these banks in vast public rebuilding schemes in Paris, in railway construction and elsewhere was an important one, but the extent to which they actually aided the process of industrialization has been exaggerated. French industry, down to the close of the Second Empire, remained (with a few notable exceptions such as the Creusot foundries and large cotton mills in Alsace and northern France) small family businesses which provided their own capital and were thus independent of the banks. This circumstance modifies the conclusion that the key to economic progress lay in the growth of credit, as the Saint-Simonians claimed and that the new financiers had provided the essential means for French industrial expansion. But no one could deny Napoleon III credit for maintaining stability at home and peace in Europe for sixteen years of the eighteen his empire lasted.

One of Napoleon III's first actions after the *coup d'état* was to find an obvious and immediately striking way of continuing the work of Napoleon I. He recognized the propaganda value of making the public buildings of Paris splendid and imposing. Napoleon III furthermore claimed that the public works which the first emperor had begun on so grand a scale had been one of the principal causes of domestic prosperity and had promoted social progress. And so work on completing the Rue de Rivoli was speeded up; but the man with whose name the reconstruction of Paris was justifiably linked was Baron Georges Eugène Haussmann, who was brought to Paris by Napoleon III in 1853 and appointed Prefect of the Seine. From 1853 to 1870, backed by the emperor, Haussmann was the driving force behind the gigantic demolitions and reconstructions which gave Paris the beautiful tree-lined boulevards, vistas, squares and parks, still enjoyed today. The cost was staggering and money was raised by Haussmann in all manner of unorthodox ways. Nor were the seamier sides of the old city of Paris banished by Haussmann. In some ways they were aggravated as the urban poor were crowded into the decaying suburbs of the city. Behind the grand boulevards could still be found the insanitary older Paris lacking sewerage and the necessities of a modern city. The 'wedding cake' architecture of the Opéra and the cosmopolitan elegance of the Second Empire Paris lived side by side with the dirt and poverty of the suburbs and with the crowded streets of the rest of the city. For this Haussmann can hardly be blamed. He did achieve a gigantic transformation of central Paris – a monument to the public face of opulence which the Second Empire presented to the world.

If the first Napoleon stood for anything it was to make France the leading power in Europe. Napoleon I was the most audacious and brilliant military leader of his age, the personal victor of battles which humbled one after another of the traditional powers of Europe. He sought to reshape the map of Europe. He did so by leading victorious armies against the Habsburgs and the Prussians and then dictating the terms of peace by virtue of superior might. France was not strong enough to set about the conquest of Europe, even utilizing the spirit of nationality to disrupt the states of her opponents. In contrast to Napoleon I, Napoleon III was not a militarist and hated the suffering and loss of life war entailed. It is not easy to reduce Napoleon III's ideas on foreign policy to some simple formula, such as territorial expansion or nationalism. Rather, he wished to transform the conduct of European international relations peacefully as far as possible to make France the centre of European diplomacy responsive to the international currents of his time. He would avoid Napoleon I's mistake and never make an enemy of Britain. With England's friendship he aimed to replace the settlement of 1815 dictated by the conquerors of France with a new settlement based on the principles he espoused. Napoleon III was his own foreign minister; Drouyn de Lhuys (1851, 1851–5, 1862–6), and Walewski (1855–60), held the title but were really little more than the emperor's executive agents. Napoleon III's policy was characterized by a certain half-heartedness and caution, a desire not to push things to their ultimate conclusion. A lack of consistency and unpredictability made the rest of Europe uneasy and suspicious without bringing France much gain. But in the 1850s Napoleon III was at least partially successful. In comparison with the 1860s this decade can be seen as his 'fortunate years'.

The assumption of the imperial title in December 1852 was intended to be symbolic for France. But it was symbolic also for the rest of Europe, a challenge to the settlement of Vienna. The allies had then by treaty – the Quadruple Alliance of November 1815 – agreed to look upon the return of Napoleon or any of his relations as tantamount to a French declaration of war on the rest of Europe. And so in October 1852 Louis Napoleon hastened in a famous speech to reassure Europe that the Empire meant peace. To the monarchs of Europe, an emperor who based his right to rule on the votes of the people, was a usurper of the imperial dignity; the 'dynastic numeral' chosen by Napoleon III added insult to injury; it recognized as 'Napoleon II' the son of Napoleon I, the unfortunate Duke of Reichstadt who had died in Schönbrunn, and so by inference Louis Napoleon denied the legitimacy of the Bourbon restoration. Not surprisingly the tsar refused to recognize the new emperor and to address him as his brother. Queen Victoria took a much more sensible view based on national interests, writing: 'Objectionable as this appellation (Napoleon III) no doubt is, it may hardly be worth offending France and her Ruler by refusing to recognize it...our object should be to leave France alone, as long as she is not aggressive'.* For reasons of state, Prussia and Austria followed the British example, merely noting that Napoleon III had expressed his readiness to uphold the territorial *status quo*.

Napoleon III counted on great power rivalries and the conflicts created by nationalism to provide him with opportunities of changing the European *status quo*. Support for the suppressed nationalities in the Balkans under Ottoman rule seemed to provide France with a worthy cause to bring about change. In November 1849 Louis Napoleon had suggested to the tsar the possibility of partitioning the Ottoman Empire as part of a scheme to remodel Europe. The tsar rejected the notion out of hand. Five years later Napoleon III found himself fighting the Crimean War ostensibly in defence of the Ottoman Empire. The alliance he concluded then with Britain certainly broke up the concert of 1815, but the war brought Napoleon III little profit and painful casualties. He ended it as soon as he decently could do so without loss of prestige. The Congress of Paris in 1856, superficially at any rate, confirmed France's new leading position in Europe; but France had neither gained territory, nor had the map of Europe been redrawn; the defeat of Russia had not ended with the creation of an independent Poland, looking to France in gratitude for its liberation. The most popular aspect of the Congress of Paris, as far as the French were concerned, was that peace had been restored. The war had required a much larger expeditionary army than originally

* *The Letters of Queen Victoria*, II, pp. 397–8

intended, it was costly in men and money and for what French gains? Drouyn de Lhuys had always suspected Britain and warned that in the Crimea France was fighting Britain's war. (See chapter 11 for a discussion of the Crimean War diplomacy.)

Italy was Napoleon III's next venture. Napoleonic tradition pointed to Italy as one of France's natural spheres of European influence. The other was the Rhine. In Italy the struggle would involve a contest with Austria, on the Rhine with Prussia. In studying the course of international relations, historians tend to pay too much attention to the making of friends and too little to the choice of enemies; but really the choice of enemies dictates which friends a country seeks. Napoleon III chose Austria as his next enemy for the sake of extending French influence in Italy. It was a fateful choice for the history of France and of Europe. It is interesting to speculate what would have happened if Napoleon III had fought Prussia on the Rhine in 1859, before the Prussian army reforms had taken effect, instead of Austria in Italy. Napoleon III probably considered the chances of success in Italy a lesser gamble than winning a victory on the Rhine. Yet the German and Italian questions were in the end tied to each other as the diplomacy of 1859 was to show.

The Italian adventure was probably one of several plans Napoleon III carried around in his fertile and secretive mind in the early 1850s. Italy was not only the scene of Napoleon I's earliest triumphs but also that of Louis Napoleon's conspiratorial youth. A move forward in Italy seemed to Napoleon III to promise the greatest benefit at the least cost; but he acted with characteristic caution and prepared the way carefully. At the Paris Peace Conference in 1856, Britain had shown the greatest sympathy for the Italian cause and to avoid British enmity remained a cardinal principle of Napoleon III's policy. Austria, furthermore in putting pressure on Russia during the Crimean War after all the help the Habsburgs had received from the tsar in 1849, had lost the sympathies of the tsar. The defeat of Austria was not therefore likely to trouble Russia unduly. If Austria was the new enemy, then Napoleon III was quite ready to switch allegiances and befriend Russia. He had already at the Congress of Paris established better relations with the new Tsar Alexander II. He continued assiduously to cultivate Russian friendship even at the expense of temporarily worsening relations with Britain. If Russia would keep a large army in Galicia, thus threatening Austria and preventing Austria from reinforcing Italy, Austria would have one hand tied behind her back: Tsar Alexander II was prepared to co-operate up to a point and a Franco-Russian agreement was eventually concluded in March 1859. But there was no genuine identity of purpose. The tsar wanted to rid Russia of the humiliating peace terms of Paris, especially of the Black Sea clauses. This had become a veritable obsession with him.

For France the fate of the Black Sea clauses were an entirely secondary interest. The Franco-Russian alignment never amounted to much
for one reason more than any other: Russia, like Britain, after 1856
was determined not to be embroiled again in a European war. It was
this fact that gave Napoleon III his opportunity to defeat Austria in
1859, not skilful diplomacy.

In January 1858, an Italian revolutionary, Felice Orsini, attempted
to assassinate Napoleon III and Eugénie who were on their way to
the opera in a coach. The emperor and empress were unhurt but the
bomb caused many casualties. This was the sort of accident Napoleon III interpreted as destiny. Orsini was imprisoned and executed
but not before Napoleon III had made use of the unfortunate man to
publicize the cause of Italian freedom.

Napoleon III saw an opportunity for France in the ambitions of
Cavour, prime minister of Piedmont. Cavour saw Piedmont's opportunity in the ambitions of Napoleon III. Of the two men, each
anxious to get the better of the other, Napoleon III was marginally
the more honest. At their meeting in the spa of Plombières in July
1858, a bargain was struck. This time Napoleon III made sure of a
tangible gain. Savoy and probably Nice also would be ceded by
Piedmont to France (p. 221). The cession would undo at least a
part of the territorial peace terms imposed on France by the allies
in 1814 and 1815. The regions, moreover, were French speaking and
had been declared French by Revolutionary France in 1792. Cavour
paid this price in return for the promise of French assistance in a war
against Austria. Future plans for an Italian Confederation were also
agreed. Piedmont would receive Lombardy and Venetia and so
become the dominant north Italian power, stretching from the Alps
to the Adriatic. The Franco-Italian alliance would be cemented by the
marriage of Napoleon III's cousin, the troublesome Prince Napoleon
to the daughter of Victor Emmanuel of Piedmont. In the south of
Italy the Kingdom of the Two Sicilies would remain undisturbed. The
future of central Italy was still somewhat vague, with the Pope left
temporal ruler of his extensive dominions; but the smaller duchies
were to form a new central Italian kingdom which Napoleon III
hoped to dominate. Finally, the Italian Confederation was to be
presided over by the pope. The inconsistencies of Napoleon III's
'nationalism' are revealed by his Italian plans. He did not wish to
create a united Italy as a powerful neighbour of France but to keep
Italy divided and looking to France. France would replace Austria,
only France would pose as liberator and friend. What Napoleon III
did not wish was to stir up popular nationalism despite all his
gestures to the sovereignty of the people. Mazzini's republicanism
was anathema to him. Napoleon III was not after all the heir of
'1848'.

Once more, as in the Crimea, the Italian policy did not work out as Napoleon III had expected. Helped by Austria's inept diplomacy the war of aggression, planned by Napoleon III and Cavour for more than a year, was made to seem a defensive war fought by Piedmont against Austria (chapter 12). Cavour had rejected the Austrian ultimatum in April 1859 and early in May Austrian troops crossed the frontiers of Piedmont. Napoleon came to Piedmont's aid as he had promised. During the month of May the French troops were moved into Piedmont utilizing the new railway lines. They won without their Piedmontese allies the Battle of Magenta on 4 June and with their allies the Battle of Solferino on 24 June 1859. French and Austrian casualties were very heavy and the Austrians withdrew their army behind the strong defensive line of the 'Quadrilateral'. But the Piedmontese military build-up had been much slower than anticipated and Italian 'volunteers' from other states failed to materialize in large numbers. This time Napoleon III had taken personal charge of the armies. He saw the dangers of another 'Crimea' looming ahead. Large French reinforcements would be needed to break the Austrian defences; the Prussians had threateningly mobilized on the Rhine. For Napoleon III the war had become too much of a gamble. Taking Victor Emmanuel into his confidence, Napoleon III concluded a speedy armistice with Francis Joseph at Villafranca on 11 July 1859. Through the French intervention in the war, Piedmont gained most of Lombardy but not Venetia and so Napoleon III renounced his claim to Nice and Savoy. The war fell short of Cavour's expectations and he resigned in rage (p. 225).

What had France gained as a result of this second war? Napoleon's quick compromise solution had saved many French lives. The French at Solferino had lost nearly 12,000 men. Napoleon III had defeated Austria and proved the superiority of French arms over Austrian. He had done 'something for Italy'. In the longer term he had done more for Italy than he and Cavour anticipated at the time. The war could not be neatly curtailed but gave impetus to the forces of change that led to the Second War of Italian Liberation in 1860. Cavour returned to power in 1860 and now prepared for the further enlargement of Piedmont at the expense of the three duchies in central Italy and of the pope's province of Romagna. Napoleon III acquiesced and this time he secured the price: Savoy and Nice were ceded by Piedmont to France in March 1860. But Napoleon III had lost the friendship of 'patriotic' Italians. Italy was unified by Italians not by Frenchmen and Italian resentment at the loss of Savoy and Nice could still be fanned into flames by Mussolini seventy-five years later. By his intervention, France had not gained but lost influence in the Italian peninsula. Hers were to be the last foreign troops to depart from Italian soil when they left Rome in 1870. For all his dexterous diplomacy and the risks taken in war, France in 1860 was in no stronger position than before. The concert of powers in 1815 had finally collapsed in the 1850s, but in the new realities of power and conflict France was to become the principal victim.

Great Britain: Cautious Reform in the Authoritarian Decade

Great Britain presents a contrast to continental Europe. For a start there was no written constitution. Custom, precedent and single legislative acts determined how Britain was governed. The powers of the monarchy had been so heavily circumscribed that the sovereign did not share power with governments formed on the basis of support in an elected parliamentary assembly, however unrepresentative of the majority of the people. There were nevertheless occasions when Queen Victoria and Prince Albert before his untimely death in 1861 did exercise real authority. They certainly made their views unmistakably known. Queen Victoria's letters are a wonderful source for understanding middle-England. 'With regards to the suffrage,' the queen wrote in 1851 to her prime minister Lord John Russell who was considering modest parliamentary reform, 'the proposals of the Committee appear to the queen to be framed with a due regard to the importance of not giving an undue proportion of weight to the Democracy. In the queen's opinion, the chief question to consider will be whether the strengthing of the Democratic principle will upset the balance of the constitution.' Nor did the queen approve of revolution and the armed overthrow of legal institutions, especially not French ones. The dangers of the events set in motion by the French Revolution of 1789, so recently demonstrated in 1848, had cast a dark shadow. The Queen was therefore outraged when Palmerston, the foreign secretary, conveyed his approval of Louis Napoleon's *coup d'état* to the French. Lord Russell seized the opportunity to get rid of Palmerston. The queen observed, 'with respect to a successor to Lord Palmerston, the Queen must state, that after the sad experience which she has just had of the difficulties, annoyances, and dangers to which the Sovereign may be exposed by the personal character and qualities of the Secretary of Foreign Affairs, she must reserve to herself the unfettered right to approve or disapprove the choice of a Minister for this Office'.*

She could not in reality exercise any such power. Palmerston was back in the Cabinet though at the Home Office in December 1852, and became her prime minister in 1855, her personal views notwithstanding. Windsor was not Potsdam or the Hofburg. Queen Victoria's influence, was by persuasion and not by 'command' though that phrase remained in formal use long after it had lost reality, symbolizing the continuity of affairs of state through changes of government.

The closest Britain came to revolutionary violence was in the later 1830s and early 1840s during the period of hardship and economic downturn. Handled wisely by the ruling Whigs who did not over-react, no legacy of extreme bitterness burdened social harmony in later decades. Both the Whigs in the 1830s and Peel's Conservatives in the 1840s faced new and challenging problems. How could social order best be safeguarded and progress best be assured. Among the ruling elite of Britain on one issue there was general agreement, not to widen the franchise further to include the masses of working men. Property and ownership were considered to be one essential attribute of responsibility. Only to men with a sufficient material stake in society would it be safe to allow any participation in government. The more property, the more influence (with the exception of the sovereign). Otherwise possessions from the attack of the envious 'mob' and 'liberty', itself the most prized right of every Englishman, was held to be in danger. 'Liberty', of course, did not then imply equal rights. The renowned political thinker and economist Walter Bagehot encapsulated this thinking in a principle that every individual had only a right to so much political power as he could exercise without impeding any other person who could more fittingly exercise power. Good government was therefore not to be attained by counting heads; mankind was selfish; in a democracy without limits a majority would tyrannize the minority. It followed, however, that the minority also had duties and obligations not to tyrannize the majority but to provide good government.

Clearly then there were beliefs and attitudes shared in Europe. But what constitutes 'good government', that was the difficult question that had to be addressed. In pre-industrial societies in the eighteenth century and earlier times, government had largely been confined to the defence of the realm, the conduct of relations with other countries, the maintenance of an army and navy, the conduct of war, the raising of money and its control, appointments to offices and the preservation of law and order. In direct concern for the welfare

* *The Letters of Queen Victoria*, vol. 2, pp. 332–3, p. 343.

of the people, government had played no large role except for the relief of destitution under the old Elizabethan poor law which required parishes, not central government, to make the necessary provision. The industrial revolution changed this. A common feature in Europe was the extension of government's traditional role.

In mid-nineteenth-century Britain the growth of towns, the spread of factories, the herding together of large numbers of people in those parts of towns close to the factories, imperilled traditional social controls of pre-industrial times. The manufacturers, owners of property, and growing numbers of members of the professions were emerging as an important group beside the predominant landed interests. Old and new, what should be the balance between them?

Two principles appeared to provide the answer: free trade and the application of the principle of utility, that is to measure any action by the test whether it would benefit the greatest number. Of the two, freedom of competition was the stronger; competition could even be cloaked in morality. Everyone should be given the opportunity to make the best of their lives, beyond this support from the state would be harmful. Theodore Hoppen has summed up this attitude succinctly, 'state intervention . . . though rarely achieving good of itself, could properly be used to remove specific abuses in order to allow the free market to work its miracles of growth'.* For the great radical liberal reformers John Bright and Richard Cobden, principal exponents of the so called 'Manchester School', free trade would bring the blessings of peace and prosperity.

State intervention raised another issue passionately debated: who was to exercise control over such legislation. At first it seemed social reformers, followers of Jeremy Bentham, men like Edwin Chadwick, who were appointed to Royal Commissions would succeed in establishing centralized controls rather than leaving the administration of the new laws entirely to local bodies. Inspectorates and boards were set up to supervise the factory acts, the new poor law and for a time health but they remained sparsely resourced. There were strong feelings against attempting to override traditional local authorities; their powers were, however, indeed increased and widened so that they carried the principal burdens of administration in mixed arrangements. Preventing government from becoming overpowerful was viewed as an issue of liberty.

Laissez-faire, a minimum of government and only where indispensable, was the general principle supported by the classical economists and political philosophers. But this was no more than a general guide. The actual approach was pragmatic, a cautions readiness for adapta-

* K. T. Hoppen, *The Mid-Victorian Generation 1846–1886* (Oxford, 1998), p. 94; and for an excellent discussion of these issues, pp. 94–124.

tion. Sir Robert Peel, prime minister from 1841 to 1846, exemplified this. In the 1840s he continued to pursue policies of free trade and to reposition the Conservatives he led to represent not only the landed interests, but also the rising group of manufacturers and the industrial needs of manufacture and trade. The increase of the nation's wealth would benefit all. But accompanying the beliefs that government should, where appropriate, promote efficiency, another strong impulse, not of cold calculation but moral, influenced mid-Victorian Britain. Religion, and Christian teaching permeated Victorian thinking.

Novel was the attempt to ascertain the true nature of particular problems. Expert Royal Commissioners were appointed to investigate and make recommendations. This more 'scientific' approach to government too reflected the times. The ideal was not government *by* the people, but taking responsibility *for* the people, especially those considered too weak to look after themselves. Social legislation of the period was thought necessary for the benefit of women and children, their health and education, in the factories and mines. Social reform of adult men was in the main confined to quite specific issues of safety. The control of disease was another area and this could not be limited by age, gender or class. Parliamentary legislation began to be passed by the Whigs after the passage of the Reform Bill of 1832 and continued by the Conservatives in the 1840s. In mid-Victorian Britain a heightened concern for 'the condition of England' became evident. Factory acts, legislation governing mines and public health, were enacted but they were limited in nature and the attempted control by a central inspectorate was inadequately resourced. The most important of the social issues relating closely to social order as well as to humanitarian needs is exemplified by Victorian provisions for the destitute.

The Poor Law Amendment Act of 1834 had not solved the problem. The widespread assumption of the better-off Victorians that the destitution of the able bodied was a *moral* failing was simply false. In times of economic downturn the most willing could find no work and their wages in good times were too low to build up sufficient personal savings to tide them over. The Act of 1834 sought to abolish outdoor relief except for special cases such as the infirm elderly. As a 'test' of genuine need it compelled the recipient of relief into a workhouse where families were cruelly broken up and living conditions following the Benthamite principle of 'less eligibility' were supposed to be worse than that endured by the poorest but independent wage earner. This could not be realistically enforced. Since the object was to get the inmates to leave and re-enter employment, reducing their health would have been counter-productive. Workhouses could not be allowed to turn into places of utter degradation. Scandals received wide publicity but they were not the rule. The Poor Law Amendment Act of 1834 was ill suited to meet the needs of society in the developing industrial age. Overall the real wages of manual workers rose only slightly in the 1850s, but more important was the availability of work. Unemployment, through no fault of their own, sickness and old age, would plunge a whole family into destitution. Although unemployment was nationally not high in the decade of the 1850s, except in 1858 when it reached over 7%, for those who were affected it was a calamity even whilst supposedly living in the Victorian 'boom years'.

The new poor law was intended to provide relief to all but the elderly and disabled only inside a workhouse. Parishes were to be combined into 643 unions, each with a workhouse. Many of the destitute preferred no relief rather than to enter the workhouse. Life in the workhouse meant regimentation and forced repetitive often senseless labour; the workhouse destroyed family life by separating wives from husbands and children and resembled prisons, depriving inmates of freedom. This was perhaps the most cruel application of the principle of 'less eligibility', though the logic behind the practice was to separate the adult able bodied from children who were to be placed in more appropriate surroundings as orphans, until their mother or father left the workhouse. As symbols of Victorian inhumanity and objects of hatred by the poor, the workhouse with its stigma, took pride of place. In practice the withdrawal of outdoor relief proved at times of high need impractical and there were in any case not enough workhouses built. Some local authorities also found provision of outdoor relief a cheaper option to providing support in a workhouse. Where workhouses could provide temporary shelter or as a workhouse infirmary providing medical treatment without requiring admission to the workhouse itself, they served an important function for the poor. Some but by no means all deserved the depiction in the novels of Charles Dickens.

The legislation enacted during the years by the government led by the great aristocratic Whig reformer, Lord John Russell the third son of the sixth Duke of Bedford, from July 1846 to February 1852, continued in the practice of passing specific reforms cautiously, rather than elaborating some grand vision. In the textile factories further safeguards in the employment of women and children were enacted in 1847, the following year a public health act was passed. This and other reforming laws were more indicative of the future than far reaching in their practical effects at the time.

The great famine in Ireland had provided Peel with the opportunity to take free trade a logical step further with the repeal of the Corn Laws. It fell to Russell to deal with the human consequences of the famine.

History, the Protestant ascendancy, disparities of landownership, with the majority owning no land or only a tiny holding, the obvious discrimination of an established Anglican Church when 80% of the Irish people were Catholics and about half of the Protestants were Dissenters, poverty and overpopulation, were all elements making up the 'Irish question'. The Act of Union of 1800 intended as a new starting point in the relationship of Britain and Ireland brought about some reforms such as Catholic emancipation in 1829 but did little to tackle the other root causes of discontent in Ireland. It is difficult to see how any government could have done given the parameters of the government's powers of intervention and its available resources in the first half of the nineteenth century. Daniel O'Connell, the Irish political leader, organized the Irish masses to provide backing in the Westminster parliament for reforms. O'Connell was no firebrand, but dedicated to peaceful change. Peel's suppression of his renewed agitation in the early 1840s and his death in 1847 led to the collapse of unified protest.

Potatoes, not bread, was the staple diet of the Irish peasant, and the staple crop. Its failure was a catastrophe. From hunger and disease more than a million perished and the population declined from over eight to six and a half million in 1851. Another million Irish families were so desperate that they left their homes to emigrate to the uncertainty of life overseas, mainly to the United States during the decade from 1845 to 1855. Population growth in Ireland, reliance on a single crop, and the large majority of landless agricultural labourers had led to the apparent fulfilment of Malthusian prediction. Even before the 'Great Hunger' years of 1846 to 1849 emigration had proved to be the only escape. Through the remainder of the century the population of Ireland continued to decline whilst that of Britain rose, so that from forming almost a third of the United Kingdom in 1841 it decreased to about one-ninth in 1901.

Faced with the magnitude of a disaster not experienced before by ministers in London, and considering Peel's reputation for fiscal prudence which regarded low burdens of public expenditure a virtue, the ministry's response before its fall in 1846 was prompt though modest in the provision of relief. During the years of Russell's Whig Cabinet attempts to provide public work in return for relief were insufficient to meet the needs of the starving millions; soup kitchens were set up. It was hopeless to imagine that workhouses would be able to cope. Outdoor relief had therefore to be granted to three-quarters of a million.

In the same period more than half a million tenant families were evicted from small holdings by landlords who were responsible for the payments of their rates. A year later the potato blight reached Scotland. The 'Highland Famine' was less devastating than the Irish;

relief was better organized and the number of people affected much smaller and deaths were largely avoided. In Ireland migration and death reduced the numbers of the landless and plots of insufficient size. The human price paid for the 'improvement' was huge. There were now more Irish farms of viable acreages. Continued migration reduced also the pressure on the land. It was by such means, not by industrialization, that the worst effects of population growth were checked. Ireland's population continued to decline. For two decades after O'Connell's death nationalism no longer took pride of place in politics in Ireland or Westminster. Instead it was the 'land question'; the tenants enjoyed increased power and through changes in the electoral franchise in 1850 more influence, than the rural poor. It was their concerns for better conditions of tenancy that were pressed in Westminster. Nationalism was driven underground. It was Irish-men in the United States who gave the movement a new lease of life by founding in 1858 a secret society, the Fenians, dedicated to revolutionary rebellion. Their offshoot in Ireland was the Irish Republican Brotherhood. The movement advocating the violent road to independence was to enjoy no practical success in the 1860s. It served as a warning nevertheless of the possible consequences of ignoring Irish grievances. It was Gladstone who would take that message to heart.

No great issues divided Liberals and Tories in the 1850s. Landowners and business interests are to be found supporting both parties. The Conservatives by tradition were the party of the country gentry allied to efficient reformers like Huskinson and Peel. But the protection of the farmers through tariffs on grain had long ceased to be an issue of practical difference with the continuing reductions under the Tories, though total repeal of the Corn Laws had caused a shock at the time. The Conservatives stood for upholding the old social structure of rural England and with it the established Church of England. On the question of the admission of Catholics and 'Dissenters', later called Non-conformists, the Whigs had proved more flexible in granting some basic civil rights such as the franchise and admission to parliament. The Whigs were no less keen than the Conservatives to maintain the social structure and also regarded the Reform Bill of 1832, if not as a final settlement, at least as a settlement for a generation, which in fact it pretty well turned out to be. The Whigs received their wider support from liberal reformers and middle-class radicals, but their zeal for any further substantial reform had abated when they returned to power in July 1846. Lord John Russell's administration surprisingly remained in power for six years. That the great families who formed the exclusive Whigs should hold the reigns of government in mid-Victorian England was not due to their dynamism but the division of the political groupings of the time. Their majorities after the general election of 1847 depended on varying support from the Radicals, themselves soon split, Liberals, the Irish and the 'Peelites' or Liberal Conservatives as they called themselves. It was a shifting basis of support from measure to measure, but sufficient as long as the Conservative opposition of some two hundred and thirty clung to protection.

Over a hundred members of his party in the House of Commons had followed Peel when he split the Conservative party over the repeal of the Corn Laws in 1846. The two hundred and twenty or so Conservatives who remained could find no allies to secure a majority and appeared doomed to permanent opposition. And so they were but for three brief interludes: for ten months in 1852, for just over a year from February 1858 to June 1859 and for almost two years from February 1867 to December 1868. A real return to power with Disraeli's second Cabinet did not occur until 1874. They thus languished in lively opposition for a total of twenty-three years out of twenty-seven. That the opposition was lively was largely due to their leader in the Commons, Benjamin Disraeli.

Perhaps it was a distinguishing mark of the Victorian gentry, the better-off middle classes and the aristocracy that they could embrace as leader a man of talent, of non-aristocratic birth, of stature and demeanour very different from that of the English country gentleman, and a baptized Jew. In no other country of Europe was this possible then, or for long after. One of his early opponents, that most aristocratic of Englishmen, the third Marquess of Salisbury, who later served as foreign secretary in his Cabinet on hearing of his death in April 1881 wrote, 'The blow is a very severe one...Lord Beaconsfield had been so long associated with the Tory Party, and of late years his popularity has risen so high, that the Party will hardly believe in its own existence without him...one can hardly talk of the death of a man of 76 as if it were a strange and unexpected event – yet now that it comes it fills me with sadness and hopelessness.'*

Disraeli's political ascent had not been smooth and easy. He was elected in 1837 in the constituency of Maidstone, with its small electorate still one of the most venal constituencies after the passage of the Reform Bill. It had been his fifth attempt to enter parliament. Continuously beset by financial difficulties in his private life, his public life did not sparkle either. He was disappointed not to be offered a place in Peel's administration in 1841. Disraeli together with a small intimate group of young aristocratic and dissident Tories, nicknamed 'Young England', disapproved of Peel's cold and

* Salisbury to Lady John Manners, 19 April 1881, quoted by J. A. S. Grenville in *Lord Salisbury and Foreign Policy* (London, 1964), p. 10.

efficient 'middle class' oriented administration. They conjured up a happy and contented past where an enlightened monarchy and nobility supported by the established Church had supposedly created a golden age. It was pure romanticism, nostalgia and an escape from the realities of the day, but no doubt enjoyable for its young aristocratic leaders. Disraeli was their most important inspiration. In his novel *Coningsby* he portrayed their personalities and aspirations. A year later in 1845 appeared *Sybil, or the Two Nations* which depicted the contrasts and evils of a society divided by extreme wealth and poverty. But 'Young England' could provide no solution to remedy the deplorable conditions produced in so many cities by the industrial age. In looking to the Church and the maintenance of the aristocratic traditions of rural England, Disraeli was condemning in this vision the Conservatives to a dwindling minority in politics. It was Peel who sought to align the Conservatives with the growth of manufacture and business. The repeal of the Corn Laws in 1846 gave Disraeli, not yet leader in the Commons, but its most effective speaker the opportunity to savagely attack his leader for betraying the party and to carry the majority of backward-looking Conservative rank and file with him.

Disraeli had rallied the country gentry, but most of the senior Conservatives with ministerial experience and ability including Gladstone followed Peel. This was disastrous for the Party, yet a circumstance that would make it possible for Disraeli to become its leader and prime minister in 1867. But Disraeli had courageously risked his political advancement by supporting Russell's administration in removing the disabilities of Jews from entering the House when Baron Lionel de Rothschild was elected for the City of London in 1847. Though the Bill passed in the Commons it was repeatedly defeated in the Lords until 1858. There were clear limits then to Disraeli's opportunism when he believed fundamental principles were at stake.

Russell's early reforming zeal soon abated. In 1847 child and female labour in factories was 'limited' to ten hours a day, at least an advance. A Public Health Board set up in 1848 displayed another social concern by the government, with little practical effect. Finally, the Poor Law Board was intended to ameliorate harsh conditions. In courting popularity in 1850 by fanning the flames of anti-Catholicism when Catholic bishoprics in 1850 were forbidden to call their sees after place names, Russell was descending to rather discreditable politics quite uncharacteristic of the reformer.

In foreign affairs, Palmerston caused great commotions without achieving much. In Europe Britain held to a policy of non-intervention and non-interference unless it was a question of bullying a small country. The opportunity arose in the so called Don Pacifico affair.

David Pacifico was a Portuguese merchant born in Gibraltar, who claimed British citizenship. In an anti-semitic riot his house was burnt down in Athens where he had settled. The police had stood by and so he claimed compensation from the Greek government. His claim was exaggerated but backed by Palmerston who sent a naval squadron to the Piraeus in 1850. In the Commons he defended his conduct with the ringing declaration that a British citizen 'as the Roman, in the days of old, held himself free from indignity, when he could say *Civis Romanus sum* [I am a Roman Citizen], so also a British subject, in whatever land he may be, shall feel confident that the watchful eye and the strong arm of England will protect him against injustice and wrong'. It was excessive but a splendid appeal to the superiority the English felt over everyone else in the world. Soon after, Palmerston's unpredictability led to his temporary downfall when he congratulated Louis Napoleon on his *coup d'état*. Russell's ministry lasted only a few weeks longer. Lord Derby then headed for ten months a Conservative minority ministry in 1852 in the Lords, with Disraeli as chancellor of the exchequer, and by now undisputed as leader in the House of Commons. In this his first spell in office Disraeli became responsible for the budget. There was to be no attempt to return to protection; instead he attempted to find some compensation for the landed interests by reducing the tax on tea and on malt and hops which cleverly also reduced the cost of beer. His complicated tax changes were less well thought out. The government was defeated on the budget and the Whigs returned to power in coalition with the Peelites in 1852.

The new government was not headed by Russell but by the Earl of Aberdeen. Gladstone now established his reputation as a consummate chancellor of the exchequer, keeping a tight rein on government expenditure (except inevitably during the Crimean War). In Victorian England it was not the role of government to supervise the nation's economy. On the contrary, the business of the nation freed from interference of tariffs was to prosper separated from government. Government's duty was to take no more in taxes than necessary to fulfil its essential functions of efficient administration, defence and limited social-related costs. Private charity, self-help institutions such as the friendly societies, were supposed to fill needs which government did not. It was also the great age of charity. While in continental Europe central expenditure grew as a proportion of national income, in Britain it remained steady amounting in 1853 to 8.6% and only reaching 10% in one year between 1853 and 1880. A hundred years later it had risen to more than 45% on the continent and 37% in Britain. Gladstone also made the Treasury a department of particular power, controlling the expenditures of all of the other departments thereby enhancing the role of the chancellor of the exchequer in the Cabinet. Gladstone's careful husbanding of the nations finances and grand plan to abolish income tax was, however, to be thrown out of kilter by the cost of the Crimean War.

It is interesting to compare government in Britain and on the continent during the authoritarian 1850s. In some respects the approach in Britain and on the continent appeared to be similar in their caution not to extend the franchise, not to admit the majority of the people to any say in government. But whereas in Britain constitutional development had undergone no violent challenges and upheavals, democracy had briefly appeared to have broken through on the continent only to be forcibly repudiated again. Liberals on the continent had taken fright at the forces unleashed in 1848. Reforms to try to reconcile the masses of the people were now attempted from above. The price of reform was acceptance of authoritarian rule. The authoritarian ministers around the crown intended to weaken such influence as representative assemblies could still exert after 1848. The armies loyal to the crown, were the guarantors of stability. The gulf between the reaction on the continent, even if progressive in some respects, and Britain could not be more clear. Contemporaries were well aware of it. In Britain, parliament had not been weakened. The military were under the firm and accountable control of the civilian government. The people, unlike on the continent, were free from political oppression, could voice their views without fear of arrest and the government was open to criticism by a free press. Elsewhere in Europe such liberties were only enjoyed in small countries: in Belgium under the benign Leopold I, Queen Victoria's 'dearest uncle' with its constitution after 1848; in Switzerland with its national assembly elected by manhood suffrage; and in Sweden, which despite a restrictive authoritarian constitution, permitted a free press, began to give rights to women and had introduced compulsory education as early as 1842. At least for a time too the Danes also had secured a liberal constitution in the aftermath of the 1848 revolutions. But in 1850, the combined populations of these more enlightened small states was less than twelve million and their influence did not compare with Great Britain's.

It was an extraordinary irony that it should be a government headed by the pacific Aberdeen that was responsible for taking the country into the Crimean War. Four decades earlier in 1813 Aberdeen as ambassador to Austria had witnessed the horror of war walking over the battlefield after the battle of Leipzig, and seen the suffering of the wounded and dying. The experience had left an indelible impression. But inside the Cabinet there were ministers in 1853 who urged a forceful response to Russian expansion in the Balkans and threats to the Ottoman Empire. The most pugnacious were

Palmerston and Russell. The Peelites including Gladstone were arguing for caution and peace. The press and the public clamoured for action. Aberdeen was not a strong leader and did no more than to try to slow the drift to war. In the end he resisted no further. How the Crimean War came about in the general minefield of the relations of the great powers over the 'Eastern Question', however, needs to be examined more closely in the chapter that follows.

12

The Eastern Question
Leads to War

The Crimean War has frequently been described as 'unnecessary' by historians. By this is meant that there were not sufficient real differences of vital interest between the powers to justify the abandonment of diplomacy and the resort to force. However, seen in that light, were not most of the wars of the nineteenth and twentieth centuries 'unnecessary'? The only 'necessary' war is one deliberately waged for the purpose of aggression, or for defence in the face of such aggression. The Second World War, for instance, was a 'necessary' war; but it is not a very useful task for historians to divide wars into these categories. What is far more illuminating is to discover how it came about that the contemporary decision-makers came to the conclusion that it was necessary to fight. What assumptions motivated the powers and, with hindsight, how correct were these assumptions?

Although the immediate cause of the quarrel concerned Catholic and Greek Orthodox monks in Jerusalem whose claims were taken up by Napoleon III and Tsar Nicholas I, two underlying issues stand out. The first was Nicholas' phobia about the dangers of the Bonapartist revival in France which he believed would spread revolution throughout Europe and so destroy the settlement of 1815. The second was the British phobia about what were believed to be the true intentions and unlimited territorial ambitions of Russia. To take the latter first, how real were British fears?

Russia had made some gains during the Napoleonic Wars: acquiring Bessarabia in 1812. This brought her to the River Pruth which separated Bessarabia from what were known as the Danubian Principalities of Moldavia and Wallachia (later unified as Rumania); in the west, Russia had retained in 1815 a portion of what had formerly been the Prussian share of Poland's partition despite the threats of Castlereagh and the secret alliance he concluded in January 1815 with Austria and France at the Congress of Vienna. That was the sum of Russia's territorial success in Europe for a century. In 1914 Russia's frontiers in Europe were still those of 1815, bounded by Germany and Austria-Hungary in the west and south along the line of Poland's partition of 1815, and then further south again along the River Pruth where Rumania was now Russia's neighbour. (For the sake of complete accuracy it may be noted that during the hundred years after 1815, Russia's frontiers in *Europe* actually underwent some small changes backwards and forwards: Russia annexed the delta at the mouth of the Danube in 1829; she then, in 1856, lost the delta of the Danube again, together with a portion of Bessarabia after the Crimean War, but secured the Bessarabian territory back in 1878 after the Russo-Turkish War, so regaining the line of the River Pruth, but not the delta of the Danube. Against the Ottoman Empire in Asia, Russia had been able to manage only a very limited expansion after 1815, gaining a small area in Trans-Caucasia in 1829 and a rather larger territory in the region around Kars in 1878. (See map p. 20.) Thus Russia's European frontiers present for a century an extraordinary picture of stability when compared with the radically-changing frontiers of the three other major European continental powers, Prussia, Austria and France. These continental changes were so fundamental that three great powers acquired new names, for after 1871 we have Germany, Italy and Austria-Hungary and from the debris of the Ottoman Empire in Europe there emerged five fully independent states.

A spectacular contrast to Russian conservatism in Europe is provided by Russia's advance in Asia during the nineteenth century. Russia's transcontinental expansion, beginning around the 1830s, brought her to the frontiers of Chinese Turkestan in 1868 and Afghanistan in 1873. Russia simultaneously expanded her Pacific power, acquiring territory as far as the River Amur. The full consequences of Russia's advance on the relations of the powers did not, however, become evident until the close of the nineteenth century when Anglo-Russian rivalry in Europe turned into a global rivalry and became an element in the new era of *Weltpolitik*. But already in the nineteenth century Britain tended to credit Russia with the desire to destroy British influence in the Near East and even of wishing to invade India.

In the 1840s and 1850s the part of the world where a collision between Russia and Britain appeared most likely was the Ottoman Empire. Both the Russians and the British were agreed that Ottoman rule could not last much longer and that its collapse could involve the powers in a general war when it came to deciding what should take the place of the empire. In these circumstances the Russians could see three acceptable ways of safeguarding their national interests: the first and preferred solution was to keep the Ottoman Empire in being but as a kind of protectorate tied closely to Russia. In 1832 and 1833 Tsar Nicholas I actually achieved this objective when the Turks had to turn for help to Russia to meet the advance of Mehemet Ali, the Pasha of Egypt. Russia then concluded an alliance with Turkey which allowed her a predominant influence at Constantinople. The second solution was to maintain the Ottoman Empire as a neutral buffer by agreement with the other powers and to safeguard Russian interests in the sensitive Straits region by an international compact. That was done when the four, and later five, great European powers, Britain, Austria, Prussia, Russia and France concluded the Straits Convention in 1841. Thus in 1841 Russia had to abandon her first preference for the second. The third solution was to partition Turkey after reaching some agreement with the powers most vitally concerned. This Russia never secured though she tried on more than one occasion to discuss the possibility. The trouble was that Britain, Austria and France could not tell which of these three policies the Russians were actually following. That is not surprising. Nicholas I was not always clear himself, especially as he attempted to combine elements of all three policies in a manner most favourable to Russia and presenting the least danger to her. This attempt to harmonize policies with quite different aims was characteristic of Nicholas' handling of foreign policy and helps to explain his Crimean blunder.

Nicholas also sought to harmonize his Ottoman policy with the objective of guarding Europe from revolutionary change led by a resurgent France. So at one and the same time he seemed to be facing in two directions at once, wishing to preserve the *status quo* in Europe whilst talking about partitioning the Ottoman Empire which the Austrians, French and British all thought might lead to a general European war and the abandonment of the *status quo*.

Nicholas saw it differently, and mistakenly as it turned out. His conservatism in Europe he believed would reassure the powers that his policies in the Ottoman Empire were not designed to harm them. He intended to work with Austria and Britain and to isolate France. He was prepared to give up virtually all territorial ambitions in Europe in order to reach this understanding. He coveted no part of Prussian or Austrian territory. The continued partition of Poland between the three monarchies he regarded as a common interest binding them together. In the Balkans, Nicholas was ready in the 1840s to see a great extension of Austrian influence; he even spoke of letting Austria as a non-maritime power occupy Constantinople and the Straits, though Russia too would reserve for herself certain safeguards such as a garrison stationed on the Bosphorous. If it came to partition Russia would take over completely the autonomous principalities of Moldavia and Wallachia (Rumania). Russia had occupied them for several years after 1829 and when Russian troops were withdrawn, continued to exercise extensive rights though they remained under Ottoman suzerainty. To reassure Austria, Nicholas promised not to cross the Danube should the Ottoman Empire in Europe collapse. But Metternich in 1843 and 1844 did not respond with any enthusiasm to these overtures. He probably rightly believed the tsar's plans could not be realized peaceably and that in the end he would be driven to occupy Constantinople which Britain would not tolerate.

In June 1844 Nicholas came to England on a state visit. It gave him the opportunity to discuss the future of the Ottoman Empire with Lord Aberdeen, the foreign secretary. The results are a good illustration of the dangers of such 'summit' diplomacy. The discussion made quite a different impression on the participants and so led to serious misunderstanding. Nicholas thought a verbal agreement had actually been reached and that in just a few hours he had succeeded in removing British suspicion of Russia. For Aberdeen the conversation was just a 'mutual expression of opinion'; but so important did this conversation appear to Nicholas that he had it written up a few months later and this memorandum was approved by Aberdeen as an accurate account when he sent him a copy in January 1845. What the tsar and Aberdeen had told each other was that Britain and Russia would try to maintain the Ottoman Empire as long as possible. But if 'we foresee that it must crumble to pieces, to enter into previous concert as to everything relating to the establishment of a new order of things'* in a way that would safeguard the security and treaty rights of Russia and Britain and the general balance of power in Europe.

Peace in the Ottoman Empire depended largely on the attitude of the foreign powers. The sultan was able to rule his own dominions in his own fashion provided there was no outside interference. A few years of quiet had followed the Mehemet Ali crisis and the international settlement of 1841, though the attempted reforms did not satisfy the foreign ambassadors at Constantinople. The most powerful of them, Lord Stratford de Redcliffe, nevertheless used his influence to give the sultan and his ministers a breathing space. He also ensured a predominant influence at Constantinople for Britain. The Russians were prepared to tolerate this state of affairs: partly because Britain commanded the situation with her naval power, and partly because Nicholas was ready to accept in good faith British assurances that Britain would not take Constantinople for herself, but wished to maintain the Ottoman Empire. By December 1852 the tsar believed the state of the Ottoman Empire had decayed even further and that foreign pressure would lead to an early crash.

* K. Bourne, *The Foreign Policy of Victorian England, 1830–1902*, pp. 258–61.

In the part of the Ottoman Empire bordering on the territory of the Habsburgs a serious crisis threatened to develop. The Turks were ruling harshly in Bosnia to suppress unrest, and when the neighbouring Montenegrins seized a town in Turkish territory, Omar Pasha, the Turkish governor, declared war on the little principality of Montenegro. Austria protested vigorously. Although the Austrians wanted to maintain the Ottoman Empire and desired it to be strong in Constantinople, they wished Ottoman rule to be weak in the regions bordering the lands of the Habsburgs. The Turkish subjugation of Montenegro, moreover, threatened to strengthen the Ottoman Empire along the Adriatic and this Austria was determined to stop. The crisis over the Turkish-Montenegrin conflict was hastily ended when the Austrians sent Count Leiningen to Constantinople in February 1853 with an ultimatum that Turkey desist from invading Montenegro. The Turks finding themselves isolated gave way and promised to end the war. Round one between a great power and Turkey when the Turks sought to strengthen their hold over a portion of their Empire had gone against Turkey.

Russia had backed up Austria at Constantinople thus emphasizing Austrian-Russian solidarity in the 'Eastern question'. But when the French made demands on the sultan that was a very different kettle of fish. Nicholas interpreted Napoleon III's backing for the claims of the Catholic monks as an attempt to replace Russian influence at Constantinople with French influence. It was not. Napoleon III had merely carried on a long tradition of French policy to gain some prestige and to strengthen France in the Ottoman Empire where she was very much the weaker power compared to Britain, Russia and Austria. Napoleon III too had his eyes on the approval of the clerical party at home. The notion of provoking a war with Russia was far from his calculations. The French enjoyed a 'local' success in December 1852 when the sultan's *firman* handed the keys, and so the guardianship, of the Church of the Nativity in Jerusalem to the Catholic monks. Matters might have rested there but where the upstart Napoleon III was concerned, Nicholas could exercise no balanced judgement. The revival of Bonapartism with its espousal of 'national' causes such as Poland he regarded as a threat which had to be met at all costs. France had been isolated in 1840 during the Mehemet Ali crisis and Austria, Prussia, Russia and Britain then had worked together to reach a settlement. Nicholas could see no reason why France should not be isolated again, and why Napoleon III, who had the audacity to call himself 'Emperor of the French' and challenged the validity of the 1815 settlement, should not be humiliated. Given this frame of mind, Nicholas looked upon any success of the emperor's in the Ottoman Empire, however trivial, as in fact the greatest significance and also as a personal affront. That is why the quarrel of the monks loomed so large.

The dispute between the Catholic and Orthodox monks had, in fact, a long and complicated history. France for centuries had been the legal protector of Catholic pilgrims travelling from western Europe to Jerusalem and Bethlehem. A number of Catholic Orders of monks had settled in the Holy Land to look after the shrines and this entitled the Catholics to worship there. Since the mid-eighteenth century, however, many of these functions had been taken over by Greek Orthodox monks and the sultan had granted the Greek Orthodox monks privileges earlier granted to the Catholic ones. The tsar established his role as protector of the religious freedom of the sultan's Christian subjects in the famous treaty of Kutchuk-Kainardji (1774). Article VII of that treaty ran: 'The Sublime Porte promises to protect constantly the Christian religion and its churches, and it allows the Minister of the Imperial Court of Russia to make, upon all occasions, representations... promising to take such representations into consideration, as being made by a confidential functionary of a neighbouring and sincerely friendly Power.' Sporadically, during the first half of the nineteenth century, the dispute over the rights to the Holy Places had flared up, with the French backing the Catholics and the Russians the Orthodox monks. What made the dispute so dangerous after 1850 was Tsar Nicholas' Francophobia and dislike of Napoleon III.

In January 1853 Nicholas judged the moment right to prepare a counter-blow against the French. It could only be done by getting the sultan to revoke decisions in favour of Catholic monks. Count Leiningen a month later confirmed how much could be achieved by bullying the Turks. Nicholas would do the same. He expected Austrian support for Russian demands in Constantinople. It never occurred to him that Austria was not in close alignment with Russia. He had, after all, proved his friendship for the Habsburgs in 1849. With Prussia too, Russia enjoyed good relations. The only problem seemed to be the likely reaction of Britain to Russian pressure at Constantinople. But here Nicholas believed he was fortunate. Aberdeen had become prime minister of a new coalition government in December 1852. The more bellicose Palmerston was shunted to the Home Office and Lord Russell placed in charge of the Foreign Office. Tsar Nicholas straightaway tried to revive his former good *rapport* with Aberdeen. He spoke to Sir George Hamilton Seymour, the British ambassador in St Petersburg, in January 1853 about Anglo-Russian co-operation and gave it as his opinion that the contingency considered in 1844 of a collapse of the Ottoman Empire had drawn near. Would it therefore not be a good idea to discuss the general principles of a partition? Russia's claims were small; he only asked that the Danubian Principalities of Moldavia and Wallachia should be placed under Russian protection; Britain could have Egypt and Crete if she wished. The crucial question, however, was the future of Constantinople. It should not be allowed to come under the control of any one great power. The Aberdeen Cabinet carefully considered its reply to this overture. It was friendly. Britain too did not wish to acquire Constantinople, Russell assured the tsar, and Britain recognized the tsar's special responsibilities towards the Christian subjects of the sultan. But the British Cabinet did not believe that an Ottoman collapse was imminent; the cabinet thought that the right policy was to continue to maintain the Ottoman Empire and to avoid undue pressure on the sultan's ministers. Aberdeen had clearly misjudged Nicholas' determination. He reported to the queen at the time that he did not think 'there is anything new in this demonstration by the Emperor. It is essentially the same language he has held for some years'.

Nicholas was quite satisfied with the British response but ignored the advice. Without pressure on the sultan, France could not be made to give way.

During the next nine months escalating pressure by Russia on Turkey was met with counter-moves by Britain to defend Turkey and by France to maintain the rights previously gained. Diplomatically the struggle naturally centred on the sultan's seat of government at Constantinople. Diplomacy was backed by military sanctions. A Russian army threatened the Turkish Principalities of Moldavia and Wallachia, and Russian warships, the Turkish Black Sea coastline. Britain and France had at their command the classical threat of ordering their fleets from the Mediterranean through the Dardanelles, the Sea of Marmora and up the Bosphorus to Constantinople and beyond to the Black Sea. This was a move the Russians did not wish to provoke. But the British Cabinet was extremely sensitive about the possibility of a Russian attack on Constantinople. A Russian expeditionary force could theoretically leave Odessa or Sevastopol and be landed on the Bosphorus. In fact we now know the tsar was considering just such a surprise blow in the spring of 1853 but was dissuaded by his military advisers because they feared that this could lead to a general war. The main Russian land advance in any case would have to be made across the River Pruth through Moldavia, Wallachia, into Bulgaria and then through Rumelia – territories all still part of the Ottoman Empire in Europe – to Constantinople. These territories lying between Russia and Constantinople formed the barriers or 'buffers' to a Russian advance. The history of the 'Eastern Question' for the next thirty-five years is marked by successive crises each one of which was in large part concerned with preventing Russia from using these countries (the Principalities, the later Rumania, Bulgaria and Rumelia) from becoming stepping-stones for a Russian domination of Constantinople. The 'by product' of such an advance would be that Russia would cross the Danube and eventually, unless halted, would reach the Aegean thereby cutting off Austria's trade and influence and ambitions south-eastwards. So Austria too was intimately involved. (See map p. 181.)

The Russians followed up the Austrian success of Count Leiningen's mission by sending Prince Menshikov as a special envoy to Constantinople to bully the sultan into acknowledging Russia's superior position in the Ottoman Empire. The sultan was to allow diplomatic negotiations to be undertaken without the Turkish foreign minister who in December 1852 had handed the keys of the Church of the Nativity to the Catholic monks there present. The Russians also demanded that a new convention should be signed to protect the privileges of the Orthodox Christians; in return Russia offered a defensive alliance to Turkey to 'protect' the sultan from French counter-pressures. The tsar and his foreign minister Count Nesselrode believed that by insisting on Turkish observance of article VII of the treaty of Kutchuk-Kainardji they had found a way of gaining predominant influence in the Ottoman Empire; the French would be ousted from any influence at Constantinople whilst the British could be reassured that Russia was only insisting on her 'treaty rights'. It was an extraordinary Russian miscalculation that Britain and France would simply acquiesce in this Russian manœuvre.

Menshikov, a professional soldier, had been deliberately chosen to present the Russian demands as uncompromisingly as possible. What the tsar desired was an abject climb-down by the Turks, not genuine diplomatic negotiations leading to a compromise. Accompanied by a Russian general and a Russian admiral, the mission was intended to convey the threat of military action if the sultan did not give way, though Menshikov was actually only permitted as a last resort to break off diplomatic relations. Menshikov arrived in Constantinople on 28 February 1853. Three months later, on 21 May he left in anger and diplomatic relations between Russia and Turkey were severed. During the intervening twelve weeks Menshikov's demands and the Turkish responses – the exchanges can scarcely be described as 'negotiations' – show the sultan and his advisers as ready to make many specific concessions. At Menshikov's behest not one but two foreign ministers were dismissed: the Turks also promised to improve the position of the Orthodox monks guarding the Holy Places, and to respect the religious rights of all Greek Orthodox subjects. All this was to no avail because the sultan rejected the basic Russian requirement of allowing Russia a large, if not a predominant voice, in the internal affairs of the Ottoman Empire. That this is what the Russians were after became clear in May 1853 when the Russians required not only that the sultan respect the religious rights of the Orthodox Christians, but that in practice he accept the Tsar of Russia as protecting all other rights the tsar might feel rightfully belonged to the Orthodox Christians, a claim entirely unjustified by any interpretation of the treaty of Kutchuk-Kainardji. Had the Turks given way, Russia's right to interfere would have been so enlarged that she would have been able to do so whenever it suited her for two out of every five of the sultan's subjects were Orthodox Christians.

How far was Ottoman intransigence to blame for the breach with Russia? The sultan's advisers were pastmasters at procrastination, of seeming to give way whilst in reality doing little. But Menshikov's deliberately offensive behaviour had aroused genuine anger, resentment and nationalist fervour against the infidel. In Paris and in London the issues were not fully understood. During the course of the Menshikov mission, when it became evident how much pressure Russia was exerting on Turkey, Napoleon III was undecided what to do and in the end half-heartedly sent the French fleet only as far as Salamis in Greece. In London there were divided counsels and Aberdeen was inclined to blame the ambitions of Napoleon III for the present crisis. The British fleet at first was not sent, but then a few days later the British Cabinet changed its mind and the Mediterranean squadron was ordered to proceed to Besika Bay just outside the Dardanelles and arrived there on 13 June 1853. A day later the French fleet reached Besika Bay also, visible evidence for the first time of the Anglo-French alignment – not alliance as yet.

Early in 1853 the experienced British ambassador Stratford de Redcliffe had returned to Constantinople from leave. Historians have debated whether the arrival of the ambassador contributed to the Turkish breach with Russia. Menshikov placed the blame for his failure on the influence of Stratford de Redcliffe and it is certainly true that Stratford de Redcliffe held to a policy maintaining British influence in Constantinople and of preventing Russia from securing predominance. This obvious rivalry of the powers played into the hands of the sultan who felt better able now to resist Russian demands. But in all probability Stratford de Redcliffe was sincere in trying to bring about a settlement between Russia and Turkey. If the dispute had merely concerned the Holy Places and the respective merit of Russian or French claims, Stratford de Redcliffe would have used all his influence to satisfy Russian susceptibilities. But when Menshikov demanded on behalf of Russia the widest and vaguest rights to interfere in the Ottoman Empire, there can be no real doubt that Stratford de Redcliffe welcomed Turkish resistance to what amounted to a Russian ultimatum. But resistance was in the circumstance a natural Turkish reaction anyway. In London too it was gradually realized that the real question did not concern the Holy Places but the future of the Ottoman Empire. There was still a general desire to avoid war, but no clear plan as to the best way to achieve a peaceful outcome.

The Austrians also wanted to avoid a general war and played a very active diplomatic role. It must be remembered that for France and Britain war would mean a war in a far-off place, whereas for the Austrians a war among the powers would threaten the existence of the Habsburg Empire as the Austrians and Russians faced each other along the long Galician frontier of more than 400 miles. To begin with Francis Joseph and his foreign minister Count Buol tried to dissuade the tsar from invading the Principalities and from starting a war against Turkey.

Austrian appeals and French and British naval demonstrations did not deter the tsar. He felt he could not bow to the pressures of the powers and after the Turks had finally rejected the Russian proposals, the Russian army on 3 July 1853 crossed the river Pruth and began the occupation of the Principalities. Even now, however, neither Russia nor Turkey declared war thus taking the final and irrevocable step.

Buol now tried to persuade all the powers to devise some formula that would settle the Russo-Turkish dispute and so lead to a withdrawal of the Russian army from the Principalities. The British, French, Austrian and Prussian diplomats met on 24 July in Vienna and with Buol concocted the Vienna Note outlining the terms of a possible settlement. Though the Russians had refused to participate in the conference, the solution now proposed by the diplomats was almost entirely favourable to Russia and the Russians accepted it. The Turks rejected the terms of the Vienna Note. In backing Turkey earlier on France and Britain had lost effective influence over Turkish policy. The Turks who would have had to submit to a united concert of Europe did not need to accept the proposals of a divided Europe.

The increasing threat of war especially alarmed the Austrians but it also had to be considered by Prussia. Prussia was nominally a signatory of the Straits Settlement of 1841, but had no interest in the Eastern Question as such. So Prussia in 1853 was again nominally involved in the Crimean diplomacy but remained on friendly terms with all the powers, especially Russia. In the long run Prussia's neutrality proved an infinitely greater gain to her interests than war on either side would have done.

The Austrian situation was quite different and decidedly uncomfortable. Any heavy military involvement in one part of Europe, such as the western Balkans, would expose the Habsburg weakness elsewhere in Italy and in Germany. It might also lead to a renewal of internal troubles. With the original dispute Austria was not concerned, only with its repercussions. Austria wanted to stop Russia from occupying the Principalities and so dominating the lower Danube.

In Constantinople during September and October 1853 war fever mounted. The sultan was determined to defend his empire, a part of which was now being occupied by the Russians. There was deadlock. The Russians would not withdraw unless the Turks accepted their demands. In London the British Cabinet believed Constantinople in danger and so ordered the British fleet to the Bosphorus on 4 October, though in an effort to preserve the peace Stratford de Redcliffe delayed calling the fleet until 21 October. This British move was a decisive step. It undermined the European basis of the Straits Settlement of 1841 to which Russia was a party. Now British and French warships would be at Constantinople but not Russian – the balance was upset. There was a final flurry of Austrian and Russian diplomatic activity; Napoleon III still wished to find a way of avoiding war. But it was not possible to move the Turks to make concessions to Russia now that the Principalities had been occupied and British and French warships were protecting Constantinople. The sultan now took the initiative when he confirmed what his ministers proposed, the despatch of an ultimatum to Russia demanding the evacuation of the Principalities. On 23 October 1853, on the eve of the expiry of the Turkish ultimatum, the Turks started hostilities. A Turkish military force crossed the Danube into the Russian-held Principalities, and the Russo-Turkish war had begun.

Now that the war had actually broken out between Russia and Turkey, Britain and France either had to admit that all their demonstrations on behalf of Turkey were bluff or go to Turkey's aid if Turkey were defeated. Aberdeen and Napoleon III tried to find a way out of the dilemma. Napoleon III even hoped the Russians would win in the Principalities, and the Turks would quickly ask for peace. Somehow the defence of the Principalities was not a sufficient rallying-cry for war. Hardly anyone in Britain or France apart from the ministers even knew where they were. Nor was there much enthusiasm for defending the Turks. With the assistance of the indefatigable Buol a new round of negotiations was attempted, to no avail. The great powers were still trying to reach some settlement without loss of prestige to any of themselves, at the expense of the Turks if need be, but now the Turks and British public opinion would not let them. The Turks took the offensive in the Principalities and in the Caucasus, where the Russian troops were weak. In the Caucasus the Russians were already fighting bands of local tribesmen. The position of the Russian forts on the Black Sea coast became indeed pretty desperate and several were evacuated by sea. The Russian Black Sea fleet relieved the situation when it met Turkish warships in a naval engagement at Sinope on 30 November 1853. The wooden Turkish warships were entirely destroyed. The news was greeted in England by the press as the 'massacre' of Sinope. At a time when the

British and French fleets were anchored in the Bosphorus, this naval engagement offensively fought by the Russians, moreover, seemed a challenge to their role as Turkey's protectors.

In Britain there were many pressure groups clamouring for war with Russia rather than for a war in defence of the Turks. Radical newspapers and pamphleteers saw the war with Russia as an opportunity for completing the work of the revolutions of '1848'. Some Polish émigrés welcomed war with Russia because they believed it would turn into a war of nationalities from which an independent Poland would emerge. More moderate and liberal opinion saw the coming war as an ideological struggle between the principles of constitutionalism championed by Britain and the autocracy of the tsar. *Punch* summed up the common denominator of all the varied opinion in favour of war in presenting the conflict in moral terms as a just war. These were not the views of the pacific Aberdeen. Aberdeen and Clarendon tried to resist the pressure, but first Palmerston resigned in mid-December and then Napoleon III threatened to act on his own.

It is difficult to make much sense of Napoleon III's erratic diplomacy during the winter of 1853. He was pushing the British Cabinet forward but also appealed to the tsar for peace. In the end the British Cabinet agreed with Napoleon III on another decisive step closer to war when the British and French warships were ordered to proceed from the Bosphorus into the Black Sea. The admirals were instructed to protect Turkish ships and to confine the Russian navy to its base in Sevastopol. Thus Britain and France were now claiming predominance not only at Constantinople but also in the Black Sea. On 12 January 1854 they informed the Russians of their decision which came close to a declaration of war. Without being defeated the Russians could not accept such a disastrous outcome of the crisis – even after their defeat they did not reconcile themselves to such a state of affairs. Even now, however, the European powers avoided taking the last irrevocable step. The tsar tried to secure the alliance of Austria in the coming conflict. So did Britain and France and their diplomatic rivalry delayed the actual outbreak of war between the European states. Buol was personally inclined to a western alliance but military calculation and the financial state of the monarchy worked against his plans and Francis Joseph did not wish to go to war with Russia.

In March 1854 Napoleon III and the British Cabinet lost patience. Domestic political pressures had overcome Aberdeen's and Clarendon's long hesitations. On 12 March Britain and France signed an alliance with Turkey pledging themselves to guarantee Ottoman integrity and independence. The sultan in turn invited France and

Britain to assist him in repelling the aggression of the Tsar of Russia and to maintain the balance of power in Europe. An ultimatum was then sent to Russia demanding that Russia withdraw from the Principalities. No reply was received. And consequently on 28 March 1854 in London and in Paris war was formally declared on Russia.

There is little point in trying to divide the blame in some proportional way between those responsible for war. But the general conditions leading to war and the motives of those who made the vital decisions are reasonably clear. Tsar Nicholas believed the issues underlying the confrontation between Russia and Turkey involved the most vital national interests. The tsar, it is often said, was mainly motivated by pride and considerations of prestige. This does him less than justice. His fears that revolution would once more spread through Europe led by the Bonapartist revival were genuine, though excessive, but what happened in the Ottoman Empire was of vital and real concern to Russia. The Ottoman Empire left entirely to itself presented no danger to Russia. A weak Ottoman Empire tempted Russia to expand at the sultan's expense; but if a feeble Ottoman Empire should become a base for foreign great powers, then Russia would be in danger. Thus a weak neighbour presents the stronger with conflicting interests of both opportunity and danger; this is a classic situation which may result in war between rival powers as it did on this occasion. The Ottoman Empire was, after all, Russia's neighbour and not the neighbour of France and Britain and so the Russians felt that its fate ultimately concerned Russia more deeply than anyone else.

The menace of French and British naval squadrons in the Black Sea in January 1854 confirmed the tsar's worst apprehensions about what would happen if he could not maintain Russian influence in the Ottoman Empire and in the Caucasus. So vital to Russia did he consider the issue to be that he was ready to risk war with France and Britain. He still hoped to keep the Russo-Turkish war, which had been in progress nearly three months, localized, by assuring Britain. Austria and France that their interests would not be harmed. That is why he had remained largely on the defensive in the Principalities. When France and Britain believed they needed to come to the defence of Turkey after the naval engagement of Sinope it was in fact the Russians who were being hard pressed in the Caucasus. The British Cabinet and Napoleon III went to war believing Sinope had placed the Bosphorus and Constantinople at Russia's mercy. By moving British and French warships into the Black Sea in January 1854, war between the European powers became virtually certain.

Turkey, France and Britain in turn had declared war on Russia, not the other way round. Britain and, to a lesser extent, France wished to restore the 'balance' in the Ottoman Empire, which in reality meant

British predominance. Could Britain and France have remained on the defensive? If the tsar had been told that any advance across the Danube or any actual attack on the Bosphorus would mean war with Britain and France, would the tsar then have moved forward or would he also have remained on the defensive? Probably the latter – but the tsar could not accept allied maritime supremacy in the Black Sea without losing all influence in the Ottoman Empire and exposing Russia to the danger of invasion. The weakness of the Aberdeen coalition government and its assessment of 'public opinion' at home, the vacillations of Napoleon III, and the sheer length of time the crisis lasted without any lessening of tensions, all these influences were responsible for the drift into war. As far as the disputes were concerned that led to the war between Russia and Turkey, it might have been possible to work out a settlement, but on the demands Britain and France made on Russia in January 1854, there could be no negotiated agreement. The tsar had to resist them. The British Cabinet and Napoleon III had responded to the crisis in the end with excessive aggression, evidence not of their strength but of their own sense of weakness at home. In these circumstances the Turks had been able to follow a national policy and to escape the influence of the great powers. In the autumn of 1853 the Turks had made the running, especially by their decision for war in October. It was not the last time that in the absence of a great power concord, such as the ideals of the 'concert of Europe' had represented earlier in the nineteenth century, the policy followed by a 'small power' could act as a catalyst and embroil the great powers in war. It was to happen again on a much more disastrous scale in 1914.

13

The Impact of the Crimean War on Europe

Once war had broken out between the three European powers, it was expected to become one of the most decisive struggles of the nineteenth century. A major war was an exciting and novel experience for Britons and Frenchmen. After all Britain and France had not fought in a European war for forty years so that only the relatively old could remember war at all. This new war with Russia, moreover, was not seen as a localized conflict confined to the defence of the Ottoman Empire. It was looked upon as a decisive struggle between two systems of government, the representative and the autocratic, in which Britain, the most progressive and industrialized power, would prove her superiority. Victory was expected before the year was out. Instead the British and French troops despatched to the East could find no Russian soldier to fight for six months. The sense of anticlimax was tremendous. The war just did not seem to get started as far as France and Britain were concerned, although casualties from disease mounted day by day. The real fighting as far as France and Britain were concerned began only months after war had been declared by them when the allies landed in the Crimea in September 1854.

The one episode of the war which is best remembered, the famous Charge of the Light Brigade at the Battle of Balaclava, characterizes an important aspect of the war: the contrast between the reckless courage of the troops and the indifferent tactical and strategic skill of the generals and officers who led them. The soldiers proved themselves to be still the soldiers of Wellington's army, but there was no Wellington. The Crimean campaign, therefore, has been regarded as an appalling example of British muddle and incompetence, relieved only by the shining example of Florence Nightingale, who succeeded in bringing some order to the hospitals in the field. In this respect the Crimean War marks a turning point in the history of modern warfare. It was the last of the eighteenth- and early nineteenth-century wars

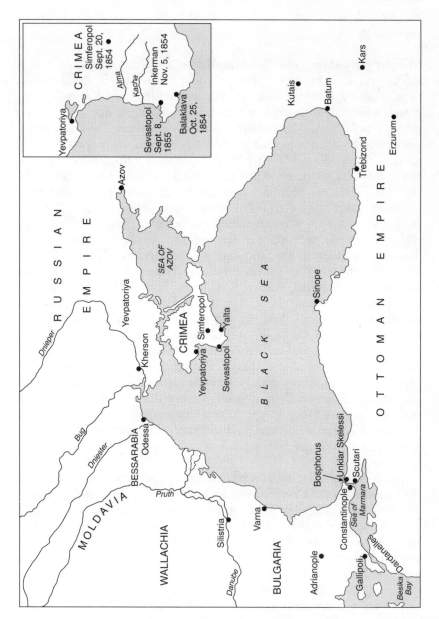

Map 2 The Crimean War

when an army lost most of its strength through epidemics and disease, not death in battle. It should be compared with earlier campaigns in this respect, not later campaigns where attention was paid to more adequate medical services and hygiene, reforms which owed much to the advances in medical knowledge and the Crimean experience.

Militarily speaking, the Crimean War is sometimes described as a minor war in a far-away place, involving a relatively small British expeditionary force of some 30,000 men under Lord Raglan's command. Certainly it hardly affected civilian life at home. Yet such conclusions about the war are wholly inadequate. They are based on viewing a European war solely from a British standpoint, and a narrow one at that. They are probably also a reflection of the contemporary British disappointment with the course and outcome of the war. The war was downgraded by contemporaries and later historians have tended to follow their example. In fact the Crimean War was a major war involving far heavier casualties than any other European war during the century from the close of the Napoleonic Wars to the outbreak of the First World War. By the time the Crimean War ended, the total number of dead of the three European combatants, Russia, Britain and France, according to most recent estimates was about 675,000. Of these there were 45,000 British dead, 180,000 French, and 450,000 Russians. There are no reliable figures for the losses of the Turks but they were probably not less than 150,000, and might well have been much more. About one man in five lost his life in battle, the other four died from disease especially typhus, cholera and various undefined fevers. The Crimean War dead of almost three-quarters of a million may be compared with the 40,000 killed in the Austro-Prussian War of 1866 and the 190,000 soldiers who died in the Franco-Prussian War. Only the death toll of the American Civil War compares in scale with the Crimean.

These comparative figures provide only a statistical impression of the grimness of the Crimean War and of the suffering of the troops on all sides. Florence Nightingale in her reports home described conditions more graphically and urged reforms. The Crimean War was also the first to be covered by 'war correspondents' sending news direct from the front. The best known was Russell of *The Times* but it was actually Thomas Chenery, the paper's Constantinople correspondent, who first revealed the deplorable state of the British medical services at Scutari. Government incompetence was probably no greater than was shown at the beginning of most wars, but never before, untrammelled by censorship, had a gifted newspaperman brought all the ghastly details of war before the most influential sections of the public, the 60,000 readers daily of *The Times*. Ten years later an historian of the Crimean War concluded, that, 'women and practical men simply spoke of *The Times*, instead of referring to public opinion.'

The disquiet at Aberdeen's conduct of the war led to a vote of 'no confidence' in the House of Commons on 29 January 1855 when a motion was passed by a large majority to set up a select committee to enquire into the state of the army before Sevastopol. Aberdeen resigned and after trying every possible candidate first, the queen in February 1855 was forced to send for Palmerston, a political leader whom she intensely disliked. Overall British military administration could not be speedily changed, but the Palmerston Cabinet improved the lot of the British soldier in the Crimea dramatically, though the total number of men who volunteered to serve remained disappointingly small. The British force continued to be led by generals who proved themselves second-rate. The Admiralty at first failed to organize adequate transport and supply ships but gradually the position improved. The Crimean campaign was at least an impressive demonstration of British sea power. Granting all the shortcomings of administration and leadership, the task of supplying expeditionary armies hundreds of miles from home was formidable and in the end more or less successfully accomplished. Although the British, French and Turks did not inflict a total defeat on Russia, Russia acknowledged that she had lost the war by accepting humiliating peace terms.

The problems the Russians faced in supplying their troops in the various actual theatres of war and possible theatres of conflict were, if anything, even worse than the problems faced by the allies. Russian mobility and capacity to fight was hamstrung by lack of communications. The allies could move supplies by sea, whereas the Russians did not possess a single railway line south of Moscow. Everything had to be moved by horse and wagon over hundreds of miles. In the autumn and spring mud made the dirt track roads almost impassable and to find an adequate supply of hay for the horses in all seasons was an even worse nightmare. The Russian forces in the Crimea by the spring of 1855 had reached 300,000 men and 100,000 animals, all needing to be fed and the majority of them placed at the furthest point of the peninsula. In the face of Russia's general administrative corruption and bureaucratic inefficiency, it was a near-miracle that sufficient supplies along the desolate roads to the Crimea were maintained. By extreme national exertion, the Russians saved themselves from total military defeat in the Crimea.

From a strategic point of view Russia's greatest handicap was the danger of attack on so many frontiers of the Empire. Field-Marshal Paskevich, Russia's Commander-in-Chief, at the beginning of the war was afraid that the Russian troops in the Principalities might be cut off if Austria declared war and her army advanced eastwards (see map p. 202). Paskevich therefore counselled caution in the Principalities and the creation of an army reserve in central Russia. Then

Paskevich feared also for the security of the Baltic and Finland after Britain and France had entered the war. Some substance to these fears was given in the spring of 1854 by Admiral Sir Charles Napier's naval sortie easily beaten off by the Russians near Hangö at the entrance to the Gulf of Finland. The engagement was insignificant but the results were important for the tsar ordered heavy reinforcements to Finland, Latvia and Estonia. The Russians were more sensitive about the Baltic than the Black Sea. A possible invasion of the Crimea was expected by the Russians after their withdrawal from the Principalities, but the Crimea was far away from the centre of Russian power and Paskevich was confident of being able to contain and pin down the allied invading force. In a sense he was right. The allies never seriously thought of any campaign inland away from the fleet. Nevertheless Paskevich's excessive caution threw away Russia's chances of winning. He should have followed a bolder course and risked the dangers from the neutrals in order to concentrate Russia's military effort where the allied armies were fighting and not dissipated his strength by guarding all possible points of attack.

From the start of the war, diplomacy and military campaign plans were closely interrelated and decisively affected each other. The first phase of the war, the purely Russo-Turkish conflict, lasted from 23 October 1853 to 28 March 1854. The Russians and the Turks fought on two fronts in Trans-Caucasia, and on the Danube, which marked the frontier between the Principalities occupied by Russia and Ottoman Bulgaria. The Turks took the offensive but their attacks on the Russian army in the Principalities were beaten back after fierce fighting; by the end of the month the Russians were in command of the mouth of the Danube. There was no dramatic breakthrough by either side. In the Caucasus region the Russians had been fighting throughout the reign of Nicholas I the hardy and fierce Moslem tribes living in the valleys and mountains, and their most dangerous leader, Shamil, invoked a 'Holy War' against them. The war with the Turks weakened the Russian position there. The Russian forts on the Black Sea coast were evacuated, but elsewhere the Russians held their own against the mountain tribesmen and a larger Turkish army. The naval victory at Sinope in November 1853 was the one bright spot for the Russians but on the whole they were nervous and apprehensive about the future. The fact is that Britain and France came to the 'rescue' of the Ottoman Empire when it was in no immediate danger.

With the British and French entry into the war at the end of March 1854, the military situation did not change for some months. Russia and Turkey continued to fight each other alone. The tsar urged Paskevich forward across the Danube to the capture of Silistria, a Turkish stronghold which could then be held if the allies landed at

Varna on the Bulgarian Ottoman Black Sea coast to aid the Turks. Paskevich hesitated. The Austrians and Prussians, under the guise of neutrality, seemed to him to be threatening the Russian rear. Paskevich expected Austria to declare war in May 1854. The tsar assured him they would not, and finally, early in May, Paskevich marched to Silistria. The Turks defended themselves stoutly and after six weeks the Russians withdrew. Not that the allies were responsible for that, but the Austrians. The Tsar was now afraid the Austrians might join the war against Russia in the summer months. He ordered a carefully-planned withdrawal from the Principalities as well. By the end of August 1854 all the Russian troops were back on their own soil. To one of his generals the tsar wrote, 'How sad and painful for me, dear Gorchakov, that I had to agree to the insistent arguments of Ivan Feodorovich (Paskevich) concerning the danger threatening the army from the faithlessness of Austria, whom we have saved.'

Austria had behaved threateningly over the question of the Principalities when concluding a treaty with Prussia on 20 April 1854, one of whose main points was that the two powers announced their intention to secure the eventual withdrawal of Russia from the Principalities. More important was perhaps the Austrian mobilization in April 1854 of four army corps in Galicia in addition to the three army corps already mobilized in south Hungary the previous autumn. On 3 June 1854 Buol sent to the Russians a note demanding that they evacuate the Principalities. Simultaneously the Austrians had secured the agreement of the Turks for Austrian troops to occupy the Principalities as soon as the Russians left. By the end of June the tsar tried to make the best of the situation by consenting to evacuate the Principalities provided Austria would undertake to prevent the British and French armies from entering them. But the tsar did not try to hide his anger at Austria's base ingratitude and lack of reciprocity for the Russian services rendered to the Habsburgs in 1849.

Meantime Britain and France had sent an expeditionary force to the East. The French were led by Marshal de Saint-Arnaud, an able general. He had been placed in command by Napoleon III as a reward for managing the military aspects of the *coup d'état* in December 1851, although in 1854 he was known to be mortally ill. The British commander was Lord Raglan, a nephew of the Duke of Wellington. The French force was well organized and led by officers who had gained some practical experience in several years of colonial fighting in Algeria. The British army was in a sad state of disarray. Raglan, after losing an arm at Waterloo, had spent thirty years behind a desk, and the experience of many of his officers was confined to the parade ground. There was also a good deal of suspicion between the two commanders and between London and Paris. On land the French troops throughout the war outnumbered the British, and accordingly played the leading military role. The Turkish 'allies' for whom the war was being ostensibly fought were regarded by both French and British with disdain. At first both Napoleon III and the Aberdeen government thought that militarily the war would be a minor affair involving perhaps 10,000 French troops and the same number of British. This underestimate was the main reason for the breakdown of the organization of supplies that followed the later decision to send large reinforcements to the expeditionary force.

The point of landing decided on by the French and British troops was the Gallipoli peninsula. The idea was to take up strong defensive positions to meet the enemy. The Russians were expected to rout the Turkish forces and then rapidly thrust through the Balkan mountains to Constantinople. The allies would then be waiting for the Russians at Gallipoli. It is hard to see how these plans could have conceived the war as anything but a major effort from the outset. It is a characteristic example of the lack of political and military co-ordination. The premisses on which the allies based their military policy were mistaken. The Russians only advanced a few miles across the Danube to the fortress of Silistria, which they besieged. Consequently there was no contact between the Russian, French and British armies encamped several hundred miles apart from each other. Silistria, under its Turkish commander, the energetic Omar Pasha, held out as has been seen and so the Russians advanced no further. After considerable delay and discussion the allies therefore decided to disembark their armies from Gallipoli where they were unlikely to meet a single enemy soldier and to convey them through the Straits into the Black Sea and then to Varna, on the Ottoman Bulgarian Black Sea coast. Once a base had been established at Varna the allies would be closer to the scene of action and in a position to send a relief army to Omar Pasha bottled up in Silistria, which lay about a hundred miles to the north of Varna. But the allies were foiled again. As they landed in Varna in June 1854, the Russians began pulling out from Silistria and in July and August from the Principalities as well. As the Austrians took over the occupation of the Principalities from the retreating Russians the allies now found themselves in the ludicrous position of facing the Austrians, potential allies, and not the enemy, the Russians.

The war on the Danube front had ended before the French and British had entered the fight. Indeed what were the allies fighting for now that the Ottoman Empire was no longer in danger and that one cause for the outbreak of war had been removed by the Russian evacuation of the Principalities? There was in Paris and London a great feeling of anticlimax and even a sense of the ridiculous. The British and French troops just had not been able to find an enemy to fight during the first five months of the war. They nevertheless suffered heavy casualties. Cholera and other endemic fevers raged in the camps and killed many of the troops. It was pointless to stay in unhealthy Varna. Morale was low. Where they would go next was one of the worst-kept secrets of any war. The Russians guessed and *The Times* knew and published the information. The allies were expected to bring the war to Russian soil by landing in the Crimea. The Russians, however, miscalculated that the attempt would not be made immediately with the autumn and winter of 1854 approaching but that the allies would wait until the following spring. Thus the element of surprise was not entirely lost.

The motive behind the expedition to the Crimea was more political than strategic. France and England wished to win at least one striking prestige victory and then to negotiate a peace. They therefore planned to capture the naval base of Sevastopol. Its fall would underline the loss of Russian supremacy in the Black Sea and so protect the Ottoman Empire. The allies did not anticipate an arduous campaign for they thought that the capture of Sevastopol could be accomplished fairly easily since the defences of the fortress guarded the approach by sea and there were none to defend the base from an attack by land. The British and French force would have the advantage of communications by sea, whereas the Russians, known to be outnumbered, could only receive reinforcements along tenuous and very long land routes. The allies expected to be in Sevastopol long before the winter set in and could then be home for Christmas. Their optimism proved entirely unfounded.

The landing began on 14 September 1854 at a point on the coast some nine days' march from Sevastopol. Three rivers crossed the terrain between that landing point and Sevastopol. They offered strong defensive positions to the Russians. Why did the allies not land close by Sevastopol? It was the first of several serious mistakes. After the landing there were more delays. Raglan was slow in getting the British troops ashore. Eventually on 19 September the order was given for the combined armies, 62,000 men, to march to Sevastopol.

Admiral Menshikov commanded the defence of Sevastopol. During the summer of 1854, with only 25,000 men available, he had constantly urged that reinforcements should be sent to him. Few were sent. Field-Marshal Paskevich regarded an attack in the Crimea as a threat far less serious than that posed by the Austrian armies. When the allied landing took Menshikov by surprise because it had occurred earlier than anticipated the Russians were outnumbered, having only some 35,000 men capable of fighting. Menshikov's best chance lay in disrupting the landing but he was over-cautious. Instead of attacking the allies as they slowly landed he decided to meet the allied army in defensive positions on the River Alma. On 20 September the allies and the Russians fought their first engagement of the war. The British and French armies showed great courage at the battle of the Alma; so did the Russians but they were badly led and defeated. Soon after the battle, Saint-Arnaud, the best and most energetic commander the allies produced during the whole of the war, finally succumbed to cancer and died, having handed his command to General Canrobert, an indifferent leader. Military historians later blamed the allies for not following up the victory of the Alma and pursuing the enemy. Without cavalry and short of supplies, it is, however, doubtful whether a rapid pursuit to Sevastopol was feasible. Raglan eventually moved forward and secured a good base by capturing the port of Balaclava, but when the allied armies reached Sevastopol they were surprised by the formidable defences facing them and decided they could not take the city by storm; they now asked for siege equipment to be sent to the Crimea and settled down around the fortress for the winter.

Within Sevastopol the defenders were inspired by Admirals Kornilov and Nakhimov to fight to the last. The most outstanding soldier in Sevastopol, however, was an engineer, Colonel Totleben. With prodigious human effort and despite a lack of tools, land defences were improvised; the approaches of the city were soon guarded by a series of crude but very effective earthworks constructed under Totleben's supervision. As the allies settled down outside the city, the defenders did not let up and constantly added to the strength of the earthworks. The most worrying aspect of trying to defend the naval base from the Russian point of view was the lack of gunpowder and other essential supplies.

To disorganize the build up of the allied armies and divert their attention, Menshikov decided to attack the British-held port of Balaclava. This relatively small battle on 25 October became legendary because of the fiasco of the 'Charge of the Light Brigade', which only occurred as a result of a confusion of orders. The brigade of 673 men suffered 247 casualties as the cavalry rode unbelievably up the valley between Russian-held hills straight towards the muzzles of a battery of guns which the Russians had earlier captured from the Turks. The Light Brigade actually succeeded in overrunning the guns and killing the gunners, but then met a huge force of Russian cavalry and so had to ride back again down the valley to the allied positions. It was an incredible charge, evidence of the high fighting morale of the British troops, if nothing else.

Reinforcements were now reaching the Russians in Sevastopol. By early November 1854 Menshikov had at his disposal an army that equalled and possibly exceeded, the combined French and British forces. He decided once more on offensive action to defeat the allies.

On 5 November 1854 he attacked the allied positions on the Heights of Inkerman. The Russian plans were badly worked out and the Russians suffered defeat as they were unable to dislodge the allies. Casualties on both sides were heavy; Inkerman indeed must rank as one of the major battles of the nineteenth century. Its main result was to produce a stalemate for many months. The Russians abandoned the hope of driving the allies out of the Crimea and the allies of taking Sevastopol by storm before the winter.

After November 1854 the Russians attempted no further offensive sorties. The Crimean War turned into a conflict of attrition on both sides. The elements and disease took a heavier toll of the combatants than the fighting. A hurricane in mid-November 1854 added to the allied disorganization at sea and on land. As winter set in the suffering of the troops on both sides was appalling. Of the two allies the British were much worse off than the better-organized French. By January 1855 less than 15,000 British troops were fit and able to fight. The French by this time had sent close to 90,000 men East, the great majority of them to the Crimea, and their hospitals and medical services were functioning well.

Before Sevastopol there was sporadic fighting; attacks on some Russian-held forts were countered by Russian sorties against the allied positions. In the spring of 1855 some 55,000 Turks, under Omar Pasha, landed in the Crimea to reinforce the allies but neither the British nor the French commanders thought them much use and feared the spread of disease. The Turks consequently did not contribute significantly to the fighting around Sevastopol. As the months dragged on without anything decisive happening in Crimea which could bring the war to a close, Austrian intentions became once more of crucial importance.

Vienna remained the centre of diplomacy during the Crimean War. The Russians hoped Austria would remain neutral. What the Foreign Minister Count Buol wanted was to bring the war to an end and he believed the best way to bring this about was to mediate 'actively' holding out the promise of an alliance to France and Britain provided they agreed with Austria on joint war aims; but Buol also intended these war aims to be sufficiently limited to induce Russia to make peace rather than risk adding Austria to her other enemies. The result of Buol's diplomatic activity was that in August 1854 Britain, France and Austria had agreed on 'Four Points' as representing the essential conditions for peace. They were (i) Russia would renounce her special rights for Serbia and the Principalities; these would be replaced by a general guarantee of the powers; (ii) free navigation of the Danube; (iii) the revision of the Straits Convention of 1841 'in the interests of the balance of power in Europe'; (iv) the renunciation by Russia of her rights as protector of the Orthodox Christians in the Ottoman Empire. Britain agreed only reluctantly to these 'war aims' in order to secure the Austrian alliance. The Russians, after the early reverses in the Crimea, accepted the Four Points at the end of November 1854 so that Austria would have no excuse to join the allied side. The war ought now to have ended in a negotiated peace. But there was always an unreality about the negotiations. Russia, France and Britain were not ready to stop fighting and Austria not prepared to start. Buol therefore simply continued to pursue his tortuous diplomacy. What he now wanted was some tangible advantage for Austria, such as a permanent Austrian occupation of the Principalities and an end to the war, without Austria actually having to fight at all. The French were more keen to secure the help of the Austrian army and to win a striking victory than to bring a war that had so far been inconclusive militarily, to a speedy end by diplomacy. Napoleon III was prepared to pay a price: the renunciation of the possibility of French intervention in Italian affairs. Napoleon III accordingly promised the Austrians his support for the *status quo* in Italy. The promise was not to prove worth much. Buol nevertheless persuaded a reluctant Francis Joseph to sign an alliance treaty with Britain and France (2 December 1854). Although the treaty was called an 'alliance' it meant even less. Austria had not agreed to join in the war against Russia but only to consult with its allies on what to do next if peace were not assured by the end of the year on the basis of the Four Points. Since the latter had already been accepted in principle by the Russians, and the Austrians did not mean to fight, the 'alliance' made little difference to the situation.

The French had taken the lead in all these diplomatic rounds at Vienna. Britain more realistically was looking for an ally to augment the much smaller than promised expeditionary army in the Crimea. Negotiations had been going on with Piedmont-Sardinia for some months. In January 1855 Victor Emmanuel, who wished to retrieve some battle honours after the disasters of 1849, agreed to join the Anglo-French Alliance. A Piedmontese expeditionary force of some 17,500 men landed in the Crimea in the spring, where they were paid for by the British and kept in the rear. They only once saw action in September and so, through no fault of theirs, contributed little to the fighting. Austria meanwhile tried to mobilize the German Confederation but was rebuffed by Prussia, represented at the German Diet in Frankfurt by Bismarck, a clear-sighted diplomat given to sarcasm and large cigars! Prussia in fact, despite her alliance with Austria and apparently anti-Russian stance, was busily sending essential war supplies to the Russians. Eventually in March 1855 a strange kind of preliminary peace conference opened in Vienna, presided over by Buol. The Russians had complied with three of the Four Points, what remained was to define the third – the revision of the Straits Convention in the interests of the balance of power in Europe. What Britain and France insisted on in the end was the 'neutralization of the Black Sea' – no Russian warships were to be permitted; nor any Turkish warships incidentally, although Turkey was ostensibly an ally. The Russians refused such a humiliating limitation to their sovereignty and broke off the conference in June 1855. Buol had come to the end of his resources. Austria's bluff was called. Instead of going to war on the Anglo-French side, the Austrian armies were demobilized. The decision for peace or war remained on the battlefield of the Crimea.

By the spring of 1855 some of the contestants had changed, but this did not at first bring peace any nearer. Nicholas I, disheartened by the lack of success of his armies and worn out by his constant labours, caught a chill and died from pneumonia on 2 March 1855. His successor, Alexander II, wished to continue the struggle but lacked Nicholas' fanatical zeal. In London, Aberdeen had fallen and Palmerston had taken office determined to pursue the war to victory. In the Crimea, General Pélissier replaced the indecisive Canrobert in command of the French army. Napoleon III, who was tiring of the war, though he was still waiting to win at least one battle, threatened to take command of the allied armies in person. The war was far from over as the Russian defenders of Sevastopol refused to accept defeat. There were times when, through disease and lack of organization, the allies might have been defeated. Instead the build-up of the allied armies after the winter had passed gave them equality and possibly superiority over their Russian opponents. The French army now numbered 120,000 men; unhappily the British volunteer army comprised only 32,000 men which was 40,000 short of the number Parliament had voted. Palmerston was desperate to raise more troops anywhere; the government paid for 5,600 mercenaries, the so-called British, German and Swiss Legions. More important were the 17,000 Piedmontese guarding the rear of the British force. Then there were 55,000 Turks commanded by Omar Pasha. In all the total available allied force in the Crimea in the Spring of 1855 amounted to about 225,000 men. Their main task was the capture of Sevastopol, defended by about the same number of Russians.

The tenacity of the defenders and the courage of the attackers makes the long siege and battle for Sevastopol an epic in military history. At the height of the battle, in one day's fighting for the great Malakhov fort, the allies lost 10,000 men and the Russians, 13,000. The heroism of the ordinary soldier on both sides, indifferently led by their generals, almost surpasses the imagination. On 8 September 1855 Malakhov was captured. The Russian commander ordered that Sevastopol should be blown up and evacuated. The fall of the city was celebrated in London and Paris. What was not realized at home was that the Russian commanders had, during the night, ferried their army and all but the most seriously wounded across Sevastopol Bay and had taken up previously prepared and strongly fortified positions on the northern slopes of the Bay.

The allied armies had won a great prestige victory, but Sevastopol was a useless rubble heap and the bay was dominated by Russian guns on the northern shore and so of no use to allied shipping. The Russian army had withdrawn in good order and remained a formidable force; more important, their new positions were too strong for the French and British troops to attempt to attack after their recent exertions. So the actual fighting in the Crimea just faded away after September 1855. It was a military stalemate for the next six months. Napoleon III had gained his victory. He was now anxious for peace. Alexander II too was more ready for peace. He felt no personal emnity for Napoleon III. His army in the Crimea was difficult to supply and to reinforce; another Russian army was fighting the Turks in the Caucasus; still another guarded the Baltic and finally a large Russian central reserve army faced the 200,000 strong Austrian army (when partially mobilized) which never came. The strain on Russia was very great and so Russia was ready for peace given the right opportunity. In Vienna the indefatigable Buol was plotting new ways of bringing the war to a close.

The Crimean War was unusual in its diplomatic aspects. Whilst the armies fought in the Crimea, the diplomats were continuously attempting to embroil or neutralize Austria depending on which side they were on. Austria tried to use her bargaining position to force the Russians and all the allies to accept a negotiated peace. Progress was agonizingly slow. In mid-November 1855 Buol and the French representative agreed on the peace terms to be presented to the Russians in the form of an Austrian ultimatum. Britain was not consulted beforehand. These terms were a vague and rather harsh interpretation of the Four Points already agreed upon in the summer of 1854 (p. 190). Russia would have to accept the complete neutralization of the Black Sea. A new condition, especially important to Austrian interests, was added to the original Four Points. So that Russia would be cut off from all access to the mouth of the Danube, she would be required to cede some Russian territory (southern Bessarabia) to the Principalities and to Turkey. But the Palmerston Cabinet was reluctant to settle for less than a peace that would not only guarantee Austrian interests in the Balkans but also British interests in central Asia. Britain would have liked to establish buffer states across Russia's path to India. But these were not objectives of any interest to Austria and France. Early in December 1855 Napoleon III secured Britain's grudging consent to the Austrian-French terms. The French war effort had remained overwhelmingly the largest in the alliance and that gave Napoleon III the influence he was now using in the interests of peace. The Austrians presented the terms in St Petersburg in the form of an 'ultimatum' on 28 December 1855. The ultimatum was the usual Austrian play with words; what the Austrians were really threatening was not war, but just a breach of diplomatic relations. Francis Joseph would not have given his consent to war; in any case Austria was in no condition to fight. Why then did the Russians agree to the peace terms?

It was not, as is so often thought, the threat of Austrian intervention in a military sense that the Russians really feared most at this stage. Austria had proved a paper tiger too long to retain much military credibility, though Russian resentment at Austria's behaviour, strong throughout the war, now reached a new climax. The Austrian 'ultimatum' and the proposed peace terms gave Tsar Alexander and his advisers the final jolt that made them realize that the question of peace or continuing the war had to be squarely faced. In St Petersburg the Imperial Council met in the Winter Palace on 1 and 15 January 1856 presided over by the tsar. Many arguments were put forward why Russia must seek peace. The most telling was the conviction that the war could not be won and was weakening and endangering the internal stability of the Russian Empire. The state councillors expressed their belief that the longer Russia fought, the harsher the terms of peace would be. Alexander II concurred and on 16 January 1856 accepted the terms of the Austrian ultimatum.

Meantime the Russian and allied armies continued to face each other in the Crimea and were doing their best to survive another winter. The provisions, equipment and hospitals of the British army had been improved out of all recognition since the previous year; but the much larger numbers of French troops now suffered terribly. Typhus broke out and the French medical services proved totally inadequate. During the first three months of 1856 admitted losses of French dead from typhus and cholera were 24,000 but in reality may have approached as high a figure as 40,000. An armistice was not concluded in the field until March 1856, and the last allied troops did not depart until July, long after the peace congress at Paris had completed its work.

The 'Congress' of Paris began its proceedings on 25 February 1856 with all the trappings of a great European event. It was the first important *Congress* since Vienna 1814–15. (Actually the Verona meeting in 1822 had been called a Congress, but since that date all the meetings of the representatives of the powers had been 'confer-

ences'.) There were some very important differences between the
Congress of Vienna and of Paris. At Vienna, in 1814 and 1815, the
great powers had redrawn the map of Europe. In 1856 France,
Britain and Austria had agreed beforehand to seek no territorial
annexations for themselves. To Napoleon III's regret there was to
be no redrawing of the map of Europe this time. In 1815 the allies
had sought to guarantee future stability by agreeing to co-operate in
peace as they had in war; although they did not represent the whole
of Europe, in the guise of the 'concert of Europe', they claimed to be
acting for the general good. In 1839–41, when dealing with the
problem of the Ottoman Empire, the 'concert of Europe' had then
been revived by the great powers. During the Crimean War it finally
broke down. There was another obvious difference between the
Congress of Vienna and Paris. At Vienna, Austria, Prussia, Britain
and Russia concluded an alliance to safeguard Europe from any new
French danger. At Paris, it was Russia that was excluded when
Austria, Britain and France concluded a secret alliance on 15 April
1856 to safeguard the new treaty settlement. In 1815 the Quadruple
Alliance intended to last another twenty years had an effective life of
about seven years before the four powers ceased to act in the spirit of
the alliance (though Russia, Prussia and Austria continued on their
own a few more years). The Three Power Alliance of 1856 on the
other hand did not even last one year; it never had any reality.

There was no 'concert' after 1856, not even one directed against
Russia. The years that followed the Congress of Paris saw the development of intense national rivalries. There were no stable alignments
between states as each sought to further its own national interests.
1856 to 1870 was an anarchic period in European international
affairs. Prussia and France co-operated for a time and began doing
so during the congress. Britain stood aside from playing a major role
in continental diplomacy for nearly twenty years. Austria and Russia
were rivals in Germany; France championed Piedmont and fought
Austria. In the Balkans the rivalry of Austria and Russia began to
take shape as the Congress of Paris ended and Russia felt deep
resentment for the faithless Habsburgs. So, despite all the talk at
Paris of preserving the 'balance of power', it neither existed nor did
the peace congress further such aims. Unlike Vienna the questions of
Europe were not settled at Paris; they were not even raised. To be
precise only one question was mentioned briefly and then only a
week after the peace treaty with Russia was signed, and that was
Italy. Lord Clarendon, the British foreign secretary, had hoped to do
something for Britain's Piedmontese ally, possibly an agreed
rearrangement of central Italy in Piedmont's favour, but all Cavour,
the Prime Minister of Piedmont, received was a nice speech from
Clarendon. Britain was not prepared to make an enemy of Austria,

opposed to changes in Italy, at the very time when Britain was on the point of signing the secret alliance with her and with France to guarantee the eastern settlement. Anyway none of the powers attending the congress, other than Piedmont, were ready for a European war for the sake of northern and central Italy. At Vienna in 1815, the four victorious powers had wanted to create a conservative stability in Europe for a generation and France of the Restoration had accepted the territorial settlement when reached. At Paris in 1856, Russia did not resign herself to the conditions imposed on her, France wished to redraw the map of Europe, Prussia to re-establish herself as a great power, and Austria nervously faced the future and the threat of renewed nationalism in her empire. Britain meantime had been served notice by Austria and France that in Asia she must meet the challenge of Russian expansion alone. So Britain left continental Europe alone but for one brief flurry in Italian affairs in 1860. There was, therefore, no meeting of minds at Paris in 1856, such as had occurred at Vienna in 1815.

In practice then the Congress of Paris was confined to the conclusion of peace terms with Russia and to imposing a European solution on the hapless Turks, who were treated more like a defeated enemy than a victorious ally. The price of western support was reform in the Ottoman Empire. The sultan acquiesced when he promulgated a new reform decree (18 February 1856). It forbade discrimination against any of the sultan's subjects on grounds of class, religion or race, the sultan undertook to protect the rights and privileges of all, confirmed religious freedom and an equitable system of taxation and much more besides on paper. The sultan's promises were incorporated into the proceedings of Paris (Article IX of the Treaty of Paris). For the tsar's right to protect the Orthodox Christians, based on the old treaty of Kutchuk-Kainardji, was substituted the general solicitude of the European powers but they expressly declared that this did not give them 'the right to interfere, either collectively or separately, in the relations of His Majesty the Sultan, with his subjects, nor in the internal administration of his Empire'. The well-being of the Christians had taken second place to considerations of international diplomacy.

The Russians had come to Paris not on the basis of 'unconditional surrender' but on the terms of the Austrian ultimatum earlier on agreed with the French and British governments. When it came to important details at the conference and after, Napoleon III sought to interpret these terms generously rather than harshly. He used his influence to limit the portion of Russian south Bessarabia to be ceded to the Principalities and to Turkey. On the other hand, British pressure secured the return to Turkey of the fortress of Kars, but was otherwise unsuccessful in checking Russia in Transcaucasia and central Asia. In the Balkans the Russians had already evacuated the Principalities, now they had to renounce their special rights in the Principalities as well; but this did not benefit Austria. France and Britain were not prepared to allow the Habsburgs to remain in occupation of the Principalities unconditionally as a reward for Austria's diplomatic assistance before the congress. Instead France and Britain declared that the Austrians could only stay in the Principalities if they were ready to give up Lombardy and Venetia. This suggestion the Austrians naturally refused to consider.

The single, most important, result of the Paris Congress was probably the growth of Balkan nationalism. It was due paradoxically to negative, rather than intentionally positive policies. By denying both Russia and Austria any extension of influence in the Balkans, conditions were brought about which permitted the creation of independent states from the decomposition of the Ottoman Empire in Europe. Whether the 'Balkanization' of this region which lasted until 1945 was a good thing for Europe is an open question, but it was bound to occur unless one or more great power took the place of the failing Ottoman Empire as suzerain power.

The fate of the people under Ottoman rule in the nineteenth century was not of prime concern to the 'great powers' except as in so far as it affected their own rivalries and interests. The one exception was Greece whose struggle for independence had fired the enthusiasm of Phil-Hellenes. Greece had declared independence in 1821 and was placed under the protection of Britain, France and Russia. The rest of the Balkans under Ottoman rule were not even regarded as part of Europe proper, but called the 'Near East'. The Ottoman sultans with some skill, a mixture of concession and brutality, managed to maintain their suzerainty over the Balkan nationalities for most of the century until 1878 and did not lose the last remnants until 1918. They exercised control by supporting the ruling nobles against the peasants, by military force, and by repressing emerging national cultures and their national churches. Religious authority for the Christians was exercised by the patriarch of the Greek Orthodox Church in Constantinople. But neither the 'great powers' nor the administrators of the Ottoman Empire in Constantinople, could prevent the penetration of western revolutionary ideas among Albanians, Croatians, Greeks, Rumanians and Bulgarians, setting Christians against Muslims, and challenging authoritarian rule.

The Serbians, with the exception of mountainous Montenegro, and the Bulgarians, had remained under Ottoman rule for three and a half centuries politically and their religion and culture was dominated by the Greek Orthodox Church. The Sultans and the Greek Orthodox Church sought to suppress Serbian and Bulgarian national consciousness. The Serbs had struggled against the Turks and won a measure of autonomy but Serbia's fate depended on the changing relations of the great powers especially Austria and Russia. The Treaty of Paris in 1856 placed Serbia under the collective guarantee of the powers and forbade Turkish military intervention without their consent. In Serbia the situation was complicated by the rivalry of the two leading dynasties Obrenović and Karadjordjević. The attempt to expel the Turks altogether in the 1860s failed. The Balkan League Prince Michael Obrenović organised from 1866 to 1868 with Montenegro, the Bulgarian Revolutionary Committee, Greece and Rumania fell apart with the assassination of Prince Michael. The young Milan Obrenović succeeded and much to the relief of Austria-Hungary, Serbian militancy quietened down until the outbreak of the rising against the Turks in Bosnia-Herzegovina in 1875 (pp. 345).

For Greece, the opportunity of fulfilling the *Megali Idea* ('Great Idea'), of uniting Greeks under Ottoman rule in Thessaly, Macedonia, Epirus, Crete and the Islands of the Aegean, seem to have come in the 1850s with the outbreak of the Crimean War. Greece and Russia were allies in their enmity to the Turks. The Greeks fermented unrest in Thessaly, Macedonia and Epirus. But Greek schemes soon foundered. Turkey's allies, Britain and France, intervened and landed troops in May 1854 occupying the Piraeus forcing the Greeks to remain neutral. The British and French only withdrew in 1857. In 1862 the Greeks deposed the unpopular king Otto I and chose a Danish prince, Christian, whose long reign as George I until his death in 1913 spans the history of modern Greece. The continuous thread linking Greek policies for more than a century remained the 'Great Idea' of unifying all the Greek people; complete *enosis* still remains to be achieved. Rarely could it be accomplished by peaceful negotiation. An exception was the cession of Corfu and the other Ioinian Islands by Britain to Greece in 1863. When in 1866 the Greeks in Crete rose in revolt against the Turks demanding *enosis*, Greek volunteers crossed over to Crete. Again it was the powers which restrained Greece from going to war and so Turkey was able to crush the rising in 1869 but made concessions granting autonomy under the pressure of the powers.

Bulgaria had been conquered by the Turks at the close of the fourteenth century, the nobles either fled or converted to Islam. For the peasant population the earlier oppressive rulers were replaced by others under Ottoman control. As rival armies, Turkish, Russian and Austrian, crossed its lands, the people suffered. In Bulgaria the spiritual and cultural domination of the Greek Patriarchate suppressed national consciousness. But the Bulgarian language had survived. Bulgarians from the late eighteenth century on were influenced by western ideas of national revival and social reform. In the 1860s underground organizations in Rumania with branches in Bulgaria were preparing for a national rising. In May 1876 the revolt broke out in the sanjak of Philippopolis and was suppressed with great cruelty, atrocities denounced by Gladstone as the 'Bulgarian massacres'.

The land that later became Rumania was divided into two principalities, Wallachia and Moldavia, which remained under Russian protection. Rumanian nationalist leaders drew their inspiration from France and in 1848 Ion Brătianu returned from Paris to head a short lived provisional government. The Rumanian national revolutionary movement/threatened both the Habsburgs whose Transylvannian Rumanian peasants demonstrated their discontent and the Russians. Joint Russian Turkish military intervention suppressed the national movement and Bratiănu was forced back into exile. The Russian and later Austrian occupation brought great hardship. Yet the mid-1850s proved to be the turning point in the Rumanian history of the two Principalities. The Crimean War led to the removal of the Russian protectorate which was replaced by a collective guarantee of their autonomous institutions by the powers signatories of the Treaty of Paris of 1856. They still remained divided under the suzerainty of the Turks. But the Turks could not militarily intervene without the consent of the powers. Rumanian desires for unity could not be denied for long. The same prince, Alexandra Cuza, was elected by the two assemblies of the Principalities thus accomplishing in all but name the union of Rumania. In 1866 Cuza was forced to abdicate and replaced by Prince Charles Anthony of Hohenzollern-Sigmaringen as hereditary monarch. A constitution on the restrictive model of the Belgian was introduced and Bratiănu became the dominant political leader. What marred Rumania's independence, affirmed by the Congress of Berlin in 1878, was the persecution of the Jews.

The Ottoman Empire had continued to decay despite periodic efforts to reform. The interventions of the 'great power' to control the turbulence were confused and ambiguous because of their suspicions of each other. They could neither agree to maintain the *status quo* nor on a plan of reorganizing a partitioned Ottoman Empire. Every time a crisis arose, piecemeal solutions had to be found. Nor would the powers wholeheartedly support nationalism in the Ottoman dominions for fear it would lead to the premature collapse of the empire and worse conflicts between them. Britain wished to protect the route to India and the Turks as guardians of the Straits. This placed Britain in opposition to Russia. Austria-Hungary after 1867 was torn between wishing to gain influence among the struggling Balkan nationality but was fearful of arousing irredentist desires since millions of Serbs, Croats and Rumanians were subjects of the Dual Monarchy. Russia was bitter over Austria's 'ingratitude' during the

Crimean War, supported Pan-Slavism and so was locked in rivalry with Austria-Hungary. The impact of the Crimean War marked a further stage in the evolution of the 'Eastern Question'. In London, Vienna, Paris and St Petersburg the one conclusion they could all agreed on was that the Crimean War had not settled the problems of the Balkans.

The part of the peace settlement that has attracted the greatest attention and which was looked upon as the most important achievement by the victors was the neutralization of the Black Sea. By this was meant that neither Turkey nor Russia, nor any other power, was to be permitted to maintain any but a few small token warships in the Black Sea, nor could any naval bases exist on its shores (Articles XI and XIII). This provision treated the Russians and the Turks equally, that is equally badly, and so seemed an equitable arrangement designed to preserve the *status quo* between the two Empires; but the facts of geography made this a very one-sided disarmament agreement. Neither the Russians nor the Turks had a navy worthy of the name left in the Black Sea at the end of the Crimean War. From now on the Russians could not even construct a navy or support its operations from a naval base in the Black Sea without breaking the peace treaty and serving long notice that they were doing so, since they could not hope to construct warships secretly. The Black Sea, moreover, was landlocked except by way of the Bosphorus, the Dardanelles and the Mediterranean, so no Russian warship could be brought into the Black Sea except past the vigilant British Mediterranean fleet. The British and French navies, though equally excluded from the Black Sea, could enter the Black Sea at will should Russia attack Turkey or break the treaty terms, since there was nothing to stop them. Britain and France could, therefore, dominate the Black Sea whenever they wished. The Black Sea clauses were a highly effective means of disarming Russia in the south, but the problem of punitive disarmament provisions is not whether they can in practice be enforced – they can, but whether the powers are ready to enforce them at the risk of war, and this they are not usually prepared to do. It is one thing to impose peace terms after a costly war with fierce determination, another to maintain the provisions after several years of peace. In 1870 the Gladstone administration was not prepared to fight Russia for the sake of upholding the Black Sea clauses. Instead Gladstone made the best of a bad situation and agreed to a revision of the 1856 treaty that was by no means altogether in Russia's favour.

The Crimean War marks a point of transition in the history of Europe. Russia henceforth gave up the notion of a general European

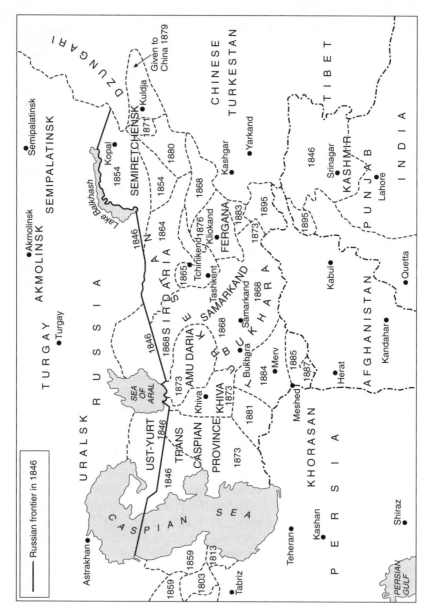

Map 3 The Expansion of Russia in Asia

mission, of preserving Europe from revolution, and of maintaining as far as possible the territorial settlement of Vienna. In 1856 'Europe' had inflicted a humiliating peace on Russia. Russia now turned her back on Europe, concentrated on a great expansion through central

Asia, and followed a national policy in general support of the Slavs
and co-religionists beyond the empire. Russia's bitterness against
Austria was extreme, but the effect of this breach of Austro-Russian
friendship on European history should not be exaggerated. Russia
did not attempt to take advantage of Austria's difficulties during
the decade of the 1860s. Furthermore, even had Russia remained
on terms of intimate friendship, it can scarcely be supposed that
Russia would have come to the aid of Austria in Italy or in Germany.
It is unlikely that Russia would have risked war in order to
maintain the Habsburg Empire beset by a combination of internal
and external threats; but when it seemed in Russia's best interests, as
during the renewed troubles in the Balkans in 1875, Russia was
soon enough prepared to work with Austria and not against her,
notwithstanding recent history. The impact of the Crimean War on
Russia nevertheless was important. Tsar Alexander gave priority to
internal reform and avoided risking another conflict with the European powers. To reverse the adverse conditions of the peace imposed
in 1856, moreover, assumed an importance in Russian eyes that
exceeded in importance all other European issues such as German
unification. Russia had never counted for so little in Europe in the
nineteenth century as during the decade and a half following
the Crimean War.

Austria gained little and neither foe nor friend respected Austria's
conduct during the war. The navigation of the Danube was freed
from Russian influence but instead of the Austrians replacing Russian influence on the mouth of the Danube, two international commissions were set up by the Treaty of Paris to guarantee free
navigation. The European Danube Commission (Austria, France,
Russia, Piedmont and Turkey), and the Danube River Commission,
represent the first, and also one of the most successful permanent
international organizations designed to ensure multi-national co-
operation for a common good. After Austria's evacuation of the
Principalities in 1857, they did not remain weak and were consolidated and assumed the national name of Rumania (1862); they
became virtually independent in the 1860s, a fact recognized by the
Treaty of Berlin (1878).

Prussia had been treated in a humiliating way at Paris and only
admitted to a part of the conference proceedings because she was a
signatory of the Straits Convention of 1841; but Prussia's real gain
was Europe's loss. All the talk about the 'concert of Europe' could
not decently cover the conflicting aims of the participants. This
international conflict created favourable conditions for Prussian
expansion in the 1860s.

Britain grumbled but signed the Treaty of Peace. Lord Salisbury
was later to say that in supporting the Turks instead of the Russians,

Britain 'had backed the wrong horse'. The Eastern question had not been solved but the next major international crisis there was at least postponed for twenty years, no negligible achievement from Britain's point of view. The respite given to the Turks was not utilized to make the Ottoman Empire safe from internal disintegration. The secret three-power alliance between Austria, Britain and France of 1856 guaranteeing the safety of the Ottoman Empire turned out to be a 'dead letter' from the start. Multi-national empires, like the Ottoman, could only be held together by force and Turkey's neighbours would not permit the sultan to exercise the force necessary to maintain his Empire in Europe.

The congress had made Paris the centre of European diplomacy. It recognized Napoleon III as a necessary pillar of any European settlement. That is one of the paradoxes of the peace conference for Napoleon III in reality wanted to reshape Europe. When, during the congress, he offered to support the Austrians in the Principalities on condition that they abandoned Habsburg territory – Lombardy and Venetia – in Italy, his initiative foreshadowed where the next European crisis would occur.

Part Three

Authoritarian Europe
Transformed

14

The Unification of Italy

Cavour returned from the Congress of Paris a bitterly disappointed man. He had gone to Paris to extend the power of Piedmont in northern and central Italy at the expense of the small duchies and of Austrian influence. He secured nothing. Piedmont gained no territory in return for her sacrifices in the Crimea. Though Piedmont had only played a small role in the fighting, nevertheless one in ten of the expeditionary force of over 17,000 never came home, victims of the scourge of disease during the winter of 1855. The international climate had not been favourable for Cavour's plans at Paris and all his intrigues and devious diplomacy, of which a Talleyrand would have been proud, could not overcome the realities of power politics.

British policy and French policy were diametrically opposed over the Italian question in 1856. Britain's main concern was to keep France out of Italy. Palmerston and his Foreign Secretary, Clarendon, would have liked Austria to depart from her Italian possessions in Lombardy and Venetia and thereby to leave Italy to the Italians, but the Austrians were determined to stay. Since the Austrians were not only recent allies, but also hopefully future partners in the task of maintaining the settlement in the East, Britain and France had not been willing to push them too hard. Nor was Napoleon III about to abandon French influence in Italy. His troops had remained in Rome after overthrowing the Roman republic in 1849 and he had no intention of withdrawing them now; British support for Piedmont and 'Italy' was limited to exhortation. The French, as has been seen, would not even go that far.

One thing had become clear at Paris. Just as there was an 'Eastern question', so there was an 'Italian question' whose development the European statesmen believed could vitally affect their national interests and the peace of Europe. What the great powers viewed as the 'Italian question', patriots in the geographical peninsula

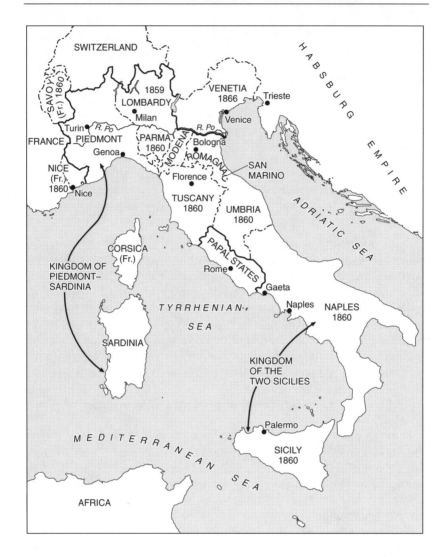

Map 4   The Unification of Italy

of Italy came to espouse as the 'Risorgimento', or to give it its literal English translation, 'resurgence'. Both the *Italian question* and the *Risorgimento* are intellectual abstractions; they have no agreed or precise meanings; indeed their definition by contemporaries gives us a clue to their thinking, rather than an explanation of actual events.

The 'Italian question', as has been seen, meant something different to the Austrians, the French and the British. They viewed it first from the point of view of their national interests and ambitions and only secondarily, if at all, from an 'Italian' standpoint, and what that meant in 1856 was still far from clear. It was in the traditional interests of both Austria and France to keep Italy relatively weak and divided. Britain's Italian policy on the other hand also conformed to the classical nineteenth-century mould of her continental diplomacy, that is to try to create independent barriers wherever rival great powers threatened to clash and to give these barrier states stability by encouraging good internal government and by providing international guarantees of non-intervention. None of the great powers at this stage thought in terms of 'Italian unification'. Clarendon arrived no nearer to that idea than wishing to see the future of Italy left to the decisions of reformed and enlightened Italian rulers. He wrote from Paris that the Italian question excited intense interest, but that everybody wished to maintain the peace. If only Britain and France could be brought to work together towards ending all foreign occupation of Italy, peacefully of course, then the Italian princes and people could be left to find their own solutions. Clarendon observed if all that happened 'then the Italian question would at once be settled'. In looking for a wholly peaceful solution of the Italian question, with both Austria and France behaving in a self-denying spirit, and Britain having to do no more than give a noble moral lead without losing anything thereby, Clarendon was indulging in large doses of wishful thinking.

Italy was to be unified only four years after the Congress of Paris, yet what is so remarkable is that unification was no part of the programme of any single Italian ruler before 1860. The idea of unity was identified with a revolutionary republican programme and so became embroiled with policies which were also directed against the sovereigns and social structure of the individual Italian states. In 1860 came the great change. In that year social and political struggles, a bewildering variety of civil conflicts, gave Garibaldi's guerrilla movement for unity the opportunity of victory in the south and became fused with the 'establishment' politics and nationalism of Piedmont. Behind the whole story lies a fascinating tangle of personal rivalries and secret diplomacy which historians have tried to unravel ever since.

The intellectual apostle of republican unity was Giuseppe Mazzini. A citizen of Genoa, and so a subject of the King of Piedmont, he was a bitter enemy of Victor Emmanuel and Cavour. Mazzini was condemned to death *in absentia* in Piedmont for his role in the unsuccessful attempt in 1833 to induce the Piedmontese army and navy to insurrection. The rising was intended as the spearhead of a revolutionary republican movement which would rid Italy of sovereigns and foreigners alike. Mazzini saved his life by living in France,

Switzerland and England but fourteen of his fellow conspirators were executed and many imprisoned. As a practical leader of insurrections, Mazzini was a failure; as the leading propagandist of Italian unity his influence on a section of Italian patriots and on his greatest disciple, Garibaldi, was enormous. Mazzini's ideas proved a live political force throughout the Italian peninsula from the 1850s onwards; his influence was greatly feared by the established conservative rulers. He addressed himself to the people not only of Italy but of Europe. He believed in nationalism as a panacea which would solve the problems of all peoples. The future of Europe should be entrusted to the peoples of Europe. His associations of 'Young Europe' and 'Young Italy' he saw as a 'Holy Alliance of Peoples'. Mazzini's programme threatened every throne of Europe. He was a true political revolutionary. He scarcely concerned himself with the ideas of socialism; his overriding aim was to achieve the foundation of an Italian republic as the realization of the popular will. Unity would be forged in revolution.

It is difficult to assess how far Mazzini's message was understood by ordinary people, the great majority of whom lacked the necessary basic education. He was probably never widely read and his claim that 50,000 people were associated with 'Young Italy' is very doubtful. As the most important member of the triumvirate of the ill-fated Roman republic of 1849, Mazzini gained more popular renown, but his greatest influence was indirect, through the education of revolutionary leaders who constantly stirred up discontents and gave it a nationalist direction. Garibaldi's Expedition of the Thousand finally exemplified what could be achieved by popular appeal and by an uprising in Sicily originally inspired by the Mazzinians.

When the Italian nation state was created in 1860 it confounded its makers. The people had played their part, but Mazzini's republic was not established. Victor Emmanuel's and Cavour's original aim had been more limited, to achieve Piedmontese predominance in northern and central Italy alone. Thus the unification of Italy had not come about according to anyone's preconceived plan. It was not the inevitable and crowning edifice of the *Risorgimento*. What occurred was the outcome of many rivalries, local discontent, and also just chance. The republicans, socialists and radicals were defeated by the conservative establishment of Piedmont; so was the Church; but political unification had not begun to solve the economic and social problems of Italy which remained regionally divided.

Many Italian historians of the *Risorgimento* have stressed the uprisings of 1848 as significant evidence of the growing national consciousness of Italian people. That an 'Italian' patriotism played a part is undeniable but, as the outstanding British historian of Italian unification, Denis Mack Smith, has convincingly shown, the degree

of national consciousness that existed has been greatly exaggerated.*
The events of 1848 and 1849 can be viewed quite differently. They
also show how deeply divided Italy was, between its old and new
rulers, between radicals and moderates, between peasants and the
urban population, between the rulers and people, each conscious of a
local nationalism. All these rivalries were both causes of 1848 and, at
the same time, explain the divisiveness of the various revolutionary
movements in Italy. Political and social protest sparked off risings of
local significance which, in the end, weakened the hold of all the
established rulers in Italy; but a wider sense of Italian patriotism
played only a minor role in 1848.

The first of the Italian risings broke out in Palermo, Sicily, on 12
January 1848, though a violent outbreak could have occurred elsewhere in the peninsula seething with social discontent and political
agitation. Rising expectations had made the hardships of the winter
of 1847–8 intolerable. With a tradition of lawlessness and conspiratorial societies, violence in Sicily was never far from the surface.
Sicilians, moreover, nurtured ideas of independence and freedom
from the hated Bourbon rulers of the Neapolitan mainland. The
authority of the royal army collapsed. The Neapolitan soldiers,
followed by revolutionary bands, pillaged the Sicilian villages before
they finally departed. King Ferdinand of Naples now granted constitutions to Sicily and Naples in a vain effort to halt the spreading
revolutionary tide. Reluctantly Italian rulers in the rest of the peninsula began granting constitutions in the face of liberal political
agitation. In mid-February 1848 the Grand Duke of Tuscany granted
a constitution, followed in March by Charles Albert of Piedmont and
by Pius IX in the Papal States.

The Italian states were unsettled even before news of the February
revolution in Paris and the March revolution in Vienna reached
northern Italy. When the large thrones of Europe were placed in
jeopardy, the rulers of the small ones felt even more insecure and
unsure as to the best way to save themselves. It was the unrest in
Milan from January to March 1848 that proved the catalyst, transforming the situation in northern and central Italy from one of
protest and demonstration to open war.

The resentment of the more militant Milanese at Austrian bureaucracy had been mounting since January. The news of the fall of
Metternich (on 13 March) sparked off a spontaneous rising when,
during the five 'glorious days' from 18 March to 22 March, the
Milanese forced Marshal Radetzky to withdraw his troops from the
city to the fortresses of the Quadrilateral. In Venice, meanwhile, a

---

* See especially, D. Mack Smith, *Victor Emmanuel, Cavour, and the Risorgimento*
(Oxford, 1971).

quite separate revolution led to the establishment of a republic; the Austrian commanding general there had pulled out his troops without a fight. Radetzky had gone over to the defensive in the face of the upheavals in the peninsula, but actually there was scarcely any cohesion among the disparate Italian movements.

The Milanese had appealed to Piedmont for help against Austria. Charles Albert hesitated. He was reluctant to throw in his lot with the revolutionary committee in control of Milan. Anyway the Austrians might very well recover and defeat the rebels in Milan. The Milanese left to themselves could, therefore, claim during the 'five glorious days' to have defeated the Austrians on their own. Finally on 24 March the Piedmontese ministers persuaded Charles Albert to act. He declared war on Austria and with his army crossed into Lombardy.

The Italian war of liberation seemed to have really begun. A hopeful Mazzini arrived in Milan. The new liberal ministers of King Ferdinand of Naples sent soldiers north to Lombardy. The Duke of Tuscany declared himself for Italy and even troops from the Papal States joined in the war to aid the Lombards. The alliance of 'Italians', however, was more apparent than real. Charles Albert remained suspicious of irregular soldiers fighting in Lombardy. He was more concerned to annexe Austrian Lombardy-Venetia, and the independent Duchies of Modena and Parma than to pursue the war against Austria on behalf of 'Italy'.

The first ruler actually to defect from the 'Italian' movement was the Pope, who had once appeared to be in the vanguard. On 29 April 1848 Pius IX repudiated the role of those of his troops who had joined in the struggle against the Austrians. Faced with the contradictory responsibilities of being the head of the universal Catholic Church and an Italian sovereign, it was the former which prevailed. As Pope he could not support war, or even revolution, and so he called on the Italian people 'to abide in close attachment to their respective sovereigns'. On the propaganda of the Mazzinians, the Pope poured bitter scorn rejecting 'the treacherous advice...of those who would have the Roman Pontiff to be the head and to preside over the formation of some sort of novel republic of the whole Italian people'.* It was the end of the myth of the patriot Pope. After 1848 the Church became identified as the enemy of liberal reform and papal sovereignty was regarded as a major stumbling-block in the way of political unification. The Pope was followed by the King of Naples. As soon as Ferdinand had regained power he withdrew his troops from Lombardy. The reconquest of Sicily was more important to him than the fate of northern Italy.

* D. Mack Smith, *The Making of Italy 1796–1870* (London, 1968) pp. 151–2.

Meantime Charles Albert was trying to defeat both republicans and Austrians. His price for helping the Lombards and Venetians was their acceptance of Piedmontese rule. Their consent did not help them. Charles Albert's army was incompetently led and Radetzky defeated the Piedmontese at Custozza on 24 July. Charles Albert fell back on Milan and after a token defence the king withdrew his disorganized forces and concluded an armistice with the Austrians early in August 1848. By its terms Piedmont undertook to give up providing military assistance to the Lombards and naval assistance to Venice. It was ironic that both Lombardy and Venetia, 'fused' so recently with Piedmont at Charles Albert's own insistence, were now abandoned by the king.

Peace did not last many months in Italy. Charles Albert was determined to avenge the humiliation of his defeat. In March 1849 he renewed the war by attacking the Austrian army. Radetzky easily defeated the Piedmontese again only a few days later at the Battle of Novara on 23 March 1849. The Austrians now inflicted some exemplary punishments on the disaffected Lombards. In Milan fifteen men and two women were publicly flogged and General Haynau, of later Hungarian ill-fame, stood out for his brutal conduct. Homes were burned, fines exacted, property confiscated and some 900 people were executed.

During the spring of 1849 the Austrians now felt themselves strong enough to suppress Italian nationalism and radicalism in central Italy as well as in the north. They moved into Tuscany, Modena, Lucca and the Papal States in April and May 1849. The cities offered resistance but the peasantry remained apathetic. Pisa, Lucca, Leghorn, Bologna and Florence all fell to the advancing Austrians. Before the Austrian army, however, still lay the formidable city of Rome.

Rome played a particularly important role in the history of the *Risorgimento* attracting to its defence in 1849 some Italians from all over the peninsula and the two most famous heroes of the *Risorgimento*, Mazzini and Garibaldi. The third of the trinity of *Risorgimento* heroes, Pope Pius IX, had fallen from grace since his refusal to join the war against Austria. He had steadily lost control of his dominions after the heady days of 1846. Appalling economic conditions in the Papal States produced continuous unrest. Furthermore, during the spring and summer of 1848 the Pope's refusal to countenance a war against Austria for Italy caused great resentment in Rome. The climax was reached when, in mid-November 1848, Count Rossi, the most prominent of the Pope's new liberal ministers and an opponent of war with Austria, was murdered by a mob. Rome passed into the hands of the revolutionaries and the Pope fled to Neapolitan territory. A few months later, in February 1849, the Pontiff's rule in the Papal States was declared at an end in Rome. After democratic elections the Roman Republic was established, though support for the Republic was largely confined to Rome itself, Bologna, and the larger towns. Meantime, Venice too was maintaining its independence. The Venetians were blockaded by the Austrians who, however, during the winter of 1848–9 made no move to attack the city. Yet between the Roman and Venetian Republics there was no attempt to co-ordinate moves against the Austrians. Perhaps no realistic military co-operation was possible.

Whilst the Roman Republic was waiting for the inevitable onslaught of the counter-revolution, it passed during its brief period of existence some admirable social and economic reforms. This was even before Mazzini reached the city. He had been appointed by the Roman Assembly to act as one of the Triumvirs to whom leadership was collectively entrusted. Mazzini arrived in Rome in March 1849. He took up residence in a small room in the Pope's palace. He was accessible to all and continued the policy of social reform. It was a brief moment of glory for the most famous 'Italian' revolutionary. So far his stay in the peninsula had been uneventful. He had first come to Milan, but until the moment of defeat the Milanese preferred the King of Piedmont and the troops he could bring. After the fall of Milan, Mazzini moved to Florence. Nowhere had his ideas prevailed or succeeded. Now he had come to Rome in desperate times; the revolutions had practically spent themselves in the rest of the peninsula.

The Utopian social republic could not survive for long in the face of foreign intervention. To the defence of Rome, besides the many friends of Mazzini, there also came Garibaldi, the greatest of the nineteenth-century guerrilla leaders. Garibaldi had been converted to the Mazzinian dream of creating the Italian nation in 1833 when he was a young merchant seaman. He had unsuccessfully conspired in Piedmont and had gone to fight for liberty in Uruguay after being condemned to death in Piedmont. His exploits as a guerrilla leader at the head of his band of Red Shirts, together with his Brazilian companion, Anita, who loved him passionately and shared all his arduous campaigns, had ensured his fame long before he had returned from South America to Italy in June 1848 to offer his services to Charles Albert. He was welcomed as a hero in Nice, but Charles Albert underestimated the importance of Garibaldi and his small band of 169 followers. Not surprisingly the king offered no place in the Piedmontese regular army to the one-time revolutionary and follower of Mazzini, but, in fact, Garibaldi's relations with Mazzini had become strained. For Mazzini the people's republic and Italian unity were inseparable. Garibaldi was prepared to follow any path, provided it led to Italian unity, and so he was ready to abandon republicanism. If Charles Albert would defeat the Austrians and lead Italy to unity then he would be a royalist. 'The great, and only, question at the moment is the expulsion of the foreigner and the war of independence,' he told a meeting of 'Young Italy', 'I was a Republican; but when I discovered that Charles Albert had made himself the champion of Italy, I swore to obey him and faithfully to follow his banner...Charles Albert is our leader, our sym-bol...There is no salvation apart from him.'* Garibaldi now regarded Mazzini as an impractical idealist. Mazzini, for his part, believed Garibaldi had been duped by the ambitions of the Piedmon-tese royal house. Garibaldi's fanatical attachment to the sacred cause of Italian unity alone can explain his readiness first loyally to serve Charles Albert, despite the king's lack of enthusiasm, and later 'treachery', and then to serve with equal loyalty, and without thought of personal reward, his son and successor, Victor Emmanuel II.

Garibaldi had reached Rome in February 1849 a month before Mazzini, though he did not bring in his tough legionaries until the end of April. Mazzini and Garibaldi collaborated closely. They were both determined to defend the Roman Republic and, if they lost to foreign invaders, to do so gloriously. The Pope in the meantime appealed to the Catholic powers of Europe to restore to him his temporal dominions. By mid-May 1849 the Spaniards, in response to the Papal appeal, had landed a small force at the mouth of the Tiber. The Austrians had occupied Tuscany and the northern region of the Roman Republic, including Bologna. The King of Naples was threatening Rome from a third direction and had occupied the south-ern region of the Republic. The decisive campaign against the Roman Republic, however, was conducted, not by a European monarch, but by the army of another republic, the French. The old Austro-French rivalry in Italy was making itself felt. Louis Napoleon, recently elected president, knew there was no time to be lost if Austria were to be forestalled. The prince-president wanted the credit at home, both for restoring the Pope, thereby earning the approval of the church, and for 'protecting' the Republic by arranging for a liberal compromise between the citizens of Rome and Pius IX. The French Assembly supported Louis Napoleon's plan of sending an expedi-tionary force to Rome; and so, on 24 April 1849, with General Nicholas Oudinot in command, 10,000 French troops disembarked at Civita Vecchia not far from Rome. In the countryside Oudinot was well received and he expected to be welcomed by the Romans as a protector anticipating the advancing Austrian, Spanish and Neapoli-tan forces; but instead of welcoming the French, Mazzini and

* J. Ridley, *Garibaldi* (London, 1974) p. 238.

Garibaldi organized the defence of the city. When the French were getting ready to enter the gates of Rome in triumph, they found themselves, to their surprise, fired on. Oudinot realized he could not hope to take the city by storm since Garibaldi held all the vantage-points. He therefore played for time. After negotiations lasting a month, a truce between the French and the Romans was concluded, but all the time these talks were going on, Oudinot's forces were being heavily reinforced. The new Napoleon could not accept a military set-back at the start of his career. Garibaldi also made good use of the breathing space by turning against and defeating the Neapolitan invaders. Garibaldi was back in Rome when on 1 June 1849 Oudinot ended the armistice. On 2 June the French began an attack on the fortified outposts of the city. Oudinot now had at his disposal a well-equipped army of 30,000 men. The Roman citizens' army and Garibaldi's men fought with extraordinary heroism, though Garibaldi's tactical skill did not match their courage. By the end of June the Roman National Assembly accepted that surrender was inevitable and that to continue the struggle would lead to needless loss of life. They gave up the city to Oudinot on 3 July 1849.

The Cardinals now speedily returned to put an end to the Republic. A far more reactionary government than before 1848 was set up in the Papal States. The French stood by helplessly. Only when all signs of liberal reform had been obliterated did the Pope, in April 1850, return to Rome. Mazzini, however, was able to leave Rome undisturbed. He managed to reach Marseilles and from there travelled to England, where he stayed as one of the distinguished band of exiles of the 1850s. Garibaldi also left Rome intending to fight on for Italy. He rallied some 4,700 of his followers and departed the day before the French came in. His plan was to gather an army in central Italy, and if that should fail, to make his way to Venice, the last 'free' Italian republic. Garibaldi was surrounded on all sides by four armies now numbering some 86,000 men. Spanish, Neapolitan and French troops were sent to pursue him. The Austrians were looking for him in the north. With a dwindling band of followers the harassed Garibaldi marched to the Adriatic. His efforts to reach safety is one of the epic tales of the *Risorgimento*. Neither Garibaldi nor his followers reached Venice. They dispersed. Some were shot; others captured and released. Their fate was arbitrary. Garibaldi managed to reach the territory of Piedmont but it was the most harrowing escape of his life. He was with his Anita, who was mortally ill. They found a farmer to hide them and Anita died. Heart-broken, Garibaldi had to make his escape even before her hasty burial. Once in Piedmont Garibaldi was briefly imprisoned and then the embarrassed royal authorities asked the most famous 'Italian' to leave the country. Garibaldi set sail in September 1849 and eventually in July 1850 he reached New York. His career seemed over, yet his greatest days were still to come.

The last embers of the Italian revolutions were extinguished when the Austrians occupied Venice in August 1849. Months of bombardment as well as the ravages of disease and famine had broken the resistance of the Venetians who had been resolutely led by Daniele Manin. When it was all over there seemed to be little to show for all the revolutionary efforts throughout the peninsula. The Austrians were more firmly in control of northern and central Italy than before. The Piedmontese army had proved no match against the Austrian. The once liberal Pope had established a reactionary régime and was protected by another foreign army, the French. In the south, Ferdinand re-established his authority on the mainland and in Sicily, and so resumed his rule of the curiously-named 'Kingdom of the Two Sicilies'. Throughout Italy, local causes, local grievances and rivalries had generally proved more important than national issues. The peasantry had shown little enthusiasm for the revolutionaries. Everywhere 'moderates' and 'socialists' were in conflict and Mazzinian republicans confronted the supporters of the existing rulers. The defence of property, or the lack of it, was a more vital question for most people than idealism and Italian patriotism. In any case, a sense of patriotism was felt more usually for a man's village, town or region rather than for any concept of 'Italy'. As elsewhere in Europe, it was difficult to imagine in the 1850s, that during 1848–9 the Italian States had been in turmoil and that for a short time it had seemed possible that the Austrians might be thrown out or that Charles Albert had really believed what he was saying when he declared *Italia farà da se*, Italy will manage by herself.

After his defeat at Novara, Charles Albert was a broken man. He gave up his throne and died in exile in Portugal. His son, who became Victor Emmanuel II, made peace with the victors; but that the young king strongly defended constitutional government and that he forced Marshal Radetzky to moderate harsh Austrian armistice terms is one of the myths of *Risorgimento* historians. In fact the Austrians treated Piedmont and its new king leniently and wished to strengthen him against the radicals he faced in his parliament at home. They also realized that harsh peace terms would only encourage Piedmont to seek the help of France. Actually Victor Emmanuel was quite capable of standing up to the radicals without Austrian support. When Piedmont's principal port, Genoa, refused to accept the peace terms, Victor Emmanuel's prime minister, a Piedmontese general, bombarded the town into submission. Victor Emmanuel, to begin with, had scant respect for the Piedmontese constitution, the famous *Statuto* which he had been forced to grant in the spring of

1848, yet the constitution survived the whole débâcle. The House of Savoy was no longer held in sufficient popular esteem to enable the king to return to absolutist rule.

Victor Emmanuel was a likeable, approachable and physically courageous man; but he was also lazy when it came to office work. He lived prodigiously, hunting game and mistresses. In manner coarse, he could yet charm diverse men, even Queen Victoria. There was a kind of rough joviality and honesty about him that Garibaldi admired. Though not exactly the gentleman soldier-hero of *Risorgimento* legend, Victor Emmanuel was no simple fool either. He was shrewd and politically skilful, reassuring the Austrians of his hatred of the liberals and radicals, working with two outstanding conservative politicians and aristocrats, first Massimo Azeglio until 1852 and then Cavour, whilst simultaneously never losing the loyalty of the wild and romantic Garibaldi. Victor Emmanuel wished to strengthen royal power, to speed the recovery of Piedmont and to build up his army so that Piedmont could fight the Austrians again, this time with real prospects of victory.

As Piedmont entered the decade of the 1850s, the *Statuto* survived intact though the Piedmontese constitution did not create a parliamentary form of government on the British model. The Piedmontese monarchy retained considerable power, but just as the King of Prussia was to discover in the 1860s, an expansive national policy precluded a return to absolutism. Victor Emmanuel, moreover, recognized that the intelligence and capacity for government, first of Azeglio and then of Cavour, were indispensable to the recovery of Piedmont.

Azeglio set the policy of Piedmont on a moderate conservative path, but the prime minister was not dependent on majority parliamentary support. This was clearly shown in 1849. The radicals who were then in a majority had condemned the peace Victor Emmanuel had concluded with the Austrians as unconstitutional. Parliament was dissolved but new elections in July 1849 returned a radical majority again still implacably opposed to peace with Austria. Victor Emmanuel and Azeglio, regardless of parliament, concluded the Peace Treaty of Milan with the Austrians in August 1849, whilst once more dissolving parliament. The autumn elections after much royal and ministerial intervention finally secured a majority in the chamber for the government and king. The danger of a royal *coup d'état* had been averted and constitutional, though not yet parliamentary, government had been preserved. That the *Statuto* remained intact was Azeglio's major contribution to the Italian national cause for it made Piedmont an acceptable leader of Italy later on.

During the period of Azeglio's premiership, the most important legislative achievement was the abolition of the extensive privileges the Church had enjoyed in Piedmont. In November 1852, Cavour, the most important minister in Azeglio's administration, replaced his chief by rather a dubious manœuvre. He assured for himself a majority in parliament by forging a political alliance between a moderate group of left/centre deputies and the moderate conservatives, his own supporters. This deal became known as the *connubio*, literally 'marriage', between groups of the centre which tended thereafter to dominate Italian parliamentary life. The Italian practice of parliamentary government usually allowed the same group of ministers to retain power for long periods, basing their support on shifting political alignments between party groups. By way of contrast in Britain, after the party confusion of the 1850s, a two-party system of government was to emerge and predominate. The means by which Cavour had achieved power were significant also for the importance of parliament was enhanced. Under Cavour's expert guidance parliamentary procedures became accepted and by the time of Cavour's death in 1861 constitutional government had developed into a form of parliamentary government.

Cavour's political realism made the unification of Italy possible, but unification did not come about according to any carefully prepared plan. Indeed, before 1860 Cavour never even conceived of the possibility of Italy as a unitary political state. What Cavour meant by 'Italian' independence, was independence from the foreign occupation and the influence of Austria. He laboured for a free Italy of independent states with an enlarged progressive Piedmont the most powerful among them. It can be said with equal justice of Cavour's policy, as a decade later of Bismarck's, that it showed him as a successful exponent of *Realpolitik*. Cavour's policy was based on the notion that means do justify ends, that to gain national objectives whatever price is necessary has to be paid without false sentimentality; he believed that advantage had to be taken of whatever opportunities arise often by chance and unforeseen. Whilst pursuing broad overall objectives, neither Cavour nor Bismarck highly prized consistency of policy for its own sake. There was no room for too fine a conscience or too acute a sense of moral scruple in their behaviour. Behind a genial unprepossessing exterior, Cavour possessed the drive, ambition and ruthlessness to seek to control all important decisions as the king's first minister and to limit as far as possible royal independence. He utilized parliament to check royal authority and royal authority, when necessary, to check parliament. Cavour was a sincere believer in parliamentary institutions but divorced these from the ideas of allowing parliament predominance. He wished to keep the franchise narrow and thus confine voting to only the wealthiest citizens. He hated Mazzini for his democratic and revolutionary programme. Cavour believed that the mass of the people needed to accept the decisions of their enlightened leaders. No wonder that one of his heroes was Oliver Cromwell. Certainly he would never have approved of the later Disraeli or Gladstone.

Cavour through the circumstances of his times entered politics only at the age of forty. Yet before his death thirteen years later he had served as prime minister for more than eight of them and gained European stature. Mazzini and Garibaldi's work for Italy extended over three decades; short-lived triumphs were followed by disasters until 1860. Cavour's influence covered a short period of time and he was brilliantly successful. His background favoured his rise in Piedmont. He was born into a well-known and wealthy aristocratic family. After a disastrous spell in a military school and a short period of service with the army, he prepared himself by studying practical reforms abroad in France and in Britain. In Piedmont there were no openings for a conservative reforming politician who wished to transform the absolutism of the Piedmontese monarch into a more limited constitutional monarchy such as existed in Guizot's France during the reign of Louis Philippe. In contemporary Piedmont there were no openings in politics for able men during the early years of Charles Albert's reign for there was no political life. Merely to carry out the king's policies did not suit Cavour's strong-willed personality or political beliefs. He stood aside from revolutionary conspiratorial politics and he devoted much of his energy to introducing agricultural improvements on the extensive family estates which he administered. But he also kept up his interests in the wider world beyond provincial Piedmont by studying the political and social aspects of the modern state.

Cavour's vitality could only begin to find a political outlet when in 1847 Charles Albert granted freedom of the press. His active interests widened during the stirring revolutionary months of the following year. He became the editor of a new newspaper *Il Risorgimento* which preached the message that the Italian rulers should co-operate to throw out the foreigner from the Italian peninsula. The *Statuto* Charles Albert had granted in the spring of 1848 enabled Cavour to stand for parliament and at the second try he was elected as a conservative deputy for Turin. He certainly backed Charles Albert's policy of attacking Austria in 1848, but was not associated with Piedmont's defeat for he was not in favour of the renewal of the war in the spring of 1849. He gained office in Azeglio's government in October 1850. He held the post of Minister of the Marine, Agriculture, Commerce and a little later Finance as well, so that he had soon emerged as the most important member of the administration. To gain power he intrigued with the parliamentary opposition against Azeglio. After relations with Azeglio had become impossible he left the government and the country for a few months. But he was recalled and in November 1852 he replaced Azeglio as prime minister. He was now able to put into practice the political beliefs he had defined for himself in 1835 when he wrote, 'the more I observe the course of events and the behaviour of men, the more I am persuaded that the *juste-milieu* is the only policy right in the circumstances, capable of saving society from the two rocks which threaten to break it – anarchy and despotism'.* He was not opposed to change, but change would have to be justified by practical needs. Though emotional in defence of his own conservative principles, he distrusted emotions in others and what he regarded as the destructive passion of party conflict. In seeking now in the 1850s to avoid such a development of party conflict by arranging for his support a central coalition of parliamentary groups he was of course misreading contemporary British parliamentary developments which he professed so much to admire.

Cavour reserved his especial hatred and contempt for republican revolutionaries, the followers of Mazzini, whose 'shameful, hateful prejudices' he believed would have to be defeated at all costs if Piedmont and Italy were to move forward to a better future. On this point he was even prepared to make common cause with the Austrians. He was determined to discredit Mazzini's insurrectionary efforts. In 1853 when Mazzini organized a rising in Milan, the Piedmontese authorities arrested his followers in Piedmont and perhaps even gave the Austrian authorities advance warning. Much to Cavour's embarrassment the Austrians publicly expressed their appreciation of Piedmontese help. This was essentially a good deed Cavour wished to perform in secret.

Compared with the rest of western Europe, Piedmont's economic development was slow, but in contrast to the other Italian states, Piedmont under Cavour's premiership took the lead, outpacing development even in Austrian Lombardy. Piedmont was overwhelmingly agricultural. The 'industrial revolution' had not got very far anywhere in the Italian peninsula. In the 1850s it was pretty well limited, in northern Italy, to Piedmont and Lombardy. Here some factories had been built where industrial processes turned raw silk into yarn ready for weaving. The silk yarn was then exported abroad. Only the smallest beginnings of a metal industry in Genoa, Milan and Turin based on the use of iron and steel had emerged before 1860. Cavour's policy of free trade and public finance certainly encouraged the growth of the Piedmontese economy but progress was slow even in railway development, which benefited most directly from government assistance. By 1860, Piedmont possessed 819 kilometres of railway line, Lombardy 522 kilometres and the whole of the rest of the Italian peninsula put together only 451 kilometres. For all

* H. Hearder, 'Cavour' (Historical Association, 1972) p. 12.

Cavour's efforts in finance and commerce it is important therefore not to exaggerate the economic progress Piedmont achieved in the 1850s.

To make Piedmont more powerful Cavour spent money to build up the navy and the army, but he realized that without foreign help, Piedmont's armed forces would stand no chance in any renewed war with Austria. Nor did he think that a popular Italian movement would be decisive in war. Such a movement, however, could be useful to Cavour in manipulating Italian opinion in northern and central Italy to create conditions favourable for his aggressive diplomacy. So Cavour seems to have given secret encouragement to a group of patriots of the left, prominent among them Manin, Giorgio Pallavicino and Guiseppe La Farina, who organized the National Society in 1857. The National Society propagated the idea that only Piedmont and its monarch could provide the necessary leadership and strength to defeat the Austrians. Republicanism and Mazzini's programme of revolution should therefore be renounced. Garibaldi was the most important leader to co-operate with the National Society and so a tenuous link was formed between him and Cavour.

Cavour thus had no illusions about Piedmont's strength. Austria would not be driven out of Lombardy and Venetia without French help. Nor would this result be achieved by diplomacy. At Paris in 1856 Cavour had learnt that Britain was averse to any European war, whereas Napoleon III, though cautious and vacillating, wished to undo the settlement of 1815. Cavour had to wait until the time was ripe for Napoleon III 'to do something for Italy'. What Napoleon III meant by this phrase was rather vague; he certainly did not intend to create a unified Italian state. Indeed he was consistent in opposing both the republicanism of Mazzini and Garibaldi's obsessions with Italian unity.

Orsini's assassination attempt in January 1858 on the emperor and empress on their way to the opera (p. 151) seems to have been the sign of destiny Napoleon III had been waiting for to pursue a more active Italian policy designed to reconstitute Italy under French patronage along the lines first carried through by his uncle. Secretly and conspiratorially Napoleon III and Cavour met at the little French watering spa of Plombières in July 1858. Here they plotted a war against Austria. From the letter Cavour sent to Victor Emmanuel, a detailed account of their discussions has survived.

Cavour reported, 'As soon as I entered the Emperor's study, he raised the question which was the purpose of my journey. He began by saying that he had decided to support Piedmont with all his power in a war against Austria, provided that the war was undertaken for a non-revolutionary end which could be justified in the eyes of diplomatic circles – and still more in the eyes of French and European public opinion.' Cavour and Napoleon III then discussed the various pretexts that might be used to goad the Austrians into war and to put them in the wrong. It was all pure cynical *Realpolitik* and in the end it worked. In that sense there was a rough kind of justice in the fact that twelve years later the emperor himself fell victim to a *Realpolitiker* just as unscrupulous but of greater skill. There is no need to consider in detail how the two finally hit on an insurrection in the territory ruled by the reactionary Duke of Modena as furnishing the best excuse. Cavour admitted that after considering each Italian state in turn to seek 'grounds for war it was very hard to find any'.

Cavour and the Emperor then considered the redistribution of territory in Italy. Napoleon III thought that Ferdinand of Naples and the Pope presented difficulties. Cavour replied that it would be easy to keep the Pope in possession of Rome by means of a French garrison whilst letting the provinces of the Romagna revolt. He added that there was no need to worry about the King of Naples; his subjects could get rid of him if they wished and Napoleon III rose to the bait saying that he would like to see Murat's son Lucien on the Neapolitan throne. And so the two 'settled the fate of Italy'. Subject to modification they agreed that the 'valley of the Po, the Romagna, and the Legations would form a Kingdom of Upper Italy under the House of Savoy'. Thus Piedmont was offered Lombardy, Venetia and part of the Papal States. 'Rome and its immediate surroundings would be left to the Pope. The rest of the Papal States, together with Tuscany, would form a kingdom of central Italy. The Neapolitan frontier would be left unchanged. These four Italian states would form a confederation on the pattern of the German *Bund*, the presidency of which would be given to the Pope to console him for losing the best part of his estates.'* Of course in the altered balance of power in Italy under such a scheme there was no doubt that Piedmont would predominate. But it is important to note that neither Cavour nor Napoleon III thought in terms of setting up a unitary Italian state. Cavour's aims were more limited: to enlarge Piedmont and to drive out the Austrians. Napoleon III then asked what France would get and suggested that Piedmont should cede Savoy and Nice. Cavour agreed to Savoy on the principle of nationality and added this same principle made the cession of Nice difficult. Napoleon III agreed to leave this, for him, 'secondary question' to later discussion. The final price Napoleon III exacted was the marriage between Victor Emmanuel's young innocent daughter to his dissolute cousin, the Prince Napoleon. Cavour and Napoleon III also examined the military aspects of how the war might be won. The emperor believed

* D. Mack Smith, *The Making of Italy*, pp. 238–47.

a considerable effort would be necessary before the Austrians could be brought to concede defeat and to give up their Italian territories. He thought an army of 300,000 men necessary. Cavour could only promise 100,000 Italian front line troops. From the start therefore Napoleon III and Cavour both accepted that the burden of fighting would fall more heavily on the French than on France's ally just as it had done in the Crimea.

It has been worth considering in some detail what had passed at Plombières, because the understanding then reached provided the guidelines which Cavour followed in his Italian policy until 1860. The Plombières understanding was formalized in a secret Franco-Italian treaty in January 1859 and Victor Emmanuel's daughter was married to Joseph, the Prince Charles Napoleon. The French-Piedmontese treaty was ante-dated to December, however, so that the delivery of Victor Emmanuel's daughter to Prince Napoleon's marriage bed should not appear to have been part of a general diplomatic and territorial bargain! The secret treaty added Nice to Savoy as France's gains and dropped the idea of an Italian federation headed by the Pope.

Despite the French alliance Cavour's task remained one of extreme difficulty. Napoleon III constantly vacillated. A popular appeal for liberation in the Italian states was a prerequisite for justifying Piedmontese and French intervention. Yet anything of a Mazzinian-style revolutionary movement was anathema to Napoleon III and to Cavour. Cavour sought some support from the left and from Garibaldi, yet he wished to curb their uncompromising views on Italian unity which ignored the European diplomatic realities. Success depended, Cavour concluded, on not alienating Napoleon III whose conditions of assistance had been clearly spelt out at Plombières.

Garibaldi secretly visited Turin at the end of February 1859 at Cavour's invitation. Cavour also brought about a meeting of Garibaldi and Victor Emmanuel. Garibaldi was told about the plans for war in the spring and offered to train and enrol volunteers. Garibaldi now abandoned the Mazzinians and agreed to obey the king. This alliance between the king and Garibaldi was to prove of momentous importance in 1860. But the plan that a war should begin by Garibaldi leading a guerrilla force into Modena did not work out and Cavour thought all was lost when the European powers intervened to preserve the peace. The Russians in March 1859 put forward the idea of a European Congress to settle the affairs of Italy. In April the British called on Piedmont to disarm in return for admission to the proposed congress. Worst of all, Napoleon III was inclined to give way and insisted that Cavour should accept disarmament; but the Austrians now wished to demonstrate that Piedmont had given way to Austria in Italy and not to the European powers which were threatening to treat 'Italy', and so Austria's role there, as a European question. The Habsburgs had no intention of being equated with the Turks. Cavour saw his chance and rejected the ultimatum. The Austrians were quite prepared to fight against the ideas of nationality, but the efficiency of the Habsburg army did not match the resolutions of the emperor. Austria declared war on 29 April 1859 and the Austrians advanced rapidly into Piedmont. On 3 May Napoleon III announced that he was coming to Piedmont's aid and declared war on Austria.

The outcome of the war of 1859 was important, not only for Italy but for Europe. Though unified, Italy counted for little more in the military balance of Europe after 1860 than Piedmont had done before; the war of 1859 marked the victory of nationalism over great power tutelage. The disintegration of the 'Concert of Europe' was manifestly gathering pace. This was also the first war in which the new railways played a crucial role in carrying troops to the front. The French emerged with the battle honours and Napoleon III's army confirmed France's reputation as the first military nation of Europe. But appearances were rather misleading. Superiority is a matter of comparison. The French war machine of 1859 was not an example of splendid organization, quite the contrary. The speed with which troops could be assembled and carried to battle in the railway age required careful planning and attention to detail well before war begins. In this respect Napoleon III failed lamentably. The French army arrived quickly enough in Lombardy, but they did so in great confusion without tents, cooking pots or even ammunition. There were no bandages for the wounded and stores had to be borrowed from the Italians. From Genoa the emperor telegraphed to Paris his dismay, 'We have sent an army of 120,000 men into Italy before having stocked up any supplies there. This is the opposite of what we should have done.' The French infantry nevertheless won the day; well trained and with experience gained in Algeria, they overcame the handicap of a lack of good staff work and Napoleon III's incompetent military leadership.

Napoleon III took personal command of the armies in Lombardy in mid-May 1859 and the best that could be said for that arrangement was that the even more incompetent military leadership of Victor Emmanuel was pushed into second place. Piedmontese mobilization plans were in worse shape than the French. There was a lack of supplies and instead of 100,000, only some 60,000 front line troops could be assembled and these only gradually.

The Austrians, however, were too badly led and organized to take advantage of the weakness of Piedmont at the outset of the war. One army corps had to be left in Hungary to cope with an anticipated Hungarian revolt. The Hungarian and Italian troops proved unreliable and many deserted. The Emperor Francis Joseph, moreover had completely miscalculated Austria's diplomatic position and military strength. He was sure Prussia as a 'German' power would join the war against France. He even believed Britain and Russia would intervene in Austria's favour. Then at the outset of the war the Austrian army, commanded by General Férencz Gyulai, failed to attack the weaker Piedmontese before the French arrived. The Austrians allowed the French to concentrate their forces and they suffered two defeats at Magenta on 4 June, a battle fought exclusively by the Austrians and the French, and at Solferino (24 June) the French, this time supported by the Piedmontese, again bore the brunt. Solferino was notable for the carnage it caused. The young Austrian Emperor was moved to say, 'Rather lose a province than undergo such a horrible experience again!' Napoleon III and Victor Emmanuel were similarly sickened by the suffering; but the war was not by any means at an end militarily. The Austrians had withdrawn in good order into the formidable fortresses of the Quadrilateral.

Napoleon must have feared getting bogged down in another Crimean situation. To keep the French army intact in Lombardy, let alone reinforce them and equip them to storm the Austrian defences, would require many more troops and a great effort. Meantime Napoleon III felt exposed on the Rhine by Prussia's partial mobilization on 14 June. The Piedmontese and Italian military contribution, moreover, had proved disappointing and fell far short of Cavour's promises. Nor could Piedmont pay the costs of Napoleon's campaign as they had undertaken to do. Napoleon III risked hostility at home if the war continued inconclusively and feared that by continuing the war he would be merely encouraging the forces of revolution in the Papal states and elsewhere. All these risks were not worth taking for the 'Italians', nor for the acquisition of Savoy and Nice. Napoleon III extricated himself with diplomatic skill. He persuaded Francis Joseph to make peace and Victor Emmanuel to accept its terms which gave Piedmont the considerable territorial gain of Lombardy though the Austrians would retain Mantua and Peschiera as well as Venetia. Victor Emmanuel, who had risked much but to his own chagrin sacrificed less than the French in battle, accepted the bargain without consulting Cavour. On 8 July an armistice was signed, then at Villafranca on 11 July 1859 the Preliminaries of Peace were concluded. To save Habsburg susceptibilities Lombardy was ceded to Napoleon III and only then handed by the emperor to Victor Emmanuel. Austria in 1859 was therefore not excluded from Italy. According to Villafranca, the rulers of the central Duchies of Tuscany, Parma and Modena were to be restored though it was not clear how. Napoleon III, who had not lived up to all the promises of Plombières, for his part did not insist that Piedmont cede Savoy and Nice to him.

Cavour only arrived at Victor Emmanuel's headquarters on 10 July, after the crucial decisions had been taken. He demanded that Piedmont should carry on the war alone. Victor Emmanuel refused. After a stormy interview Cavour in a great rage resigned. Cavour's judgement was at fault in more than one respect – Villafranca did not end the movement leading to Piedmontese expansion and the eventual unification of Italy. Later on Victor Emmanuel and Cavour gave credence to the legend that Napoleon III had behaved treacherously behind the backs of the Piedmontese in reaching agreement with the Austrians to end the war. This version of *Risorgimento* history conveniently concealed Victor Emmanuel's own consent to end the war, the military shortcomings of the Piedmontese and the almost total failure of 'Italians' from beyond Piedmont to rally to the Italian cause.

Cavour was out of office from mid-July 1859 to mid-January 1860 believing his work of making Piedmont predominant on the peninsula was ruined. Austria had lost a battle and territory, but he thought not her position as an Italian power. Cavour did not realize that he had accomplished far more than the terms of Villafranca allowed for. The key to the future expansion of Piedmont lay in the fate of the central Italian Duchies. The Austrians after Magenta and Solferino could no longer hope to restore by force the rulers of Parma, Modena and Tuscany. Of these Tuscany, with its capital of Florence, was the most important. The outbreak of the war between Piedmont and Austria in April 1859 had been the signal for revolution in Tuscany and Grand Duke Leopold had fled from the Duchy. A provisional government was formed and offered the 'dictatorship' – a respectable and honourable office at that time – to Victor Emmanuel. Aware of the susceptibilities of Napoleon III, Victor Emmanuel refused but accepted nominal command of the Tuscan army. In mid-June 1859 the Duchess of Parma and the Duke of Modena went the way of the Grand Duke of Tuscany. Without accepting formal leadership, Victor Emmanuel sent in Piedmontese administrators and occupied the territory. Piedmontese occupation also extended to the northernmost region of the Papal dominions known interchangeably as the Romagna or the Legations whose principal cities, Bologna and Ferrara, had appealed to Victor Emmanuel to assume control.

After Villafranca the Piedmontese army withdrew from the Romagna and the three Duchies. But Piedmontese agents and influence remained, working through local leaders, the most important of whom was Baron Bettino Ricasoli; these agents prepared the way for Piedmontese annexation later on. In August 1859 the provincial government of Tuscany held elections and convened an assembly which voted that Tuscany should be annexed by Piedmont, Villa-franca notwithstanding. By the time the final Peace Treaty of Zurich was signed between France, Piedmont and Austria on 10 November 1859 the rights of the rulers of the Duchies were upheld in theory only; the treaty contained no practical provisions for their restoration. In fact their chance of restoration was negligible unless Napoleon III had insisted on it. The Duchies became the scene of complex intrigues between opposing factions during the autumn and winter of 1859.

It was Cavour, when he returned to power in January 1860, who finally completed the diplomatic manœuvres leading to the annexation of the Duchies and the Romagna. Napoleon III's preference for the terms of Villafranca had so far barred the way. British support for the Piedmontese policy of annexation helped to persuade Napoleon III, but Palmerston was furious when he discovered that Cavour had struck his own bargain with the French. Cavour had once again offered Nice and Savoy to the emperor in return for his support to annexe the Duchies and the Romagna. Plebiscites were organized in March 1860 and the Duchies and Bologna overwhelmingly voted for annexation to Piedmont. In the meantime the French made sure of Savoy and Nice by occupying these territories first and then, in April, arranging plebiscites after their occupation. Little was now heard about setting up an Italian federation, but as late as the spring of 1860 Cavour did not think a unitary Italian state a realistic possibility.

No period of the *Risorgimento* was more extraordinary than its dramatic climax. The web of intrigue and double-dealing now became so complex that historians have argued ever since about the relationships and motivations of Victor Emmanuel, Cavour and Garibaldi. The evidence that exists can be made to fit several patterns. The patriotic version is that Cavour was wise and prudent; that to prevent European intervention he pretended to stop Garibaldi whilst secretly helping him and supporting the Expedition of the Thousand. Alternatively Cavour can be shown as a determined enemy of Garibaldi and above all of the whole Mazzinian dream of revolution and unification because the two were inseparably bound up with each other. Thus whilst pretending to help Garibaldi's expedition he secretly did all he could to ensure its failure. What there can be little doubt about is the personal sense of rivalry Cavour felt for Garibaldi. The kind of Italy which Cavour envisaged was very different from the kind Garibaldi and those who surrounded him hoped for.

In April 1860 Garibaldi was ready for new action, this time in defiance of Victor Emmanuel and Cavour. Garibaldi was incensed at the Piedmontese intention to cede Savoy and Nice. He planned direct intervention; he would lead an expedition from Genoa to Nice and destroy the ballot boxes on the day of the plebiscite. But instead of steaming to Nice, Garibaldi was persuaded to attack the royal Neapolitan forces in Sicily where a rising had precariously begun. It was later to gain hold because of the Sicilians' hatred for the Neapolitans and the peasants' for their landlords. Garibaldi asked the Piedmontese authorities for help, above all for modern rifles and ammunition. Cavour denied him all assistance. But faced with a crisis in Turin over the cession of Savoy and Nice, Cavour did not dare add to his unpopularity by publicly vetoing and preventing Garibaldi's departure. According to another later account, Cavour tried to persuade Victor Emmanuel to arrest Garibaldi, but was too late as Garibaldi had sailed. The lack of Piedmontese co-operation had in any case delayed Garibaldi's departure until 5 May 1860. By then, however, Garibaldi's volunteers had increased from the original two hundred to just over a thousand.

On his way to Sicily Garibaldi landed a small diversionary force in Tuscany with instructions to attack the Papal States, thereby alarming Napoleon III without achieving anything. On 11 May Garibaldi's Thousand, or to be precise 1,090 if we include his mistress, the one woman of the expedition, landed unopposed on the coast of Sicily at Marsala. He faced some 25,000 Neapolitan troops on the island. Yet in just under a month, on 6 June, the Neapolitan army was first defeated and by the end of July had agreed to capitulate and evacuate Sicily. Garibaldi's was one of the most extraordinary victories won by an ill-equipped guerrilla force in the history of warfare, perhaps most aptly compared with the sixteenth-century exploits of the *Conquistadores*. Garibaldi's bold leadership and the incompetence of the Neapolitan generals is one explanation. Another important one is the nature of barbaric civil war. Fear was created in the Neapolitan army by bands of merciless Sicilians seeking vengeance for the brutality of the Neapolitan soldiery. It was a bloody and terrible struggle not confined simply to rival troops. The rising of peasants against the oppressions of their landlords supported by the Bourbons was more important in overthrowing Bourbon rule than patriotic feelings.

Although Garibaldi had left Genoa as the self-proclaimed champion of 'Victor Emmanuel and Italy' he now refused to hand over the island straight away to his monarch. His reasons were sound. He needed Sicily as a base from which to attack the mainland and he was sure that Cavour would stop him if Sicily were administered by Piedmont. So Garibaldi made himself 'Dictator' of Sicily. As dictator he now refused to countenance the social peasant revolution that had so powerfully contributed to the overthrow of the Bourbons. Garibaldi had only one obsession – Italian unity. The contest between

Cavour and Garibaldi reached new heights. Cavour was surprised that Garibaldi's mad adventure of conquering Sicily had succeeded. To forestall Garibaldi's conquest of the rest of the Neapolitan Kingdom, Cavour attempted unsuccessfully to inspire a conservative revolution in Naples in favour of Victor Emmanuel. The Piedmontese navy meantime was ordered to prevent Garibaldi and his Red Shirts from crossing the Straits of Messina. Cavour wished all the credit for the conquest of the Italian states to go to Piedmont and its constitutional and conservative monarchy. Unification based on a revolutionary movement led by the charismatic Garibaldi, even if in the name of Victor Emmanuel, would dwarf Piedmont's rule, so Cavour believed, and Piedmont's enlightened conservatism and institutions would be swept aside by the revolutionary spirit.

The British were actually just as worried. Palmerston feared that Garibaldi's adventure would in the end lead to an extension of French influence in the Mediterranean as Cavour might strike a new bargain with Napoleon III to help him stave off further victories by Garibaldi in the south. Thus the enthusiasm of the British people was not shared by their realistic prime minister calculating the effects of the unexpected changes in Italy on the balance of power. Napoleon III meantime was as much opposed as Cavour to the revolution Garibaldi was arousing. Garibaldi's success in defeating and clearing out the remaining Neapolitan troops from Messina in July 1860 galvanized Napoleon III, Victor Emmanuel, Cavour and the British Cabinet into more frantic planning. The British and French cancelled each other out due to their mutual suspicions. Britain would not agree on a joint naval action with France to prevent Garibaldi from crossing to the mainland. Napoleon III hesitated to act on his own. The intrigue now becomes so dense it will probably never be possible to establish what happened with certainty. Cavour followed at least three alternative and contradictory policies secretly. His monarch's actions were equally devious. On 22 July 1860 Victor Emmanuel sent his orderly officer, Count Litta, with a letter to Garibaldi in Sicily ordering Garibaldi not to cross to the mainland. But many years later among Litta's papers a second *unopened* letter was found in which the king told Garibaldi to disregard the first letter. One plausible explanation is that the first letter was written on Cavour's instructions and the second was a secret message to Garibaldi verbally delivered, to be confirmed by actually handing over the letter only if Garibaldi insisted. Another explanation is that Victor Emmanuel was backing and deceiving both Cavour and Garibaldi in his determination to be on the side of the winner in the end. Or perhaps Cavour knew all along that the king sympathized with Garibaldi.

Garibaldi put an end to speculation and cut the Gordian knot by the rapidity and directness of his military moves. With 3,360 men and two steamers the *Torino* and *Franklin* he outwitted the Neapolitan navy and carried his little army across the straits to Calabria where he landed at Melito on 19 August. After some fierce fighting during the early days, Garibaldi received reinforcements from Sicily and although heavily outnumbered by the royal Neapolitan troops defeated them; the poor peasants of southern Calabria were all on Garibaldi's side. Military opposition simply collapsed in the face of the peasant revolt and Garibaldi's reputation. He hurried north to Naples ahead of his main body of troops. Early in September 1860 the king withdrew from Naples to the north. Garibaldi's triumphant entry had a touch of comic opera about it. Taking a fantastic risk he accepted control of the city, and travelled ahead of his troops along one of the few Italian railway lines from Salerno to Naples. He arrived with just 30 companions on 7 September to a tremendous welcome to accept the transfer of this city of half a million inhabitants. Until he handed over power to Victor Emmanuel on 8 November 1860, Garibaldi ruled the Kingdom of Naples as Dictator except for the royal stronghold in the northern region. Garibaldi was able to contain the Bourbon troops loyal to King Francis but they were too strong to pass and so barred Garibaldi's way into the Papal States. The continued loyalty of the Neapolitan troops to the Bourbons enabled Cavour to regain the upper hand.

The only way to re-establish Piedmontese predominance was for the Piedmontese army to advance through the Papal States to the Neapolitan kingdom and for Victor Emmanuel to take command even at the risk of civil war. Napoleon III was half persuaded to permit this great extension of Piedmontese rule to stop Garibaldi's revolution but he remained unpredictable. Cavour took the risk. In mid-September Piedmontese troops invaded the countryside still under Papal rule. Those of the Pope's subjects who resisted the invasion were shot as traitors. Italian unification thus was not to be achieved simply as a glorious popular movement. Thousands of 'Italians' fought for their rulers, so that the full story of unification includes aspects of civil war with all its customary bitterness and savagery. However, the British Cabinet in Russell's famous note of 27 October 1860 defended the actions of Victor Emmanuel in overthrowing the Italian rulers and this gave Piedmont some support among the generally hostile reactions of European monarchs. Plebiscites were the device which legitimized Victor Emmanuel's aggression. They were held in Sicily and the Neapolitan mainland (also in the Papal States occupied by Piedmont) and returned results overwhelmingly in favour of annexation by Piedmont.

In October Piedmontese troops reached the Neapolitan Kingdom and on 26 October Victor Emmanuel and Garibaldi met. It was a dramatic moment. Garibaldi took off his hat and greeted the monarch theatrically with the words: 'I salute the first King of Italy.' Victor Emmanuel's prosaic reply was an anti-climax, as is the rest of the history of the *Risorgimento*; 'How are you, dear Garibaldi?' Garibaldi was now, for the first time, in a subordinate position. He soon found this difficult to accept and the royal Piedmontese army did not make it any easier by treating the motley collection of Garibaldini with scant respect. On 8 November Garibaldi resigned his dictatorship and handed over power formally to Victor Emmanuel. The next day he quietly left for his simple house on the island of Caprera, having refused the honours the king wanted to bestow on him. His contribution to Italian unity had been immense but Victor Emmanuel was just as determined as Cavour that Garibaldi must be made to retire from active political life with many honours if he so wished, or without them if not.

When Garibaldi left Naples his useful work for Italy was ended though he lived another twenty-two years. In 1862, at Aspromonte, the incorrigible revolutionary leader attempted another insurrection to win the Papal States. This time he was defeated and wounded by Italian troops. He spent a brief period in prison and was then released. He had become a legend, a heroic historical figure of the past.

For Cavour there were not many months of life remaining after unification; but Cavour saw Mazzini's ideas defeated. The Piedmontese constitution was extended to the rest of Italy. A parliament was elected and on 17 March 1861 Victor Emmanuel was proclaimed King of Italy. It was Garibaldi who had forced Cavour to embrace the cause of Italian unity. But neither Piedmont nor 'Italy' could have accomplished the defeat of Austria. The French alliance made unification possible and this was Cavour's achievement.

Cavour's work long outlived his death on 6 June 1861. His traditions and political outlook were followed by his successors. Italy remained a monarchy and did not become a republic. The anti-clericalism of Piedmont was extended to the rest of Italy. As in Piedmont during the era of Cavour, so in Italy, government was constitutional, centralized and based on a parliamentary assembly. However the franchise for the Italian parliament was as narrow as that for the Piedmontese had been. It gave the right to vote to only half a million out of twenty-two million inhabitants and only 300,000 actually voted. The practice of basing governments on majority centre groups in coalition also continued. It stifled party development; instead parliamentary life was splintered into small groups and personalities bargaining for a share in power, a system inherently unstable, in the absence of any one strong political leader.

During the 1860s the process of unification was virtually completed. Those Neapolitans who were still struggling for the restoration of the Bourbons were suppressed in what the royal authorities called the 'Brigands' War'. Venetia became Italian as a consequence of the Austro-Prussian-Italian war of 1866 (p. 257). The Pope was deprived of Rome when his protector Napoleon III had to withdraw the French troops to defend himself against the Prussian onslaught in 1870 (p. 320). But for the Alto-Adige (South Tyrol), Italy had to wait until the dissolution of the Habsburg Empire in 1918.

With unification, Italy became the first of the new nation states. Nationalism had triumphed despite, rather than because of, the attitudes of the majority of the people. Italy was not to become one of the foremost great powers but judged by the ideas and movements which originated and were developed in the Italian peninsula during the nineteenth and twentieth century, Italy's role was one of European importance.

15

Russia and the Reforms of Alexander II

Even Russia experienced an authoritarian decade of reform though it occurred in the 1860s, ten years later than in western Europe. The more enlightened conservative attitude of Alexander II was in certain respects similar to the attitudes of conservative reformers elsewhere in Europe, in Prussia, France and Italy. Reform would preserve the social structure; to resist it was to invite unrest, even revolution. More remarkable even than the reforms themselves perhaps was this widespread recognition among conservative rulers that there was a need for change. About the reforms in Russia, however, there was one distinctive feature: everywhere else in Europe social reform went hand in hand with political reform. In Britain pre-eminently, but also in France, Prussia, Austria and Piedmont reform involved a diminution of the sovereign's authority, a movement away from absolutism to a constitutional monarchy and the simultaneous growth of popularly-elected parliamentary assemblies which participated increasingly in government; in Britain, of course, parliament dominated government. In this respect Russian reformers differed sharply from the rest of Europe. Not only was it the tsar alone who could initiate reform – that was not so unique a feature, it was also true of Napoleon III – but Alexander II just as much as his predecessors was rigidly opposed to the minutest introduction of constitutional government. Alexander II was determined to preserve intact the tsar's autocratic powers he had inherited from his father Nicholas I. To describe him in any meaningful sense as a 'liberal' is thus very misleading. Alexander II admired his father's stern personal rule and also his father's desire to bring about practical reforms, above all in the conditions of the serfs. In his later reforms Alexander II could therefore justifiably feel that he was following in the footsteps of Nicholas I.

Alexander II became known as the 'Tsar Liberator'. But as the historian Florinsky has so aptly put it, he was singularly ill-qualified by education, convictions and temperament for the role of the reformer he was fated to play. Little of the enlightenment had rubbed off on the young Alexander who was tutored by the poet Vasili Zhukovsky. It is interesting that Nicholas I should have approved so humanitarian and literary a programme as that devised by Zhukovsky. But Alexander simply was not interested in the arts and literature. He was far more attracted to the other indispensable aspect of his education, the army. Here it was the uniforms, ceremonies and military parades that attracted him rather than the deeper mysteries of military science. On his travels in Europe, Alexander acquired a good grasp of languages and he also travelled extensively in Russia itself to places as distant as Siberia. His education was completed through his introduction to various military commands and membership of the State Council and Council of Ministers during the decade of the 1840s. There was no conflict between father and son and it is evident that Nicholas I had taken great pains to prepare Alexander II for the succession.

In view of Alexander's character – he was rather indolent and indecisive and despite public displays of emotion and kind-heartedness capable of maintaining a severe police régime with all its attendant cruelties – it is surprising that it was especially his reign that became associated with the period of great reforms in Russian history. To the extent that in an autocracy good deeds are credited to the autocrat personally, he earned the title of 'Tsar Liberator'. Nevertheless his personal contribution to reforms was far less positive than his more admiring biographers would have us believe. In many ways his influence impeded the practical realization of reforms which had become law. He was indecisive and throughout his reign alternated between reforming impulses and reaction. As his advisers he selected both reformers such as Dimitri Milyutin and extreme conservatives, men such as Dimitri Tolstoy, and he kept both in office simultaneously. It was only with reluctance that Alexander took up the root cause of Russia's social ills, the problem of the serfs. Once a programme for emancipation had been devised, the other practical reforms of his reign followed from that.

In 1855 out of a Russian population of some 60 million, serfs together with their families numbered more than 40 million. Russia was backward and sunk in perpetual poverty and frequent famine. The serfs led a brutish existence, floggings and utter dependency on their masters being considered the norm. Industrialization had made little headway in mid-nineteenth-century Russia and until towards the close of the century had made little impact on the people. But bad as the condition of the serfs was, service in the army was worse – torn for most of his adult life from his village and family, the conscript lived a penal existence. Masters could send recalcitrant serfs to the recruiting office – a threat sufficiently powerful to quell all but the most desperate characters. The 'great reforms' of the 1860s did not liberate the Russian people. That process was so gradual, and the contrast between aspirations, the laws of the state, and the realities of the situation were so stark, that the degree of discontent was raised more by the hope of reform than satisfied by their application. In the end the process was so slow that the dependence of the majority of the peasants on the tsarist bureaucracy was replaced eventually by dependence on the Stalinist bureaucracy. Yet the vast Russian masses remained attached to their country and their tsar by notions of patriotism, superstition, false expectations of the tsar's beneficence and perhaps sheer apathy. Their stoicism in the face of unbelievable hardships is possibly the most remarkable feature of Russian society.

The position of the serfs differed greatly. The majority were peasants who worked on the land. The land belonged to the estates, about half of all the *male* serfs in 1859 (10.7 million) laboured on the estates belonging to the nobility. The estate was generally farmed by an administrator or the landowner. The serf would be permitted to farm part of the land for himself but in return was required either to pay for this privilege or to provide free labour services. The proportion of labour services or payment a landowner required would depend on whether or not he wished to farm large tracts himself. Where he did not wish to farm the land, he would permit the serf to hire himself out elsewhere in return for a payment to the landowner. Whatever limited rights the serf possessed on paper they counted for little in practice. The serf, and his family's dependence on the landowner economically, socially, and in matters of punishment was virtually unlimited. The law of the state was more concerned to back the landowner than the serf. The usual punishment frequently meted out was flogging; indeed floggings in the stables were an everyday occurrence in rural Russia. It is difficult to realize in describing the situation that it is the nineteenth century and not the thirteenth we are writing about. The domestic serfs were little more than slaves. Of course in defence of the system the need for some form of paternalism over ill-educated and backward people can be argued. There were also kindly masters and the behaviour of the landowners was not necessarily always arbitrary. Then favourable comparisons have been made between the condition of the Russian serf and the American negro slave in the south. Finally the point can be made that whereas emancipation led to civil war in the United States, in Russia emancipation was carried through peacefully. Autocracy thus seemed to have advantages too. But all this is rather special pleading. The evils of serfdom had long been recognized in Russia itself.

Alexander II was not predisposed to reform and in the 1840s had rather taken the part of the nobility. But the humiliation of the Crimean War and the wretched state of Russia on his accession probably convinced him that something needed to be done to modernize Russia so that she could take an equal place among the powers of Europe. But it was far from his mind to attempt anything like a 'revolutionary' change in Russian society. The nobility was, with the army and the church, a pillar of the throne. Alexander did not intend to shake the foundations. In an address to the Moscow nobility he explained his point of view in 1856; he had no intention of emancipating the serfs immediately, 'but, of course, you understand yourselves that the existing order of serfdom cannot remain unchanged. It is better to begin to abolish bondage from above than to wait for the time when it will begin to abolish itself spontaneously from below'. Not surprisingly the nobility which derived such profit from the institution of serfdom did not respond to the tsar's lead. The process followed before the emancipation of the serfs was proclaimed on 19 February 1861* was slow and laborious. In 1857 the tsar took advantage of the different situation prevailing on the estates of the Polish nobility to create a large number of committees of enquiry. He next obliged the nobility elsewhere in Russia to co-operate with a general scheme of emancipation. After interminable delays and modifications the emancipation statutes were proclaimed in 1861.

The fact that the emancipation statutes created more unrest than joy provides a true indication of their impact. The notion that henceforth, that is from 1861 onwards, the serfs were emancipated was a cruel joke. In many respects the immediate effect of the emancipation statutes was to worsen, not to improve, the lot of the peasant. Nor had he in fact received any guarantee of personal freedom but was held in a new kind of bureaucratic and economic bondage for years. The bulky volume of 360 pages comprising the emancipation statutes was so complex, obscure and ambiguous that few understood how to apply them let alone the serf how to read what rights he now could claim. There was complete confusion about what the peasant should be required to pay, how much land he would receive. Acceptance of the land by the peasants had to be made compulsory – a necessary measure since the financial burdens that went with this granting of land were more onerous than the peasant farmer could sustain. The nobility, themselves heavily in debt, tried to recoup from the 'emancipated' serfs. They resented having to give up about a third of their land to the peasantry; they regarded this as little short of confiscation. In return for giving up land the landowner received bonds from the government to some

---

*   3 March 1861 western calendar.

eighty per cent of the value of the land. The peasant was supposed to pay the remainder, but frequently this proved impossible and the landowners accepted that fact. The general effect of emancipation was to impoverish the landowners further. Economically the peasants were frequently worse off too. The land they now received was appreciably less than the land they had previously been able to farm in return for labour services or cash. And as in practice (though not in theory) the landowner received an element of compensation for the loss of labour services, the debt payments imposed on the emancipated serf were far too heavy. The government provided the peasants with the necessary credit which had to be repaid in 49 years. The peasants did not even hold most of the land personally. They were organized into village communes and under one of the systems of tenure prevailing the land was allotted to the commune which divided the land among the households and even sometimes redistributed it periodically. The commune was administratively responsible for taxes and all the other business of the state. It was run by government officials so that the majority of emancipated serfs, now called 'free village dwellers', exchanged bondage and dependence on the landowner for that scarcely less onerous dependence on the commune. They were generally not free to go where they wished or to farm their own land.

For their loss of control over the serfs, the nobility were to some extent compensated by being admitted to participate in local government. The proposals for reform took the customary long time of bureaucratic committee discussion, several years, before being settled by the statute of 1864 which created provincial and district *zemstvos*. The district *zemstvos* consisted of an executive board and an assembly elected for three years by a three-class system which favoured the propertied. The district *zemstvo* assemblies in turn chose the members of the provincial *zemstvo*. The assemblies elected their executive boards. They met once a year, but possessed no real executive functions for which they had to rely on the tsar's police and other officials. The *zemstvos* concerned themselves with discussion about purely local economic matters, hospitals, roads, education, agriculture and the relief of the poor. They served as 'schools of administration'. But their creation was not a step towards a sharing of the function of central government with an elected assembly. The reform which applied only to the purely Russian province did not make the Russian Empire less autocratic than before. In 1870 city institutions similar to the *zemstvos* were created. Russia uniquely lacked among the great powers a national assembly. This the autocratic tsars would not concede until half a century later. Yet the *zemstvos* despite all their shortcomings did useful work and, though very hedged about, the principle of elected assemblies dealing with questions of local concern marked a move into modern times.

The need to reform the administration of the law became urgent once the landowners' personal rights over the serfs had been severed. Another committee prepared the way for the reform of 1864. Western principles of law were for the first time established, but in practice an independent judiciary, where everyone enjoyed equality before the law, could not be allowed to function as long as the tsar was determined to maintain autocracy and the surveillance and control of the population by a secret police. Yet here too the establishment of new courts marked a great step forward.

The army as has already been noted was the most dreaded and hated institution of the state. Army service was for 25 years, and communities had to provide their quotas of recruits. Exemptions could be secured by the nobility and the better-off, but only rarely by the poor and never by the serfs. The army law of 1874 was the work of General Dimitri Milyutin. It followed the principle of reforms first adopted by the Prussian army in the 1860s. In place of the huge standing army with long-term service, a smaller army composed of six-year service was formed, which together with nine years with the reserve provided a large trained reserve of manpower. Furthermore exemption could no longer be claimed on grounds of social class. Every able-bodied male of twenty was theoretically liable for service, but selection depended on a ballot, exemption also being possible for pursuit of higher education or the needs of dependants, for instance if a man was the only support for an old widowed mother. The army reform was far-reaching in practice and made a tremendous difference to the life of ordinary people in Russia. Taken together with other reforms introduced in the universities and also with a lightening of censorship, the reign of Alexander II marked a watershed between the old Russia, and the modernized autocratic Russia that was to be severely challenged in 1905.

The 'plight' of the Poles caught the imagination of romantic western Europe. Radicals in Britain saw in the struggle of the Polish people a fight for personal and democratic rights against autocracy. Napoleon III championed their cause and in Britain 'public opinion' obliged Palmerston to offer mediation between the revolutionary Poles and the Russians in the summer of 1863. But neither France nor Britain had the slightest intention of fighting for the Poles and Russia was already assured of Prussian friendship. The prevailing view, that of long-suffering Poles rising against their oppressors the Russians, was a grossly oversimplified one. The British people had no more understanding of the Polish situation in 1863 than of the Czecho-Slovak in 1938. These were all 'far off' countries for which the masses would never have gone to war. 'Public opinion' in this context was the skilful creation of brilliant propagandists, such as Alexander Herzen, who had settled in London and of a group of radicals, rather than the genuine movement of the masses, more interested in problems nearer home.

Tsar Alexander had actually begun his reign with the best intentions towards his Polish subjects. Nowhere in the Russian Empire was the 'thaw' more in evidence. Prince Michael Gorchakov was sent as Viceroy to Poland in April 1856 and by various cultural, religious (Poland was of course Catholic Slav, not Greek Orthodox Slav like the Russians), economic and political measures attempted to conciliate the Poles. As in Russia, the peasant question was the most fundamental facing Polish society. In Poland the *Code Napoléon* still prevailed and the Polish landlords claimed that no reform was really necessary. They did not wish to give the peasants land. But radical groups, whose strength lay in the towns, wished to bring the peasants to their side in a struggle to create a Polish nation by much more widespread land reform. They proposed that an insurrection should be started and that its leaders would immediately grant the peasants their land unconditionally whilst compensating the landlords from a state fund. By and large the landlords placed their economic interests first and were content to collaborate with the Russian administration provided the land reform adopted did not harm them.

Alexander persevered with a conciliatory policy despite periodic disturbances in 1861. At the head of the administration he placed Alexander Wielopolski, who managed to offend all sections of Polish society, including the Catholic Church, which resented his policy of toleration towards the Jews. In May 1861 Gorchakov died and was replaced in 1862 by the moderate Grand Duke Constantine, the tsar's brother. The growth of radical strength as well as the fears of the better-off Poles, who did not wish to appear antagonistic to the Polish national spirit, led to a loose co-ordination of insurrectionary planning by the Polish National Central Committee in Warsaw. A Russian decree introducing conscription aimed to wipe out the radical organization in Warsaw and in the larger towns brought the crisis to a head. The date of 21–22 January 1863 was set by the National Central Committee for the start of the rising.

It was a very different affair to 1831. There were no large-scale battles. The Polish insurgents fought in bands in the countryside with the acquiescence of the landlords but without the general support of the peasantry. The rebel leaders were divided and individual acts of courage could not alter the fact that the rebellion was a hopeless cause. It was repressed by the tsar in about a year with great severity, especially where, as in Lithuania, it had spread beyond the confines of the Polish kingdom.

Curiously the consequences of the insurrection were of benefit to the peasantry and worked out to the disadvantage of the Russians. Nicholas Milyutin was sent by the tsar to introduce the agrarian reform of March 1864. The settlement was favourable to the peasants.

Some 700,000 Polish families secured their freeholds and retained their rights to the use of forest and pasture-land without compensation to the landlords. These were better terms than the Polish peasants could have expected from a Polish victory! But it did not reconcile them to the vigorous programme of Russianization now begun. With the land question that divided peasant and landlord out of the way, all Poles now tended to combine against the Russian bureaucracy that oppressed them.

It is a paradox that although Alexander II's reign was chiefly remarkable in foreign affairs for the humiliation which Russia suffered in war with England and France in the Crimea in 1855 and 1856, and for many months in 1877 in Bulgaria at the hands of the Turks, that nevertheless during the decades from the 1850s to the 1870s the basis of Russia's trans-continental power was laid. Two setbacks span Alexander's reign, the Congress of Paris and the Congress of Berlin. On both occasions Russia was confronted with a coalition of powers blocking her expansion southwards at the expense of the Ottoman Empire. As far as her western frontiers were concerned, Russia was a satiated power; she had enough trouble with the Poles not to wish to add to them. In the Baltic, Alexander II was happy to continue with his father's conciliatory policy towards the Finns which allowed them a great deal of autonomy; what is more this was the only part of the Empire where the tsar, as Grand Duke of Finland, was prepared to rule constitutionally with the advice and consent of the Finnish Diet.

Through the sale of Alaska in 1867 Russia abandoned American colonies she could not defend against a determined British or United States attack. Simultaneously Russia expanded through Central Asia to India and through Siberia to the Far East. Nicholas Muraviev, the Governor-General of Eastern Siberia, was responsible for the drive to the Pacific. Territories under Chinese control were wrested from her by the treaties of Aigun in 1858 and Pekin in 1860. These regions, along the Amur and the Ussuri rivers, are now central to the Russo-Chinese dispute, as the Chinese argue that imperialistic treaties are invalid. In central Asia Russia also expanded on a vast scale. A well-co-ordinated military effort conquered the independent Muslim states and Russia reached the frontiers of Afghanistan. The scene was set for the rivalry in the Middle East and Asia between Britain and Russia that dominated Anglo-Russian relations during the last quarter of the nineteenth century. What had happened was a kind of domino theory in reverse. Typical of the imperialist process else-where, the search for defensible frontiers had led the Russian soldiers and administrators on from one territory to the next. Much of their expansion was unplanned and even disapproved of in far-away St Petersburg. But ambitious governor-generals, like General Kaufmann in central Asia, paid little attention to counsels of restraint and caution when they reached them. In terms of ultimate power, Russia benefited enormously. Alexander II presided over the expansion, which pleased him personally, but he was not its initiator (see map p. 200).

The revision of the Peace of Paris was the obsession of Alexander II and Gorchakov, his Chancellor (p. 320). The momentous events in central Europe culminating in the unification of Germany were viewed, not from a European point of view, but a narrow Russian one. Ungrateful Austria was hated by Alexander and his ministers for her hostile role during the Crimean War so that her defeat in 1866 caused little concern. The tsar was more disturbed by the Prussian annexations of the minor north German states following on the Austro-Prussian war of 1866 (p. 262) because they offended his principle of legitimacy. When war next broke out between Prussia and France in 1870, what seriously alarmed the tsar was the prospect of a Napoleonic victory. The French Emperor's espousal of the Polish national cause in particular, and nationalism in general had turned him, in the tsar's eyes, into Russia's greatest enemy. The tsar was even prepared to consider co-operation with Austria to check that danger (p. 319). So the traditional friendly policy towards Prussia was continued during Alexander's reign despite Gorchakov's personal misgivings about Bismarck. This friendly non-interventionist attitude on Russia's part had the greatest consequences for European history as it was one of the essential conditions making possible the unifica-tion of Germany.

16

The Struggle for Supremacy in the German Confederation

The decade of the 1850s witnessed the defeat of two great powers, Austria and Russia, but their reaction to military disaster was very different. The Habsburgs were more determined than ever to hold on to the basic tenet of their policy; not to recognize the *political* claims of the many nationalities making up the empire. They were offered no more than cultural equality. The Habsburgs had fought and lost in Italy in 1859. But they had not lost badly and so had been able to conclude a compromise peace which left them in control of Venetia and nurturing the dream of reversing the Italian decision. The Habsburgs in the 1860s now set themselves against the victory of nationalism in Germany. Despite the weakness of the Habsburg Empire in finance, military capacity and internal cohesion, Francis Joseph and his ministers pursued a European policy far beyond the empire's strength with disastrous consequences. Defeat led Alexander II in a different direction to Francis Joseph. Alexander II abandoned a European policy, and concentrated on internal reform whilst avoiding any further possibility of war with the European powers (p. 240). In the short term the tsar's policy served Russia well and allowed the Russian Empire to make some progress, whereas Francis Joseph's obstinacy and inflexibility led the Austrian Empire to be defeated again in 1866 both in Italy and Germany.

In the transformation of the German states into Germany we can see two forces at work. In one respect unification was the outcome of a traditional struggle between dynastic states, with the populations of the state following their rulers in war. These dynastic conflicts had been common since the Reformation. When viewed from this point of view the struggle for supremacy in Germany was a conflict between German rulers with the most powerful, the King of Prussia, coming out on top after defeating his weaker rivals. Thus the King of Prussia assumed the title of German Kaiser, a hereditary emperor at the apex of a feudal structure. In this sense Prussia absorbed the rest of Germany either by outright annexation or by dominating the other states. As some historians see it, Germany was not so much united as Prussia enlarged. There is no denying this aspect of the conflict among the German states in the 1860s. Contemporaries tended to view the conflicts in terms of past dynastic struggles. Bismarck did so too, paying lip service to 'German nationalism', 'democracy', 'liberalism', as expressing mere sectional interests, or professorial propaganda, which could be utilized in the service of his policies. But in fact Germany did not just become an agglomeration of states dominated by Prussia. Prussia did not absorb Germany. It was the other way around. Germany in the end absorbed Prussia and all the other states.

In the process of unification there was also another force at work which was revolutionary and anti-particularist. It had surfaced in '1848' and gradually became dominant in twentieth-century Germany This was popular nationalism which found its focus not in particularist state institutions, rulers, administrations or parliaments but in German institutions, the Kaiser, the *Reichstag* and the combined German armies. At the turn of the century 'imperialism' became a German movement and was not identified with any particular state; it was a German navy that came into being, not a Prussian. German unification was far more complete than Bismarck in a sense ever intended or imagined it to be. This was because it was the German people who decided that their individual states counted for less than Germany as a whole and that local allegiances and associations were cultural or largely sentimental historical relics. Only united could Germany be a great power militarily and industrially among other great powers; indeed united she would be the leading European power. *Deutschland, Deutschland Über alles*, took precedence as Germany's national anthem over the Prussian *Heil dir im Siegerkranz*. The needs of industrial growth and the climactic development of German nationalism burst the nineteenth-century shackles which Bismarck believed he had so ingeniously placed on his creation. Thus the story of German unification and Bismarck's role in it is analogous to that of the sorcerer's apprentice. Bismarck released powerful forces and in the end found they had a life of their own too strong for his successors to control.

The declining fortunes of the Habsburg Monarchy is the reverse side of Germany's rise. In the Habsburg Monarchy the force of nationalism was tearing apart an empire based on loyalty to a dynasty. The Hungarians wished to recover their historic rights including domination over Slovaks, Slovenes, Croatians, 'Saxons' and Rumanians (in Transylvania); they acknowledged Francis Joseph as their ruler in the sense of King of Hungary. The main objective of the Czechs was to reduce the influence and power of the 'German'

Austrians and this they did by emphasizing the reality of the Austrian Empire as a whole for in it the German Austrians would form a minority. Each nationality worked for its own benefit only using the argument of imperial unity where it suited particular national interests. Loyalty to the emperor varied after 1859 from the disaffection of his remaining Italian subjects to the comparative loyalty of those minorities who looked to him for protection, the Poles, the Czechs and the Rumanians. It was not an inconsiderable achievement in the face of the prevailing nationalism of the age that the Habsburg Monarchy survived until the close of the first World War.

After the Italian defeats of 1859, made worse by Italian unification in 1860, even Francis Joseph recognized that some modification of policies hitherto pursued had become unavoidable. On his return from the northern Italian campaign the emperor therefore promised to utilize peace at home to place Austria's welfare on a solid basis 'by appropriate development of its rich spiritual and material resources, and by modernizing and improving its legislature and administration'. It took two years to give these vague assurances some concrete form in the February Patent of 1861. With extreme reluctance Francis Joseph made concessions to liberal constitutional demands. The administration was dominated by ministers, Johann Bernhard von Rechberg (foreign minister), Karl Ludwig von Bruck (commerce and trade) and Anton von Schmerling (interior). Francis Joseph refused to concede a 'constitution', hence the February 'Patent'. But in practice Francis Joseph had taken the first steps away from absolutism. A real measure of local autonomy and local representative institutions, the *Landtage* was introduced. But the spirit of the centralized *Gesammt Monarchie* was very much retained. Of the central institutions the *Reichsrat* became a genuine parliamentary assembly. The Lower House of Deputies was composed of 343 delegates sent by the locally elected Diets (*Landtage*). The Upper House consisted of the archdukes, hereditary nobles, princes of the Church and the monarch's nominees. Legislation including finance required the consent of the *Reichsrat*, though the retention of an 'emergency paragraph' in theory permitted the monarch to revert to absolutist rule whenever he thought it necessary. On the other hand the emperor had conceded that his ministers were responsible both to him and the *Reichsrat*. The empire had settled into an ambiguous state of constitutionalism, a half-way house.

There were two serious flaws in these constitutional and administrative 'reforms'. The finances of the empire continued in a parlous state as the Hungarians remained irreconcilable opponents of the constitutional settlement embodied in the February Patent. The Hungarians were led by Deák in a policy which denied the validity of centralized institutions for the monarchy such as the *Reichsrat*. Not a single Magyar representative took his place in that body. The crown was admonished to honour the April Laws. The link between Hungary and the Hereditary Lands, Deák asserted, was as between one free nation and another each acknowledging its own sovereign, Francis Joseph. On the eve of the conflict with Prussia over the future of Germany, Francis Joseph suddenly changed course. He sought a compromise with the Hungarian moderates, the Deákists. Rechberg and Schmerling were dismissed; promises were made which seemed to go some way to meeting Hungarian objections to the centralized institutions of the February Patent. All was still in flux and nothing settled when the war broke out with Prussia in the summer of 1866. As usual, Francis Joseph's timing had been thoroughly unfortunate. The continued uncertainty of Hungary's loyalty and the certainty of Italian disloyalty was a fatal handicap to an already weakened Habsburg Empire when it came to the contest with Prussia in 1866. Lack of finance at the same time had prevented more modern equipment such as breech-loading rifles, from being issued to the army, which itself was left under strength. The army estimates were constantly pared down by economy-minded ministers and actually reached their lowest point in 1866.

The state of the Austrian army was in great contrast to the Prussian at this time. In Prussia the liberals were defeated on the issue of army reform and expenditure. In Austria the ministers successfully diminished the funds the army needed. During the crucial years of the contest for the supremacy in Germany, Prussia was in a constitutional crisis just as was Austria, but it was a very different kind of crisis. In Prussia the conflict was one with liberal politicians; it was a political crisis and 'patriotism' proved stronger than political principles. The majority of the people turned away from the politicians to acclaim Bismarck's victories and most of the politicians, mixing expediency and patriotic feelings, followed suit. In Austria the constitutional crisis was not one between the monarch and leading politicians but above all with the Hungarian people. It sapped the confidence and strength of the empire. In Prussia the army blindly followed the king. In Austria, the emperor felt some doubts about the loyalty of German, Austrian and Hungarian troops let alone Italian in all circumstances. Everywhere Francis Joseph was too late in making concessions which, if they had been voluntarily made with good grace, might have brought some counter-advantage. Francis Joseph played a difficult hand badly; Bismarck played a strong hand with great skill and total lack of scruple.

From the moment Bismarck became the first minister of the Prussian crown in September 1862, his words, his actions, his conflicts and alliances, dominated first the Prussian, then the German and later

European affairs for nearly three decades in a way no other European statesman of his age succeeded in doing. That is not to claim that the history of Prussia and Europe conformed to some gigantic master-plan conceived by Bismarck. All a great political leader can achieve is to have a major impact on his own times. As for the future, new faces will shape events beyond the vision of the founding fathers of nations.

It is no longer fashionable among historians to ascribe to any individual an overwhelming influence on the particular course history takes. Political leaders need men of ability to second their efforts; Bismarck's success depended on Roon, the war minister, and Moltke, the brilliant strategist. The powers political leaders are able to exercise are circumscribed by the society in which they function and which sets limits to their freedom of action. Thus Bismarck was dependent on the goodwill of the sovereign whose theoretical power he had done so much to preserve, whereas British prime ministers depended on an unpredictable electoral process and the vagaries of parliamentary majorities. Largely uncontrollable external influences, the effects of the trade cycle, the consequences of unexpected military defeat, a thousand and one events, all can radically alter political fortunes. The very call to office is usually the result of a particular combination of circumstances which might have led to a different outcome if just one element in that combination had been different. The manner in which Churchill replaced Chamberlain in May 1940 is just one example. In 1862 William I would probably not have considered such a complete outsider, and embarrassingly extreme royalist, as Bismarck had the king not reached a point of near-despair in his conflict with parliament over the reform of the Prussian army, the details of which had become a royal obsession. In these circumstances, foreseen by Roon during the previous summer, a pre-arranged conspiratorial telegram had been sent to Bismarck in Paris on 18 September urging him back to Berlin. The telegram read: *Periculum in mora. Depêchez-vous* and was signed by Roon as '*L'oncle de Maurice Henning*'. Even so William I was at first only prepared to accept Bismarck provisionally, and his formal appointment as prime minister was delayed until October.

It is not difficult to show that political leaders do not think up entirely original ideas and policies of their own which they then proceed to act upon. Like everyone else they borrow ideas and make them their own; different aspects of their political programme can be traced to others. Thus the determination to assert Prussia in Germany militarily, diplomatically and economically was not a course of action first thought up by Bismarck. The antecedents of these policies can be traced to his predecessors (see especially chapter 9). All this has to be borne in mind and deepens our understanding of how historical changes come about. But if this line of reasoning is taken too far, then the importance of an individual leader is diminished to the point where the emphasis on his lack of originality, on his dependence on chance, and on the work of others, his inconsistencies and mistakes, no longer square with the obvious that nevertheless there have been individuals who can clearly be shown to have altered the course of history.

Literally thousands of books have been written about Bismarck. Historical judgements have varied from Golo Mann's conclusion that there 'is no other instance in the development of western Europe of one figure who changed a nation's destiny',* to Helmut Böhme's view that at 'a distance, longer or shorter... from national patriotic idea-s... it has become possible to avoid seeing the development of (German unification)... as only part of the national achievement of a single man, Bismarck, and to look to right and left of the hero figure; to turn one's attention... to the *conditions* in which his individual policy was conducted'.† These are not mutually exclusive conclusions, it is all a question of balance and perspective.

Bismarck himself was always conscious of the limitations of what it was possible for one man to achieve and how dependent the future was on the unpredictable reactions of others as well as on mere chance. 'Politics is neither arithmetic nor mathematics,' Bismarck wrote many times; 'To be sure, one has to reckon with given and unknown factors, but there are no rules and formulae with which to sum up the results in advance;' and he added with characteristic scorn, 'only Professors can create scientific laws.' On another occasion he wrote, 'By himself the individual can create nothing; he can only wait until he hears God's footsteps resounding through events and then spring forward to grasp the hem of his mantle – that is all.'‡ In his memoirs, written in fits and starts during the years of his retirement, he rearranged history to suit the Bismarck legend he then wished to propagate of a statesman who foresaw events and brilliantly achieved his goals although surrounded by enemies and intriguers. He leaves his readers in no doubt that the lion's share of the credit for Prussia's achievements belonged to him. Yet despite all the distortions and the unreliability of these memoirs, they do offer insights into the workings of Bismarck's mind and the methods of his statesmanship. Bismarck's correspondence and writings assembled in the fifteen volumes of his collected works (the *Friedrichsruhe Ausgabe*) published in Berlin during the years 1912 to 1935 are an even more fruitful source. The Bismarck revealed here shows that

*   G. Mann, *The History of Germany since 1789* (Penguin, 1974).
†   H. Böhme, *The Foundation of the German Empire* (Oxford, 1971).
‡   O. Pflanze, *Bismarck and the Development of Germany* (Princeton, 1963) p. 87.

questions often asked about his policies and aims frequently over-simplify. For instance one of the old chestnuts is whether Bismarck 'planned' German unification and the three wars which brought it about. Bismarck frequently denied the possibility of such precise planning. He wrote that in politics, and Bismarck used the word in its broadest sense to include diplomacy, 'there are no rules and formulae with which to sum up the results in advance.' Or again about the task confronting statesmen: 'Politics is not in itself an exact and logical science, but it is the capacity to choose in each fleeting moment of the situation that which is least harmful or most opportune'.* In the closing passage of the posthumously published third volume of his memoirs Bismarck observed that the problem confronting the statesman is to assess as accurately as possible what others in certain given circumstances will do. Yet as he wrote elsewhere: 'One must always reckon with the possibility that the opponent will at the last moment make a move other than that expected, and act accordingly.' The conclusion he drew from this realistic assessment allows us a real insight into his method of conducting policy. 'In other words,' Bismarck continued, 'one must always have two irons in the fire.'† Historians have convincingly unravelled the logic that lay behind the sudden changes of policy that so bewildered Bismarck's contemporaries and earned him a Machiavellian reputation. Bismarck's particular genius was to place more irons in the fire simultaneously than anyone else succeeded in doing and yet not to lose the confidence of the men he was dealing with. He would delay his choice between options until he was certain where Prussia's maximum advantage lay coupled with the least risk. 'Many paths led to my goal,' he later wrote; 'I had to try all of them one after the other, the most dangerous at the end. It was not my way to be single-handed in political action.'‡

From these quotations the shape of *Realpolitik* can be discerned. Bismarck's view of diplomacy was the antithesis of Gladstone's. He did not believe that broad ethical and moral precepts governed diplomatic actions. Bismarck believed in an overall divine purpose. Nations struggling for growth were part of the divine plan. Whatever contributed successfully to that growth was justifiable. Bismarck's Christianity was Lutheran; he believed in free will. When applied to international affairs this meant that success and failure were not predestined. The diplomat, he believed, must make use of all his talents to assure a successful outcome for his own state in the continuing struggle between nations. He believed in morality as

* Pflanze, *Bismarck*, p. 89.
† Pflanze, *Bismarck*, p. 91.
‡ Pflanze, *Bismarck*, p. 91.

something that certainly applied to private life, but equally looked on moral considerations as having no relevance to politics. He distinguished between questions that concerned individuals and those that affected the interests of groups, be they social classes, political parties, or nations. Bismarck believed that provided he could show that an action served the interests of the state no further justification was needed.

A lust for power characterized Bismarck's own political life though he was kept on the periphery of political power away from Berlin until the king entrusted him at the age of forty-seven with the principal ministerial office in 1862. To describe him as a 'typical Junker' is not very meaningful. To hang a label on a man of outstanding capacities which seeks to identify him with the supposed outlook and attitudes of a particular class or sectional interest is again to oversimplify. Great intelligence transcends such confining barriers. Bismarck was a man of many parts and that of Junker or landed squire was just one of them. His attachment to his landed estates, which a grateful nation considerably enlarged, was genuine and typical of the landed Junker families of Prussia from which he had descended on his father's side. Characteristic of these Junkers too was their sense of paternalism to the peasants on their estates, a feudal loyalty to the monarch, and a self-confidence amounting to arrogance. A rigid code of honour earned them respect even though they were bound to become something of an anachronism in the developing modern industrial society. They survived as a caste astonishingly long; indeed in debased form until the German débâcle of 1945, the majority serving Hitler. Bismarck represented this same attitude of service to the state and to its monarch; it was not so much a personal loyalty as loyalty to the Prussian state, for Bismarck was fully aware of the limited vision of William I and the foolishness of the Kaiser his grandson. For his gravestone he chose the inscription, an adaptation of one of Schiller's poems: 'A faithful German servant of Kaiser William I.' His service to William II he deliberately passed over in silence.

On his mother's side his forebears were intelligent middle-class professionals, many of them educated, professors of law and civil servants. Bismarck was conscious of this, the other 'half' of his inheritance, and seems to have been ashamed of it. He never lost an opportunity to play the 'Junker' in an exaggerated way and to deride 'professors', 'bureaucrats' and intellectuals. Although Bismarck reacted against efforts to impose an education on him in his youth, he became a master of the German language spoken and written. He was a good linguist, fluent in French and good in English and had taught himself Russian. As a student he lived a rather dissolute life, but passed his law examination with ease. He spent a short time reluctantly in army service and at the age of 24, after his mother's death, helped his father run the family estates. High-spirited, but somewhat unbalanced and given to melancholy, young Bismarck's intelligence was recognized, as was his extreme laziness.

Ambition and a thirst for power transformed Bismarck and enabled him to subordinate the defects which stood in his way even though he never entirely overcame them. He suffered from periods of indolence, excessive eating and drinking, hypochondria and nervous prostration. Vindictiveness and intolerance of even the slightest opposition, a ruthlessness in gaining his ends, personal as well as those of the state, are the least attractive aspects of his character. But his mind was razor sharp, he could be cruelly and devastatingly witty; he was clever at assessing the weaknesses of his opponents. His successes and his failures were on a grand scale. He did not 'plan' in the sense of mapping out a specific sequence of moves, but rather sought to reach limited and clearly defined goals, one at a time, by taking advantage of situations that he either helped to create or that presented themselves to him by chance. He could be patient, waiting for the right opportunity, but brutally fast when he thought the rewards were worth the risk. Once he had made up his mind to a particular course of action he became irresistible, cajoling or blackmailing everyone around him, including the king, into doing what he wished. Clever, self-assured, incapable of playing second fiddle, always determined to be the leader, to have everything revolve around him, these were some of the characteristics of the 'Iron Chancellor'. In the end all these characteristics and others, were typical not of a class, the 'Junkers', or of Prussians in general, but were uniquely combined in the make-up of an individual, Bismarck.

Bismarck became involved in politics as a representative of the landed gentry to the United Landtag in session in Berlin in 1847. The revolution of 1848 found him back on his estate all ready to rescue the king from the popular mob and the barricades. As a parliamentary representative to the parliament elected in 1850 under the three-class system he soon became notorious as an extreme reactionary. What mattered to him was Prussia. For the German parliament at Frankfurt in 1848 he had nothing but scorn and he characterized the learned assembly as the 'German sham' (Schwindel), the smaller German courts and princes he regarded in the same light, just a sham, not to be compared with the royal house of Prussia. The French revolutionary legacy such as the rights of man and nationalism in the sense that the state expressed the will of the people, all such ideas were anathema to Bismarck. Only later did he make skilful use of these 'contemporary' movements to serve his own purposes.

In 1851 Frederick William IV chose Bismarck to serve as Prussia's Ambassador to the revived German Diet. For six years he studied at first hand German affairs and the options which were open to Prussia and Austria in dealing with them. He travelled to Vienna and Paris widening his experience and meeting Francis Joseph and Napoleon III. With the mental collapse of Frederick William IV in 1857, Bismarck's position, which had depended on the goodwill of the king, was undermined. He was 'promoted', but shunted away from Frankfurt where the vital questions facing Prussia in German affairs and in her relationship with Austria were being discussed, to serve as ambassador in St Petersburg. The knowledge he gained of Russia and the respect for its potential power was to influence him throughout his later career. But Bismarck also made sure of not being forgotten by frequently returning to Berlin where he was openly labelled a careerist. William I did not much like him. In the spring of 1862 Bismarck transferred to Paris and it was from there, as has been seen, that Roon in September 1862 called him to Berlin. Whether this was done with or without the king's knowledge is not certain. Bismarck's readiness to carry on and push through the army reforms desired by William I even without a majority in the parliament decided the king to entrust him with government. In his wildest dreams William I could not have imagined in 1862 that the man he had appointed temporarily as chief minister was not to relinquish that office for twenty-eight years, outlasting the king's own long life. Nor with all his self-confidence could Bismarck have foretold what lay before him.

His appointment aroused general indignation. Bismarck's hostility to a liberal and constitutional-minded parliament was taken for granted. A day before proroguing parliament, which refused to pass the estimates, he had bombastically declaimed to the finance committee of the Lower House, 'It is not by speeches and majority resolutions that the great questions of our time are decided. That was the great mistake of 1848 and 1849. It is by iron and blood.' Later the phrase in reverse order, 'blood and iron', became famous; at the time it was regarded as a wild and provocative challenge to domestic and international tranquillity. The king feared Bismarck would provoke revolution. Many thought the *Landwehr* lieutenant had spoken presumptuously of war. It was not an auspicious start. What his remark revealed was contempt for the parliamentary constitution. For Bismarck the constitutional conflict was not a matter of principle but of power and that was on the king's side.

The first step to Prussia's renewed rise to great power status Bismarck saw quite clearly was to make Prussia the master of Germany north of the river Main. Practical statesman that he was he did not trouble his mind about possible second steps. He always followed limited goals. One step at a time. What were the obstacles? For the independence of the smaller German states and their princes he had no respect as has been seen. They too were in his eyes all '*Schwindel*', shams. If they could be isolated from Austria and the rest of Europe did not intervene these states and free towns could not hold out against Prussia's economic and military power. In dealing with the various chessmen on the European diplomatic board Bismarck showed his cleverness and total lack of scruple during the early years. To each he presented Prussian interests and policies in the light most likely to appeal. To the Emperor Napoleon III, Bismarck intimated that both France and Prussia were dissatisfied powers who cared not a fig for the Vienna Treaty settlement of 1815. They should support each other to suitably re-draw the map of Europe. To Francis Joseph, Bismarck presented Prussian policy as being based on the tradition of the old alliance between Prussia and Austria and the *equality* of the two states in German affairs as against the pretensions of the smaller German sovereigns; Prussia, like Austria, so Bismarck assured the Austrian ministers, cared nothing for public opinion or national sentiments and would make policy according to its dynastic interests. To the Tsar of Russia, Bismarck emphasized Prussia's traditional friendship and the interests the two monarchies shared in the suppression of Polish nationalism. The irons were all ready to hand to lay in the fire which Bismarck knew just how to fan at the appropriate moment.

During his first years of office Bismarck's aim, far from strengthening 'German' institutions and by this means strengthening German unity, was to attempt to discredit the German Confederation in every possible way, to show its impotence when faced with 'real' states such as Austria and Prussia. In December 1862 he explained his point of view to William I in a secret memorandum. The more Prussia was bound by German federal treaties and agreements the less her real power would be, for Austria could organize the members of the German Confederation against Prussia. This was an acute assessment of the Habsburgs' German policy which opposed Prussia's growth of power especially in the economic sphere through the *Zollverein*. The customs-union had recently (in 1862) been strengthened when France and Prussia signed a commercial treaty. Prussia was not interested in any of the reform proposals brought before the German Diet at Frankfurt. What Bismarck tried to do was to wean Austria away from aligning herself with the smaller German states to an alliance with Prussia against them. Bismarck was not particularly successful in achieving his goal in 1863. The Austrians could not be persuaded to 'desert' their allies in Germany. But Bismarck was already making good use of the inflammatory material at hand. Napoleon III's ambitions and restlessness continued to worry the

Austrians. The Polish revolt in Russian Poland in January 1863 increased Austrian fears. But for the moment Bismarck miscalculated. He sought to gain Russia's friendship for the future by sending General von Alvensleben to St Petersburg to promise Prussian help in the suppression of the tsar's Polish rebels. When it came to the Poles, Bismarck was afflicted by the phobia of seeing them as the mortal enemies of Prussia. Their spiritual resilience deeply disturbed him and in a private letter he even referred to the need to 'extermin-ate' the Poles, though he did not mean this literally in the twentieth-century Hitlerian sense. So there was more to the Alvensleben mis-sion to the tsar than diplomatic calculation. Bismarck had allowed his personal feelings to affect his good judgement. It all turned out badly. The tsar's ministers did not need Prussia's help. Alvensleben sent back a Convention which would have allowed Russian troops to pursue the Poles from Russian Poland on to Prussian territory. Napo-leon III took up the cause of 'Poland' and Britain and even Austria sent protests to Russia on the harsh treatment of the Poles. Protests too showered in on Berlin against the Convention and Bismarck defended himself saying that the Convention did not exist as it had not been ratified. This in turn angered the Tsar of Russia. It was a failure for Bismarck. But the Polish involvement proved an even greater setback for Napoleon III who in the end was distrusted by everyone, the Russians, the Austrians and the British.

The renewal of trouble over the future of Schleswig-Holstein in the autumn of 1863 gave Bismarck another opportunity to win Austria's alliance and so her tacit abandonment of the anti-Prussian policy in German affairs. Bismarck promised to come to an arrange-ment with the Austrians over the tariff question now that the *Zoll-verein* had triumphed throughout the German states thus proving Prussia's economic predominance over *Kleindeutsch* Germany. Eco-nomic considerations, he assured the Austrians, would be subordin-ated to political. But if the Austrians refused to abandon their alliance with the smaller German states against Prussia, then Prussia would summon to its aid German nationalism and call for another parliament elected by the German people to take the power from the Habsburgs and the lesser German princes. Bismarck would ally with the spirit of Frankfurt of 1848. The inevitable outcome would be as in 1849, the little Germany with the King of Prussia at its head. This was no sudden brainstorm. Bismarck was never afraid of taking even the most serious risks when the stakes were high. He had thought of allying the Prussian crown with German nationalism as one 'iron in the fire' for several years and considered that working men and peasants could be combined with the crown to form a common front to defeat the liberal bourgeoisie. No alignment at home or abroad was rejected by Bismarck on grounds of ideology or of principle. It was just a question for him of whether immediate interests were served.

The year 1864 was more successful from Bismarck's point of view than 1863 had been. The liberal opposition in parliament was expecting to recover its rights not by offering resolute resistance at home against Bismarck's unconstitutional acts but as a by-product of the expected failure of Bismarck's German policy. Instead the reverse happened. For sheer virtuosity and lack of scruple, Bismarck never excelled his handling of the Schleswig-Holstein question to Prussia's advantage. The Schleswig-Holstein question in all its juridicial complexities was tailor-made for Bismarck's diplomatic conjuring tricks. The great powers thought they had settled the issue by the Treaty of London in May 1852 in a way that solved the succession question and the integrity of Denmark. The childless Danish King Frederick VII would be succeeded by Christian of Glücksburg, who was the heir of the Kingdom of Denmark, but owing to different succession laws, not heir to the Duchies of Schleswig-Holstein. Christian would nevertheless also succeed as ruler of the Duchies. The other claimant heir, the Duke of Augustenburg, had agreed on behalf of himself and his family not to disturb the peace of the Duchies or to oppose the settling of the succession of the Duchies; he never was asked, however, formally to renounce his claim to the Duchies. This was the first ambiguity of the treaty of 1852. The second was the arrangement whereby the powers agreed that the Duchies and the Kingdom of Denmark should be united into one well-ordered whole, whereas the King of Denmark had promised Prussia and Austria to respect the separate rights of the Duchies. Finally Holstein remained in the German Confederation whilst Schleswig linked to Holstein was not a member.

When Christian ascended the throne of Denmark in November 1863 he also signed a new constitution which the German states declared infringed the promises of 1852 for it incorporated Schleswig into the Danish Kingdom, or so they claimed. It was a repeat performance of 1848–9. The cause of the Duchies was the means of emphasizing German nationalism. The son of the Duke of Augustenburg now claimed the right to the succession of the Duchies which his father had not explicitly signed away in 1852. The very situation which the Treaty of London in 1852 had thought it had solved had now arisen. The smaller German states of the Diet of the German Confederation proposed that in support of Augustenburg as the rightful duke, Holstein should be occupied by an army of the Confederation. Bismarck made every effort to defeat this plan. Instead he won over Austria to drop the Augustenburg claimant, to recognize Christian as rightful heir, but to act against Denmark on the grounds that the new constitution set aside the rights of the Duchies which

King Frederick had promised Prussia and Austria to maintain. In January 1864 Bismarck finally induced the Austrians to sign an alliance with Prussia against Denmark. The army of the Confederation had occupied Holstein without Danish opposition. The Prussian and Austrian armies now moved through Holstein and on 1 February crossed into Schleswig. The Danes this time resisted and so Denmark, Austria and Prussia were at war. The unequal struggle could not last long; by mid-April 1864 the last strong Danish defensive line at Düppel fell. The signatories of the Treaty of London convened a new Conference in London ostensibly to preserve Denmark and restore peace. But in 1864 the powers were no longer united. Bismarck changed front at the conference. Austria and Prussia declared themselves for the separation of both Duchies from Denmark and for the Augustenburg succession. The war had been started in the name of the Treaty of London; it was to end by reversing its provisions. The Danes would not accept, hoping vainly for British support, and the great powers abandoned the pretence of imposing an international settlement. The conference broke up on 25 June and the war continued the following day.

Bismarck had no intention of handing the Duchies over to Augustenburg. Within days of declaring that this was his aim, he persuaded William I to abandon the 'ungrateful' Augustenburgs. Denmark, denied support by the powers, had to ask for peace. In August 1864 the King of Denmark ceded his rights in the Duchies to Prussia and Austria. The Danish war was over. The fuse for the greater war between Austria and Prussia was laid. There can be little doubt that Bismarck intended to exploit further the issues involved in the future of the Duchies to secure their annexation to Prussia and Prussian predominance north of the Main. If this meant war with Austria, he was ready for it. Meantime he widened the breach between Austria and the German states. The Duchies were not handed over to Augustenburg, championed by the German states, but jointly ruled by Austria and Prussia. The troops of the Confederation were ignominiously forced to leave Holstein in the autumn of 1864. Bismarck with all the advantages of Prussia's geographical propinquity also made Austria's position in the Duchies increasingly difficult.

By the spring of 1865 Bismarck's policy required another somersault. Before he could persuade William I to envisage the annexation of the Duchies his sense of honour had to be satisfied. A council of crown lawyers provided the means by declaring that the King of Denmark had been the rightful Duke of Schleswig-Holstein at the outset of the war and so the Duchies now belonged to Prussia and Austria by right of conquest. Bismarck had expected and probably worked for this outcome. But at the Crown Council on 29 May 1865 he argued against a policy of an immediate breach with Austria and against the annexation of the Duchies. For almost a year, until the end of February 1866 Bismarck's policy remained tortuous and conformed to nothing like a clear plan of war with Austria for the supremacy of Germany. This was really characteristic of Bismarck's diplomacy. Bismarck was uncertain. He was a great believer in the intuitive process which he believed would tell him when the best moment for action had arrived. Until then his skill was not to bind himself irrevocably to one course of action. By the summer of 1865 tension between Prussia and Austria reached a critical point. William I was all for Prussian annexation and the Austrians irritatingly backed the pro-Augustenburg agitation. But nothing was allowed to interfere with the annual rite of 'taking the waters'. William I and Bismarck departed to the gloomy Austrian spa of Gastein, highly fashionable and favoured by the Emperor Francis Joseph. Neither the Austrians, more than usually bankrupt, nor Bismarck, wanted war in 1865. When, therefore, the Austrian Count Blome arrived in Gastein to negotiate with Bismarck a settlement offering concessions, the outcome was the famous Convention of Gastein of 14 August 1865. The joint administration by Austria and Prussia of the Duchies was ended. Instead the once indissoluble Duchies were divided; the administration of the Duchy nearest to Prussia, Holstein, was assigned to Austria, and the administration of Schleswig to Prussia. The German states and Europe professed to be indignant at this division of the spoils. But even now the question had not been settled for the Austrians had insisted that the partition of the Duchies should only be provisional.

During the six months from the Convention of Gastein to the Prussian Crown Council of 28 February 1866 which virtually decided on war with Austria, Bismarck did all he could to strengthen Prussia's position *vis-à-vis* Austria. The Danish war had convinced him that Britain and Russia were unlikely to intervene in a conflict between Austria and Prussia. Italy might be induced to act as ally. The key was held by Napoleon III whose benevolent neutrality would leave Austria isolated. Bismarck met the emperor at Biarritz in October 1865. Historians have conjectured ever since exactly what passed as Bismarck's own record of the conversations in Biarritz and Paris is brief and vague. That Bismarck reduced his options by agreeing with Napoleon III on France's price of neutrality in the event of an Austrian-Prussian war seems unlikely. More probably Bismarck left Napoleon III with a general impression that a friendly policy towards Prussia would bring dividends to France, for if it came to some rearrangement of the map of Europe, France too would benefit and be able to extend its rule to wherever French was spoken (i.e. Belgium). Bismarck may even have vaguely spoken of the Rhine frontier. But to anything definite he certainly never committed himself. Napoleon III did not commit himself either and responded with general expressions of sympathy. He repeated Bismarck's own remarks made in Paris earlier, 'one must not try to create events, but let them ripen; they will not fail to occur, and then they will furnish proof that Prussia and France are the two states in Europe whose interests make them most mutually dependent...' and so on. Nothing decisive was achieved at Biarritz.

During the winter of 1865–6 Bismarck contributed to a further deterioration of Austro-Prussian relations. The details matter less than Bismarck's intent and that became clear at the meeting of the Crown Council on 28 February 1866. Bismarck frankly avowed that war between Prussia and Austria had become a matter of time. The ground was shifted away from the Schleswig-Holstein to the greater German question. Bismarck was not very precise about his solution of the German question. William I with his scruples was still reluctant to overthrow any other German prince, but Bismarck well knew that in the flush of victory the king's sense of honour could be managed. The crown prince was a much more determined opponent. He deplored the struggle for Germany as a war between brothers. But Bismarck got his way. He was authorized to seek an Italian alliance and assurances from Napoleon III should the purpose of the war turn out to be for more than the future of the Duchies. The Prussian military advisers, Moltke and Roon, were confident of victory.

The secret alliance between Prussia and Italy was not concluded until 8 April 1866. The Italians did not really trust the Prussians. Though entitled 'offensive' and 'defensive', its provisions were purely 'aggressive'. Article II provided that if Prussia's plans for reforming the German Confederation according to her own wishes failed and Prussia took up arms then Italy would *follow* Prussia in declaring war on Austria. Italy and Prussia would only conclude peace by mutual consent (article III). The war would end when Austria agreed to Prussian conditions over the German question and Venetia had been ceded to Italy. Most interestingly Italy stipulated that the alliance would lapse unless Prussia declared war on Austria within three months of the signature of the treaty (article V). This clause restricted Bismarck's freedom of action and avoided Italy becoming merely Bismarck's diplomatic tool, which is what Victor Emmanuel feared would otherwise happen. Bismarck had less success tying down Napoleon III. It was true that Napoleon III had made the Italian alliance possible because Victor Emmanuel would not sign it unless Napoleon III favoured this step. Napoleon III gave his private assurance though in rather a hedged-about way. But Bismarck probably realized the French would insure themselves with both major contestants. In this he was right. Napoleon III continued to send general expressions of goodwill to Berlin but he sent precisely similar messages to Vienna. He had made sure that Italy would gain Venetia if Prussia won. On 12 June he concluded a secret treaty with Austria, that if Austria won in Germany, Austria would cede Venetia to France (and Napoleon III would hand it then to Italy) and if Austria won in Italy that she would respect the *status quo ante bellum* (article II). In return Napoleon III promised French neutrality and if possible Italian neutrality (article I). Austria also bound herself to reach an understanding with France before sanctioning territorial rearrangements which would upset the European equilibrium. In an additional note Austria promised not to establish Austrian hegemony over a united Germany. Napoleon III's aim was first to maintain the division of Germany and secondly to secure 'compensation' for France if either Austria or Prussia won and there is no doubt that what the French wanted was the Rhine frontier of 1814. But unlike in 1859 Napoleon III had failed to specify the payment France was to receive in any of these agreements. He expected Austria to win eventually. He also believed that during the war there would be a better opportunity to exploit France's neutrality than before it had begun.

The last diplomatic moves of Napoleon III vacillating as always between allowing war to break out between Prussia, Italy and Austria or trying to preserve peace, between the offers of mediation and the calling of a European Congress to settle the dispute, delayed the outbreak of war for just over two months. They were all ineffectual and Bismarck even managed to put himself in the position of accepting pacific proposals rejected either by Italy or by Austria. He hoped neither ally nor enemy would save Prussia from peace and if they did, then he had the patience to wait and work for another opportunity.

An examination in detail of the diplomatic machinations of the German Diet in Frankfurt sheds no new light on the origin of the Austro-Prussian war. The other German states struggled to avoid a war breaking out where they would be forced to take sides and in which they would risk their very existence. Austria sought their alliance. Bismarck was content with their enmity which would give Prussia the excuse of annexing their territory. Bismarck's weapon against the German Confederation, an alliance of sovereigns, was to threaten to place Germany's future in the hands of a German parliament elected on the basis of universal suffrage – an alliance of people against the princes who stood in the way. Then only the King of Prussia would remain. Bismarck's clear aim was to exclude the Habsburgs from any say in German affairs. Prussia by sheer force of size, economic and military power would then dominate 'smaller' Germany. The precise institutional forms this domination would be expressed in, outright annexation or a confederation permitting local tradition to persist whilst having all real decision and power in the hands of the King of Prussia, Bismarck had not worked out. He was inclined to prefer the maintenance of outward tradition and so confederation, but the first time he ever used the phrase 'North German Confederation' was on 9 July, after the war had been won. War had become inevitable when the Austrians became convinced of Prussia's lack of sincerity and refused to concede the primacy of Germany to Prussia without a struggle.

Count Mensdorff, the Austrian Foreign Minister, decided on the fateful step of breaking off negotiations with Prussia over the future of Schleswig-Holstein and on 1 June he handed the decision of what should be done with the Duchies to the Diet of the German Confederation. Bismarck countered by denouncing the Austrians for breaking the Convention of Gastein whereby Austria and Prussia agreed to deal with the Duchies exclusively themselves. He failed to mention that Prussia had already broken it by concluding a secret alliance with Italy. These were just manœuvres. Austria hoped for allies among the smaller German states; Bismarck threatened them. Bismarck also ordered the occupation of Austrian-occupied Holstein. But the chivalrous attitude of the Prussian commander, much to Bismarck's chagrin, permitted the Austrians to withdraw peacefully. Nor did Bismarck have any success in persuading the Italians to start the war. But the Austrians saved him further trouble by proposing to the German Diet of the Confederation that all the German states except Prussia should be mobilized. A Bavarian amendment excluded the mobilization of the Austrian army as well. Although mobilization was therefore not directed solely against Prussia, the Prussian delegate at Frankfurt had already received his instructions to announce Prussia's withdrawal from the Confederation and to issue an invitation to the German states to form a new alliance with Prussia (14 June). On the following day Bismarck delivered ultimatums in Hanover, Electoral Hesse and Saxony demanding that the three north German states side with Prussia or that they would otherwise be regarded as enemies. It was naked aggression and the ultimatums were rejected. The Prussian army moved in and with scarcely a fight – except in Hanover – occupied all three states before the end of the month. Meantime the army of Saxony had joined the Austrian army in northern Bohemia, whilst the most powerful of Austria's German allies, Bavaria, maintained her army in isolation within her own frontiers. The future of the struggle for supremacy in Germany would be decided in the campaign about to commence between Prussia and Austria. The war had begun when Prussian troops took the offensive and without any formal declarations.

In Germany and Bohemia hostilities actually lasted only three weeks. The Italians who vainly tried to win an engagement prolonged the war a few weeks. The outcome came as a great surprise to the rest of Europe. The Prussian army was not held in high esteem. The victory over Denmark in alliance with Austria, another great European power, after weeks of hard campaigning had not added to its reputation. Only with hindsight can it be seen that since the shambles of the partial mobilization of 1859, the fighting capacity of the Prussian army had been continuously improved not by any one reform, or suddenly with a stroke of a pen, but gradually. Backed by Bismarck, William I and Albrecht von Roon carried through the army reforms despite parliamentary opposition; the effectiveness of the regular Prussian army was much improved by 1866. The *Landwehr* now formed a second-line reserve force. The Prussian armies were organized by Helmuth von Moltke, the most gifted military mind since Napoleon and Wellington. Moltke was appointed Chief of the Prussian General Staff in 1857. A man of education and breadth of mind, he was a new kind of general; a professional specialist who organized a team of specialists to the very highest standards of efficiency and made the Prussian General Staff a model for army reform in Europe and later even in the United States. Service on the staff and in the line created in the long run a close relationship and understanding between headquarters and the officers in the field armies. The special concern of the General Staff was the preparation of the army for war and the drawing up of war plans which included the arrangements for efficient mobilization. In the age of the railway the necessary planning had become very exacting. Even though Prussian planning worked imperfectly in 1866 it was superior to Austrian mobilization. Thanks to Bismarck's diplomacy, Prussia also enjoyed the advantage that the Austrian forces were divided. The northern army assembled in Bohemia where the territories of Prussia and the Habsburg Empire met. The southern army operated in Italy. Moltke was the king's principal military adviser in 1866 and responsible for the war plan which defeated the Austrians, even though the Prussian commanders of the three armies which invaded Bohemia were reluctant to be bound by the Chief of Staff's plan. Mistakes were made, but the errors of the Austrians were worse. Crushingly defeated in one battle, the Austrians had lost the whole war on both fronts.

Sadowa, or Koniggrätz as the Prussians called it, was in its consequences one of the most decisive battles in modern history. Moltke's plan was to surround and annihilate the Austrian army. General Benedek, despite his protestations that he was not fitted for the task, commanded the northern Austrian army in Bohemia. On 2 July he telegraphed to Francis Joseph that peace should be sought at any price since the destruction of the army was unavoidable. On the following day the Austrians fought stubbornly but were defeated by the better led and armed Prussians. It was a large-scale battle with a total of more than 400,000 men being involved. Twenty-four thousand Austrians were killed or wounded and thirteen thousand fell as prisoners into Prussian hands. Prussian ascendancy in Germany had been decided on the battlefield. But even more than that was decided. If Prussia had lost the battle, Bismarck, Moltke and Roon would have fallen from power and the conflict between crown and parliament would have taken a different course. Instead their partnership remained unchallenged and gained for Germany the ascendancy in Europe. Even the majority of the Prussian parliament now joined in the chorus of praise and hailed Bismarck as the hero of the day. It did not help the Austrians that they defeated the Italians on land at Custozza on 24 June and out at sea as well a month later off Lissa. The Italian alliance with Prussia guaranteed Italy's ultimate success at the conference table without regard to the Italians' lack of military success. For the victorious Prussians the road to Vienna lay open. William I, who had been so reluctant to make war on his fellow German monarch, now wished to spare him no humiliation. The King of Prussia was an old soldier with a simple faith in the righteousness of the God of War. The battlefield was the final arbiter of questions of honour as far as he was concerned; not so for Bismarck. No one better exemplified Clausewitz's famous dictum that war was 'only a continuation of state policy by other means'. Austria was beaten. Bismarck anxiously scanned the European diplomatic scene to discern what new dangers threatened Prussia now that her lightning victory had upset the calculations of her continental neighbours and the mythical 'balance of power' was seen to be disturbed.

Bismarck's moderation when concluding peace with Austria has always been praised as an example of the highest quality of statesmanship. The German states north and south of the river Main were at the mercy of the Prussian armies. The Habsburg Emperor could have been forced to cede a portion of Bohemia. There was a stormy 'war cabinet' meeting on 23 July with William I and his generals loudly protesting against Bismarck's policy of no annexations of Austrian territory, and Bismarck overcome by nervous exhaustion weeping in an anteroom. Bismarck's will prevailed: the Prussian army was halted and the Habsburgs were not asked to cede an inch of territory to Prussia. Significantly during the actual course of the war the civilian power of the Prussian state as represented by Bismarck had won the upper hand over the military. Bismarck recalls how at the meeting of 23 July, he had been the only person present not wearing a uniform. No doubt he felt that a uniform would have falsely placed him in a junior rank! William I finally conceded on 24 July. Bismarck had found an ally in the crown prince. William I commented bitterly, that he, the victor, despite the splendid feats of his army, would have 'to bite into the sour apple'.

Prussia and Austria concluded an armistice and a preliminary peace at Nikolsburg in Bohemia on 26 July 1866, only just three weeks after Sadowa. Prussia promised to withdraw from Habsburg territory which was to remain undiminished except for the Venetian Kingdom (article I); the German Confederation was dissolved and the Emperor of Austria agreed to his exclusion from the new German organization; a closer union north of the Main was to be founded by the King of Prussia, and a union of the south German states, whose relationship with the Northern German Confederation remained to be settled later (article 2). The territorial status of Saxony, (Austria's most loyal ally) was preserved intact (article 5). The Emperor of Austria recognized the various territorial changes in northern Germany including the Prussian annexation of Schleswig-Holstein, but the Danish-speaking inhabitants of northern Schleswig were promised a plebiscite and the choice to be united with Denmark (articles 3 and 5). The King of Prussia would seek Italy's approval to the peace preliminaries as soon as the Venetian Kingdom had been handed over to Italy by Napoleon III (article 6). Austria was also required to pay a war indemnity (article 4). In short, Prussia annexed Hanover and three smaller north German states with some four million inhabitants and despite the 'territorial integrity' of Saxony, the 'independence' of the remaining north German states was soon lost – except for a measure of local autonomy – in the North German Confederation, formed under the leadership of the King of Prussia.

The interesting question facing historians is why with all the German states at his mercy and Austria unable to offer further resistance, Bismarck did not help himself to more, for instance the whole of 'smaller' Germany. The answer he gives in his *Reminiscences* is that his moderation was due to the intervention of Napoleon III and his misgivings of continuing the war with both Austria and France ranged against Prussia. It is a part of the truth, but not the whole. Bismarck is unlikely to have made any firm plans as to what kind of peace to impose when he began the war. Characteristically he preferred to wait for the situation to unfold. A week after Sadowa he seemed to have been bent on destroying the Habsburg Monarchy by encouraging nationalist revolts in Bohemia and Hungary. In Paris, Napoleon III presided over divided counsels. Drouyn and the Empress Eugénie were war-like, Rouher pacific, warning Napoleon III not to set himself against the principle of national self-determination. Napoleon III chose a half-way course. He would not threaten Prussia by mobilizing an army on the Rhine, but on 5 July offered his friendly mediation to the Kings of Prussia and Italy, saying that the Emperor of Austria had ceded Venetia to him. Bismarck as usual seems to have followed contradictory policies. On the one hand he was working for a rapid peace giving Prussia direct dominance in

northern Germany, and indirect domination over the southern German states. The southern German states were to be isolated and the
dualism of Prussia and Austria in Germany ended by Austria's exclusion. But in his anxiety to be prepared for any alternative, even the
worst, a hostile European coalition against Prussia, based on an
Austrian-French alliance possibly with Russian support, he had
made plans to set off disruption throughout Europe through appeals
to revolution and to nationalism. This second course of action, quite
unnecessary at the time, angered the tsar and induced him to call for
a European Congress. In fact even in the summer of 1866 Bismarck's
excessive caution led him to suffer from 'nightmares of coalitions'.
The tsar was unprepared for war and so was Napoleon III, psycho-
logically and militarily, for the rapid and decisive Prussian victory
had robbed him of any actual power to influence events. On the night
of 11 July 1866 the French Ambassador Benedetti arrived at the
headquarters of the King of Prussia with Drouyn's instructions insisting on an immediate armistice. But already on 9 July, Bismarck had
written instructions to the Prussian Ambassador in Paris to be laid
before Napoleon III limiting Prussian demands to predominance in
north Germany. The southern German states were to be permitted to
form a union and guaranteed an independent international position.
The stumbling block was William I's craving for annexation of north
German territory, but Napoleon III's reluctant agreement was won on
the eve of the signature of the Nikolsburg preliminary peace. If
Bismarck really did give way to Napoleon III in July 1866, he
probably need not have done so. But Bismarck was never a man to
take unnecessary risks. It is therefore possible to conclude that the
Austro-Prussian settlement of 1866 in reality fulfilled his wishes at
that time.

The preliminary peace had made no mention of the southern states'
'independent international position', as the French were not slow to
notice. By the time the peace of Prague was signed on 23 August
1866 the emperor had won this assurance that France would not face
a united Germany north and south of the Main – or so it seemed.
Behind Napoleon III's back, Bismarck had already prepared the way
for a close alignment of the south German states with Prussia. Bismarck had begun by demanding territory and large war indemnities
from the south German states. He then proposed an alternative. The
southern states should conclude secret alliance treaties with Prussia
beyond the usual defensive alliance provisions. If Prussia should find
herself involved in a war which threatened her territorial integrity,
then the southern states would not merely fight with Prussia but place
their armies under the command of the King of Prussia. In a military
sense they would thus have given up their independence. Precisely
what induced the southern Germans to sign away their unfettered

sovereignty is still not completely clear. Certainly the fear of harsh peace terms and their sense of isolation was an important motive; it may well be that Bismarck threatened them, saying that if they would not be allies then he would feel free to strike a bargain with Napoleon III instead, at their territorial expense. Bavaria might end up like Poland, a victim of partition. In any event the southern states capitulated without much resistance to Bismarck and the secret treaty between Prussia and Bavaria was signed on 22 August 1866, a day before the peace of Prague with its now empty promise of respect for the southern states' independent international existence! And this clause was intended to represent the only success of Napoleon III's mediation, for France received no territorial compensation for her consent to the alteration of the map of Europe in northern and central Germany. In August Benedetti had been sent away by Bismarck empty-handed with general assurances and promises that he, Bismarck, would support the emperor's designs on Luxemburg and Belgium. After the conclusion of Nikolsburg, Napoleon III simply had no leverage to force Bismarck to concede anything he did not wish.

After the annexations of Hanover, Hesse-Cassel, Nassau, Frankfurt and Schleswig-Holstein without benefit of the consent of their populations, Prussia was greatly enlarged. In the north, Prussia had not 'unified' Germany as much as conquered German territories. But among the 4 million new Prussian subjects the king acquired, there were many who opposed the forcible Prussianization. The dominance of the kernel of old Prussian power, Protestant Brandenburg-Prussia, was further diluted. There were many more Catholic Prussians after 1866 than before, as well as large groups of people in the Polish provinces and in Hanover whose loyalties were not given to the Prussian King. The annexations of north Germany continued that process of the transformation of 'Prussia' into Germany and the loss of a purely Prussian identity. To have annexed the southern German states would have swamped Prussian traditions even further and this may well have been the reason why in 1866 Bismarck preferred a policy leading to domination over them rather than total absorption. However, Bismarck could not halt the process of the absorption of *Prussia* into Germany, a process to which he himself so powerfully contributed by his successes in 1866.

17

The Unification of Germany
1866–1871

Bismarck returned to Berlin in triumph. During the victory parade he rode on a charger through the Brandenburg Gate with Moltke on one side and Roon on the other. He was no longer regarded as the political gambler who had led the royal government in defiance of the constitution and then started a war which many had predicted would end in Prussia's defeat. In just seven weeks Bismarck and the Prussian army had destroyed the assumption of a century or more, that Prussia was one of several German states and that in Germany her choice of policy lay between co-operation with Austria or challenging her influence. Only in the economic sphere had the latter policy shown any signs of success. More usually Prussia had acknowledged the Habsburg Emperor as the senior member of the Confederation.

During the war of 1866 many of the smaller, and all of the larger, German states had allied with the Austrians. There were some exceptions, where the rulers of some small northern and central German states unwillingly 'allied' with Prussia to escape an otherwise inevitable Prussian occupation. To be counted among Prussia's less enthusiastic allies were, in the north, Oldenburg, Mecklenburg-Schwerin and the Hanseatic cities; Brunswick and Mecklenburg-Strelitz agreed to Prussian 'reforms' and were permitted to remain neutral. Bavaria, Württemberg and Baden joined Austria but engaged only in little fighting. Mutual jealousies prevented them from co-ordinating their forces with each other or with the Austrians. Only Saxony, which in the nineteenth century displayed a lemming-like capacity for always choosing the losing side, proved a resolute ally. Apart from Prussia the most important northern German state was Hanover which resisted and fought the Prussians. Since the accession of Queen Victoria, Hanover was no longer ruled by a British sovereign and so Bismarck did not hesitate to force a war on the state.

A crucial stage in the unification of Germany was, therefore, brought about, not because the German states wanted unity under

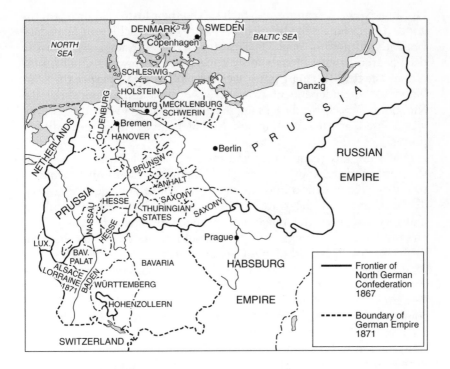

Map 5 The Unification of Germany

Prussian leadership, or because the spirit of the German people had manifested itself irresistibly as in 1848. Quite the reverse is true as is shown by the evidence of 1866. Bismarck's Prussia had imposed its will by force. Later patriotic myths have obscured the fact that Prussia in 1866 made war, not only on Austria, but also on the majority of the German states.

If Bismarck is rightly praised for his moderation towards Austria in victory, it should not be forgotten that he behaved as a conqueror in northern and central Germany dethroning princes who refused to give up their sovereignty. Why? Both attitudes can be explained in a rational way as part of a calculated policy to cajole or terrify, in order to bring home to the German rulers that any state not whole-heartedly on Prussia's side would be treated as an 'enemy' without regard to any supposedly common German bonds. A notorious example of this treatment was the prosperous Free City of Frankfurt. It had done no harm to Prussia, but the citizens were maltreated and collectively fined and annexed to Prussia, their ancient rights extinguished. Hanover was annexed and Prussianized and the infirm King George was driven from his throne; the Elbe Duchies, Schleswig-

Holstein, were also annexed which solved their historical problem for good. The promise of the plebiscite in northern Schleswig was conveniently forgotten. The small states of Hesse-Kassel and Nassau disappeared to give Prussia more coherent shape. Some small northern and central German states were permitted by Bismarck the semblance of an independent existence, the most important being the Kingdom of Saxony. For them the 'North German Confederation' was devised, an alliance of unequals, which gave Prussia the reality of power.

It was not any scruple that had stayed Bismarck's hand in 1866 in the north and the south. Bismarck deliberately sought an alternative to outright annexation and for this there could only be one reason. To have annexed the states of Weimar, Mecklenburg, Oldenburg and Saxony, after the much larger annexation which Prussia had already carried through in 1866 would have posed no internal problems for Prussia, but with his eyes on the southern states, Bismarck wished to show how considerate Prussia could be to allies. Prussia's policy in northern and central Germany depended on Bismarck's view of how best to develop future relations with the south German states. He did not, moreover simply wish to annexe Bavaria and Württemberg with their predominantly Catholic populations and non-Prussian cultures and traditions. They were to be drawn into Prussia's power orbit under the guise of an alliance or federation. In short, the North German Confederation only makes sense if it is seen as an experiment, or blueprint, which it was intended could be applied later to a wider confederation involving the whole of 'smaller' Germany.

What had been achieved under Bismarck's leadership in 1866 was the exclusion of Austria from the future development of German affairs. Without Austria, Prussia was bound to dominate because of her overwhelming size and strength. Bismarck believed that in good time the southern German states would fall like ripe fruit into the Prussian basket. One German civil war was enough; Bismarck preferred an alliance with the south Germans to outright annexation. It was a process which to begin with he felt need not be, and should not be, hurried. The first task was to digest what Prussia had gained and to provide a new momentum for Prussian policy at home and abroad.

The Prussian victory of 1866 transformed the politics of Prussia and destroyed the possibility – admittedly a slender one – that Prussia might become a constitutional monarchy. That is what the solid liberal opposition and its allies in the Prussian parliament had been striving for. But they expected to follow the British example only partially. They attempted to gain control over the budget and were asking for a 'responsible' ministry. They wished the ministers to be legally accountable to parliament, not to be dependent necessarily upon parliamentary majorities. They were prepared to recognize the extensive powers of the crown but were looking ideally for a half-way house where power would be shared by king and parliament. For four years the parliamentary opposition had held fast, in the face of royal threats and Bismarck's campaign of intimidation. After Sadowa the extraordinary thing that happened was that this majority of steadfast and honourable men turned themselves practically into a government party, supporters of Bismarck, after they had gained some concessions on the scope of parliamentary government. They placed the 'national question' first. Not for the last time experienced and intelligent men believed they could make a distinction between the 'good leader' and the 'bad leader'. They would support Bismarck in 'solving' the problem of German nationalism for they wished to see German power enhanced in the world; but they would oppose Bismarck whenever he tried to ride roughshod over those liberal principles they held dear. That was the theory and it overlooked the fact that in contributing to Bismarck's success abroad they would make him all-powerful at home as well. Some sixty years later Germans similarly sought to distinguish between the good and the bad Hitler with far more calamitous consequences for themselves and Europe.

A new Prussian parliament had been elected in July 1866 during the excitement of the war; in fact polling took place on the very day of the battle of Sadowa. The Conservatives gained 114 seats and became the strongest party with 142 seats. The liberal opposition parties, the Progressive Party and the Left-Centre Party, had been reduced from 253 to 148 seats. Early in August Bismarck appeared before the parliamentarians not in arrogance, as might have been expected after his success, but with apparent magnanimity. He appealed for a reconciliation between the royal government and parliament in the greater interests of Germany. He asked for an 'indemnity' on behalf of the government for any actions committed, and payments made in past years, without parliamentary consent; but Bismarck avoided any actual admission of guilt. As he put it a month later in a speech to the lower chamber of the Prussian parliament (on 1 September), 'During the last four years nobody on one side has been able to convince anybody on the other. Each has believed he was acting right in acting as he did...We (the royal government) wish for peace in this domestic conflict but not because we are not equal to the struggle. On the contrary, the tide is flowing more in our favour at this moment than it has done for years...We wish for peace because in our view the Fatherland needs it at the present moment more than ever before.'* Bismarck then held out the prospect that the royal government would 'discharge the tasks, which remain to be discharged, with you jointly'. The opposition was tempted. Past conflicts had no relevance for the present or for the future, so Bismarck now claimed, as he invited all men of good will to join him in building the new Germany. William I had reluctantly consented to the introduction of an 'Indemnity Bill' as it went against his sense of divine right to ask his parliament for any indemnification of royal actions. It is difficult to withhold a kind of admiration for this stiff-necked Prussian monarch who seemed to lack the most elementary political instincts and who for honourable and traditional reasons always would at least begin by trying to act in the way which to him seemed right. He often finished less honourably by acquiescing to the wishes of his first minister. Compromise with the people did not belong to the vocabulary of a Prussian king, but Bismarck always gained the upper hand over the old gentleman who then consented to do what he had earlier opposed.

Bismarck also succeeded in winning over the majority of liberals and conservatives. The Indemnity Bill was passed with a majority. To a bill introduced by Bismarck which provided for financial grants to the victorious generals, parliament next added the name of Bismarck and made him a gift of a large sum with which he purchased the estate of Varzin in Pomerania. Only a minority of parliamentarians refused to indemnify Bismarck and to continue in opposition. They were the rump of the once-large Progressive Party. A larger group of the Progressive Party split off and in 1867 took the name of the National Liberal Party. They undertook to support Bismarck in his national German policy but declared they would maintain themselves as a 'vigilant, loyal opposition' should the royal government ever threaten liberal principles, the maintenance of a parliamentary constitutional state, the rights of individuals and, in economic policy, free trade. The Conservatives too split. The traditional Conservative Junker party could not accept Bismarck's 'revolutionary' German policy; they opposed the loss of Prussia's identity in the new 'smaller' Germany, the diminution of royal prerogatives, and naturally opposed the idea of a parliamentary assembly elected by secret ballot and on the basis of universal manhood suffrage. So for the old conservatives Bismarck was too liberal, and for the progressives not liberal enough; but the conservative industrialists, the more liberal-minded Silesian noblemen, the bankers and professors now dissociated themselves from the original Conservative Party and formed their own party group

* Böhme, *The Foundations of the German Empire*, p. 170.

known as the Free Conservatives (later on they called themselves German Imperial Party, *Deutsche Reichspartei*). Together the National Liberals and Free Conservatives gave Bismarck, for more than a decade, the backing he needed to lay the foundations of the German Empire whilst observing most, if not all, of the constitutional proprieties.

The North German Confederation only lasted four years. It then gave way to the German Empire, but the constitution devised for it settled the main features of the constitution of the German Empire. It continued to influence German constitutional development even after that and ideas basic to it can be traced to the present constitution of the Federal German Republic. Its peculiarity lay in the nature of the federal unity it established between the states composing the North German Confederation (and later those which made up the German Empire) and the central Imperial power. The associated states had rights far more extensive than local regional rights. The rulers of the states continued, in name, their reigns as sovereign dukes or kings. They were governed according to their own laws and constitutions with their own parliamentary assemblies and civil and judicial service; the administration, the churches, the schools were all administered according to state laws and state taxation was levied to meet these costs. These extensive separate state rights, of course, also left intact those of the largest German state – Prussia. The central federal authority was exercised by the *Bundesrat* (the Federal Council). The representatives of the state government sat in the *Bundesrat*, but with a voting strength according to the size of their states. Prussia possessed seventeen votes, Saxony four, Mecklenburg-Schwerin and Brunswick two each and the remaining eighteen states one each. Decisions were reached by simple majorities in secret session, the delegates voting according to instructions from their governments; a simple majority of 22 votes out of the total of 43 votes was required. In practice Prussia could always gain a majority and so completely dominated the *Bundesrat*. The King of Prussia assumed the modest title of President of the *Bund* and the real function of Commander-in-Chief. He appointed, and could dismiss, the Federal Chancellor. He controlled foreign policy and could declare war and conclude peace. The army of the Confederation was Prussianized. Besides the Federal Council or, to use its German name, the *Bundesrat*, the constitution provided for the election of a *Reichstag* by a vote as democratic as any at that time in Europe, universal manhood suffrage. The Federal Chancellor, however, was not responsible to the *Reichstag* or dependent upon majority support from it (as in Britain), but responsible to the President of the *Bund*, that is the King of Prussia, and to the *Bundesrat*. In the draft of the constitution as presented to a Constituent Parliament, Bismarck had created a grand façade of 'allied governments', and a national democratic parliament which left all real power and decision-making in his own hands as the Prime Minister of the King of Prussia. He did not at first aspire to become Federal Chancellor, which he regarded as a symbolic office for public consumption. He had conceived the 'Chancellor' as the King of Prussia's representative on the *Bundesrat* who would follow Bismarck's instructions.

The so-called 'allied governments' were in no position to offer any serious opposition to Bismarck's plans. Two small principalities, nevertheless, did so foolhardily. Their rulers were treated drastically: the Duke of Saxe-Meiningen was deposed, and the state of Reuss was occupied, but Bismarck did not wish to create the impression south of the River Main that the 'allied governments' were of no account. By cajolery, a few peripheral concessions, and by threats, he secured their 'willing' consent to the constitutional draft during the winter of 1866. The opposition of the constituent *Reichstag* proved more formidable.

The constituent *Reichstag* was elected by universal man hood suffrage in February 1867. A high proportion of the electorate exercised their rights. Just as in '1848' there were few ordinary people among the elected representatives of the people; a royal prince and some fifty dukes and barons were elected. Supporting Bismarck without reservation were 39 Free Conservatives, and 27 Old Liberals. The Progressive Party was reduced to 19 and the old Conservatives to 59. Some seventy members were divided into many parties opposed to the Confederation: Poles, Schleswig-Holsteiners and loyal Hanoverians or 'Guelphs' as they were known. Bismarck could count on the absolute support of the Conservative groupings and the old Liberals, some 125 votes. The Progressive Party and Bismarck's particularist opponents could muster together about 90 votes against him. The balance was held by 79 National Liberals, who were the largest single party in the new *Reichstag*. It is they who won some concessions from Bismarck.

The National Liberals wanted to make the whole of the Federal Executive, that is all the ministers, responsible in a limited legal sense to the *Reichstag*. Bismarck in the end compromised by agreeing that the chancellor alone should countersign all draft ordinances and laws after the kind had signed them. In agreeing to add the chancellor's signature, Bismarck satisfied the requirement of legal responsibility, though what this really amounted to always remained rather abstract and ambiguous. It did not mean that the chancellor was 'responsible' in the sense of dependent on a majority view taken by members of the *Reichstag*. The Liberals also succeeded in securing more concrete rights, such as strengthening the immunity of parliamentary members from arrest, the right to new elections within 60 days of a dissolution of the *Reichstag*, and the adoption of a secret, instead of an open, ballot when elections were held. The *Reichstag* also won the right to pass annual budgets, but financial control over government – the central power of modern parliaments – was not as complete as it appeared. The greatest struggle between Bismarck and the National Liberals in the *Reichstag* was over the military budget, over which the *Reichstag* had no control. This comprised most of the Confederation's expenditure. A compromise solution was reached which allowed the amount of the military or 'iron' budget for four years to remain outside parliamentary control. After that date, 1 January 1872, the number of recruits to be called to the colours, that is to say the amount of money to be spent on the army, was to be fixed by a law for which the *Reichstag*'s consent would become necessary. All laws required the approval of the *Reichstag*, the *Bundesrat* and the king, and the signature of the chancellor. Both the *Bundesrat* and the *Reichstag* enjoyed the right to initiate legislation.

The Constitution was finally approved by the *Reichstag* on 16 April 1867 by a majority of 230 to 55. It created nothing like a parliamentary government on the British model. Political development in Germany was crippled by Bismarck's undisputed hold over the chief ministerial office of the state for 28 years. On the other hand the *Reichstag* was no façade or simple talking-shop either, which is probably what Bismarck had first intended it to be. Political parties did emerge with some gifted and respected leaders though they could not control the emperor and the imperial executive with the chancellor as its head, and despite the compromise reached on the military budget in 1867, the *Reichstag* never gained control over foreign policy or over the enormous expenditure on the army and, later, the navy. The most vital decision of government remained in the hands of the civilian and military leaders enjoying the emperor's confidence. Until 1890 Bismarck towered above them all.

Bismarck did not need to 'plan' German unification. The North German Confederation already comprised two-thirds of the whole of Germany now that Austria had been excluded. The remaining third could not really lead an 'independent sovereign existence' as envisaged in the Treaty of Prague. About that contemporaries were not in any serious doubt. The south German third was not even united but Württemberg, Baden and Bavaria were as suspicious of each other's intentions as they were afraid that their territories could become pawns in Bismarck's power game. Why then did they so willingly put their heads in a noose by signing the secret treaties with Prussia in 1866? The contradictions of south German diplomacy are frequently glossed over by historians, but given the position in which the south German states found themselves after Austria's defeat their policies do make a certain amount of sense.

They were under pressure from all sides. Now that the former condition of Austro-Prussian rivalry in Germany had been replaced by Prussian predominance, the 'middle states' could no longer maintain their independence by manœuvring between the two major 'German' powers. Austria, after 1866, could not be relied on as a counterweight to Prussia. Nor could the south German states turn to France for support. Bismarck had not been slow to point out to the south German governments that Napoleon III hankered after the left bank of the Rhine and had proposed that territory from the south German states would compensate France for the further growth of Prussia in Germany. Clearly Bismarck had intimated that he could always strike a bargain with Napoleon III if the south German governments remained recalcitrant. Thus there seemed to be no choice left to them but to settle with Prussia on the best terms they could obtain.

If we now examine the position from the Prussian side, Bismarck, had he wished, could easily have overcome south German resistance by force and could have done so provided he was prepared to 'compensate' France for maintaining her neutrality in the conflict. He probably had no objection on principle against abandoning some Bavarian or other German territory to Napoleon III, but since he had decided against acquiring southern Germany by force, there was no need to agree to any territorial compensation for France. However, it was characteristic of Bismarck not to reject French approaches out of hand when the French Ambassador, Benedetti, conveyed Napoleon's suggestions during July and August 1866. To maintain Napoleon's hopes gave Bismarck another 'iron in the fire'. So Bismarck parried Napoleon's projects to acquire the Bavarian and Hessian portions of the left bank of the Rhine, which would have regained for France the 1814 frontier; Bismarck dropped broad hints that Napoleon should look for compensation to the French-speaking regions, Belgium and Luxembourg. Napoleon did not press his demands for the 1814 frontier but concentrated on Luxembourg. In the meantime Bismarck had pocketed the Benedetti 'draft' which mentioned 'Belgium' for possible future use. He used it effectively in July 1870 when he published it in *The Times* but omitted the date of the document, thus making it appear that Napoleon III had immediate designs on Belgium.

There is no conclusive evidence which allows us with certainty to expose Bismarck's motives. It is unlikely that he had a clear-cut plan to bring about a war with France. As has been seen, if a union between the north and the south had been his only aim, Bismarck could have achieved it without a war with France, but Bismarck was not willing to make the necessary concessions to the south German states, or to Napoleon III, to win their co-operation for a policy of

German union. Bismarck was in no particular hurry. In October and November 1866 he was a sick man. When he returned to Berlin that December, the North German Confederation still had to be given a constitutional form. Prussia had her hands full absorbing all the king's new subjects. In any case, time, Bismarck believed, was on Prussia's side. He would make good use of it to strengthen Prussia's domestic and international position whilst undermining the will of any potential opponents to offer effective resistance.

At least on one point Napoleon III seemed to have made some headway – the plan to acquire Luxembourg with Bismarck's assistance. Napoleon III needed a diplomatic and territorial success to offset Prussia's increase of power. Public opinion in France, though pacific, demanded that France should continue to provide proof of her primacy in continental Europe. The acquisition of Luxembourg would not be much but it was something. The purpose of Bismarck's policy on what became the 'Luxembourg' question is particularly difficult to unravel. At first he helped Napoleon III by putting pressure on the King of the Netherlands, the sovereign Duke of Luxembourg, to divest himself of the Duchy. With the example of the 'personal union' of Schleswig-Holstein before him, William III of the Netherlands was ready to do what he was asked. Prussia also had some standing in the Duchy as she possessed the right to garrison the fortress of Luxembourg which had formed a part of the defunct Confederation. By December 1866 Bismarck became decidedly less friendly to France. He now referred to Luxembourg as 'German' and privately wrote that the French alliance would be 'too dearly bought' if purchased 'by a humiliating injury to German national feelings'. Bismarck now believed the best way to consolidate the North German Confederation with the south was 'through the excitement of national feelings' and that could only mean the encouragement of anti-French prejudices. At the same time he posed as the injured friend when talking to Napoleon III's emissaries, blaming the emperor for his clumsy diplomacy.

Napoleon III, scathingly attacked by the opposition at home (p. 294), was desperate to prove that his friendly policy towards Prussia, and his sympathetic attitude towards German national consolidation, would pay dividends for France. He also boasted in Paris that Prussia had been halted at the gates of Vienna by France in 1866. The emperor was promptly answered by Bismarck in Berlin. Bismarck could not tolerate the French claim implying that his policy in 1866 had been tied to Napoleon III's apron strings, and so, on 19 March 1867, he released the texts of the secret Prussian alliance treaties with Bavaria, Württemberg and Baden concluded in the previous year; they made it appear that the barrier of the River Main, for which Napoleon III took the credit, was illusory. Bismarck and Napoleon

III were now set on a diplomatic collision course. Napoleon III, playing on the Dutch king's fears that Prussia hankered after Dutch territory, offered to guarantee the Dutch frontiers in return for the cession of Luxembourg to France. William III agreed to 'sell' Luxembourg but only if the King of Prussia agreed! For the subsequent crisis Napoleon III must share the blame. He was not likely to gain that consent whilst French agents in Luxembourg were going around inciting the local population to escape the 'hated domination of Prussia' and to declare themselves for France. In Berlin during the crucial debates in March 1867 over the constitution of the North German Confederation, nothing suited Bismarck's purpose better than to divert attention by whipping up national fervour. He inspired the question by the National Liberal leader, the Hanoverian Bennigsen, on 1 April which called on the government to stand firm over Prussian rights in 'German' Luxembourg. Justifying his change of front by referring to the national excitement, Bismarck now proceeded to ruin any chance Napoleon III had of completing the negotiations successfully at The Hague by threatening the Dutch king with German retribution if he injured the 'national sense of honour'; yet surprisingly for a time, even at this late stage in April 1867, Bismarck considered the possibility of bargaining with Napoleon III; he would help France acquire Luxembourg after all in return for Napoleon III's agreeing to release Prussia from the Nikolsburg treaty condition requiring a plebiscite in north Schleswig. Bismarck did not persevere with this idea. One thing, however, was clear, neither he nor Napoleon III were prepared to go to war in 1867 over Luxembourg or anything else. Bismarck, therefore, became an internationalist and resorted to the good offices of the European powers, signatories of the treaty of 1839, to settle the question. The outcome of the London Conference which followed was that Luxembourg was declared neutral under a 'collective' guarantee of the great powers. This was no effective guarantee since its breach by any one of the signatories released the others from their obligations. Cynics might, therefore, call it a 'scrap of paper'. Still it fulfilled its immediate aim of preserving Luxembourg from French absorption. Prussia withdrew her garrison and Napoleon III was left with no alternative but to abandon the plan of acquiring the Duchy with Prussia's secret consent.

The outcome of the Luxembourg question could be presented as a compromise with Bismarck and Napoleon III both making concessions, but in reality it was a much heavier blow for Napoleon III. The Luxembourg crisis marks a significant stage in the evolution of Bismarck's policy on the German question. It was not, as is sometimes argued, that he had progressed from a Prussian patriot to a German patriot. Bismarck would have regarded such descriptions as being empty phrases. It was all a matter of tactics to him. The attraction of a diplomatic bargain with France had never been strong; it seemed even less inviting to Bismarck in 1867. Better results, he came to feel, could be achieved by stirring up German national feelings, but even now, in the spring of 1867, Bismarck was not ready to commit himself finally to one particular course of action. He still intended to keep as many options open as possible. Bismarck's success in the end lay in his ability to harness the nineteenth-century force of nationalism to the traditional cause of the Prussian crown.

Austria was a staunchly conservative power in Europe. The experience of '1848' had made Francis Joseph more, not less, conservative. In facing the tide of social revolution, Russia and Prussia were Austria's natural allies; but there was also a link between the revolutionary tide and nationalism in Italy, Hungary and Germany though revolutionaries and nationalists were frequently uncomfortable partners. The Habsburgs' wisest policy would have been to sever the tie between revolution and nationalism by satisfying the aspirations of one or the other, but Francis Joseph regarded real concessions to either as unthinkable except at the point of defeat, and so the Habsburgs were defeated in 1859 and 1866 by the enemies of Austria who cynically exploited the weakness of Habsburg policies. The Habsburg Empire was not strong enough to support a policy which refused accommodation with Magyar and Italian nationalism within the empire whilst simultaneously facing the assault of France and Piedmont in the south and Prussia in the north. Yet Francis Joseph could not bring himself to satisfy Piedmont in northern Italy or Prussia in the German Confederation where Austria sought to maintain her in a subordinate position. With hindsight it is not difficult to reach such a logical historical judgement, but what great power has ever willingly and gracefully given up its influence, let alone territory forming part of the state without an armed struggle? There are a few examples of the abandonment of influence peacefully. Britain abandoned its influence to the United States in the Caribbean and Central America at the close of the nineteenth century, but this involved no territorial cession. Infinitely more difficult was it to strive for a settlement in Ireland. The Habsburgs did not believe themselves so weak that their empire and its cohesion was doomed. It survived another two generations and fought creditably for three years in the greatest of land wars. The right policy in the 1860s appeared to be one of strength rather than appeasement.

The shock of defeat in the war of 1866 with its loss of Venetia and exclusion from Germany was tremendous. It was the second lost war in a short space of time; nationalism was advancing rapidly. What would happen if there were a third war in a few years? On the eve of the war with Prussia, Francis Joseph's ministers had begun to retreat from the policy of centralization. This retreat could be represented as a return to traditional Habsburg rule laid down by the Pragmatic Sanction, but concessions to the Hungarian 'rebels' was a bitter pill for Francis Joseph to swallow. That he was prepared to do so shows that glimmers of realism had penetrated his mind already before the war of 1866. Francis Joseph was prepared to learn from his mistakes though only slowly. He always placed a sense of duty to the empire before any personal feelings. The empire could not be maintained by defeating recalcitrant nationalities piecemeal although for this task it had proved strong enough in 1848, 1859 and in 1866. It simply was not enough to defeat Magyars and Italians because the nationalists within the empire could forge alliances with neighbouring great powers which, to advance their own national interests, did not scruple to follow revolutionary policies in foreign policy of a kind they would never have tolerated at home. Francis Joseph conceived it as his sacred task to ensure the survival of all the considerable territories left to the Habsburg Empire and to restore its status as a great power. He needed peace. He also had to face a period of reform, political, constitutional and military.

For once Francis Joseph made a rather inspired choice of the statesman necessary to guide the policies of the empire through these difficult years. Friedrich Ferdinand von Beust had served the King of Saxony for twenty years as foreign minister. Bismarck insisted on his dismissal in the summer of 1866. The following October Francis Joseph appointed Beust to the much more important post of foreign minister of Austria. He entrusted him not only with foreign affairs but soon after with the constitutional reorganization of the empire. Beust's wider functions received imperial recognition when, in 1867, he was accorded the title of Chancellor which only a few great Austrian statesmen had borne (Kaunitz, Metternich).

Beust has suffered from the comparison with Bismarck, a comparison of which he was only too painfully aware himself. Judged in his own right, Beust's realism and liberal outlook, his ability to look at the embittered national problem of the empire with the fresh eyes of an outsider, his energy and diplomatic skill, served the Habsburgs well. He could not restore Austria's fortunes in Italy and Germany as the war party at court desired. No one could have done so. What he did was to save the empire from further defeat and then to redirect its international purpose to acting as a bulwark against the advance of Russia in the Balkans whilst advocating, in 1871, alliance with the new Germany.

The constitutional federal arrangements were worked out with surprising rapidity considering all the complexities involved. Beust acted as intermediary in negotiations with Deák. He was assisted by Count Julius Andrássy, once a condemned follower of Kossuth, who had taken advantage of the amnesty to return to his homeland. The 'Compromise' establishing the Dual Monarchy, henceforth Austria-Hungary, fell far short of Kossuth's demand for independence but it did give Hungary internal autonomy and an important influence over the policy of the empire as a whole. The residual powers of the crown remained virtually untouched. Negotiations for reaching a compromise with Hungary had been already well advanced when they were interrupted by the outbreak of war in 1866. They were resumed early in 1867. Beust and Andrássy got along well; Andrássy persuaded the more circumspect Deák and enlisted the help of the Empress Elizabeth to overcome the reluctance of Francis Joseph. The Hungarians accepted the indivisibility of the Habsburg Dominions and gave up Kossuth's policy of complete independence. Deák recognized that Magyar political domination over the nationalities, which comprised the lands of the Hungarian crown, was best maintained within the framework of the Habsburg Empire and accepted the validity of the Pragmatic Sanction (1723) which had declared the dominion indivisible and inseparable (*indivisibiliter ac inseparabiliter*). The 'Compromise' received the consent of Francis Joseph in the summer of 1867 and by the end of the year it was accepted and the necessary laws were enacted, both by the Hungarian *Reichstag* and the Austrian *Reichsrat*.

The competence of the *Reichsrat* no longer extended over the whole empire. The sovereign ruled over both halves of the empire as Emperor (Kaiser) of Austria and King (König) of Hungary. He was separately crowned in Hungary. Three areas of government were designated as concerning both halves of the empire, foreign affairs, military affairs, and finance to the extent that it dealt with common imperial financial and economic interests. These imperial or common Ministries (*Kaiserlische* and *Königliche*, or K and K for short) were created. The joint ministers who were all appointed by the emperor were responsible to the 'Delegations'. The Delegations were composed of 60 delegates each from the Austrian *Reichsrat* and the Hungarian *Reichstag* who had to agree; their agreement then required the consent of the emperor to give them the force of law. Periodically discussions over their respective financial contributions caused great tension between the Hungarian and Austrian representatives. On the whole the Hungarians fared well. Their influence on imperial affairs was equal to the 'Austrian' but their contributions to joint finance smaller. Both the 'Austrian' half of the monarchy and the Hungarian possessed its own prime minister and government with competence over all matters not specifically reserved as an 'imperial' or common responsibility.

Dualism did not allow for an equal *political* role to the Slavs of the empire. They were promised cultural rights but politically were represented as various minorities in the Hungarian *Reichstag* and the Austrian *Reichsrat*. The Czechs to begin with refused to collaborate and so during the first decade after the Compromise, the Austrian-German liberals exerted a predominant control over internal Western or Austrian government, but even so the Compromise did not allow the Austrian-Germans more usually the kind of dominance enjoyed by the Magyars in Hungary. The Austrian-Germans were later on frequently successfully challenged by combinations of the nationalities – Poles, Czechs, South Slavs and Italians. Only the Poles of Galicia achieved some concessions to autonomy and a dominant position over the Ruthenes. Of the nationalities comprising the lands of the crown of Hungary, only the Slav-Croats received a measure of autonomy. They in turn abandoned the South Slavs to Magyar dominance.

In practice these complex institutions functioned reasonably well when judged in the light of the problems besetting the government of a multi-national empire, though they did not satisfy the majority of the Slav peoples (except the Poles who made no common cause with Czechs or other Slavs). The concessions made to the Magyars were considerable. In foreign affairs the prime minister of Hungary, responsible to the Hungarian parliament, had a constitutional right to be consulted on questions of foreign policy which the prime minister of the Austrian western lands of the monarchy did not possess. It was a right that was exercised and no important decision on foreign affairs could be taken without the Hungarian prime minister's knowledge and consent. The three Common Ministries which functioned in theory separately from the government of Austria and Hungary in practice could not carry out many major decisions in foreign, financial or commercial questions without consulting the relevant ministers in Hungary and Austria.

The emperor sought to uphold the rights of the Common Ministries, especially anything affecting military matters, but the business of the empire could only be carried on with the help of an informal conference of ministers. The ministers would work for the necessary constitutional agreements of two parliaments, of two governments and the Common Ministries. The foreign minister (only Beust ever received the title of 'Chancellor') presided over the conference when the emperor did not himself attend. Its precise membership would vary according to the business being discussed, but a full conference would include the three common ministers for foreign affairs, finance and war, the prime ministers of Austria and of Hungary, the Austrian and Hungarian ministers of finance, sometimes other ministers and often the chief of staff. There the real power lay rather than with the Delegations which met only briefly. Inevitably the checks and balances created by the Compromise of 1867 resulted in the empire following cautious policies representing the lowest common factor of agreement between rival interests. It precluded an ambitious policy of attempting to recover the empire's German or Italian position.

During the closing years of the decade of the '60s, the reshaping of Europe was completed and the European balance of power fundamentally altered. The defeat of France and the consolidation of Germany, which became industrially and militarily the leading European power, signified a great change of direction in the history of Europe. Years after the event the leading participants were sorely tempted to represent these developments as fulfilling their carefully-planned policies. Bismarck was especially successful in the role of 'auto-historian', to coin a new word. The twenty-first chapter of his reminiscences entitled 'The North German Confederation' is a masterly episodic treatment, with the omissions as interesting as the contents, telling us much about Bismarck's outlook and methods. Bismarck gave himself credit for remarkable foresight. He had not earned it. We often find that contemporaries are not aware that they are living on the brink of momentous events. These are seen as momentous only in retrospect. On 3 July 1870, on the eve of the Franco-Prussian War, the head of the British Foreign Office observed to the foreign secretary that he had never known 'so great a lull in foreign affairs'. It did not seem an inappropriate judgement at the time. Since the short Austro-Prussian War of 1866 only two relatively minor issues had ruffled the diplomatic calm, the future of Luxembourg and the future of Crete, and the powers had settled these questions by 1870. There were always tensions between the powers, each fearful that another state might gain some unilateral advantage at the expense of the other powers and each pursuing its own aims of seeking not only to maintain, but to expand, its influence. These tensions and rivalries must have appeared less acute during the closing years of the 1860s than they had been during the previous two decades which had witnessed a European war in the Crimea and a continental wave of revolutions. So the curious fact is that all the powers were following conservative and hesitant foreign policies from 1868 to 1870. Bismarck too made the point frankly enough when he wrote that he had overestimated France's military strength and so was concerned to postpone a showdown between the two powers.

The diplomatic moves of the individual powers from 1868 to 1870 are really of negative interest in that they were all to a greater or lesser degree studies in failure. Francis Joseph did not straightaway abandon the idea of recovering Austria's influence in Germany. His appointment of the defeated Saxon, Beust, was interpreted as a gesture of defiance. In practice, however, he recognized that the empire needed several years of peace to consolidate at home and to reform the military machine. On the German question the Austrians could only engage in diplomatic sparring. Beust sought to strengthen the desire for independence of the south German states. Without a coalition, Prussia would never be pushed back. There is little point in examining in detail the negotiations between Francis Joseph and Napoleon III on this issue. The insuperable obstacle was that the only basis for an alliance with France against Prussia was one that sacrificed south German interests. It would hardly serve, therefore, to strengthen Austrian influence with the south German states at the expense of Prussian influence. The hostility of the German Austrians to a pro-French and anti-German policy would, in any case, have caused a grave crisis within the Austro-Hungarian Empire, nor could the Austrians win French support for an anti-Russian policy in the Balkans.

There was much royal coming and going. Francis Joseph and Napoleon III met in Salzburg in August 1867; the Austrian Emperor visited Paris in October but the discussion led nowhere. The attempt to draw in Italy in 1868 and 1869 failed also for the Austrians would not give up territory in the south Tyrol and Napoleon III would not leave Rome and abandon the Pope. All that came of these long-drawn-out negotiations was an exchange of letters between Francis Joseph and Napoleon III in September 1869, promising each other assistance if attacked, but there was no real commitment despite the cordial language. Austria-Hungary was isolated. There was no basis for an agreement with France, no desire for an agreement with Prussia and scarcely-concealed hostility towards Russia. The south Tyrol divided Austria and Italy, and Britain followed her own specific interests – Belgium and the 'Eastern question' – and these did not include an active concern for changes in the balance of power on the continent.

Russia too was isolated. Tsar Alexander was unable to come to closer terms with Austria. The 'Eastern question' increasingly divided the two empires. From 1866 onwards it exerted an intermittent but, at times, a powerful influence over the relations of the powers. With the revolt of Crete in summer of 1866 against Turkish rule and desire for union with Greece, the movement for independence from Ottoman rule gained new impetus. This phase of the diplomatic crisis petered out in 1869 with the 'concert of powers' agreeing on the least dangerous course which was to postpone the 'Eastern question' and in the meantime to support Ottoman rule. The ambitions of Russia and Austria-Hungary in the Balkans on the one hand, and the attempts of Prussia and France to take advantage of Russia's and Austria-Hungary's involvement in the east in order to advance their own aims in the west on he other, led to much confused diplomatic activity from 1866 to 1869. A number of short-lived abortive alignments were formed in quick succession between Russia and France, Russia and Prussia, and Austria, Italy and France, but none of them had any lasting effect. In 1870 the neutral great powers were as suspicious of each other as of the belligerents France and Prussia. When the Eastern question became pressing in 1875, the European situation had been completely changed in the interval by the victory of Germany over France.

Bismarck was not particularly successful either, though he improvised with masterly virtuosity. His actual behaviour during the Luxembourg crisis, whether premeditated or not, created an irreparable breach with France after 1867. Another string to Bismarck's bow was his pro-Russian policy. Bismarck attempted to assure for Prussia the continued benevolence of Russia, so as to insure Prussia against an Austrian *revanche* and a hostile Franco-Russian alignment. The Russians, for their part, were anxious to secure Prussian support against a coalition of Austria-Hungary and France in the Balkans; but just as Tsar Alexander was not keen to back Prussia against France so Bismarck was not keen to back Russia against Austria. The result was that in the spring of 1868 they reached an informal understanding supposedly assuring Prussia that Russia would prevent Austria joining France in a war against Prussia by stationing troops menacingly on the Austrian frontier. This Prussian-Russian military agreement was typical of the agreements of these years – a not wholly reliable understanding, despite the language used. Russia would follow her own national interests when the time came and she did. From the foregoing account it will be clear that a detailed examination of the diplomacy of 1868 to 1870 is singularly profitless. Every move was cancelled out by a succeeding move, leaving each great power in isolation. That suited Bismarck well and he was very lucky to be operating in these conditions.

Bismarck's efforts to draw the southern German states together with the North German Confederation met with mixed success. The Luxembourg crisis in the end did more to encourage particularism in the south, than promote national unity. With the revelation of the secret treaties with Prussia, the 'Patriot Parties' in the south bitterly criticized their sovereigns and ministers for deceiving the people. They saw in the North German Confederation, with some justice, not the nucleus of German unity but the Prussian military state and its efficient bureaucracy territorially enlarged masquerading as a new German spirit. From Stuttgart, capital of Württemberg, and Munich, the capital of Bavaria, the response to a war with France over Luxembourg was decidedly lukewarm.

Having failed to 'win' the south during the Luxembourg question, Bismarck now wielded the economic stick of the *Zollverein*. Prussia would only renew the treaties essential to the economic well-being of the southern German states if the *Zollverein* were 'reformed'. He proposed elections throughout all the German states for a gathering of a *Zollparliament* or Customs Parliament. Bismarck's motive was not commercial reform, even less concern for parliamentary institutions. The *Zollparliament* was a means to an end. He hoped that once this all-German assembly had met in Berlin it would extend its jurisdiction over non-commercial questions. Bismarck was disappointed. The elections for the Customs Parliament in February 1868 turned in the south on the question of closer alignment with the North German Confederation or independence. The Patriot Parties in Bavaria won a majority of the votes, only narrowly lost in Baden; in Württemberg the 'anti-Prussians' swept the board. The Customs Parliament, which met in Berlin in April 1868, thus contained a strong particularist group from the south and never did fulfil Bismarck's wider national aspirations; he soon lost interest in the delegates' useful commercial and tariff work. Early in 1870 Bismarck failed again. He hoped to secure the consent of the German sovereigns and of Europe to the Prussian king assuming the title of *Kaiser.* The project proved a non-starter. The south German states had thus shown that they were not the ripe fruit bound to fall into the Prussian basket. Their fervour for German unity and fear of Prussian power had both receded. Bismarck observed it might take decades to complete unification. Unfavourable as the public political appearances were, behind the scenes Prussia had succeeded not only in co-ordinating commercial policies but also had made headway in the integration of military plans. What was clear to Bismarck was that left to its own momentum unification could be a matter of decades. Only a great national war would transform the situation. This was his judgement of the situation in 1870 when the Hohenzollern Crown candidature crisis broke on an unsuspecting Europe.

The contrast between the long-laid 'fuse' of the crisis – it originated in September 1868 when a revolution in Spain drove the reigning queen out of the country – and the sudden climax in July 1870 when the candidature of a Hohenzollern prince to the throne of Spain first became known in Paris, has led to much historical investigation and speculation as to whether Bismarck had deliberately intended to provoke France to war. This question, like so many 'Bismarck questions', is too simple. Much happened between September 1868 and July 1870 in Spain and in the attitudes of the Hohenzollern family that was incalculable. Bismarck did not control the whole affair from start to finish. What he did was to intervene and take advantage of misunderstandings and ambiguities, to push forward the Hohenzollern candidature at decisive points – but to what purpose? Characteristically Bismarck conceived a range of possibilities, from scoring merely a diplomatic victory over Napoleon III to provoking war; at the worst the candidature could always be abandoned as long as it was treated as no more than a family business which had nothing to do with state policy. The one possibility that Bismarck knew he could exclude was that the candidature would *improve* the relations between Prussia and France. It was one of many irons he kept in the fire. Chance, French blunders and Bismarck's opportunism raised the crown candidature into the issue of war between Prussia and France. Had Bismarck wished it, he could have prevented it. Instead he made sure that feelings would be exacerbated to the maximum. He was suspicious of Napoleon III and the new Liberal Empire, whose chief minister, Émile Ollivier, might plunge France into war to satisfy public opinion.

The idea of approaching a Hohenzollern prince to ascend the vacant throne was not Bismarck's. The leading minister of the Spanish revolutionary government, Marshal Juan Prim, seems first to have initiated the approach after others had declined the offer. The Prussian ruling house was related to the Catholic southern Hohenzollern branch of Sigmaringen, whose head at this time was Prince Charles Anthony of Hohenzollern-Sigmaringen. Prim's choice was Charles Anthony's son, Prince Leopold. Rumours of Leopold's candidacy reached Paris in May 1869, but Bismarck told the French Ambassador that the prince had declined to be considered. Bismarck always claimed that until the crisis broke in July 1870 he had had nothing to do with the candidacy, which was entirely a family affair of the Hohenzollerns. The secret documents of the German foreign ministry tell a different story. They show that the Spanish offer to Leopold was presented to Prince Charles Anthony in February 1870. As head of the house, Charles Anthony's consent was required. He referred the request to William I, adding that he would counsel Leopold to accept if William I 'commanded' him to do so in the interests of Prussia and the dynasty. Nothing is clearer, that if the matter had been left to William I the candidacy would have expired. William I throughout was pacific and fully aware that to proceed with the candidacy would be a provocation of France. But in March 1870 Bismarck intervened and did his best secretly to persuade William I to consent for the sake of Prussia and the dynasty. He sent the monarch a powerfully argued memorandum. This gives the lie to his claim that he had nothing to do with the question. William I was 'utterly against the affair', but in the end weakly reached a compromise with his importunate chancellor. He *would* consent provided Leopold chose himself to accept the throne. This did not fulfil Charles Anthony's condition and Leopold did not wish to go to Spain. It seemed to end the candidacy.

Bismarck meanwhile had secretly sent agents to Spain to further the candidacy. He then sent these emissaries to the Hohenzollern princes to persuade them to accept. In mid-June 1870 the intrigue succeeded. Whilst Bismarck discreetly withdrew to his estate in Varzin, his secret moves had induced Prince Leopold to accept the candidature and on 21 June William I, much annoyed by the manœuvres behind his back, added his formal consent. So much for Bismarck's non-involvement. In the end a misunderstanding ruined the success of Leopold's candidacy. The Spanish parliament, the Cortes, whose function it was to elect the king, had been prorogued owing to a mix-up over the date when Leopold's formal document of acceptance was expected to arrive in Madrid; but the secret of Leopold's acceptance could not be kept. The news reached Paris on 2 July 1870. That was not part of Bismarck's plans which had supposed Napoleon III would be faced with a *fait accompli*. The French emperor now had a chance at last to best Bismarck and to show him up as troublemaker and disturber of the peace of Europe. But he had already made his first mistake in his choice of foreign minister, Antoine duc de Gramont, who had replaced the pacific Count Napoleon Daru shortly before the crisis broke. Gramont who had served as ambassador in Vienna was violently anti-Prussian and determined to back Napoleon III in winning a great diplomatic victory. Inflexible and lacking in judgement, he served his master who in fact was fully in charge despite a recurrence of his bladder illness. Ollivier was altogether more pacific and hoping to avoid war. Only two days before news of the crown candidature had reached Paris, he had sent an optimistic message to the Legislature that he viewed the European situation with equanimity, 'at no epoque was the peace of Europe more assured'. But feelings of French pride and patriotism also blinded his judgement. He had been prepared to accept the unification of Germany by peaceful means but was not ready to accept any further French humiliations. Yet Napoleon III must bear the principal blame. Nothing was done without consulting him and he played a full and final role in all the French moves after 2 July: Gramont's angry enquiry on 4 July whether the Prussian government had had knowledge of the candidacy and Ollivier's message to the Legislature two days later belligerent in tone; French honour was at stake and the equilibrium of Europe; if the candidacy was not abandoned, Ollivier declared, 'we shall know how to discharge our duty without faltering or weakness'.* Strong stuff, but behind the scenes Napoleon III was trying to reach a peaceful solution. The trouble was that ministerial rhetoric had only heightened the clamour of the press and public excitement, giving vent to anger at Prussia's presumption.

* J. F. McMillan, *Napoleon III* (London, 1991), p. 156.

William I, meantime, an honourable though not outstandingly clever monarch, was deeply disturbed over the whole wretched business. He did not want war. For once, he did not listen to Bismarck. The king was taking the waters at Bad Ems. He did his best to defuse the crisis. Prince Leopold unaccountably could not be reached, on vacation somewhere reputedly in the Alps; his father, Karl Anton, equally troubled at the cause of the crisis, now renounced the candidature on behalf of his son. The crown of Spain was in any case hardly a great prize. Meantime Gramont had instructed Benedetti, the French ambassador, to follow William I and travel to Ems to seek personal assurances from the king. William I managed to keep Benedetti at bay with assurances of his pacific attentions. Then on 12 July the crisis should have ended. News had reached Paris of Karl Anton's renunciation on behalf of his son, a great diplomatic victory that plunged Bismarck into deep gloom. He had hastened to the *Wilhelmstrasse*, and angrily spoke of resigning and humiliation worse than Olmütz.

Napoleon III at first appeared satisfied. But the clamour in Paris did not lessen. Gramont persuaded Napoleon III that the renunciation by the father was not enough. Benedetti was sent new instructions from Paris agreed by Napoleon III, Ollivier and Gramont. He was to see William I again, to secure from the king personally a renunciation of Leopold's candidacy, and having secured it to demand an 'assurance that he will not authorize a renewal of the candidacy'. The excuse for this undoubtedly insulting demand, implying that the king was not to be trusted in the future, was that only by giving these assurances could French public opinion be calmed. Benedetti followed his instructions and there occurred on 13 July the famous episode in the *Kurgarten* of Ems. William I greeted Benedetti cordially saying, 'I am delighted to encounter you'; but the friendliness evaporated when Benedetti importunately demanded the additional assurances and William I sternly refused. Later that same day Benedetti received instructions from Gramont to seek an apology from the king for Leopold's candidacy. William I now realized for certain that his attempt to preserve peace had failed.

Bismarck that evening of 13 July was dining with Moltke and Roon in Berlin. He was determined on war and enquiries in the south German capitals of their likely response had been completely satisfactory. When that evening the telegraphic account from Ems reached Bismarck in Berlin, describing the morning's audience in the *Kurgarten* between William I and Benedetti, Bismarck saw his opportunity. By condensing this telegram he made William I's behaviour appear far more abrupt than it was. Bismarck's version of the famous 'Ems despatch' the chancellor himself handed to the newspapers for publication in a special edition in Berlin and he also sent it for publication abroad. Moltke and Roon, when they saw Bismarck's handiwork, with characteristic understatement commented, 'Yes, that will do.'

In Paris, among Napoleon III's ministers there was division and confusion. Ollivier maintained that even if Benedetti did not secure William I's guarantee, the crisis should be regarded at an end. The atmosphere was changed entirely by news of the 'Ems telegram' on 14 July. Ollivier still argued at first in favour of peace at a hastily called council meeting presided over by Napoleon III at St. Cloud. He recognised that no insult had been intended by William I. But others, including the war minister, Marshall Leboeuf, and Gramont, urged war. It seemed the peace party had won when a decision was taken to call a European conference. Why at a later meeting the decision was reversed is not clear. Perhaps Napoleon III had concluded he could no longer resist public pressure. In any event, the clear intention to fight became public when on 15 July the Legislature was asked to approve war credit. Only ten deputies rejected the credits, two hundred and forty five approved ignoring Thiers' impassioned objection,' Do you want all Europe to say although the substance of the quarrel was settled, you decided to pour out torrents of blood over a mere matter of form'. Ollivier in a less memorable phrase reassured the deputies that he accepted war with 'a light heart',* famous last words he would not be allowed to forget. On 19 July, France declared war. The outcome changed the face of Europe.

Bismarck's own readiness for war can be demonstrated clearly. Bismarck had planned other moves, including an appeal to the *Reichstag* to bring about a war should the French not oblige by declaring war on Prussia. For Napoleon III it was a question of 'prestige' on which he believed the survival of his régime depended. For Bismarck the war with France enabled him to complete the work of unification at one stroke. His particular genius lay in creating situations which afforded opportunities for decisive action. He was like a tiger waiting to spring. He deferred the decision for the moment of action to a period only briefly before he intended to act. In that sense he had no 'long term' plans. In talking and writing to contemporaries in the months before the outbreak of the war, he rehearsed various arguments, both in favour of war and rapid unification, and in favour of a policy of patience until unification evolved of its own account in years to come. His statements do not provide contradictory evidence as much as evidence for his way of exploring different avenues of reaching the same goal. He used letters to, and discussions with, other people to reason aloud. Thus no single letter or statement should be seen as reflecting the actual policy he was following at

---

* J. F. McMillan, *Napoleon III*, p. 160.

the time. About his goal since 1866 there can be no serious doubt, but only in the spring of 1870 did he use his talents to provoke a war; only then had he committed himself to action, calculating that delay was the riskier course for Prussia to follow. By the time of the French declaration of war on 19 July 1870 he had even contrived to make it appear that all the blame for the war was French. This mattered in one vital respect: it created conditions which activated the military alliance between Prussia and the south German states. A quarrel between Prussian and French ministers had been turned into the great German patriotic war in defence of the Fatherland. Of course it was a 'sham' to use one of Bismarck's favourite phrases. Had the Germans wished it, Germany could have been unified without a war with France. Bismarck was not waging a defensive war, as he claimed, but an offensive one and that was to be equally true of the military conduct of the war. What enabled Bismarck to risk Prussia's and Germany's future was his confidence in Prussian arms and his calculation that he need fear no intervention.

18

From the Authoritarian to the Liberal Empire in France 1860–1870

How 'authoritarian' was Napoleon III's France in 1860 and how 'liberal' ten years later? Labels must always be used with care and this is particularly true of the closing decade of the Second Empire. Liberal did not mean in France what it meant in contemporary Britain; the French legislature was not the British parliament and Napoleon III had no intention of permitting all power to reside with a parliamentary assembly. There was no tradition in nineteenth-century France that regarded the parliamentary assembly as faithfully representing the views and wishes of the French people; or a general belief that the French people would desire all power to be handed over to the politicians who had been elected. The republicans of 1848 regarded the legislature with more contempt than many royalists as capable of corruption and manipulation and placed their faith in universal suffrage, though they were not agreed how a strong executive might best be established. Through all the dynastic changes of the nineteenth century the predominant tradition in France was that of a strong executive which could act separately from the legislature: that executive power in the person of Napoleon III was powerfully based on the popular will as expressed in the three plebiscites of his reign. So 'Liberal Empire' did not mean a parliamentary monarchy on the British model. Nor did 'authoritarian' imply the loss of all individual liberties as in a twentieth-century dictatorship. Certainly in the wake of the *coup d'état* of 1851 socialists were arrested wholesale and exiled, but this harsh policy was soon relaxed. A few deputies – the famous five including Émile Ollivier – were returned to the legislature openly in 1857 as republicans. Finally in 1859 a general amnesty was granted by Napoleon III to his political opponents, even eventually to the fiery '1848'er, Ledru-Rollin. What Napoleon III attempted to achieve was to place his dynasty on sure foundations, to transform purely personal rule, which would come to an end with his death, to one that granted France institutions which would satisfy the majority of Frenchmen and so assure for his young son, the Prince Imperial, a secure throne during his years of minority. A favourite question that is discussed by historians is how far progress towards the liberal empire of 1869–70 was voluntary or how far it represented the attempt of a bankrupt ruler to save his régime. But the question put this way is too crude. There is a great deal of evidence to show that Napoleon III recognized that the problem of even the most successful ruler is how to assure that his work should not be undone by his successors. Napoleon III had a quite extraordinarily strong sense of history which he believed should guide leaders to avoid the mistakes of the past. In France antagonistic cycles since the French revolution had succeeded on each other. The Empire now stood for a reconciliation of all but extremists, a broad umbrella under which Legitimists, Orleanists, Republicans and Bonapartists all could find shelter provided they placed the broad interests of France before those of any sectional interest. Thus the empire was to become the form of government that divided Frenchmen the least!

This meant a gradual relaxation of control, a willingness on the part of Napoleon III to share power genuinely and not merely to create a façade of sharing. It is always easier to acquire absolute power at a stroke than willingly to give it up. Napoleon III was intellectually convinced that a time would come when he should relinquish some of his authority. Change was an inevitable condition of history. The emperor wished to anticipate it and not stand as an obstacle in its way. Those who, like Metternich, had attempted the latter had been swept away. At the same time when it came to the point, Napoleon III was very reluctant to act. He had no strong ideological commitments and his hesitation and lack of resolution increased with advancing age and illness during the closing years of his reign. When it came to timing he was purely opportunist; He held on to as much power as he could contrive by skilful political manoeuvre throughout his 18 years of rule; the 'liberal' was a pretty late development even in 1870 his powers remained strong. In foreign affairs it was downright disastrous. No doubt his failures in foreign affairs after the mid '60s damaged his prestige, made the opposition more strident, and so persuaded him towards the close of the decade that the time for inaugurating change had come. So his comparative lack of personal success and his bouts of illness did influence his timing. Nevertheless it is also true that the fundamental commitment to change had already been made by the emperor before the 1860s. When he heard the news in 1851 that the plebiscite had overwhelmingly endorsed his authoritarian rule (p. 141), he had already then fore-shadowed change, saying, 'to give satisfaction to the needs of the present by creating a system which reconstitutes authority without harming equality and without closing any door to improvement, means laying the true foundations of the only edifice capable of later supporting sensible and beneficent liberty.' Not until 1860, however, did he make a modest beginning in building up that edifice.

In 1859 and 1860 Napoleon III began to move away from his autocratic position on the right to seek the support of groups in opposition to him hitherto, the Orleanists, some of the notables and better-to-do, as well as the workmen in the towns, where he faced the toughest political resistance. The influence of Persigny, the ruthless functionary who had managed the autocratic years declined until this loyal servant of the emperor was suddenly dismissed in 1863. Then the Empress Eugénie, who urged Napoleon III to be resolute and autocratic and to defend the most extreme claims of the ultramon-tane section of the church, could not hold up the changes of policy once the emperor had decided on them. The star of Napoleon III's half-brother, the Duc de Morny who had been appointed President of the Legislative Body, was rising. By the time Morny died in 1865, the prestige of the Legislative Body had been greatly increased and Morny had also established the links between the republican deputy Emile Ollivier and the emperor which led to their eventual collabora-tion.

In 1860 Napoleon III felt himself strong enough to defy the ultra-montanes and the industrialists in his search for broader political support for the empire. Peace and prosperity, more than anything else, would reconcile the masses to the empire. Freedom of com-merce, Napoleon III believed, would contribute to those ends. France had hitherto been rigidly protectionist. In the mid 1850s Napoleon III cautiously began to lower some tariffs. He fell under the spell of the Manchester free-traders; he was introduced to Cobden by Michael Chevalier, a follower of Saint-Simon's ideas; secret discussions led to the conclusion of the Anglo-French trade treaty usually known as the Cobden Treaty in January 1860. Despite the vociferous opposition of the protectionists, Napoleon III in the succeeding years concluded free trade treaties with Prussia and many other European countries. That he persevered was a sign of strength, not of weakness as is so often claimed. Similarly his Italian policy was intended to serve the interests of France not that of any section. No doubt it was not a 'glorious' policy to conclude a compromise armistice with the Aus-trians at Villafranca in July 1859 (p. 224), but it was thoroughly practical and sensible. Much had been achieved and it would have been senseless to waste countless French lives for the sake of Venetia. The movement for Italian unification in the following year, 1860, took everyone by surprise. Napoleon III again followed a cautious policy. He acquiesced in Cavour's plan to stop Garibaldi by allowing the Piedmontese army to fight its way through the papal states to Naples. Napoleon III was not prepared to risk French lives to maintain the papal dominions inviolate. He saved for the Pope what could be saved until he finally withdrew the French garrison from Rome in the extremity of the national emergency of 1870. But instead of earning the gratitude of the Church the emperor was unjustly and hysterically attacked by the ultramontanes. Undeterred Napoleon III pursued a balanced policy. As Pius IX adopted a more extreme stance to preserve his temporal position in Italy, so the emperor reverted to supporting the traditional spirit of independence of the Gallican Church: the Pope was not consulted before bishops were nominated, state as opposed to clerical schools were expanded and religious orders no longer enjoyed all the advantages they had hitherto taken for granted. This was nothing like an anticlerical policy and most Catholics saw no reason to disapprove of the emperor's policies.

On 24 November 1860 the emperor announced the first instalment of a series of measures which liberalized the constitution. The proposals were modest but they increased the rights of the legislature. As Emile Ollivier recognized what mattered was the fact that the first step had been taken in the right direction. The opposition deputies of the legislature greeted these measures with a barrage of abuse but Ollivier, an avowed republican rose in the chamber to express his approval in a brilliant speech. In placing himself above party interest Napoleon III sought to reconcile 'men of good will' to the empire because like Ollivier he hoped they would come to see that the empire provided the best avenue to liberty with order and security. In 1861 other measures were introduced providing for a closer scrutiny by the legislature of the budget and allowing more freedom to the press. But that was as far as Napoleon III was prepared to go for the time being.

A bolder course might have served him better. Instead the next step forward followed his lack of success in foreign affairs and so inevitably was seen as unwillingly conceded rather than as freely granted in fulfilment of the emperor's vision. The elections of 1863 still returned an overwhelming number of supporters of the régime but also a few powerful new and old faces, politicians of subtlety and skill who could damage Napoleon III by their opposition, the experienced Thiers among them. The republicans increased their representation and it was clear that the emperor had not won over Paris or the few large towns. Nevertheless Napoleon III continued to woo the workers, permitting them limited rights of association and strike action in 1864, and four years later workers were allowed to form unions. But in constitutional matters he turned to Rouher, a determined opponent of liberalism. Napoleon III seemed always to be taking two steps forward and then at least one back again. Finally in January 1867 the constitution was modified again and further rights were granted to the legislature; yet Rouher remained the emperor's principal adviser. For all the world it looked as if the emperor was dribbling out reforms like drops of water from a sponge.

The mid-1860s were not a happy period for the empire. The unorthodox banking policies led to some spectacular failures, such as that of the Péreire brothers. The press, freed from many restrictions in 1868, criticized and wittily and savagely lampooned the empire. Nevertheless there can be no doubt that the great majority of Frenchmen continued to support it and favoured none of the possible alternatives: an Orleanist or Legitimist restoration, let alone a socialist republic. The elections of May 1869 showed the tide in favour of liberal constitutional reforms running strongly. The big cities remained unreconciled to the empire yet the republicans in the chamber were only a small group. A large number of deputies were returned who wished to combine support for the empire with constitutional reform: they desired a ministry whose policy would be dependent on the consent of the legislature. That was the policy Ollivier also espoused.

In November 1869 Ollivier and the emperor met secretly. A few weeks later in January 1870 Ollivier formed a new ministry. The liberal empire was moving to its last stage of evolution which was only cut short by the outbreak of war with Prussia. The emperor had now appointed a cabinet which enjoyed the support of the chamber. But the 'Liberal Empire' fell far short of the idea that the ministry, that is the executive, should be solely responsible to and dependent on a majority of the chamber as in Britain. Under the constitution of 1870 Napoleon III retained considerable powers. He remained the head of the government and appointed the ministers and presided over their meetings. He also kept his right to veto, and held to his claim that he was directly responsible to the French people to whom he could appeal when he chose by plebiscite. On the other hand the new constitution obliged him to rule in co-operation with ministers and the legislature, whose rights were further extended. Both houses could now initiate legislation. His ministers were defined as not only dependent on the emperor but also 'responsible' to the legislature – whatever that meant. But the checks on the popularly-elected lower house were still strong; the upper chamber, the senate, could veto legislation passed by the lower house and its members were nominated by the emperor and his ministers. Would the reconciliation of parties the emperor and Ollivier aimed at have succeeded? Could a constitution work with dual roots to the people: with an emperor who could base his actions on a direct appeal to the people through a plebiscite as well as with a legislature whose lower house was elected by manhood suffrage and so could claim to speak for the people?

The compromises and tensions between the popularly-based legislature and executive underlie much of modern French political history. It was a compromise between an autocratic one-man rule, whether imperial or presidential, and the parliamentary sovereignty of a large number of deputies. The attempted solution of 1870 was to be repeatedly tried in various forms with varying degrees of success in the twentieth century. Indeed contemporary France with its strong presidential tradition has sought to strike the right balance as did the emperor and Ollivier in totally different conditions a hundred years earlier. The constitution of 1870 was overwhelmingly approved by the French people on 8 May 1870 with 7,358,786 votes cast for it and only 1,571,939 against. After the plebiscite Ollivier claimed that despite the opposition of republicans, liberty had rejuvenated the empire. For Napoleon III this was a massive vote for the continuation of the empire; his support in 1870 was only ten per cent less than the majority he had secured in 1851.

Napoleon III greatly extended French influence overseas. But his successful image became tarnished after 1866 by a series of fiascos and diplomatic failures, the failure to secure 'compensation' after the Austro-Prussian War, the failure of Mexico and the failures of his diplomacy before the outbreak of the war with Prussia in 1870. At the same time it has to be admitted that the judgements of historians are often unconsciously hypocritical – backing the winners and condemning the losers. Supposing the French army had proved superior during the Franco-Prussian War leaving Napoleon III in the position of imposing a wise and moderate peace on Prussia in 1871. What would historians then have had to say about the years 1866 to 1870? They might well have commended Napoleon III for his idealism and wise restraint preferring to accept diplomatic setbacks rather than inflicting on the French people the sufferings of a major war until finally a showdown could no longer be postponed. Responsibility for the war of 1870 would have been, and usually still is, blamed more on Bismarck than on the emperor. Instead of dying in exile, the emperor would have died in 1873 at the height of success, the first statesman of Europe, the man who had been responsible for the peaceful transformation of France itself. Of course this was not the scenario. French military incompetence relative to the Prussians brought down the empire. It is however, important to remember that the opposition to the empire at home was never strong enough or enjoyed sufficient popularity to provide an alternative framework for the government of France. Prussian bayonets did that.

Seen in this context the impact of the failures of foreign policy on the survival of the régime should not be exaggerated. Napoleon III was rather half-heartedly acting on his conviction that the true statesman anticipated and worked with and not against the great forces of his age. He perceptively recognized that nationalism was the most powerful force in nineteenth-century Europe. It was characteristic of the emperor's strength and weakness to discern with profundity many of the problems of the years to come and yet to fail to act wholeheartedly on his understanding and to shape his policies accordingly. He lacked the ruthlessness and decisiveness of the successful political gambler especially in his later years. In 1863 by taking on the role of champion of the Poles, he offended the Russians without helping the Poles. More seriously Napoleon III failed to appreciate that German 'nationalism' would create a powerful rival for France. But nearly everyone else had made the same mistake before 1866 and underestimated Prussian power. After Austria's rapid defeat in July 1866 he belatedly accepted to preserve the balance of power by limiting Prussia's enlargement. But counsels in Paris were hopelessly divided. There were two groups. The traditionalist pro-Austrians, the empress, Drouyn de Lhuys, and some French marshals who wanted to intervene forcibly if necessary to prevent the defeat of Austria and her exclusion from Germany; then there was the so-called Italian faction, the Prince Napoleon and Rouher who argued in favour of a friendly policy towards Italy and Prussia whose success would destroy the detested settlement of 1815. Napoleon III decided on an unsatisfactory compromise. He got the worst of both worlds. The French offer of mediation irritated Bismarck and subsequent discussions of 'compensation' for France, such as the Rhine frontier down to Mainz or Luxembourg, ended in the fiasco of the Luxembourg crisis of 1867 (pp. 273–4). With the publication of the Prussian secret treaties with the southern states even the division of 'Germany', Napoleon's 'achievement' of 1866, was seen to be far from complete. After 1867 there was no longer any possibility of friendly Franco-Prussian co-operation, but Napoleon III did not pursue whole-heartedly any alternative policy.

Overseas Napoleon III enjoyed considerable success which later was overshadowed by the Mexican disaster. The colonial dependencies of France were reorganized and extended. His view of economic policies was liberal as he set great store on expanding world trade. In Algeria he pursued the policy of subjugation initiated during the Orleanist years and completed the conquest. Algeria was intended to be the brightest jewel in the French colonial crown – 'we will never renounce this conquest', Napoleon III declaimed in 1852 and France did not do so until more than a hundred years later. But risings, plagues and disease made Algeria difficult to rule as well as unprofitable. By way of contrast French financial intervention in Egypt proved profitable for generations. Napoleon III backed Ferdinand de Lesseps, who had founded an international company to construct the Suez canal. Napoleon himself became a shareholder and put pressure on the Sultan to permit the construction of the canal. Begun in 1859, the Suez Canal was ceremoniously opened in 1869 in the presence of the Empress Eugénie. French diplomacy was also active at Constantinople and in the Levant. France thus became a Mediterranean power second only to Britain. In West Africa France greatly extended her hold in the 1850s. Finally in the Far East, in China and Indo-China, France established the basis of a colonial empire during Louis Napoleon's rule.

The most ambitious overseas project, however, was the Mexican misadventure. The American Civil War had provided an opportunity for European intervention without risk of clashing with the United States. Napoleon III now intervened in the intermittent civil war in Mexico against the clerical 'Liberal' leader, Juárez. The pretext was Juárez's suspension of payment on the debts to foreign bondholders. With the agreement of Britain and Spain, the French mounted an expedition to compel Juárez to pay, but Napoleon III's real object was to overthrow Juárez and to bring about a Catholic monarchical restoration looking for support to France. Napoleon III had offered this crown to Archduke Maximilian, the younger brother of the emperor Francis Joseph. In July 1862 Napoleon III ordered his French commander to capture Mexico City and to arrange for a Mexican assembly to invite Maximilian to accept the imperial crown. The Mexicans resisted with a good deal of national fervour, but Mexico City was eventually captured and in 1864 the 'Emperor' Maximilian was duly installed.

Maximilian remained totally dependent on the French troops. Unfortunately for him, beset by difficulties in Europe in 1866 and by American hostility after the close of the Civil War (1865), Napoleon III decided to withdraw the French troops and to leave Maximilian to his fate. However it is perhaps unfair to saddle Napoleon III with the entire blame for the tragedy that followed. Maximilian (no more than the Pope) could expect permanent French protection of 'his' dominions. He should have abdicated and returned to Europe. Instead he chose to stay on, enamoured of his spurious dignity. He bravely suffered the consequence of his folly and vanity. Taken prisoner by Juárez and placed against a wall the poor 'Emperor' was executed before a firing squad. It was a tragedy that caught the romantic imagination of Europe. The blow to Napoleon III's standing was great. He suffered from charges of having deserted Maximilian after having been responsible for the whole escapade. His relations with the Habsburgs were damaged, furthermore, just when he was hoping for support against Prussia.

The collapse of the Second Empire itself was not long delayed. *The Hohenzollern* crown crisis in July 1870 induced Napoleon III and Ollivier to embark on a war with Prussia (for the crisis see pp. 282–6). The most fateful mistake of the Second Empire proved to be omission, a failure to reform the army adequately and in time. Napoleon III did not expect to be at war in 1870 and was not ready for it. By 1866 some of his military advisers had become alarmed at France's numerically inferior professional army when they compared it to Prussia's army. Resistance to the introduction of a conscript army, which the emperor urged was great. Traditional generals rejected the value of conscripts; the prefects reported conscription would be unpopular; and the 'liberal' opposition in the legislature objected to any increase of the emperor's military power at home. Nevertheless the emperor entrusted Marshal Niel to carry through necessary reforms in collaboration with the legislature. In the process of negotiation and argument Niel's proposals were watered down so that the hoped for force of a million trained men could not be attained. Thus Napoleon III's efforts to move away from autocracy to the Liberal Empire which strengthened the régime at home came fatally to weaken it abroad. The technical improvements introduced in the 1860s, especially the manufacture of the superior *chassepôt* rifle and the *mitrailleuse*, could not in the end counterbalance Prussia's numerical superiority at the outset of the war. With the reserve of trained conscripts, Prussia and the German states mobilized 850,000 active men; the French, calling up annually only 80,000 conscripts, relied on the professional army for its manpower and so could not mobilize much more than half that number and also lacked adequate reserves. A combination of faulty diplomacy, faulty assessments and military incompetence brought to an end one of the more hopeful and successful periods of French domestic history.

19

'Pax Britannica' at Home and Abroad

On the eve of the war between Prussia and France in the spring of 1870 Lord Clarendon, the foreign secretary, proposed that France and Prussia should reduce the strength of their armies. The confrontation of the powers on the continent of Europe was creating, he observed, a state neither of war nor peace, an atmosphere 'so destructive of confidence that men almost desire war with all its horrors in order to arrive at some certainty of peace ... [such a condition] is cruel, it is out of harmony with the civilisation of our age and it is pregnant with danger'. The idea had originated in Paris, a fact hidden from Bismarck when the disarmament proposal was made to him in Berlin by the British ambassador. Napoleon III had enough problems at home and was not at all anxious for a big conflict. Bismarck gave Clarendon a dusty response. Would Britain also reduce her navy? You 'live in a happy island and have not to fear an invasion... We are surrounded by three great Empires with armies as large as our own, any two of whom might coalesce against us'.*

This interchange is a good illustration of the profound gap of attitudes between Britain and the European nations on the continent. Historians have frequently emphasised the *Sonderweg*, the separate and singular evolution of German history. It would be more pertinent to speak of a *Sonderweg* of British history in the mid- and later Victorian age. Nowhere else among the great powers of Europe was liberty so deeply ingrained. In mid-nineteenth century Europe, Britain was a model of tolerance of freedom of speech, a free press and free representative institutions. No parliament had been dispersed with bayonets for centuries like the rump of the Frankfurt Parliament. No wonder England was admired by the politically hounded, by revolutionaries as diverse as Garibaldi, Kossuth and

---

* Quoted by K. Hildebrand, *Die Pax Britanica und Preussen 1865/6–1869/70* (Oldenburg, 1997), p. 364.

Karl Marx. Napoleon Bonaparte after Waterloo had even dreamt of retiring to a Scottish castle and Napoleon III comfortably settled in exile with wife and son in Chislehurst.

During these decades the right to vote changed from the basis of material means to something approaching adult manhood suffrage. That fundamental shift had not quite reached its logical conclusion in 1884. Nevertheless in the third Reform Bill exclusions from the franchise were now specific rather than general. Granting votes to women, that is, universal suffrage, too had by the 1880s been placed on the agenda and attracted significant parliamentary support.

Democratic government does not, of course, depend on the franchise alone. The *Reichstag* had been elected by manhood suffrage since 1867, long before the British House of Commons. But Bismarck had severely limited its power of controlling expenditure and taxation and in the German Empire the first minister, the chancellor, was appointed by the monarch and was not bound by a party but could choose his support from any combination that suited him. Control of taxation was also vested in the parliaments of the federal states which continued to be elected by the undemocratic three class franchise in Prussia. In short, the German constitution was not intended to create a sovereign parliamentary democracy. In its struggles with the executive after Bismarck's fall in 1890, the *Reichstag*, it is true, did gain influence, but the German parliamentary system remained deeply flawed (pp. 325–8). What was true of Germany was also true of Austria after the *Ausgleich* of 1867. In Russia elected parliamentary participation was delayed until the twentieth century. Nor was the survival of Napoleon III's 'liberal' empire assured, and after 1871, with its division of power and multiplicity of parties, the early years of the Third Republic did not resemble a stable parliamentary democracy.

Constitutions were not suddenly scrapped from above to be replaced by others as on the continent. The evolutionary process made progress secure. In later Victorian Britain previously firmly held views weakened to be replaced by pragmatism and manoeuvring for party advantage. This hastened the pace of reform which in turn overcame prejudice and fears. Reassuringly the widening of the franchise to most working men did not lead to any decisive political change except to strengthen the Conservative party. Late Victorian politics were not dominated by class after 1884 but by the issue of Ireland. And so it turned out very differently to the expectations and aprehensions of mid-century. Britain's progression to democracy was not planned by either of the dominant Liberal grouping or the Conservative party. Pressure was exerted by middle-class radical MPs; successive governments were not averse to extending the franchise to 'responsible' working men and artisans; in the 1850s and 1860s, parliamentary reform did not excite popular outbursts of such intensity as had preceded the 1832 Reform Bill. For a generation after the collapse of Chartism, the settlement of 1832 held. But Britain was changing, with large movements into towns as industrialization spread and intensified. The unrepresentative distribution of seats which had continued after 1832 became still more unrepresentative. Something would have to be done, but there was lacking any sense of urgency. There appeared to be always other, more pressing, issues to be dealt with first. The votes in rural constituencies and the smaller boroughs were open to influence and bribery. Local interests could dominate, rather than national. The social composition of the House of Commons changed little in mid-Victorian Britain. To repeat a much over-used description, Britain really was passing through a transitional phase from the older parliaments representative of interests excluding the majority, to the more democratic parliaments of the late Victorian era.

There was not one step in this process but several. When the Conservatives briefly came to power in 1866 and 1867, Disraeli searched for a good party issue. Traditionally franchise reform was expected from the Whig-Liberal coalitions. Now Disraeli who was chancellor of the exchequer and leader in the House of Commons, the most dynamic member of Derby's minority government, seized on electoral reform as the issue on which to outbid the Liberals. The bill produced in 1867 by Disraeli was hardly a genuine step in the direction of democracy but a clever attempt to give it that appearance. The franchise would be extended to all householders, but this was to be balanced by allowing a much more restricted electorate of wealthier men multiple votes. Other 'safeguards' made the bill far less radical than it seemed. In the parliamentary battles that followed many of these 'safeguards' were successfully knocked away by the majority of the House. Disraeli and Derby were determined to remain in power and stay on top, so the amendments were accepted including extending the franchise to lodgers. The system of voting in the counties was different to the boroughs and the rental qualification was only slightly lowered. Cleverly in the end Disraeli had been most generous in extending the franchise in the boroughs dominated by the Liberals so that those entitled to vote more than doubled while in the counties it was extended by under half. The limited redistribution of seats resulted in far fewer votes being needed to elect a Conservative member of parliament than a Liberal. Even so the Conservatives could not hope to become a majority party as under half of the members in England and Wales were returned by the counties. Votes granted in the large towns, Disraeli hoped, would benefit the Conservatives. The goal of securing a majority eluded the Conservatives until 1874. The path to a fairer parliamentary representation reflecting the wishes of the majority of the people still had a long way to go, requiring further redistribution and a universal suffrage. Publicly the political leaders virtuously declared 'trust the people', but that is precisely what in private they lacked.

As important as redistribution and the franchise was the reform of corrupt practices. The Conservatives were ahead in mobilizing their supporters with the assistance of party agents. These gentlemen were professionals not necessarily themselves holding any consistent political convictions. Elections in the 1860s could still be boisterous affairs and where competition was real and keen, free beer was one of the less serious forms of bribery. The introduction of the secret ballot in 1872 and the Corrupt Practices Act of 1883 which limited and audited election expenditure did much to clean up British politics. The Third Reform Bill of 1884 extended the franchise to all householders paying rents, not only in towns but also in the country, including Ireland for the first time. Complicated qualifications designed to restrict the franchise were still retained. They were indeed quite effective, depriving two out of five adult males of the vote in England and Wales and more in Ireland and Scotland; mainly the poorer working men and the poorest of all, the paupers, were excluded. But the writing was on the wall. The following year there was a further redistribution of seats. Manhood suffrage could not be denied forever. There was also a substantial minority ready to allow women to vote. Full democracy, however, would not be attained until well into the twentieth century.

In 1866 the Tory *Quarterly Review* happily concluded, 'our wealth is overflowing, our commercial prospects are unclouded, save by the excess of our own activity and nothing seems likely to disturb either the peace of Europe or the profound contentment which this island is enjoying'.* 'England', the *Annual Register* observed a year later, 'owes her great influence not to military success, but to her commanding position in the arena of industry and commerce. If she forgets this, she is lost', the author warned, 'the signs for those who can read, are present, and can be plainly seen'.†

The quotations illustrate the two sides of Victorian Britain, one more confident and self-congratulatory, the other apprehensive about the future. At home Britain's prosperity was growing steadily though unevenly. The middle and upper strata of society took a larger share of the increase than the lower though all did benefit. The 1850s and 1860s have been called the Victorian 'boom' years. Wages of workers

---

* E. J. Feuchtwanger, *Democracy and Empire Britain 1845–1914* (Arnold, 1985), p. 5.
† Robert Rhodes James, *The British Revolution. British Politics 1880–1939* (Hamish Hamilton, 1976), p. 15.

rose by about a third. But there were regional variations. More important than the level of wages was the availability of employment. Unemployment reached high levels of over 7% in 1858, 6% in 1862 and 1878 and over 10% in 1879. During the American Civil War (1861–65) thousands of factory operatives in the Lancashire cotton industry were thrown out of work for lack of raw cotton. It was not 'boom' for all in Victorian Britain. Poverty was regarded as an inevitable and natural state, yet Britain was still by far the wealthiest nation in the world. Her trade outclassed that of all other countries; she ruled over a great empire, but her supremacy as the 'workshop of the world' was passing. There would be competitors in the future as the continental European nations and the United States became industrialized. There was no room for complacency.

Only a Britain at peace could promote industry and commerce and avoid wasteful military expenditure and so secure her future prosperity. The muddles and shortcomings of the military enterprise during the course of the Crimean War (1854–56) only reinforced this general desire to abstain from continental conflicts. This did not rule out jingoism. The belief that Britain was endowed with a superior civilization was assumed by virtually everyone. The uncivilized backward races needed to be reminded from time to time to respect Britain and punished when they did not do so. The opening of trade in Asia and the defence of empire were pursued with vigour and force. During the decade of the 1850s, British power in India was consolidated after the Mutiny (1857) which had come as a great shock. In defence of India, Britain sought predominant influence in Afghanistan and declared war on Persia. The threat of Russia in Asia was Britain's prime concern. In China, Britain allied with the French, occupied Canton and forced on China the 'unequal' Treaties of Tientsin (1858) which opened more of China to western trade, imposed foreign supervision over her maritime customs and legalized the importation of opium. In 1860, the Summer Palace outside Peking was burnt down, further indemnities imposed, and the Russians annexed the maritime province and founded the port of Vladivostock. Non-intervention in Europe, aggression in Asia, makes intelligible Disraeli's remark that Britain was more of an Asiatic power than a European! In all of this there was little to distinguish Conservatives from Whigs and Liberals.

At home, after the fall of Aberdeen in 1855, for most of the decade that followed Palmerston, now a veteran in his seventies, was prime minister (1855–58, 1859–65). The fluidity of the early years between the party groupings by the 1880s period had evolved into two principal parties: a Liberal party led by Gladstone facing Disraeli's Conservatives. This was still not so evident during the intervening years. The Liberals for much longer than the Conservatives had remained a much looser coalition of Liberals and Whigs and other supporters with little party organization outside Westminster. Governments sought to legislate for practical reforms. Each reform worthwhile in itself without conforming to any broader ideological intent. It was not considered to be the business of government to promote great changes. A divorce court replaced the need to secure divorce by an act of parliament, reforms of the criminal law, reforms of the Poor Law, and the needs of health for families living in the towns subject to epidemics began to be addressed. Prevention of disease was critical as medically there was little advance in curing cholera, typhoid, small pox and tuberculosis, the leading killer. Compulsory vaccination finally overcame smallpox after the last serious outbreak in 1870. Cholera epidemics had regularly broken out in 1848–49, 1853–54 and 1866; better sanitation began to tackle the root cause.

From the 1830s to the 1880s Royal Commissions produced statistics and investigated problems, suggesting solutions. It was an age of committed social reformers who like Lord Shaftesbury had sponsored factory legislation in parliament, supported measures to improve public health, housing for the working poor and free schools for destitute children. He must stand for the whole group of reformers in and out of parliament who were motivated by religious faith and a strong social conscience; reform not just from above but as a result of the pressure from committed individuals and groups, distress alleviated by self-help and charity.

Trying to make life better for the disadvantaged whilst lacking the drama of a single issue reveals these years as not barren of progress. Marx looked in vain for class conflict and a revolutionary socialist spirit. Trade unionism in this period was not militant, did not aim to overthrow society but was intent on preserving the position of the skilled workers and their pay advantage over the less skilled. Bargaining was local. The majority of working men did not belong to any trade union and for female workers there were no unions to join. The general quiescent attitude of working men with some rare exceptions made the widening of the franchise with many safeguards therefore a less hazardous prospect to contemplate.

There seemed to be no great issues that distinguished the Liberal grouping from the Conservatives. The Conservatives in the 1850s and 1860s were the more cohesive party. The price of that cohesion was a state of seemingly permanent minority in parliament unless one of the groups supporting Palmerston's Whig-Liberal administrations voted with the opposition to let the Conservatives in for a short while. By launching the Second Reform Bill Disraeli had only succeeded negatively, the Liberals were no longer seen as the main champions of parliamentary reform. But it was not part of Disraeli's thinking in 1867 that he would seek to create a national party attracting the support of all classes; the Liberals could then have been attacked as a party supporting the special interests of those business interests that supported them and of the Non-conformists. In the 1860s Disraeli was still defending the 'aristocratic constitution' based on rural society and the established Church of England.

In July 1865 the electorate once more gave Palmerston and the Whig-Liberals a modestly increased majority. In October the indomitable veteran fell from his horse and soon after died. Earl Russell succeeded as prime minister but unlike Palmerston could not keep the varied support for his administration together. After the Conservatives' spell in power, Gladstone alone had the necessary standing to lead the Liberals despite Whig apprehensions. Whig leadership in politics was over. The Whig grandees would continue to play a role but were no longer dominant.

Gladstone had shown his gift as a 'modern' politician, courting the newspaper press, meeting delegations, delivering speeches to electors in the provinces, and by these means turned himself into the 'People's William'. Disraeli and Gladstone have both gone down in history as the archetypal Victorian prime ministers of the later Victorian years yet, each in personality was very different. Their famous confrontations in parliament reflecting deeply different outlooks gave an appearance of much sharper party differences than in fact was the case. Disraeli's rise has already been discussed (pp. 161–2). Gladstone's was also full of twists and turns.

Gladstone began his political life as a Conservative and his political instincts remained fundamentally conservative. He did not share Disraeli's romantic nostalgia for rural England; he was more in tune than Disraeli with modern Britain; he viewed the desirable role of government as minimalist, interfering as little as possible; his resolve was to provide an efficient executive. To secure a majority he sought support from all the groups who for one or another reason were opposed to the more narrowly focused Conservatives. He looked for votes from Liberals, Whigs, Non-conformists, Radicals, the Irish, business interests and from those members of the landed gentry not supporting the Tories. Gladstone projected a public image of robust leadership and certainty of moral purpose. His private diaries revealed a more complex personality. He subjected himself to ruthless self-examination, particularly in his younger years in the 1840s and 1850s. He suffered the tortures of conflict between the high sense of moral standards he set himself, his deep religious faith, orthodox and Anglican, and a sexual drive that deeply troubled him. He sought out prostitutes to persuade them to give up their way of life. But he revealed in his private diaries that what also drew him to this Christian work was sexual excitement and frustration. In the privacy of his home he would whip and scourge himself to purge his feelings, recording each occasion with a symbol in his diary. H. C. G. Matthew the distinguished biographer and editor of the diaries concluded, 'it is impossible to know the exact nature of Gladstone's relationship with the prostitutes he visited. The language [in his diaries] is guarded, but occasionally suggestive'.* Interesting as all this is from the point of view of a glimpse of common male double standards in Victorian England, where Gladstone differed from most was in regarding his feelings a sin.

Gladstone was able to compartmentalize political, family and private life. As he reached the summit of political power in the 1860s, his attraction to prostitutes in general was replaced by intense feelings for a few women: an artist's model and others who were not part of his circle of rescued young females. Besides these personal traumas, Gladstone also struggled with family financial problems, unlike Disraeli's, not of his own making. Yet burdens that might have blighted the lives of many a man, Gladstone took in his stride. He was no less of an effective politician because of them.

Gladstone's belief was that the business of government was not to do things for the people, but to place them in a position where they could best do things for themselves, to liberate the disadvantaged from their unequal status by providing them with the means to help themselves – minimalist government in other words, that today is coming back into fashion. A desire for greater social justice was reinforced by his religious convictions. An obvious case for reform was the position of the Anglican Church in Ireland. Its support from the compulsory rates as the established State Church was unjust. It was endowed as the national Church of the Irish people when in fact it served no more than one-eighth. Three-quarters of the Irish were Catholics and half the remaining quarter Non-conformists. The small measure of support for the Catholics, the grant to the seminary at Maynooth, only served to heighten the injustice. The disestablishment of the Anglican Church in Ireland was only part of Gladstone's aim, as he explained in 1868 to the electors of Lancashire, 'the Church of Ireland... is but one of a group questions', ... 'there is the Church of Ireland, there is the land of Ireland, there is the education of Ireland, there are many subjects... they are all so many branches of one trunk, and that trunk is the tree of what is called the Protestant ascendancy... We, therefore, aim at the destruction of that system of ascendancy'. Gladstone had found a cause to identify and hold his Liberal and Nonconformist supporters together. Disraeli too was ready to introduce reform, but Gladstone's disestablishment was bolder and a radical settlement in

* H. C. G. Matthew, *Gladstone 1809–1874* (Oxford, 1986), p. 93.

1869. The same reason for disestablishment did not apply with equal force to Britain where the Church of England was the largest denomination. The bill disestablishing the Church of Ireland in a spirit of some compromise provided compensation handing back more than half of what was taken. The remainder, £6 million, was invested in Irish welfare projects and in higher education.

The Irish Land Act in 1870 sought to tackle the thorny issue of tenant grievances; according to Irish traditions, tenants had partial ownership rights and could sell their tenancy; as long as they paid their rents, which they demanded should be 'fair'; tenants insisted on security to hold the property and to pass it on. If tenant demands and needs in Ireland were granted by legislation this raised the spectre that property rights in Britain could be questioned. Somehow a compromise had to be reached. The Land Act of 1870 was more important symbolically. The property rights of Irish landlords were no longer sacrosanct, but the rights of tenants, despite safeguards in the Act, could be circumvented by the landlords. Gladstone's attempt to reconcile the different denominations in higher education failed altogether when the Irish University Bill was defeated in 1873. Two bills and one measure aborted constituted Gladstone's first attempt to 'pacify' Ireland, to reconcile all the Irish people to the Union at a time when the Fenians gave notice that failure in Ireland could lead to violence. Gladstone's efforts despite their limitations did make plain that the government in Britain recognized the special claims of Ireland and was prepared to address them. Reform not repression, was held to be the proper response to the needs of the Catholic majority in Ireland who within the United Kingdom as a whole formed a minority. Gladstone's ministry tackled other thorny issues in a similar spirit of practical compromise. The reform of elementary education was bedevilled by conflicts between the claims of those who saw the need for a national system, those who insisted on local control, the secular and the different denominations. Royal Commissions had pointed to the urgent need to improve private and public education. The Prussian example was much admired for training an efficient workforce. The outcome, the Education Bill of 1870, imposed no authoritarian solution with state control over all schools, but a complex mixed arrangement of assisted voluntary schools, run by various religious denominations which received Treasury support, and of state schools subject to local authorities, financed from the rates without religious instruction specific to any one denomination. The circle could not be entirely squared, but the arrangement lasted into twentieth century. Compulsory attendance and the abolition of fees had to wait for a few years longer. Other reforms covered the universities (1871) where academic posts at Cambridge and Oxford were opened to all without religious tests; interestingly, Gladstone personally had little enthusiasm for this reform and would have preferred the academic body, not the students, to be reserved for Anglicans. Other measures dealt with competition for entry into the Civil Service (1870), a series of military reforms and reforms dealing with the administration of justice (1873).

The Trade Union Act of 1871 safeguarded union funds. It sought to strike a better balance between the rights of workers and their employers. Trade unions, however, remained severely handicapped by provisions against violence, threats and obstruction, which enabled employers to mount criminal prosecutions claiming that picketing had not been peaceful. Notable as Gladstone's reforms undoubtedly were, it is clear they were also cautious, still reflecting much apprehension in conceding too much to the 'lower classes'.

On the continent of Europe the decade of the 1860s was decisive in the contest of power. Successive British foreign secretaries, Russell, Stanley and Clarendon, conducted Britain's foreign policy skilfully yet making little impact on the larger course of events. Britain did not intervene in any of the wars that reshaped Europe: the Italian wars, the Prussian defeat first of Denmark in 1864 then of Austria in 1866 and France in 1870. The general line of British policy was to offer benevolent mediation without the threat of armed force. Mediation could only succeed and prove helpful, however, when the contestants had in any case concluded a peaceful outcome was preferable to war, as they did over Luxembourg in 1867 and the Belgian railway dispute in 1869.

Was there any alternative to the policy of 'non-intervention? Britain had only a small army stationed at home, the rest were in India and the colonies for the defence of her global empire. Russia was the principal threat in Asia. To meet the danger Britain sought predominance in a great arc of 'buffer' lands from Ottoman Asia Minor through Persia and Afghanistan. In North America advocates of 'manifest destiny' urged the annexation of Canada. In Mediterranean Egypt and south-east Asia the imperial rival was France. On the continent of Europe Britain could not militarily intervene without an ally. It was obviously out of the question to side with Austria against Prussia or with either France or Prussia in their conflict. While peace best served British interests, it also served her interest to await the outcome of war on the continent. In any case there was a general support for aspirations of national unification. Once completed, a more peaceful era was expected to follow.

France appeared more of a threat than Prussia. Bismarck's moderation in not annexing any Austrian territory in 1866 clearly pointed to the *kleindeutsche* solution of German unity which would not break up the Habsburg Empire. To create a stable German entity in the heart of Europe had been the aim of Castlereagh at the Congress of Vienna and now the prospects of its fulfilment created no alarm. A strong Germany would aid the balance of power in Europe. That it would actually upset the balance could not be foreseen two generations before this occurred.

Thus British policy was ready to defend specific British interests on the continent by diplomacy, and if necessary beyond Europe by force. At the same time pacific understandings over spheres of influence were always preferred to war. So Russia was both warned and forestalled in Persia and Afghanistan, but also conciliated when Britain agreed to revise the Black Sea clauses of the Peace of Paris, allowing Russia again to establish a naval force in the Black Sea (p. 341). That Britain's intentions towards Napoleon III's France were entirely pacific was underlined by the conclusion of a commercial treaty, the Cobden Treaty, a decade earlier (1860). With the United States a settlement of American claims arising from the supply of vessels to the Southern Confederate States during the Civil War (the Alabama Case) and of other issues was reached in the 1871 Treaty of Washington. Fears of an American invasion of Canada were not, however, totally banished. War plans, as late as 1900, were still worked upon, involving a descent by a British force on Cape Cod. Of course, by then any real danger had passed and shortly thereafter Britain and the United States completed the removal of all causes of conflict between them.

Gladstone, unlike his more sophisticated foreign secretary Clarendon, saw foreign relations in moral terms. In October 1870 in an anonymous contribution to the *Edinburgh Review* he set out his views:

> Certain it is that a new law of nations is gradually taking hold of the mind, and coming to sway the practice of the world; a law which recognises independence, which frowns on aggression, which favours the pacific, not the bloody settlements of disputes, which aims at permanent and not temporary adjustment; above all, which recognises as a tribunal of paramount authority, the general judgement of civilised mankind. It has censured the aggression of France; it will censure if need arise, the greed of Germany...It is hard for all nations to go astray. Their ecumenical council sits above the partial passions of those, who are misled by interest, and disturbed by quarrel.[*]

Gladstone's expectation of a Europe following Christian teaching, and of Britain as the ethical model, proved not only a noble illusion but also revealed how far the gulf had widened between Britain and the continent since 1848. Disraeli in his Crystal Palace speech in June

[*] H. C. G. Matthew, *Gladstone 1809–1874*, pp. 181–2.

1872, had no truck with such grandiose cosmopolitan ideas. But he too separated British interests from those of the continent. The role of British statesmen, Disraeli asserted, was to look after Britain's own interests, and these were imperial. It was a policy supported by all classes, he insisted, including the working class, who too were Conservative in the 'purest and loftiest' sense. Disraeli declared that he believed that they 'are proud of belonging to a great country and wish to maintain its greatness – that they are proud of belonging to an imperial country, and are resolved to maintain, if they can, their empire'.† But there was a link between Britain and the continent as the new crisis in the 'Eastern question' in 1877–78 was to show (pp. 345–8). Britain could not divorce herself entirely holding to 'non-intervention' on the continent. This tension between continental and imperial interests is a thread that runs through the whole period to 1914.

The gulf between Britain and the continental powers was nevertheless real enough. It might have seemed in the year of the Liberal apprehensions that the danger of allowing the mass of the people an overriding voice, that is, accepting democracy, were shared on both sides of the Channel. In Britain over a generation as experience allayed fears simple immobility was no option. In any case, there was no authoritarian monarchical alternative. On the continent the liberals, afraid that the revolution if continued would endanger their position and property, did have a choice; they chose to compromise with the old order. In France in 1860, after the establishment of the 'Liberal' empire, Napoleon III could still rely on support for his authority as the plebiscite in 1870 demonstrated. In the German empire the reins of power continued to be held by Bismarck. He derived his authority not from the *Reichstag* but from William I. The war with France and its outcome so raised his prestige that he remained in unchallenged power for two decades, immune to the outcome of elections, but not in the end in 1890 immune from the whims of a young new monarch.

† Robert Blake, *Disraeli* (Eyre and Spottiswoode, 1967), p. 523.

20

The Franco-Prussian War

About the Franco-Prussian War there is one historical peculiarity; there is no general agreement among European historians what to call it, Franco-Prussian or Franco-German. It is not just a question of words. The war can be viewed both as predominantly Prussian or as the first genuine 'German' war. Bismarck dominated the diplomacy of the war and Moltke the military command and organization. The three armies in the field were also commanded by Prussians. Prussian troops outnumbered by a wide margin the troops of all Prussia's allies combined; a huge force of 850,000 Prussians and German allies was assembled by the end of the war. Unlike 1866, all the German states fought for Prussia this time. They included those which had no choice, because they had recently been forced into the North German Confederation as well as the still independent south German states. But at the beginning of the war the national enthusiasm Bismarck banked on was not universal. In Hanover and the south there were those, minorities to be sure, who hated Prussia more than France. But as the war proceeded, shared battles, shared victories and losses changed all that dramatically. The war became a national crusade. On both sides feelings of patriotism and hatred for the enemy were deliberately fanned. The war ended with the unification of Germany and linked with this great event, a legacy of bitterness unparalleled in the relations of any two great powers in the nineteenth century. The Franco-Prussian War began as the last 'dynastic' war but before it was over it had become the first of the people's mass wars.

The 'German' armies possessed two decisive advantages over the French: a large superiority in *trained* manpower and Moltke and the general staff organization he had created. From the outset the Germans were stronger and the overall handling of the German armies was also infinitely superior to the French. The conduct of the German and French mobilizations magnified this basic disparity.

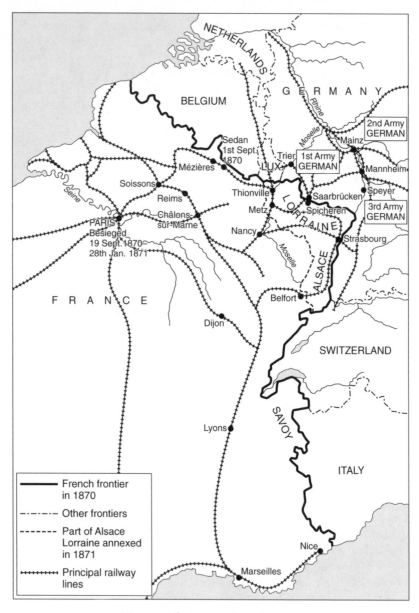

Map 6   The Franco-Prussian War

Moltke's plan was to concentrate three armies at different points in the Rhineland and the Bavarian Palatinate. The plan provided for the use of the six available railway lines to bring together a force of 300,000 to 450,000 within three weeks. All the details had been worked out to perfection. On 15 July 1870 the king was finally persuaded to order mobilization. Bavaria, Baden and Württemberg followed on 16 and 17 July. By 5 August 462,000 men and their supplies had been transported and concentrated in the Prussian Rhineland and the Palatinate poised to advance into Alsace. The force was divided into three armies under the commands of the Crown Prince Frederick, Prince Frederick Charles, the king's nephew, and General von Steinmetz. Although the royal commanders were indifferent generals and Steinmetz turned out an unmitigated disaster, Moltke nevertheless succeeded in retrieving most of their mistakes through a series of brilliant improvisations.

French mobilization was not only slower than the Prussian, it was also chaotic. The order of mobilization had gone out on 14 July, a day earlier than the Prussian. Last-minute changes of plan by Napoleon III had increased the dislocation of troop movements and supplies. By the end of the month of July, when Napoleon III took personal command of the 'Army of the Rhine' as it was called, it had reached only 238,000 men and was concentrated on a short front between Metz and as far along the railway line as the French frontier. Just beyond it was Saarbrücken in the Prussian Rhineland. Instead of enjoying independent commands, three French marshals, Bazaine, Canrobert and MacMahon were given subordinate commands of corps of the 'Army of the Rhine' whose supreme command had been assumed by the emperor. It proved a disastrous and ill-coordinated arrangement. The French military plan had called for a swift French offensive into the Palatinate, or alternatively an offensive further south, across the Rhine into Baden. The southern offensive was intended to co-ordinate a French advance with the anticipated Austrian offensive. As the likelihood of Austria-Hungary joining in the war receded, the offensive into Baden was abandoned. The offensive into the Palatinate was also abandoned, or rather it took the form on 2 August of a token advance of a few miles as far as Saarbrücken just within the Prussian Rhineland.

Moltke's plan dispersed the three armies under his direction, and planned to move them forward so that they would converge later. It was a repetition of the war plan of 1866; it was easier to handle the supplies of three smaller armies separately than of one huge combined army. He concentrated the 134,000 men of the Second Army, commanded by Prince Frederick Charles, on the Rhine between Bingen and Mainz and then ordered them forward in a south-westerly direction to the Saarbrücken region. The First Army of 50,000 men under Steinmetz had been assembled at Trier and was then moved south to Saarbrücken. The Third Army (125,000 men), which included the south German forces and was commanded by the Crown prince, was assembled at Speyer further south in the

Palatinate and able to move west to converge with the other two armies at Saarbrücken or south to threaten Strasbourg. The contrast between the way the German and French armies were deployed reflected the entirely different thinking of the French and Prussian commands. The French concentrated their main forces in one small area around Metz with a smaller force at Strasbourg and relied on impregnable fortresses for defence and on superiority of numbers for an offensive. The three separate and widely spread out smaller German armies made for flexibility and speed of movement; they could be used to outflank enemy forces always *provided* that the individual commanders acted according to the directions they received from Moltke's headquarters. Moltke was prepared to adapt his plans rapidly to take advantage of changing French dispositions and the fortunes of battle.

During the opening phase of the campaign Moltke's grand strategy was bungled by the 'initiatives' of the individual subordinate commanders. Moltke planned to coordinate the second and third armies to defeat the numerically inferior French in one great battle. Instead the armies fought piecemeal engagements before they had converged. On 6 August the First and Second Armies, contrary to Moltke's orders, attacked the French in the neighbourhood of Saarbrücken. The result of the confused battle of Spicheren Heights, where both sides fought fiercely, was that the French withdrew. With better leadership, bringing all their superior numbers here to bear on the Prussians, the French might have inflicted a crushing defeat on the rash Prince Frederick Charles and on Steinmetz. Further south the Crown prince had moved the Third Army across the frontier at Wissembourg and after a battle to capture the town, met MacMahon's smaller force entrenched at Froeschwiller a few miles further west. On 6 August the Third Army stumbled into battle. The Germans won, but the price was heavy, 10,500 casualties. MacMahon's losses were the greater, though, with 11,000 casualties and 9200 prisoners of war. What these early battles had demonstrated was that though the French possessed a rifle, the *chassepôt*, greatly superior to the Prussian, Prussian artillery restored the technological balance. The *mitrailleuse*, a primitive machine gun, was a French weapon of potential value but it was never effectively used during the war; these engagements also revealed that French military commanders blundered even more than the Prussian. With hindsight the two unplanned battles of Spicheren and Froeschwiller can be seen as marking early on a turning point in the war; the French offensive spirit was broken for good as it turned out. To the surprise of the whole of Europe, the Prussians were invading France, not the other way around.

The effect on Napoleon III of these early setbacks – for they were no more than setbacks, the French soldiers had fought magnificently – was catastrophic. Physically in an appalling state, his willpower collapsed. On 7 August he took the fateful decision to withdraw the bulk of the 'Army of the Rhine' into the fortress of Metz and to leave the entire initiative to the Prussians. Five days later the emperor appointed Marshal Bazaine Commander-in-Chief. Bazaine's general incompetence as a commander of large forces condemned a large army of 180,000 to virtual ineffectiveness until he eventually surrendered it on 27 October. Bazaine's failure seemed so inexplicable that he was later wrongly suspected of treachery. The truth is that he was totally unfit for high command. Military good sense would have dictated a speedy withdrawal of the French troops from Metz and their concentration on the Meuse or further inland on the Marne. But from Paris the empress warned that to withdraw was politically impossible and that Napoleon III must not return a defeated man. Bazaine dithered. Only on 14 August did he order the withdrawal. Moltke without knowing it had anticipated him and the three German armies fanned out in a general advance seizing crossings over the Moselle and expecting to follow Bazaine. Instead they were unexpectedly enveloping Bazaine in a net between Metz and his line of retreat. Moltke's genius thus lay not in the conception of the envelopment which was unplanned, but in his instant recognition of the opportunities the new situation offered. Two more confused battles were fought, a minor engagement at Vhionville on 16 August and a major battle at Gravelotte on 18 August with Bazaine attempting to withdraw from Metz northwards. At Gravelotte the German armies (188,000 men) met the bulk of the French (113,000 men). Blunders were committed by both sides and the Germans suffered 20,000 casualties and Bazaine admitted to 12,000. Prussian mistakes almost lost the battle of Gravelotte, but the campaign judged as a whole was a complete Prussian success, for Bazaine withdrew his army into Metz. The fate of the empire was sealed by this decision. The empire's finest troops never regained any freedom of manœuvre.

Napoleon III had left Bazaine in the nick of time on 16 August and got back to Chalôns on the Marne. Here under MacMahon's command a new 'Army of Chalôns' was formed. From Paris the empress and ministers urged him not to fall back but to advance and to 'rescue' Bazaine. Partially swayed by political considerations, MacMahon set out on 23 August with an improvised army of 130,000 men to find Bazaine. But at no time were MacMahon's moves and Bazaine's actually coordinated against the Germans. MacMahon was seeking to locate Bazaine who had promised to break out of Metz and to join him in a battle against the Germans to the north-east of Metz in the direction of Sedan.

MacMahon's doomed army marched north-east with the emperor among its baggage. Moltke rearranged the dispositions of the German forces. Whilst one army invested Metz, the other forces were combined to meet MacMahon. The trap was carefully sprung once Moltke had succeeded in locating MacMahon's cumbersome and slow-moving army. Bazaine's half-hearted effort to break out of Metz failed. The battles in which the 'Army of Chalôns' was destroyed began on 30 August at Beaumont; the French were routed and fell back in a disorderly retreat on Sedan. On 1 September the imperial force was destroyed as a fighting instrument in the battle of Sedan, one of the most calamitous defeats of modern times. The troops that had not fallen were made prisoners as Napoleon III decided on 2 September on capitulation in preference to wasting French lives. The Germans took 104,000 prisoners including the emperor. After only five weeks of actual campaigning one imperial army was shut up in Metz and the other had surrendered. There were no imperial armies left. The empire was swept away by a bloodless 'revolution' in Paris on 4 September. Nothing now stood in the path of the German armies marching to Paris and by rights the war should have ended. This was what Bismarck and the generals expected. Yet it lasted another six months.

In Paris a new republican government of National Defence was formed and inspired resistance. Without any real chance of reversing the military verdict, they held the Germans for another six months. The extensive fortification of Paris was defended by a few regular troops and a citizen army. Moltke, whose forces reached Paris in mid-September, settled down to starve the city into surrender. The defenders of Paris banked on disrupting the tenuous communications of the large German armies, on raising fresh French armies in the south to relieve Paris, and on the intervention of the great powers. Their heroism in the end was in vain. What France lacked were trained soldiers, non-commissioned officers to form a disciplined nucleus for new armies to be formed. Sheer numbers were not enough against the Prussian armies. The failure of military reforms in the 1860s now meant that a reservoir of skilled manpower simply did not exist. The new minister of the interior, the fiery republican Léon Gambetta left Paris by balloon – to raise new armies. Alphonse Thiers toured the courts of Europe for help and Jules Favre, the foreign minister, declared that not the smallest fraction of France would be ceded to the enemy. The heroic defence caught the imagination of Europe. But the defeat of Gambetta's ill-trained and ill-equipped army of the Loire, and the exhaustion of supplies in Paris, in the end forced the government to accept the inevitable and to sign the armistice terms of capitulation on 28 January 1871.

The last six months of warfare had witnessed a new ferocity of the 'nation in arms'. The *Franc-tireurs* units operated as guerrillas in the rear of the Germans and when captured were hung as criminals. Paris, so recently the centre of an elegant Great Exhibition, had suffered great hardship and bombardment. The whole country had been aroused against the invader. The Germans were equally bitter about their casualties. They blamed the French for senselessly prolonging the war. The last months of the war left a legacy of bitterness which survived for three generations. That the King of Prussia had been proclaimed German Kaiser on 18 January 1871 just ten days before the armistice not in Berlin, but at his head-quarters, the Palace of Versailles, added insult to injury. The stage-managed ceremony in the Hall of Mirrors, when William I to his disgust was actually proclaimed 'Kaiser William', symbolized the new power of Germany and the prostration of France.

Bismarck has tried to propagate the legend in his *Reminiscences* that Napoleon III's intervention in 1866 had made war with France inevitable for Napoleon III would not allow the natural completion of German unification. There is much evidence to suggest that Bismarck did not really work for war against France for that reason. What made war necessary in Bismarck's view was not so much the policy of France but the state of Germany. Despite Prussia's overwhelming economic and military strength, despite the existence of genuine national feelings in all the southern German states, especially in Baden, the southern German states had not fallen like ripe plums into the Prussian basket. Had the royal governments of Württemberg and Bavaria desired unification with a North German Confederation, how could France have prevented it? When the process of national unification in Italy was carried beyond the limits agreed by Napoleon III and Cavour the French did not intervene. Ten years later could Napoleon III have intervened if the process of German unification had been completed *peacefully*? To be sure these are hypothetical questions. What can be shown is that Bismarck had failed to unite Germany peacefully during the years immediately following the war with Austria and the German states. In 1870 he resorted to violence. He preferred to go to war with France at the head of a German coalition rather than declare war on the southern German states; the south German states for their part, when it came to the crunch, preferred the alliance with Prussia and war with France to 'peaceful' unification possibly entailing territorial compensation at their expense to satisfy the French Emperor. What made the war with France inevitable was Bismarck's decision to solve the German question, not gradually by evolution, but quickly by force. He counted on a great change of public attitude in the southern German states as a result of waging war with France. His judgement in this respect was proved sound.

The feelings against France were so strong and unreasoned that they could be played on to solve the German question in Prussia's interests. This anti-French feeling was a relatively recent nineteenth-century phenomenon though it was presented as of 'hereditary' origin stretching back to Richelieu, who, so it was claimed, had followed a traditional policy of benefiting France at Germany's expense. There is no limit to the historical nonsense that is believed especially when propagated by professors of history when they venture to make history serve the interests of their state.

The war with France created a tidal wave of German national feeling. But Bismarck was still faced with the particularism and jealousies of the south German rulers. The young visionary King Ludwig II of Bavaria gave him the greatest trouble. The House of Wittelsbach was more ancient than the Hohenzollerns and had once borne the imperial crown of the Holy Roman Empire itself. Bavaria, moreover, had prided itself on its independence as a German 'middle state'. Here feelings against Prussia had always been strongest. Bismarck made use of every weapon in his armoury, divided his opposition, threatened, cajoled, and finally actually agreed to pay a veiled bribe – in the form of secret compensation – to the improvident castle-mad Bavarian monarch as well as a commission to his emissary.

The negotiations to bring the south and north together in one German Empire were conducted by Bismarck on the one hand and the German rulers (including William I!) on the other, whilst the German armies were besieging Paris. They required weeks of patient diplomacy during a time when Bismarck feared foreign intervention and was fuming at the generals for not acting more ruthlessly and so forcing Paris to surrender sooner. Simultaneously also Bismarck had to frame peace terms with France and to negotiate with the representatives of the French government of National Defence who came to see him at Versailles. He kept all these balls in the air at one and the same time. It was a period of great strain for the chancellor. He could only manage to find sleep by drinking many bottles of beer having first induced a thirst by eating large quantities of caviare. Bismarck was determined to impose the constitution of the North German Confederation on the new German Empire. In all that really mattered to Bismarck, the conduct of foreign policy, and the control of military power, the constitution of 1867 provided for centralization; these affairs of state were placed in the hands of King of Prussia and his chancellor. To permit the 'independent' states of the North German Confederation considerable domestic autonomy, their own administrations, courts and parliaments, appeared at the time as a concession, but in fact enabled Prussia to maintain its own independence in these questions. For instance the *Kulturkampf* against the

Catholic subjects of William I, which Bismarck unleashed after 'unification' was overwhelmingly Prussian policy (p. 365), approved by a Prussian parliament elected on the three class system of voting (constitution of 1850), predominantly protestant. Such a religious-political campaign could not have been carried through in Germany and the *Reichstag* played only a minor role. Bismarck wished to preserve 'Prussia' as well as to wield the power of 'Germany' in Europe. The desire to preserve Prussia was even more essential now that Bismarck was working out the terms of German unification with the predominantly Catholic states of the south. Just as later in his diplomacy, so in his domestic policy, Bismarck sought a balance between Prussian independence and German unity. He opposed the Bavarian aim of merely re-creating the former German Confederation of states with the King of Prussia as titular Kaiser. But he was ready to allow genuine as well as purely ornamental rights to the south German states.

Bismarck won the struggle with the individual German rulers. He was bound to. He did not hesitate to play his trump card that he would call on the German people to remove those rulers who now stood in the way of unification. They were isolated and could only count on minority local support. So Bismarck tempted them with concessions provided they accepted as the basis for the empire the constitution of the North German Confederation. By the end of the year 1870 all the parliaments and rulers had agreed to the package devised by Bismarck. Some of these concessions were 'paper' concessions; they looked impressive but meant little in practice. Thus the powers of the King of Prussia, as German Emperor, seemed to be more restricted in 1871 than in 1867. He was still commander-in-chief. He could, however, only declare war with the consent of the expanded *Bundesrat* (unless *Germany were attacked*). In other ways too, the Kaiser's authority appeared to be restricted by the *Bundesrat*. But in the *Bundesrat* the voting procedures and distribution of votes in practice allowed Prussia to gain a majority whenever she wished. The chancellor presided over the *Bundesrat*, composed as before not of elected representatives, but of delegates sent by the governments of the states. In practice the *Bundesrat*, whose powers under the constitution of 1871 were so extensive, amounted to no more than a rubber stamp for Bismarck's policies. Consequently the special rights Bavaria enjoyed as chairman of the foreign affairs committee of the *Bundesrat* were illusory. Bavaria and Württemberg retained other special internal rights such as their own postal service; Bavaria's army was permitted to remain a 'self-contained unit' under the command of the King of Bavaria in peacetime. Even so it came to be largely officered by Prussians in later years. Except in matters of internal administration the special rights of the southern German states were really decorative. All the rulers kept their titles. The *Reichstag* was far more important. It was elected by manhood suffrage as under the constitution of 1867 and Prussia returned 235 deputies out of the total of 397.

The formal ceremony proclaiming the Empire at Versailles on 18 January 1871 was something of an anti-climax. William I hated the idea of giving precedence to a 'German' crown over the Prussian. But he could scarcely refuse it if it were offered by the King of Bavaria. The reluctance of the latter was partly overcome, as has been noted already, by the secret annual payment of 300,000 marks derived from the private fortune of an exiled fellow monarch – King George V of Hanover. Bismarck had confiscated this fortune earlier on and it provided him with a secret fund which he disposed without parliamentary control. Even so, Ludwig II would not come in person to Versailles. William was offered the imperial dignity by mail, so to speak, in a letter signed by the King of Bavaria. The title offered was not 'Kaiser of Germany', but what Ludwig II regarded as the lesser dignity, 'German Kaiser', not so threatening to the sovereignty of the other German princes. Bismarck did not care about the precise form of words, but William I was deeply offended. On the chosen day, 18 January, the birthday of the Prussian monarchy, not one of the other ruling German Kings – Bavaria, Württemberg, Saxony – attended in person. The Grand Duke of Baden had the honour to proclaim the Kaiser. Even on the day it was not clear how this was to be accomplished. Bismarck insisted on German Kaiser because that is what he had agreed to in a treaty signed by him after much difficulty with the Royal Bavarian government; William I adamantly would accept nothing less than Kaiser of Germany. The Grand Duke adroitly solved the difficulty by proclaiming him as 'his imperial and royal majesty Kaiser William!' When William indignantly stepped down from the daïs he passed by Bismarck without a word or handshake. Bismarck accepted his monarch's displeasure philosophically, commenting humorously in private that the 'kaiser-birth' had been difficult and that kings at such times had their odd desires.

Ten days after the proclamation of the German Empire an armistice was concluded with France. A period of intense strain was over for the Germans. For the French in defeat one crisis was exchanged for others; the need to find a stable form of government, the agony of a Prussian occupation, the loss of territory French for centuries, the war indemnity, and the *Commune*.

The diplomacy of the European powers during the Franco-Prussian War clearly illustrates what nonsense it is to suppose that nations shape their policies in order to 'uphold' the 'Balance of Power'. This had been Thiers' vain hope when he appealed for help on his tour of European courts. At the time when war broke out, the French were generally expected to win; nevertheless all the great powers had then assumed an attitude of 'wait and see'. The Russians approached Austria-Hungary with a proposal that the two empires should agree together on how best to safeguard their interests in the event of a French victory. Austria-Hungary rejected this proposal. Russia did not wish to be involved in war again but to localize the Franco-Prussian conflict. Britain was determined not to intervene; the cabinet was equally determined to localize the war and preserve Belgian independence. The publication by Bismarck of the Benedetti draft of 1866 in *The Times* after the outbreak of the war alarmed the cabinet. The cabinet therefore sought and obtained treaty assurances from Prussia and France that they would respect Belgian independence and if necessary defend it in alliance with Britain against whichever power attacked Belgium. In fact, appreciating Britain's sensitivity in this region of Europe, neither France nor Prussia was ready to risk infringing the neutrality of Belgium in 1870. At first Prussia enjoyed more sympathy than France. But as the war dragged on Gladstone became indignant at Prussia's bombardment and starvation of Paris; he was even more outraged by the peace terms involving as they did the forcible annexation of Alsace and southern Lorraine without benefit of consulting its population. Mere moralizing is not of much effect. What really mattered was that Britain followed a policy of strict neutrality and played no part in the reshaping of continental Europe during this crucial period.

In Vienna Francis Joseph and Beust had flirted with the idea of an alliance with France against Prussia. But when it actually came to the point Austria-Hungary stood aside as well. The emperor had summoned a crown council on 18 July 1870 the day before France's formal declaration of war. Beust advocated a policy of 'watchful neutrality' and was supported by the Hungarian prime minister, Julius Andrássy; this policy won the emperor's support also. In any case the Austro-Hungarian army could not have been prepared for war in less than six weeks. By then the battle of Sedan (1 September) had seemed to settle the military issue. The Austrians were not going to take on the victorious Prussians, especially not in order to come to the help of a French republic. Austria-Hungary abandoned her half-hearted military preparations and Beust in December 1870 assured Bismarck that Austria-Hungary would not raise treaty objections if the southern German states joined the North German Confederation. It was the final Habsburg renunciation of influence in Germany.

Two powers took advantage of the Franco-Prussian war to further their own national aims. They were Italy and Russia. For Garibaldi, Italian unification was not complete without Rome and there were many Italians who shared these feelings. But as long as Italy desired to maintain friendship with the French Empire, Rome would remain in papal hands. When war broke out between France and Prussia, the sympathies of the king and his ministers were all for France. In 1866, Victor Emmanuel had been on the winning side; now in August 1870 he believed this meant backing France against his former ally, Prussia. Sedan marked the turning point in Italian policy as it did in the policies of the other continental powers. French troops had been departing from Rome to reinforce the imperial armies facing the Prussians and the Italians had promised to respect the agreement with France to preserve the independence of the reduced papal state. No sooner had the news of Sedan reached Florence (the Italian capital), however, than the ministers began a series of continuous discussions which ended with the decision to defy the Pope and to annexe Rome. This breach of international law was subsequently covered up by arranging a plebiscite which voted in favour of annexation after the event.

The Russians utilized the Franco-Prussian war to present to Europe Bismarck's blank cheque to support Russia in the unilateral abrogation of the 'Black Sea' clauses. A Russian Council of Ministers decided on this step on 27 October 1870 and on 31 October sent their famous circular to the powers. But Gladstone would not accept such a *fait accompli*. Gorchakov, the Russian Chancellor, was therefore obliged to submit the question to a conference though he was assured of Bismarck's support beforehand. Bismarck felt nervous about the gathering of any European conference before he had the peace terms with France in his pocket; the best he could achieve was to insist that the conference should restrict itself to a consideration of the 'Black Sea' clauses. He also prevented any French representative from attending the opening session. At the Conference of London (December 1870–March 1871) the Russians then won a paper victory. The objectionable Black Sea clauses were abrogated. But, and this is usually overlooked, Gladstone secured a modification of the traditional rules of the Straits. The Straits were no longer to be closed to warships when Turkey was at peace. Henceforth, should the Sultan feel threatened, he could call on allied warships for support whilst himself remaining neutral. Since Russia would not have a fleet for years, this change gave a decisive advantage to Britain possessing as she did the dominant naval power in the Mediterranean.

The occupation of Rome and the new settlement of the Straits were important but incidental consequences of the Franco-Prussian War. The annexation of Alsace and the eastern half of Lorraine was the most controversial direct result. More than anything else it reinforced ideological commitment to a belief in the 'hereditary enmity' between France and Germany on both sides. Why did Bismarck inflict a peace on France, whose territorial terms, unlike the financial, were bound to prove permanently humiliating? The French only acceded to a treaty which involved cessions of the sacred soil of the Fatherland which is how Alsace and Lorraine were regarded, after suffering a whole series of military disasters. The republicans, who dominated the government of National Defence, had pinned their faith on history repeating itself. They looked back to the glories of 1792 and 1793. But now they faced a determined and ruthless foe 850,000 strong, and history does not and did not repeat itself. The invaders were firmly entrenched in France. But despite Gambetta's fiery spirit and the patriotism of many Frenchmen it is hard to believe the French would have fought on so desperately during the winter of 1870 had they been offered an 'Austrian' peace of no territorial cession though coupled with the acceptance of the fact of German unification. A generous and conciliatory peace in 1871 would have raised Bismarck's prestige as a statesman to unprecedented heights. Why did it not happen?

No historian can with certainty plumb the motives of the participants, least of all Bismarck's, yet an answer should be attempted. To begin with it would have been vastly more difficult in 1871 than in 1866 to persuade William I and the generals to make a peace without seeking to 'punish' the enemy. The whole of Bismarck's German policy had depended on painting Napoleon III and the French people in the blackest colours as Germany's hereditary and implacable foes. The war was presented to the German people as one in defence of Germany against French attack. It is doubtful whether Bismarck really persuaded himself of this. But the weapon of propaganda is double-edged. The more successfully it is wielded the more it traps its instigator. Having determined on this means of unifying Germany, it robbed Bismarck of his famous options when the war was ended. Since the unity of Germany was built on French guilt France could not be 'forgiven' now. A harsh peace alone would demonstrate France's guilt even though Bismarck realized this would mean conflict for generations. Secondly, with hindsight we assume that Bismarck in 1871 regarded his work of unification as complete and irreversible. Bismarck's caution and tendency to see *les choses en noir* is well known and at times affected his good judgement. A glance at the map showed him that Berlin was further away from Munich and Stuttgart than Strasbourg was from Munich. Alsace and Lorraine he saw as pointing a dagger at Germany. If the French in years to come were to launch an offensive they would split the north from the south; could the loyalty of the southern sovereigns in those circumstances be counted on? Later Bismarck stressed that 'geographical considerations', not an appetite for annexation, had determined his policy. On other occasions he argued that defeat in war, irrespective of the peace terms, had turned France into an irreconcilable enemy, hence it followed that the future leaders of France would only be deterred from renewing the conflict if France were so weakened as to give her no chance of success. Finally, though contemptuous of 'professors" talk, Bismarck himself probably wished to see the 'old imperial city' of Strasbourg in German hands. For the French government in Paris, unsure of its undisputed control of France, a harsh peace was doubly difficult to accept. After the failure of his mission Thiers had returned to Paris and on his way back he briefly saw Bismarck. But just at that time, in October 1870 an uprising in Paris made it clear to the Government of National Defence that Prussian peace terms involving territorial cession might lead to its repudiation. The point of French desperation was not reached until January 1871. When there was no more hope left of saving Paris, an armistice with the Prussians was rapidly concluded on 28 January. It was the first of the three steps which ultimately led to the Peace of Frankfurt. The terms of the armistice were relatively lenient. It was to last three weeks (later extended) and applied to the whole country except Belfort and the three eastern *départements*. It came into force on 31 January. Unfortunately Jules Favre failed to inform Gambetta of the delay or of the geographical exceptions with the result that the armies of the east halted and were defeated by the Germans. Paris capitulated, was partially disarmed, and agreed to pay an indemnity, but in return was permitted food supplies. With great difficulty Bismarck prevailed on William I and the generals to forgo the triumph of a victory parade through Paris. It was also agreed that elections throughout France would take place and that the elected Assembly would then authorize and ratify a regular peace treaty.

It fell to Thiers, the 74-year-old veteran of the Orleanist era, elected 'chief of the executive power' by the Bordeaux Assembly to conclude peace. He returned to Versailles on 21 February 1871. He was confronted by Bismarck in his most ruthless mood. Bismarck threatened to renew the war to induce Thiers to give in. But Thiers negotiated tenaciously and won a few concessions. It was a harsh preliminary peace that was concluded five days later on 26 February. France lost Alsace and eastern Lorraine including the city of Strasbourg, the Mulhouse textile centre, the Saarbrücken coalfield, the iron works of Thionville; the inhabitants were given a choice of nationality. An indemnity of five billion francs payable in instalments between 1871 and 1874 was imposed and linked to Prussian evacuation of French territory in stages. Thiers had failed to save Metz for France; as compensation France retained Belfort, but Thiers had to acquiesce in a limited Prussian victory parade in Paris. After further haggling in Brussels the definitive Treaty of Frankfurt was signed on 10 May 1871.

The German victory and the imposition of a victor's peace shocked Europe. 'The war represents the German revolution,' Disraeli declared, 'a greater political event than the French Revolution of last century... There is not a diplomatic tradition which has not been swept away. You have a new world... The balance of power has been entirely destroyed...' What had become clear to Europe was that primacy had passed from France to Germany. In other respects too Germany took the place of France. It was now the new imperial Germany that had to cope with international fears induced by Germany's own strength. For Germany this was very much a mixed blessing. The year 1871 marks the beginnings not only of a new Franco-German enmity but also of the recurrent German nightmare of 'encirclement'. After the foundation of the empire it became Bismarck's preoccupation, at times amounting to an obsession, to meet these new dangers both real and imagined. Britain's position was more fortunate for not having become embroiled in the national wars of the continent, unburdened by historical enmities, able to defend her own interests, but also where possible to act in the general interests of peace.

21

The New Constellation of Power in Europe 1871–1878

The German *Reich* in 1871 was recognized as the leading military power in Europe. Economically, Germany was still far behind Britain, the first industrial nation of Europe. The dynamic development of German industrial strength after 1871 was even more remarkable than her military achievements. By 1900 Germany overshadowed France and had the largest iron and steel industry in Europe, having overtaken Britain. In science and technology and in the arts Germany occupied a position second to none. But the political development of the German colossus did not match its economic and military strength.

The relationship of the different components of this new modern nation did not work smoothly together. They were in a state of separateness, at times in a kind of antagonistic imbalance. Bismarck contrived in these conditions to retain personal power for twenty years but he did not by himself create the basic political and social conditions of the empire. They could not be simply arranged by one man, even one of Bismarck's calibre, to suit his own purpose.

The nineteenth century saw the two 'German nations' emerging, just as under the impact of industrialization everywhere, in Britain earlier than elsewhere, the 'two nations' developed. The small group of the privileged and propertied, who had monopolized political power, was being challenged by an increasingly larger group of the less privileged who recognized that social reform necessitated political power. They were ill-organized and the political activist leadership was divided. They were also, on the whole, disinclined to revolution and violence, hoping to gain their ends by better organization and persuasion. The division between the 'two nations' was, of course, not as sharp as Disraeli's famous description implies. There were many in between and no stratification by simple 'class labels' stands up to historical analysis. Nevertheless the supreme problem facing those who held political power in nineteenth-century Europe was how to deal with the aspirations of the masses of the people forming the nation but not sharing in its government or prosperity. Britain, France and Italy took one broad road, Germany another; Austria-Hungary followed its own pattern dictated by its internal multi-national condition and Russia yet another of almost pure reaction.

In Britain and France during the third quarter of the nineteenth century the franchise was extended to the masses and government depended on organizing a majority of support in parliament. In Italy the adoption of manhood suffrage was delayed until 1911 and 1912. Before 1914 in all these countries a parliamentary assembly, popularly elected, had become the basis of the authority of the government. Social and economic questions fell within the spheres of government, and military power was subordinated to its will. Over questions of foreign policy it is true parliamentary assemblies rarely exerted direct control; but indirect control there was since the ministry in power was dependent on a majority in parliament. This presents a picture in the broadest brush strokes for the differences between Italy, France and Britain were enormous.

Britain during the 1860s and 1870s and 1880s, witnessed the evolution of an effective form of popular parliamentary government. Simultaneously in a way closely interrelated, the modern Liberal and Conservative Parties emerged seeking power by appeals to an electorate, in which most the adult males had been granted the vote – a vote which because it could be secretly cast, was no longer purchasable by corrupt practices. This consummated the reconciliation of government by the privileged with the broad masses in a system within which both were prepared to work. Britain had been fortunate in her history and in the freedom the British people had enjoyed from revolution and from warfare on her own territory. The popularity of the crown increased as its influence on policy declined by the close of the nineteenth century. The link between crown and the military forces of the nation was severed and they were subordinated to the parliamentary will. Even perfect constitutional arrangements do not guarantee wise decisions by those charged with the responsibility for making them, but the conflict between different interest groups are channelled and in the end resolved by the overall powers of cabinet and parliament.

Bismarck in common with many Germans was opposed to the British 'model' of government which reduced the crown to symbolic significance. Indeed Bismarck conceived a personal hatred for the British representative system which he transferred to any who supported it, Gladstone, the English wife of Crown Prince Frederick, and practically the whole female entourage of the court, which he believed was plotting against him. Yet paradoxically, it appears, Bismarck was chiefly responsible for insisting that the *Reichstag* should be elected by universal manhood suffrage. His reason was not to increase the standing and power of parliament but to undermine it. This he succeeded in doing but not in the way he had imagined. The liberals, representatives of the better-off, the new middle 'class' groups of Germans, feared that their determination to resist social change would be undermined by universal suffrage and by the influx of the people's representatives, the socialists. It was by this very fear that Bismarck hoped to chain the bulk of the liberals to support his policies. If the liberals proved obstinate, however, and desired real power then, Bismarck believed, the crown would forge an alliance with the people against this selfish class. The masses, Bismarck thought, revered the tradition of the crown above that of parliaments and would respond to a loyal appeal. Bismarck wrongly calculated that the domestic situation involving all the people could be as easily manipulated as he manipulated the few men who controlled the chancelleries of Europe in foreign affairs. He applied the same method and lack of principle in dealing with home as foreign affairs.

There was a great deal of perception in Bismarck's assessment that the *Reichstag* was an isolated body of squabbling politicians without real roots. Few Germans in the 1870s and 1880s would have wished that control should be taken out of the hands of the crown and of Bismarck and handed over to one of the parliamentary leaders, Bennigsen the National Liberal, or Windthorst of the Centre Party, let alone the Socialist Bebel, simply on the grounds that they could form a government based on a majority among their *Reichstag* colleagues. There was no widespread conviction that all power should be derived from the parliamentary assembly. The prestige and rights of the Prussian crown had not been undermined as in Britain. There was a reverence and respect for the Prussian sovereign, such as had long disappeared in Britain. It took many years of foolish behaviour and silly public appearances and speeches on the part of William I's grandson, the Kaiser William II, before the awe that surrounded the throne began to be dissipated in the first decade of the twentieth century. Even then the Kaiser still retained great powers. That is why, although the German Empire possessed in the *Reichstag* a democratic institution, it would be wrong to see the Germans as progressing inevitably towards democracy. All the major parties, even the early socialists, accepted and in a way respected, the standing of the Prussian crown. None had any intention of bringing about a revolution whatever their ideology. Nor was there support for a revolution among any sections of German society before 1914. It is therefore a mistake to regard Bismarck as the chief obstacle to a constitutional progress to which even the liberal parties did not aspire. What the Liberal and Catholic Centre Party stood for were in general personal freedoms and rights, and a share and influence on government. They did not expect to be *the* government; they never really believed in their own right to rule and to subordinate the crown, the army, and all other important pillars of the German state to their collective parliamentary will. Here is the essential difference between Germany and Britain.

There was no demand either among the broad mass of people for parliamentary sovereignty. To have brought about a great change of attitude the chancellor would himself have had to play a leading role in guiding the country towards it, and this Bismarck had no intention of doing. He clashed with the Liberals over the degree of influence parliament should enjoy. He wished to keep it to a minimum and so to manipulate the political situation that the *Reichstag* like the *Bundesrat* would be no more than a decorative addition, giving the federal states and the German people a sense of participation without any power.

The *Reichstag*, during the years of the Bismarck era, was neither a sovereign parliamentary assembly nor simply a pliant instrument in the hands of the chancellor, but something in between. There was much co-operation between the parties and Bismarck but also some vehement conflict. In the nature of the situation, the crown and the chancellor on the one hand and the *Reichstag* on the other were not in an inevitable harmony as is the ministry and the majority of the House of Commons in Britain, but two separate organs of government more like the United States President and Congress except that the *Reichstag* did not enjoy the powers of prestige of the United States Congress. Whenever the *Reichstag* proved difficult, Bismarck could claim he was responsible to the allied German governments in the *Bundesrat*. No parliamentary leaders could become ministers in the imperial government without giving up their membership of the *Reichstag*; chancellor and ministers thus confronted the *Reichstag* and negotiated with it without being a part of it; the chancellor could address the *Reichstag* but the separation of chancellor and ministers, the *Bundesrat* and the *Reichstag* was imbedded in the constitution as an insuperable obstacle to the development of a British-style parliamentary sovereignty.

The army remained a separate estate in Germany, its prestige held in unhealthily high regard. The whole of society was deeply coloured by this admiration for military virtues, obedience, the soldier's code, and an acceptance that military needs must always come first. The king was venerated as commander-in-chief. Uniforms abounded and at court predominated. King and chancellor appeared usually in uniform. In Bismarck's time, the decisions of state were taken by the chancellor. Some of Bismarck's hardest struggles in Prussia from

1862 to 1871 had been over the issue of asserting his supremacy over the generals at headquarters. Bismarck succeeded. His successors did not. The needs of the army and later the navy became a distinctive and by 'civilians' unchallengeable influence on policy-making and the direction of the army remained the preserve of the Junkers. Where did industrial Germany fit in?

The great industrial barons, like the Krupps, whose spectacular rise belongs to the decades which followed the foundation of the empire were a law unto themselves. They on the whole hated parliamentary government and of course social democracy. They believed that theirs was the Germany that really mattered. The government of the state should therefore be influenced and manipulated in their economic interests. They were internationally-minded as German trade in chemicals, manufactured engineering products and armaments found markets throughout Europe. They were the least bound by a narrow patriotism. Krupps never scrupled about selling weapons and licences for production of arms not only in Germany but to Germany's enemies too. What was good for them they believed was good for Germany. Towards their work force they often extended a feudal paternalism. They had no settled political convictions but sought to manipulate government to suit their ends. Unscrupulous and dynamic, big industry was not a 'lobby' as much as another power in the state. So the empire's progress and government came to depend on separate, sometimes uncoordinated and antagonistic elements in the state, the crown, the chancellor, the *Reichstag*, the army controlled by the Junkers and big industry. Bismarck overshadowed all these disparate forces for a time through sheer force of will and the enormous prestige he enjoyed. But the situation was inherently unstable behind the splendid façade of the empire. In later years it was hard to tell, and historians dispute the question still, where real power lay. Consequently the whole of Europe became uncertain as to the real aims and directions of German policy. In that respect the first and last years of the empire resembled each other. Bismarck in the years immediately following the Franco-Prussian War was suspected in Europe of maintaining the army in order to fight his fourth war. It took time before Germany's neighbours became convinced of his peaceful intentions.

In his domestic policy from 1871 to 1878, Bismarck relied in the *Reichstag* on the National Liberals. But with William I now regarding him as indispensable to the state, Bismarck's position was unassailable and he intended to be the master and the National Liberals were to assume the role of subordinates. The administration which was staffed in its senior ranks by Junker families and the professional middle class were the instruments of his policies. This administrative middle class was granted honours and titles and if senior enough 'ennobled' to the extent of being granted a '*von*'. The imperial era became obsessed with titles and decorations in every profession. Bismarck, supported by the National Liberals, the Free Conservatives and individual groups in the *Reichstag* passed much useful and necessary legislation promoting imperial unity in economic and legal matters. On this they could agree. But the National Liberals never submerged themselves entirely to Bismarck's will. The left wing of the party led by Eduard Lasker maintained a watchful opposition whenever it believed liberal principles were endangered.

This became clear over the renewed conflict in 1874 when the question of the military budget had to be decided. It had been agreed in 1867 between the Liberal opposition and Bismarck that the military budget should be fixed until January 1872. During the course of the Franco-Prussian War the military budget was extended until 1874. Then the National Liberals were confronted by the issue once more. Without control over the military budget, they would lose control over the greater part of the budget altogether. The National Liberals stoutly defended parliamentary rights. Bismarck deliberately steered a middle course; he was probably glad that the generals and the king would now recognize that they could not manage without the chancellor. He fiercely attacked the National Liberals, especially Lasker's wing, accusing them of wishing to weaken his position in Europe and he threatened them with the patriotic reaction of the people if an election should prove necessary. The majority of the National Liberals were intimidated and glad to accept the compromise he offered which conceded a great deal. The military budget would not be fixed permanently but for seven years at a time. Parliamentary control over government spending was thereby very much weakened. It was a heavy defeat for liberalism.

Principles of liberalism were threatened even more by the so-called *Kulturkampf*, or struggle for culture. If the liberals stood for anything it was the rights of individuals and the equality of all citizens before an impartial law. Bismarck's onslaught against Catholic institutions and Catholic religious leaders in the 1870s smacked of earlier supposedly less civilized centuries. The *Kulturkampf* failed in the sense that Bismarck for political reasons abandoned it, in the face of firm Catholic opposition. But with the hindsight of the twentieth century it was ominous that the prejudices and passion of a majority could be turned against a religious minority who were step by step deprived of basic rights.

The *Kulturkampf* has its origins not in Germany but in Italy, in the struggle between the papacy and the secular Italian state. Although the Italian constitution decreed the Catholic religion as the only religion of the state, Cavour was determined to destroy the political influence of the Church. Monasteries were dissolved in Piedmont before they were dissolved in Prussia; clerical privileges in law were abolished. What brought the conflict to a climax was Pope Pius IX's determination to uphold the spiritual supremacy of the papacy and also its temporal power. He declared war on Italian nationalism by virtually collectively excommunicating all its supporters. As Pius IX came to be increasingly hard pressed in the 1860s by the combination of nationalist and anti-clericalist political forces in Italy, so he reacted with more and more vehemence against the spirit of the new age. In December 1864 the papal encyclical *Quanta cura* was devoted to a 'Catalogue of the Principal Errors of our Time'. It condemned not only socialism and nationalism but rejected the proposition that the Pope could come to terms with what was called 'progress, liberalism, and modern civilization'. Successive conservative Italian governments, despite papal opposition, continued with their anti-clerical policies, dissolving religious orders, confiscating church funds and declaring only civil marriages valid. It was a spiritual civil war with the overpowering political strength of Italy ranged against the Pope. The final destruction of his temporal power, in September 1870, followed Prussia's victory over the emperor's army at Sedan (p. 314). Pius IX, now 'the prisoner of the Vatican', counter-attacked with spiritual weapons. It was for this reason that when the Vatican Council in July 1870 adopted the dogma of the infallibility of the Pope there was tremendous excitement in Europe. Was the Pope challenging the authority of the state and encouraging civil disobedience of the Catholics not only in Italy but throughout Europe wherever the policies of the state did not conform to the Pope's wishes? Of course all this fuss about loyalties and papal dangers was without real foundation at least outside Italy. But secular governments and liberalism appeared to be facing a sudden confrontation and many Catholics were deeply troubled.

In Germany, Bismarck gave this conflict an added political and national twist. Throughout 1870, Bismarck was not in the least disturbed by papal policies and pronouncements, viewing them with a proper sense of proportion. He was even ready to offer the Pope political asylum in Germany should he wish to leave Rome! But, as he explained to the papal emissary, the Catholic Prussian Archbishop of Posen, Ledochowski, 'the Pope must do something for us in return'. He did not object to the Pope's political influence over Catholics, provided it was exercised in Bismarck's favour! Thus he saw the Pope as a useful political ally.

In Prussia and later in the empire at this time, a Catholic political party was being formed which became known as the Centre Party. Its ties with priests were close and so it could reach the masses. The party stood for the freedom of religious rights and the rights of

independent associations within the state including Catholic organizations. The Centre Party believed that the state should act as the
protector of the rights of its citizens, not that citizens should be
subordinated in all questions to the dictates of the state. The Centre
Party also held that the state should be concerned with social conditions of the less well-off. There were aspects of the Centre Party's
policies which were in accordance with both conservative and liberal
beliefs. Under the skilful leadership of the Hanoverian Ludwig Windthorst, the Centre Party soon revealed itself as a disciplined, powerful
and independent parliamentary group prepared to work with Bismarck on some issues but not ready to subordinate itself to his will.
Having secured fifty-seven seats in the *Reichstag* elections of 1871
the Centre Party showed that it was a political force to be reckoned
with.

An important aspect of the Centre Party's policy was to preserve
the federal nature of the empire and to resist any unitary tendencies.
In this they clashed with Bismarck. The Pope could not or would not
help Bismarck to bring the Centre Party to heel. And so Bismarck
whole-heartedly threw himself into an indiscriminate anti-Catholic
campaign. Bismarck condemned Windthorst's opposition as motivated by 'enmity to the Empire', *Reichfeindlich*; Bismarck was unable
to distinguish between resistance to his own will and the good of
Imperial Germany. What gave some plausibility to this charge was
that the Centre Party tended to attract to its support other minorities
of the empire besides Guelph Hanoverians, the Poles, and the unreconciled, still pro-French, inhabitants of Alsace and Lorraine; they
wished to maintain their traditions intact as far as possible. Bismarck
was bent on Prussianizing the Polish minorities. In his *Reminiscences*
he claimed it was the Polish aspect that was decisive in his thinking
about the *Kulturkampf*.

From 1872 to 1875 anti-clerical legislation was passed by the
Prussian parliament mainly in spheres of religious organization,
secularization of bishoprics, education – and all matters within
state competence; but there was also legislation in the *Reichstag*,
such as the dissolution of the Society of Jesus and the banishment
of all, including German, members from the empire – a fundamental
infraction of the liberty of the individual German. Yet in all this,
Bismarck had the support of the majority of the National Liberals
who believed they were fighting for progress against the medieval
pretensions of the Church. The repressive legislation only increased
support for the Centre Party. In the 1874 *Reichstag* elections the
Centre Party had increased its strength to 94 deputies.

After 1875, Bismarck became tired of his unsuccessful political
campaign against the Catholic Church, but he had to wait until
1878, for a new Pope, Leo XIII, before he could repeal much of the

Kulturkampf legislation and make his peace with the Church and the Centre Party. It was part of the domestic political upheaval of 1878/9 which left Bismarck presiding over new policies supported by a different political combination in the *Reichstag*. Nobody questioned the propriety of the same man remaining chancellor though his policies had radically altered.

Bismarck created bogy-men at home or abroad to maintain his system of government; in turn he warned of the dangers of an international Catholic conspiracy, of the French spirit of revenge, and to these he added in the mid-1870s, the Social Democrats. It is unfortunately often easier to gain co-operation in confronting a common enemy than to establish bonds of common agreement. It was no unique discovery of Bismarck's that when no enemy exists it is possible to invent one. He was quite ready to sacrifice the development of mutual trust and good relationships to gain his immediate ends. During the year 1875–6 Bismarck heightened tensions and painted new enemies in lurid colours before the eyes of the German electorate. A French 'war scare' (p. 342) coincided with his need to gain approval for the military budget; during the spring of 1876 Bismarck introduced legislation to limit the rights of the Social Democrats to organize their political party. This too failed. The legislation seeking to limit the rights of the Social Democrats to organize their party was too much even for the National Liberals to accept. Then in the spring of 1878 there was an assassination attempt on William I. Bismarck viciously blamed the Social Democrat Party for being responsible. There was not the slightest justification for this accusation and the National Liberals again refused to pass an anti-Socialist Bill. A second assassination attempt on William I a month later came opportunely. There was no connection between the criminal and the Social Democratic Party. Bismarck alone linked the two. He insisted that the *Reichstag* should be dissolved and blamed the National Liberals for opposing the Socialist Bill.

In the new *Reichstag* the Liberals were weakened and the conservatives strengthened. The Centre Party remained firm and opposed the Socialist Bill. In October the National Liberals caved in and joined the conservatives in passing the bill. It did not help them. Bismarck was preparing to change the domestic and economic policy of the German Empire. The National Liberals had not proved sufficiently pliable. The free trade policy, for which the National Liberals stood, came under criticism with the recession of the mid-1870s. The change came in December 1878 when Bismarck switched to protectionist policies and broke with the National Liberals. What Bismarck had demonstrated by 1878 was that he was above party, able to choose enemies and friends regardless of consistency, and that the democratic electorate could be manipulated by vicious propaganda.

But the chancellor's power was not absolute. The *Kulturkampf* had ended in complete failure. The same fate awaited his anti-socialist legislation and by a twist of fate it became in 1890 a pretext for his dismissal by Kaiser William II.

What was France in 1871? An empire without an emperor, a monarchy without a king, a republic without a president or constitution? France found itself in a constitutional vacuum. The empire had come to an end with the capture of Napoleon III. It had always depended on his leadership and so in 1870, with or without a war, its days were numbered. Napoleon III had attempted to provide for the future by making constitutional changes in the spring of 1870 (p. 292); the 'Empire' might then have continued without an emperor, during the years of minority of the Prince Imperial – he was 14 years old in 1870 – but the young emperor would never have assumed the powers of Napoleon III; it is inconceivable that Eugénie, the empress could have exercised real powers after Napoleon III's death. So some change was inevitable.

What the great majority of Frenchmen did not want is what they got, a republic. Napoleon III's constitutional empire had received a massive vote of confidence in May 1870. The overthrow of the 'empire' in Paris the following 4 September was just as inevitable with the emperor in captivity. The empire was replaced by a 'republic' because there was nothing else that could fill the vacuum at the time quite apart from the hoped-for historical parallel. The republicans in France remained in a minority because republicanism was associated with hostility to property and with anti-clericalism. But shrewd opponents of the republicans, such as Thiers the veteran politician of the July monarchy, were not averse to the 'republic' being saddled with the ignominy of defeat.

Though the transfer to a republican Government of National Defence was a very un-revolutionary proceeding in a Paris, which itself was soon cut off from the rest of the country, the changes that followed from these events were real enough. Léon Gambetta, minister of the interior, and after his dramatic departure by balloon from Paris to Tours early in October, minister of war as well, was the most dynamic and leading spirit of the government. He was young, energetic and a convinced republican. He was determined to infuse republican ardour and a hatred of the enemy into the conservative rural masses longing for peace. With the help of a civilian and professional engineer, Charles de Freycinet, he organized new peasant armies; but they fought in vain against the superior professional Prussian army. After their failure, Gambetta resigned. But Gambetta's short tenure of power left its mark.

The ministry of the interior controlled the provincial administration. It was staffed by a bureaucracy ready to serve any form of government. The highly-centralized administration of provincial France was under the control of the prefects. Gambetta dismissed wholesale the prefects who had served Napoleon III and replaced them with republicans. This political move strengthened the republic but made no contribution to efficiency as inexperienced men took the place of the imperial prefects. They were the loyal servants of the state, so that when Thiers gained power in 1871 he in turn replaced the prefects installed by Gambetta. All these rapid changes created considerable uncertainty about the future. The principal political issue in September 1870 was when elections should be held to provide the constitutional sanction of the French people for the still provisional republic. This question, however, soon became an academic problem for the need to continue the war came to overshadow everything else. At home and abroad the Government of National Defence was accepted as the *de facto* government of France and Bismarck negotiated the armistice with it.

The government in Paris announced the conclusion of the armistice and instructed the ministers who had sought safety in Bordeaux to arrange for the election of a National Assembly to meet in Bordeaux on 12 February 1871. Its first task would be to ratify the armistice terms. The elections in war-time France, parts of it under German occupation, were thoroughly confused. The elected representatives somehow made their way to Bordeaux. Thiers had been elected in 26 *Départements* and was the natural leader to whom the majority now turned. He was expected to reconcile the Orleanist and Bourbon royal party supporters; in the meantime the 'republic' was a stop-gap. The assembly even hesitated to appoint a president as head of state of a republic and would not invest Thiers with this office, nominating him 'Chief of the Executive of the French Republic'. On 1 March 1871 the assembly ratified the harsh terms of the peace preliminaries by a vote of 546 to 107. Then the assembly decided to move to Versailles, not Paris. Before the monarchical parties could consider the future restoration, the urgent task of pulling France back from the brink of chaos had to be undertaken. Thiers was determined to establish firm and strong government without which France could not recover, pay off the indemnity, and so rid itself of the German occupation. At times it had seemed that the Government of National Defence had been the prisoner of Paris. Thiers' government was determined to be its master and the turbulence during the many months of siege boded trouble now that a common enemy no longer had to be faced.

In March 1871 Paris was a powder keg. Predominantly republican in sentiment, the majority of Parisians had seen authority pass into the hands of the moderates who had appointed themselves a provisional Government of National Defence. The more militant radical leaders viewed the government with suspicion but all effort during the months of war had been subordinated to the task of defending Paris against the invader. With its tradition of urban unrest, and memories of the brutal suppression of the June Days of 1848, revolutionary clubs and neighbourhood political action were already being organized in Paris during the siege to forestall the possibility of a counter-revolution from the right. The National Guard held the key to power in the city. The need to utilize all available manpower in defence of Paris had brought about its transformation so that now it included a majority of the poorer Parisians, who since all industrial activity had ceased were dependent on their pay as members of the National Guard to keep their families alive. The National Guard eventually became an armed revolutionary force. In October 1870 and early in January 1871 National Guard battalions from the poorer sections of Paris had attempted insurrections to replace the provisional government with a *Commune de Paris* inspired by the Jacobin mobilization of 1792 and 1793. A republic reflecting the social and political needs of the majority and defending the country against the common enemy was their aim. Thiers' capitulation to the Germans came as a tremendous shock. Efforts to save the republic from its internal enemies now became the main motive of the deprived and disheartened Parisians. By March 1871 three radical organizations in Paris, the Federation of Trade Unions, the Delegation of the twenty *arrondissements* of Paris and the International provided an embryonic organization for an alternative government in Paris, challenging the authority of Thiers and his executive and the predominantly monarchist 'Bordeaux' Assembly. Paris had blazed the trail for France before; why should it not do so again?

Thiers had arrived in Paris on 15 March. He meant to force Paris to submit and could not have anticipated the fierce reaction to the National Assembly's policies or he would hardly have risked exposing himself to the Parisians. On 18 March he ordered that a number of guns seized by the National Guard to keep them out of Prussian reach should now be removed by the regular army from the National Guard. Many Parisians also faced economic ruin. The National Assembly cancelled the moratorium on the payment of rents and commercial bills which had lasted through the war; they now threatened to suspend the pay of the National Guard as well. But recalcitrant Paris was immensely heartened by what happened next. On 18 March units of the regular army sent to seize the guns fraternized with the National Guard; revolution looked as if it might succeed even before it had really been attempted. Thiers was powerless in Paris, and a change of government in Paris had previously always meant a new régime for France. Not this time. Thiers slipped away from Paris to Versailles and transferred his administration there.

The recently formed Central Committee of the National Guard suddenly found it held power in Paris. It had no plan what to do; no organized attempt to set up a revolutionary Marxist government was made. Yet the city with its formidable force of a quarter of a million armed men, supported by the majority of the Parisians, was in the hands of the committee. They behaved in a most unrevolutionary way decreeing that elections should be held in Paris to create a legitimate *Commune de Paris*. On 26 March in response, 229,000 Parisians voted representing about 70 per cent of the electorate. The government of the *Commune* for the first time contained a sizeable number, though not a majority of *ouvriers*, but it was no 'working class' directorate. Its legislation was reformist rather than communist; free education, anti-clericalism and measures to improve the life of working people were the main objectives. Paris wished to set France an example, a return to the spirit and values of the French Revolution of 1789. There were divisions and quarrels within the *Commune* and the moderates gradually gave way to more extreme and radical leadership. But order was maintained within Paris. Life continued as usual with theatres and concerts entertaining the public and people thronged in the Boulevards.

This peaceful scene was transformed two months later. The reduction of Paris in May 1871 is reminiscent of Windischgraetz's subjugation of Vienna. Thiers reorganized the army in Versailles aided by the release of French prisoners of war. Paris was besieged again on 2 April. But fierce fighting did not commence until May. On 21 May the Versailles army was in Paris. It was only during this last stage of the civil war that barbarity and savagery gained the upper hand on both sides with hostages being shot including the Archbishop of Paris. The Versaillais massacred the *communards* at the barricades and murdered their prisoners. Nothing in the Franco-Prussian War matched the abandonment of all civilized conduct witnessed during these last stages of the battle of Paris. It ended appropriately among the graves of the cemetery of Père-Lachaise. More than 20, 000 Parisians were killed during the week beginning on 21 May and thousands were sentenced during the following four years of trials to long terms of imprisonment or death. The workers of Paris had been defeated far more savagely in May 1871 than in June 1848. The hatred of class wars was what Thiers bequeathed France in the long run, though in Paris, as in some other bigger cities, by ending the *Commune* he had succeeded in smashing the resistance of the workers for years to come.

The defeat of the *Commune* had made the republic led by Thiers more respectable and acceptable to the peasants and the better-off. It was clearly not going to be a republic that would threaten property

or privilege. Thiers' own position was ambiguous. He was at first
seen by the monarchists as the man who would cleverly arrange a
restoration. Perhaps Thiers saw himself in that role to begin with.
But the old man was an adept politician and played his cards close to
his chest. He saw no reason to diminish his powers or to have to
manage the affairs of France under any sovereign when it was
already difficult enough to manage them without one. The ravages
of war had to be made good, production restarted and increased,
international credit had to be re-established and the war reparations
to the Germans paid off so that the Prussians would evacuate the
remaining regions of France they held in surety. His task was made
easier by the divisions and squabbles of the monarchists.

In the Bordeaux Assembly they found themselves in a large majority, possibly some 400-strong altogether, though the various party
groupings were indistinct. The largest group of some 200 hoped for
an Orleanist restoration and so desired a constitutional monarchy.
They were mainly the well-to-do, practical and moderate men, liberal
in their ideas. The claimant they supported was the Comte de Paris,
the grandson of Louis Philippe. But they were divided too; there were
those who were pure Orleanists and those ready to make a deal with
the rival Bourbon claimant Henri, Comte de Chambord, a grandson
of Charles X, regarded by his followers as Henri V. These 'legitimists'
were some 100-strong in the assembly, the majority of them regarding the Orleanists as traitors and usurpers. Many of them were
unknown country gentlemen, and some came from the professions,
hankering after the return of the old order and tradition; so between
them they lacked practical political experience. Then there were
some 180 'royalists', moderates, of no particular allegiance and
also just a handful of Bonapartists. What made the royalists so
ineffective was the unbending devout 'Henri V' who refused all
compromise with political reality. The Comte de Chambord was
not only devout but also childless. The historian Bodley wrote of
him that he 'displayed in the circumstances of his life and his death
that there are heights of virtue and perfection to which it is expedient
that the secular leaders of people should not attain'. He insisted on a
restoration which acknowledged the White Bourbon Standard as the
ancient Bourbon emblem (which it was not, having been introduced
after 1814), and by his absurd purism indicated that he would deny
all France's past glories associated with the *tricolor*. This was too
much for all but the die-hards to swallow. The French people really
desired an amalgam of the best of all their traditions. Efforts to seek
a sensible solution by allowing the Comte de Chambord to rule, and
on his death passing the throne to the Comte de Paris and his heirs
were useless when confronted by a man of such pure principle as
the Comte de Chambord. And so it came about that the republic

survived because no alternative could be agreed upon and was practicable even though in the spring of 1871 there was only a heterogeneous group of republicans, certainly less than 200 in all who had gained a place in the National Assembly.

By the time of the elections of 2 July 1871 to fill the seats fallen vacant in the assembly by the *Commune*, the trend showed a strengthening of the centre, moderate republicans not by positive conviction but for want of a better solution, at the expense of the extreme left and right. Even 'extreme' Paris replaced fifteen of the twenty-one seats held by *communards* with conservative republicans or moderate royalists. This remained the trend during the following years; gradually the monarchist majority was eroded and replaced by conservative republicans. But in May 1873 the royalists were still strong enough to combine and revenge themselves on Thiers for failing to promote a royal restoration by voting him out of office.

Although the royalists were still planning a restoration, they inadvertently strengthened republican institutions instead. Marshal MacMahon, vanquished at Sedan, became president; the head of the government, a post now separated from the presidency was the Orleanist Duc de Broglie. The year 1873 proved significant in the history of the Third Republic. The financial recovery of France had enabled Thiers to arrange for the payment of the final instalments of the indemnity and the last German soldier left French soil in September. Two months later, in November, even Broglie had to accept that there was no immediate prospect of a royalist restoration and so the Republic, with MacMahon as president and head of state, was voted into being not permanently but for seven years. It was a republic without a constitution, its institutions being improvised. This was achieved first by the *amendement Wallon* on 30 January 1875 carried by 353 votes to 352. The two Chambers of the National Assembly arrogated to themselves the right of providing a constitutional framework for the republic. The two most important constitutional laws were passed on 24 and 25 February 1875. In these the Presidential powers were ambiguously defined. The President was responsible for exercising surveillance over the executive, but he could not act without the counter signature of the responsible minister. Whether the individual ministers were responsible for government policy as a whole was unclear. The Chamber of Deputies was elected by a complex system of manhood suffrage. The Senate was indirectly elected in an even more complicated way, representation being weighted in favour of rural France. The President, the Senate and the Chamber could each initiate legislation. The President, however, enjoyed one clear right: he could dissolve the Chamber before the expiration of its four-year term with the consent of the

Senate. What the 'constitutional laws' avoided was how to resolve a conflict between the President responsible for the Executive and the Chamber.

It was virtually inevitable that a political crisis would develop to decide this issue. MacMahon lacked political finesse; he was an honest man but, in common with the army and church, hated the republic of the 'Left' represented by such men as Gambetta. He appointed as his ministers men from the 'Moderate Left', the 'Centre' or the 'Right'. When elections to the Chamber were held in 1876, they produced a large majority of the Republican 'Left', divided into three major groups. Thus the ministers and the Chamber were soon at loggerheads, creating an unworkable situation. Two Presidents of Council, chosen by MacMahon, succeeded each other after only a few months. The second, Jules Simon, resigning after receiving a letter of criticism from the Marshal dated 16 May 1877 – hence the name of the crisis that ensued. The Republican 'Left' challenged the presidential power to choose ministers; they wished the Chamber of Deputies to dominate. With the consent of the Senate, more evenly balanced politically than the Chamber, MacMahon hit back and, acting constitutionally, dissolved the Chamber in June 1877. The new elections returned another large Republican 'Left' majority. MacMahon struggled on with a succession of ministers for a few months, but the Chamber would pass no legislation. In December the Marshal was forced to capitulate. Henceforth the President of the Council would choose his ministerial team which required the support of the Chamber. Presidential power to dissolve the Chamber was retained intact theoretically, but never exercised again. Parliamentary democracy had triumphed. On the other hand, assured of four years of undisturbed power and lacking the discipline of a two-party system, the dominant Chamber created and destroyed ministries at a dizzy speed; ambitious deputies played musical chairs with ministerial office. Between 1879 and 1914 the average life of a ministry was less than one year. Political instability was the price France paid for the destruction of presidential power.

So much seemed uncertain in the changed conditions of Europe after 1871. How would the German Empire exercise its new-found power? Could a continental balance of power ever be restored in Europe? And on top of all these anxieties, the complex problem, which had become known to the powers as the 'Eastern question', was soon to enter a new and dangerous phase. The German victory forced the great powers to re-examine how their national interests could best be pursued in the new condition of things.

At the *Ballhausplatz* in Vienna, where the foreign ministry adjoined the emperor's *Hofburg*, Beust pondered about Austria-Hungary's future. What stood out clearly was that the empire would have to live within its means. A re-entry into Germany was impossible. The future lay in the east. In a memorandum of 18 May 1871 Beust advised the emperor to accept a reconciliation with Prussia so that the two empires could stand side by side, dominant in central Europe and safe from external and internal danger. Italy was also to be drawn into the friendly contract. The fundamental European alignment between Austria and Germany that prevailed until 1918 was thus initiated on the Austrian side by Beust. Indications of a new spirit of reconciliation between Germany and Austria-Hungary soon became evident when in August 1871 William I and Bismarck met Francis Joseph and Beust at Bad Ischl in Austria. A few days later at Salzburg, Bismarck and Beust promised each other friendly co-operation – an alliance was not necessary, they believed. Finally Bismarck assured the Austro-Hungarian chancellor that Germany had no designs on the German-speaking Austrians. A few weeks later in November 1871, Beust was forced to resign as chancellor for purely domestic political reasons. The Beust years were characterized by a liberal approach at home and Austrian commerce and finance recovered and were in a better state in 1871 than they had been for decades.

The 'new course' in foreign policy inaugurated by Beust was continued by Count Julius Andrássy his successor as joint foreign minister. As a Hungarian, Andrássy wanted no increase of Slavs in the empire and the German Austrians shared this attitude. This outlook explains Andrássy's foreign policy of refusing to consider any schemes of territorial expansion in the Balkans at the expense of the Turks. But he equally wished to deny Russia any increase of influence and hoped to align Germany in a more definite anti-Russian stance. His policy therefore had to be to try to preserve the *status quo* in the Balkans. This was certainly true of his aims when coming to office. But then, despite his suspicions of Russia, he agreed to far-reaching schemes of reorganization of Turkey in Europe in the event of Ottoman power collapse. There was thus a certain ambivalence about Austro-Hungarian foreign policy from the start. The same is true of Russian policy.

In Russia the previous decade of the 1860s had witnessed the growth of a panslavist movement. Its adherents differed in ideas but found common ground in their attitude that Russia should protect the Slav people. This would entail support for independent Slav national movements in the Ottoman and Austro-Hungarian Empires and so inevitably threatened their destruction as great powers. The views of the panslavists were romantic, mystical, but often also genuinely humanitarian. They also had far-reaching implications in foreign affairs. Ignatiev, the Russian ambassador at Constantinople since 1864, supported a panslav programme because it would lead to a great extension of Russian power in Europe. But Tsar Alexander II and his Chancellor Gorchakov were opposed to any foreign policy adventures. Russia was undergoing a period of change and reform and needed peace. Revolutionary, liberal and national movements in the Balkans were aspects of panslavism just as abhorrent to supporters of autocracy in St Petersburg as in Constantinople. The one goal the tsar wished to attain in common with panslavism was the abrogation of the humiliating Black Sea clauses of the Treaty of Paris. At the same time Gorchakov instructed Ignatiev to assure the sultan that Russia had no designs on the empire, would not support insurrectionary Balkan movements, and hoped for intimate friendship. But the Sultan's ministers did not wish to become solely dependent on Russian goodwill and so turned for advice to the other powers. The outcome was the conference of London from December 1870 to March 1871 (p. 320). The Russians got their way as far as the abrogation of the Black Sea clauses were concerned. But they had to reaffirm the validity of international treaties, including the Treaty of Paris of 1856, and to concede a strengthening of the position of the sultan and of the western powers whose fleets could now be called to the Straits by the sultan in time of peace if he felt the integrity of his empire threatened. This was clearly a check on Russia. The tsar's readiness to accept this provision provides further evidence that he had no aggressive intentions at this time. He recognized that in western Europe, Germany's victory too had altered the balance of power. Although the tsar infinitely preferred a German to a Napoleonic victory, the war-in-sight crisis of 1875 revealed that he and Gorchakov were anxious lest German power became even more dominant and so a danger to European peace.

The change in Britain's policy from isolation to a narrowly-defined continental involvement did not occur immediately after the Franco-German War but was delayed until the change of government in 1874 when Disraeli returned to power. Gladstone meantime emphasized the ethical foundations of foreign policy and the common civilized concern of Christian Europe. All his talk was about as effective as Alexander I's about a Holy Alliance. But at the same time Gladstone was practical in his pursuit of Britain's national interest. The London Black Sea Conference can be regarded as a success for his policy. On the whole he believed it was a time for Britain to limit strictly her commitments in the Ottoman Empire and elsewhere in Europe rather than to extend them. He hoped for a 'balance of continental Europe' that would enable Britain to continue to follow her own peaceful interests.

When we come to consider Germany after 1871, the most noteworthy fact is that Bismarck had placed the German Empire in an immensely strong position. He now made the most important decision of his career. Germany would seek no further territorial expansion on the continent of Europe, or to use his phrase, she had become a 'satiated' power. This was the decision of the calculating gambler who knew when to quit. He would not repeat Napoleon I's mistake. Recent research on Bismarck's foreign policy has emphasized how frequently the chancellor hesitated, which is undoubtedly true. But Bismarck's particular genius lay in defining and limiting his objectives and in matching the means at his disposal to the aims he pursued. Bismarck's decision reversed Germany's role in Europe. In the 1860s his restless diplomacy had contributed to three wars and a radical reshaping of the map of Europe and of the balance of power. Henceforth after 1871 Germany would act as the pre-eminent conservative power of Europe throwing her weight on the side of peace and stability.

When Bismarck considered how this stability could be brought about he rejected the idealistic concepts of the Castlereagh tradition and of Gladstone who in some senses was the contemporary exponent of that tradition. With some justice Bismarck regarded the latter's idealism as a disturbing, irrational, and a dangerous factor in European diplomacy. Bismarck believed that conflicts between the powers over territorial questions and their competition for influence were as permanent a feature of the international scene as the seasons. These very conflicts, however, could be utilized in the interests of peace. Bismarck strove to achieve a condition of balanced tension in which Germany would act as the 'honest broker'. He presupposed that the nations of Europe would remain heavily armed, their military strength acting as a deterrent on each other. On the whole he pursued a conciliatory policy towards France. At the same time he regarded French enmity of Germany as irremovable in the foreseeable future. Furthermore he regarded the instability of the French republic with some anxiety in case a new royalist or Bonapartist French leader sought to gain internal popularity by espousing a chauvinistic policy towards Germany.

The so-called war-in-sight crisis in Franco-German relations during April and May 1875 was the culmination of Bismarck's campaign to intimidate France. France had rapidly recovered. Now the French army was being reorganized and it was clear that France stood at the crossroads. Over the years, if France were allowed to regain her strength, Germany could be faced again with a formidable enemy determined to reverse the verdict of 1870–71. Bismarck organized a press campaign against France including the article in a Berlin newspaper, *Die Post*, sensationally headed 'Is War in Sight?'. Bismarck gratuitously forbade the export of German horses to France which the French were rumoured to be seeking to re-equip their army. He never intended actually to go to war, just to make France believe Germany would do so unless France remained subservient to Germany and virtually defenceless. He also expected that the other European powers would put pressure on France to give up the idea of military reorganization for the sake of peace. His plan badly misfired. The powers hastened to put pressure on Berlin and not Paris. Decazes, the French foreign minister at the end of April 1875, had countered by sending a circular to the powers informing them of German threats and appealing for their help. Rome and London sent cautious notes in favour of peace to Berlin. The tsar and Chancellor Gorchakov happened to be visiting Berlin early in May. Gorchakov, jealous of Bismarck's success, took advantage of the situation by asking the chancellor to give him assurances that Germany had no designs on France. He then took credit for having made certain of peace. The war scare was over.

Bismarck was furious. He had been tagged with the label of wishing to disturb the peace when in reality he had only pretended to do so. During the spring of 1875 he was altogether in a bad state of nerves and over-excited; the *Kulturkampf* was going badly and now he had to accept a set-back in foreign policy. Though he bore personal grudges to the end of his days, Bismarck was too realistic and intelligent a man not to draw lessons from this misadventure. France could not be kept perpetually in a state of subservience. Nor would mere German threats be sufficient to keep her isolated in Europe. More than ever, German policy had to be calculated on the assumption that other European powers would only follow policies which served their immediate national interests. Germany, Russia and Austria had been bound since 1873 by an informal alignment known as the Three Emperors' League. But this conservative alignment of three monarchs would not hold together one moment longer than it served the respective national interests of the partners.

The Three Emperors' League had come about almost accidentally and was certainly not part of a carefully conceived Bismarckian diplomatic plan. The Austrians not the Germans had taken the initiative. The Austrians wished to assure themselves of Germany's friendship thereby pre-empting the possibility of a German-Russian agreement which might be turned against them. Andrássy followed up the reconciliation between the German and Austrian emperors formalized by their meeting in the Austrian spa, Bad Ischl, in August 1871, by accompanying the Austrian emperor on a return visit to Berlin in September 1872. The Russians meantime when they heard the Austrians were going to Berlin were afraid of being left out in case an anti-Russian alignment was formed and so practically invited themselves to Berlin as well. There were friendly talks and in the following year a German-Russian Convention was concluded; a

Russo-Austrian Convention was also signed and to this Germany a few weeks later, in October 1873, acceded; together these agreements provided the written basis of the Three Emperors' League. The motivation of Austria and Russia in concluding it had been mainly negative. For Bismarck too the Three Emperors' League served the negative function of isolating the French Republic and so he emphasized the conservative, monarchical solidarity of the three empires. For Bismarck these mutual agreements between all three empires were also a way of avoiding having to choose sides between Austria-Hungary and Russia in the Balkans. Finally Bismarck expected that by means of the Three Emperors' League he would be able to influence both Austrian and Russian foreign policies. What we have in the Three Emperors' League is the germ of the idea of Bismarck's later very elaborate treaty diplomacy of the 1880s. Alliances then became not so much treaties between 'friends' against potential 'enemies', as treaties between 'potential enemies' to ensure that their rivalries could be contained.

During the early years of the post-Franco-Prussian War period Bismarck preferred the looser, less definite arrangements of the Three Emperors' League – not to be confused with the Three Emperors' *Alliance* of 1881.* The League allowed Germany a free hand. The great change in Bismarck's diplomatic tactics did not occur until 1878–9 immediately after the Congress of Berlin, under the impact of the tensions created by the renewed crisis in the Eastern question. Gradually, almost reluctantly, Bismarck ceased to play the role of a spectator of European diplomacy, following Germany's particular interests, taking advantage of situation or at least trying to, and in 1878 once more himself became one of the principal participants and manipulators.

The Eastern question played a crucial part in the relations of the great powers in the second half of the decade of the 1870s. Rather surprisingly the years from 1871 to 1874 were a period of unusual calm. The tsar and Gorchakov were satisfied with their achievement of revising the Black Sea clauses. Unlike the panslavists, official Russian policy refused to encourage unrest among the subject nationalities of the Ottoman Empire. Russia wanted and needed peace. Russian policy aimed at maintaining the *status quo* as long as possible. The Austrians for their part, though still seeing in Russia the power most likely to threaten them, also wanted peace and the maintenance of the *status quo*. On this mutual basis of agreement Austro-Russian relations greatly improved.

---

* The confusion arises from the similarity of the name of these two treaties in German: *Dreikaiserbund*, Three Emperors' League; *Dreikaiserbuendnis*, Three Emperors' Alliance.

With hindsight the renewal of the Eastern crisis can be precisely dated to the revolt in Bosnia against Turkish rule in July 1875. At the time, this revolt seemed no more serious than countless other troubles facing the Turks, and Andrássy expected the Turks to master the situation speedily. He had little sympathy for the Christian Bosnians and their revolutionary activities. He was far more sensitive to any Slav 'crusade' which might seek to 'liberate' not only the Slavs under Ottoman rule but also turn its attention to the Slavs in the Austrian Empire. The Austrians hoped the Turks would suppress their rebellious subjects without too much trouble. The revolt itself was a complicated business. The Slav peasant farmers of Bosnia and Herzegovina were both Catholic and Greek Orthodox, their feudal lords were Muslim and the social, economic and administrative structure of the Ottoman rulers was designed to keep the Catholic and Orthodox peasants in subjection. Unintentionally the visit of Emperor Francis Joseph to neighbouring Dalmatia had sparked off the rising, though as has been seen, the rebels were quite mistaken in thinking they enjoyed the sympathy of the Austrians. The autonomous neighbouring Montenegrins also fostered general unrest.

The characteristic features of the Eastern crisis from 1875 to 1877 were, first, the spread of the revolt from Bosnia and Herzegovina to Bulgaria in April 1876; then Serbia and Montenegro joining in the struggle against the Turks in July 1876. A great part of the Ottoman Empire in Europe was thus in revolt. Secondly, the Ottoman rulers in Constantinople reacted with great determination and ferocity to maintain the integrity of the empire. They were successful. The Bulgarians were suppressed, more than 12,000 inhabitants were massacred. By October 1876 the Serbians had been defeated and were on the point of collapse. Left to themselves the Turks would have suppressed all the risings, an achievement all the more remarkable as Constantinople was in turmoil. One Sultan had been deposed in May 1876, and his successor shared the same fate only a few weeks later; Abdul Hamid II, who succeeded him in September 1876, was the third Sultan in power that year. The third feature of the crisis was the ineffective intervention of the great powers, the signatories of the Peace of Paris of 1856. The growing distrust between Britain on the one hand and Russia on the other prevented any concerted action between them to force reforms and a settlement on the Turks. Thus whilst the powers condemned Turkish atrocities mutual suspicion between two out of the three most immediately involved prevented any effective action. Finally, and in many ways this was the most remarkable aspect of the Eastern crisis, the Russians and the Austrians succeeded for three years in working closely together despite their earlier suspicions of each other.

In view of Britain's generally isolationist policy and traditional support for Turkey, Russia was the only power able to put military pressure on the Turks to force them to grant more independence to the predominantly Christian subjects of the Ottoman Empire in Europe if that should prove to be the only way of restoring peace in the Balkans. But Alexander II and Gorchakov were determined to avoid the mistake of Crimea. Russia must never allow herself to become isolated again. If Austria could be reassured and brought to agree with Russian policy then Bismarck would remain benevolently neutral. Thus Britain, not Russia would find herself isolated if she chose to oppose Russian policy. For a time Russian policy succeeded very well. In May 1876 Gorchakov and Andrássy on a visit to Berlin agreed on the so-called 'Berlin Memorandum' urging the Turks to grant an armistice to the rebels and to carry through reforms. At Reichstadt in July 1876 they came to a much more far-reaching agreement. By now the fighting had spread to Serbia and Montenegro. Andrássy and Gorchakov made plans for two eventualities. If the Turks won they should be prevented from altering the status of Serbia and Montenegro. If on the other hand they lost, then they would be expelled from Europe; Austria-Hungary would take Bosnia; Greece, Serbia and Montenegro would all gain territory; Bulgaria, Roumelia and Albania would be made autonomous and Russia would regain southern Bessarabia. What happened was that the Turks won; so in conformity with the spirit of the Reichstadt agreement, the Russians threatened the Turks with intervention if they did not grant an armistice to Serbia and Montenegro. In October the Turks gave way and later that year once more allowed a conference of powers of Constantinople to propose reforms. The powers failed to act together so the reforms came to nothing.

During the course of the following year, 1877, Russian policy began to waver. The unprecedented outburst of panslav enthusiasm and propaganda in Russia may have had something to do with this. More likely Alexander II was tempted by the continued turmoil in the Ottoman Empire to try to regain southern Bessarabia for Russia and to undo this aspect of the Paris peace settlement of 1856; but whether Russia could risk going to war with Turkey would depend on Austrian acquiescence and the continued isolation of Britain. Russian policy appeared to be successful. Andrássy and Gorchakov came to two new agreements in January and March 1877, the Budapest Convention. These stipulated that Austria-Hungary would not object to Russia going to war with Turkey, provided she only fought in the eastern Balkans; Russia would receive southern Bessarabia and Austria-Hungary, Bosnia and Herzegovina; all the Balkan states would become autonomous as was already agreed at Reichstadt. Accordingly, on 24 April 1877 the Russians declared war on Turkey. They fought simultaneously in Trans-Caucasia and in Europe by advancing into Bulgaria from Rumania; but by defending the fortress of Plevna the Turks succeeded in holding up the Russian advance in Bulgaria from July to December 1877. In the end, in January 1878, Turkish resistance collapsed. The military disaster was so great that the Turks were forced to accept the terms of a Russian armistice. The armistice was followed on 3 March 1878 by the signature of the harsh peace of San Stefano. The treaty created a large autonomous state of Bulgaria which included Roumelia. This powerful Balkan state, the rest of Europe expected, would remain a close ally, even a satellite of Russia. Montenegro was greatly admired, Serbia less so, and the two states together with Rumania were granted independence. We need not trouble to enumerate all the details of the treaty soon to be challenged and revised. The treaty terms represented a victory for panrussian and panslavist ideas. But in fact Russia had overreached herself. By ignoring after all the spirit of her agreements with Austria, and by alarming the British cabinet which feared a Russian domination over the Ottoman Empire, Russia brought about the very thing she had striven to avoid – her isolation.

In London a period of hesitation was brought to an end by news of this treaty. Disraeli appointed a new foreign secretary, Lord Salisbury, who on 1 April 1878 issued a famous circular despatch to the powers which made it clear to Russia that the terms of San Stefano were unacceptable and would have to be submitted to a Congress of the European powers. Backed by the fleet sent into the Straits, the British stance convinced the Russians that they would have to back down. In Vienna, Andrássy had been just as incensed by San Stefano which he regarded as evidence of Russia's faithlessness. Russian efforts in March 1878 to calm Austrian fears did not succeed, though the possibility of a revision of the Russo-Turkish peace settlement was amicably enough discussed by Andrássy and Ignatiev who came to Vienna on a special mission. Bismarck's own position was in some ways the most interesting of all. He wished to avoid becoming involved as a principal in territorial disputes in the Balkans which he held were of no direct concern to Germany; he also wished to maintain good relations with both Austria and Russia and so offered his diplomatic mediation as 'an honest broker, who really intends to do business' in a speech to the *Reichstag*.

Caution gained the upper hand in St Petersburg. The tsar and Gorchakov had never seriously contemplated defying Europe over the 'Eastern question'. Rather they had hoped that Europe would acquiesce in a *fait accompli*. When it turned out that Britain would not accept the settlement of San Stefano, Gorchakov was prepared to revise the terms. As Britain was the chief enemy, it was with Britain the Russians decided to deal. Salisbury wished to safeguard what he could of European Turkey in the most sensitive Straits region by pushing Russia back. He therefore objected to the proposed larger Bulgaria. The skilful Peter Shuvalov, the Russian ambassador in London, was empowered to negotiate on the differences between Russia and Britain and Shuvalov conceded this point. The big Bulgaria envisaged by San Stefano was to be divided at the strategically defensible line of the Balkan mountains, and the region nearest to Turkey, now called 'Eastern Roumelia', was to be garrisoned by Turkish troops. The Anglo-Russian agreement of 30 May 1878 on this question in fact conformed reasonably closely to the earlier Austro-Russian agreements of Reichstadt and Budapest. Salisbury was less successful in obtaining Russian agreement to move back in Asiatic Turkey from the advances made by Russian troops in the Caucasus region. At the Congress of Berlin later on, a formidable clash between the viewpoints of the two powers developed on this question. To strengthen Turkey's position in Asia, Salisbury concluded the Cyprus Convention with Turkey in June 1878, whereby Britain obtained the Cyprus base, in return promising to defend Turkey against Russia – not that the Turks actually sought such protection at the price. In fact the Turks were treated without respect by all the powers. An agreement between Austria and Britain completed the diplomatic moves between the powers before the Congress met.

Bismarck was the reluctant host of the Congress of Berlin. He was anxious lest the coming together of the principal statesmen of the great powers, their clashes and their conflicts, might in the end lead to new diplomatic alignments inimical to Germany's interests. What Bismarck wanted was to preserve the Three Emperors' League, the working together of Germany, Russia and Austria and the isolation not only of France but also of Britain for he feared that if Austria looked to England for support then she would no longer need Germany's friendship and he would lose his hold over her. He therefore followed the Anglo-Austrian co-operation at the Congress with much anxiety.

The Congress of Berlin opened on 13 June 1878 and was over in exactly a month on 13 July. All things considered the Russians did well at the Congress and they enjoyed Bismarck's goodwill which was of some help as they were confronted by Austria and Britain working closely together. Russia was not humiliated. She retained southern Bessarabia, an important psychological and material gain, and in any case she had already agreed to the major concession over Bulgaria now confirmed by the Congress. Nevertheless not all was smooth sailing. After some dramatic days of crisis, the details of the Bulgarian issue were finally settled along the lines of the Anglo-Russian agreement of the previous 30 May. Disraeli and Gorchakov were the colourful principals in these disputes, but the patient work of hammering out practical agreements behind the scenes was left to Peter Shuvalov and Salisbury. Andrássy strongly backed Salisbury on the Bulgarian issue. And Salisbury backed Andrássy, who insisted that Bosnia and Herzegovina should be occupied (though not annexed) by Austria-Hungary. Serbia, Rumania and Bulgaria all achieved their formal independence. The disputes over the settlement of frontiers in Asiatic Turkey between Disraeli and Gorchakov centred on the Russian occupation and use of Batum as a naval base. The Russians got most of what they wanted and Salisbury felt that only the strong anti-Russian public feeling which developed in Britain at this time could explain the exaggerated importance accorded to this issue. As for peace and stability in the future, Disraeli and Salisbury pinned their hopes on yet another reform scheme for Turkey and on an interpretation of the Straits Convention (as revised by the London Conference in 1871, see p. 320) which would have allowed the British fleet to enter it at will.

The Congress of Berlin symbolized the new status of the German Empire and the new 'pecking order' of the European great powers. In the history of diplomacy it marks a convenient point to pause. The Eastern question was not solved. None of the participants had expected to solve it. What had been achieved was that the progressive decay of the Ottoman Empire had not involved any of the great powers in war with each other over the division of the spoils of territory and influence. By luck and statesmanship war over the decay of the Ottoman Empire was avoided altogether. When war came in 1914 it was for different reasons, the weakness not of Turkey but of the surviving multi-national empires, the Russian and the Austrian, had become a major factor of instability in Europe. These weaknesses were already evident in 1878, but the Three Emperors' League had provided a semblance of international stability. The Austro-Russian differences at the Congress shattered the Three Emperors' League. In attempting to reconstruct it, Bismarck by the end of the year 1878 stood at the great divide of his post-1871 diplomacy. He abandoned, in 1878–9, his reliance on informal alignments and set up an original structure of deterrent alliances in peace time. Such alliances are still with us; they have become a permanent feature of international relations to the present day. In 1878 also, for the first time since 1856, Britain re-emerged as a first-class power in Europe. A final point about the crucial changes that divide the pre- and post-1878 periods: though there were indications before 1878 that imperial rivalries would play a role in the relations of the great powers, this role only became an important one after 1878.

During the thirty years covered by this volume the changes in Europe domestically and internationally were startlingly great. One is finally left with an impression that these years mark the 'take off' period when Europe began to hurtle at an ever-accelerating pace towards the cataclysmic changes of the twentieth century.

Further Reading

General histories

There are a number of sound general histories. Two volumes in the American *Rise of Modern Europe* series cover this period: they are Robert C. Binkley, *Realism and Nationalism 1852–1871* (New York, 1935) and William L. Langer, *Political and Social Upheaval, 1832–1852* (New York, 1969). Volume x of *The New Cambridge Modern History, 1830–1870*, ed. by J. P. T. Bury, is useful but suffers a little from attempting to cover too much in the space available so that the major aspects of political and social history have been very compressed allowing for little interpretation. A good French synthesis is vol. XVI in the *Peuples et civilisations* series, by Charles H. Pouthas, *Démocraties et capitalisme 1848–1860* (Paris, 1961), and vol. XVII by H. Hauser, J. Maurain, P. Benaert, *Du libéralisme à l'imperialisme, 1860–1878* (Paris, 1952). A German general history is the *Propyläen Weltgeschichte*, volume VIII, edited by Golo Mann (Berlin, 1960). Among the best treatments of nineteenth-century European history by British historians is R. Leslie, *The Age of Transformation 1789–1871* (London, 1964), H. Hearder, *Europe in the Nineteenth Century 1830–1880* (London, 1966), and D. Thomson, *Europe since Napoleon* (Harmondsworth, 1966). R. Gildea, *Barricades and Borders: Europe 1800–1914* (Oxford, second edition, 1996), offers a thematic approach covering wide issues, culture, race, society, less on political and diplomatic, but with an extensive bibliography.

The best account of European economic history is the *Fontana Economic History of Europe*, ed. Carlo M. Cipolla (London, 1953). The nineteenth century is dealt with in two volumes, nation by nation, by a number of authors, and has not generally been superseded. A useful textbook is S. B. Clough and C. W. Cole, *Economic History of Europe* (Boston, 1952). Sound but heavy going is A. S. Milward and S. B. Saul, *The Economic Development of Continental Europe*, vol. I (London, 1973); the best single volume economic histories as introduction, S. Pollard, *Peaceful Conquest. The Industrialisation of Europe 1760–1970* (Oxford, 1982), M. Teich and R. Porter editors, *The Industrial Revolution in National Context: Europe and the U.S.A* (Cambridge, 1996) and for Britain, P. Mathias, *The First*

Industrial Nation: An Economic History of Britain 1700–1914 (London, 1983); on the impact of war, G. Best, *War and Society in Revolutionary Europe* (London, 1982).

A general account of political thought is to be found in John Bowle, *Politics and Opinions in the Nineteenth Century* (London, 1954). George H. Sabine, *A History of Political Theory* (New York, 1950) is a sound introduction. For nationalism, Boyd O. Shafer, *Nationalism: Myth and Reality* (New York, 1955) provides an exhaustive analysis which reveals the difficulties of definitions. Hans Kohn, *Prophets and Peoples: Studies in 19th Century Nationalism* (New York, 1941) is stimulating; the same author's *Nationalism: its Meaning and History* (New York, 1955) is an excellent introduction with readings. A good summary of ideas and reflections on nationalism is Carlton J. Hayes, *Essays on Nationalism* (New York, 1966). Also interesting is E. Kedourie, *Nationalism*, 3rd edition (London, 1966).

Socialism, as a broad movement, can be studied in G. D. H. Cole, *A History of Socialist Thought*, vols. 1 and 2 (London, 1953); for the liberal tradition, G. de Ruggiero, *History of European Liberalism* (Oxford, 1927); Irene Collins, *Liberalism in Nineteenth Century Europe* (London, 1971) is a useful introductory essay published as an Historical Association pamphlet. George Lichtheim, *Marxism* (London, 1961) is a stimulating analysis and O. J. Hammen, *The Red '48ers* (New York, 1969) places Marx, Engels and their associates in their contemporary historical setting.

A general textbook of international relations is R. Albrecht-Carrié, *A Diplomatic History of Europe since the Congress of Vienna* (London, 1958). For a Soviet view see V. P. Potemkine, *Histoire de la diplomatie*, translated from the Russian (Paris, 1946–47); the distinguished French historian, P. Renouvin, in two volumes covers *Le XIX siècle* (Paris, 1954–55) in the series *Histoire des relations internationales*. A. J. P. Taylor's *The Struggle for Mastery in Europe 1848–1918* (Oxford, 1954) analyses the period with originality and insight. E. J. Hobsbawm, *The Age of Capital 1848–1875* (London, 1975), is a vivid analysis and personal interpretation of the changing 'Capitalist Economy' and of its impact on society.

General national histories

FRANCE: There is a good choice of one- or two-volume histories covering the nineteenth century. Alfred Cobban's *A History of Modern France*, vol. 2, *1799–1871* and vol. 3 *1871–1961* (Harmondsworth, 1961) is a pleasure to read and provides insights and interpretations. There is also J. P. T. Bury, *France 1814–1940*, 3rd edition (London, 1959), and J. P. Plamenatz, *The Revolutionary Movement in France, 1815–1871* (London, 1952). More recent two excellent histories are R. Magraw, *France 1815–1914: The Bourgeois Century* (London, 1983) and P. McPhee, *A Social History of France 1780–1880* (London, 1992); an entertaining and illuminating brief guide to the cycles of French history and their tenacious hold on French imaginations, is P. M. Jones, *1789 and All That: Constructing Identity in Modern France* (Birmingham University, 1985); F. Furet, *Revolutionary France 1770–1880* (Blackwell, 1996).

GERMAN STATES: From a number of available histories the following are all good: W. Carr, *A History of Germany 1815–1990* (London, 1991); Hajo Holborn, *A History of Modern Germany 1840–1945* (London, 1969); K. S. Pinson, *Modern Germany* (2nd edition, London, 1966); R. Flenley, *Modern German History* (London, 1964); A. Ramm, *Germany, 1789–1918* (London, 1967); G. Mann's *The History of Germany since 1789* (Harmondsworth, 1974) is in a class of its own; it is a very personal and brilliant commentary on the course of modern German history. An illuminating interpretation is J. Breuilly, *The Formation of the First German Nation–State 1800–1871* (London, 1996); for the best comprehensive authoritative accounts, two Oxford histories, J. H. Sheehan, *German History 1770–1866* (Oxford, 1889) and G. Craig, *Germany 1866–1945* (Oxford, 1978); E. D. Brose, *German History 1789–1871* (Berghahn, 1997).

ITALIAN STATES: D. Mack Smith, *The Making of Italy, 1796–1870* (London, 1968) covers the period in documents and long-linking commentaries. It is followed by the same author's *Italy, a Modern History* (Ann Arbor, 1959); R. Albrecht-Carrié, *Italy from Napoleon to Mussolini* (New York, 1950), H. Hearder, *Italy in the Age of the Risorgimento 1790–1870* (London, 1983) is an excellent overview.

HABSBURG EMPIRE: The best single volume work in English is C. A. Macartney, *The Habsburg Empire 1790–1918* (London, 1968). The best study in German is Erich Zöllner, *Geschichte Österreichs* (4th edition, Munich, 1970). Also of value are A. J. P. Taylor, *The Habsburg Monarchy 1815–1918* (London, 1941). A. J. May, *The Habsburg Monarchy 1867–1914* (Cambridge, Mass., 1951). R. Kann, *The Multinational Empire: Nationalism and National Reform in the Habsburg Monarchy 1848–1918*, 2 vols. (New York, 1964). A. Sked, *The Decline and Fall of the Habsburg Empire* (London, 1989) and F. R. Bridge, *The Habsburg Monarchy among the Great Powers* (Oxford, 1990) update the classic histories. From a Hungarian focus, Jörg H. Hoensch, *A History of Modern Hungary 1867–1994* (Longman, 1996) is brief and basic but useful.

RUSSIA: The outstanding general history is M. T. Florinsky, *Russia: A History and an Interpretation*, vol. 2 (London, 1947). For detailed analyses and narrative, H. Seton-Watson, *The Russian Empire 1801–1917* (Oxford, 1967); a good and briefer recent survey is J. N. Westwood, *Endurance and Endeavour: Russian History 1812–1992* (Oxford, 1993).

BRITAIN: Asa Briggs' *The Age of Improvement, 1783–1867* (London, 1959) is an outstandingly good survey. E. L. Woodward's *The Age of Reform 1815–70* (Oxford, 1938), though inevitably dated, is still useful. Readable and stimulating still is E. Halévy's four-volume, *A History of the*

English People in the Nineteenth Century (London, 1926–34). K. T. Hoppen, *The Mid-Victorian Generation 1846–1886* (Oxford, 1998) fills a need for an authoritative broadly conceived history of the period, significant too, for giving due attention to Scotland, Wales and Ireland; E. J. Fenchtwanger provides a judicious synthesis in, *Democracy and Empire: Britain 1865–1914* (London, 1985). A good survey is R. Shannon, *The Age of Disraeli 1868–1881: The Rise of Tory Democracy* (London, 1992).

OTHER COUNTRIES: Raymond Carr, *Spain, 1808–1939* (Oxford, 2nd edition, 1982); H. V. Livermore, *A New History of Portugal* (Cambridge, 1966); E. Bonjour, H. S. Offler and G. R. Potter, *A Short History of Switzerland* (Oxford, 1952). B. J. Hovde, *The Scandinavian Countries, 1720–1865*, 2 vols. (Boston, 1943). L. S. Stavrianos, *The Balkans since 1453* (New York, 1958); R. W. Seton-Watson, *A History of the Czechs and Slovaks* (London, 1943). R. W. Seton-Watson, *A History of the Roumanians* (Cambridge, 1934). B. Lewis, *The Emergence of Modern Turkey* (London, 1961). J. C. Beckett, *The Making of Modern Ireland, 1603–1823* (London, 1966). D. Dakin, *The Unification of Greece 1770–1923* (London, 1972). E. H. Kossman, *The Low Countries 1780–1940* (Oxford, 1978); two outstanding studies are R. Clogg, *A Short History of Modern Greece* (Cambridge, 1979), and C. M. Woodhouse, *Modern Greece. A Short History*, 4th edition, (London, 1986); a classic in translation is, O. Haleki, *A History of Poland* (London, 1986) and the excellent second volume by Norman Davies, *God's Playground: A History of Poland* (Oxford, 1987); R. Okey, *Eastern Europe 1740–1985* (London, 1986) is a reliable survey; R. Crampton, *A Short History of Modern Bulgaria* (Cambridge, 1987); M. S. Anderson, *The Eastern Question, 1774–1923* (London, 1966).

The revolutions of 1848–1849

It is difficult to find a one-volume history which deals equally well with all aspects of the revolutions and succeeds in making any penetrating generalizations. Priscilla Robertson, *Revolutions of 1848: a Social Study* (Princeton, 1952) is a lively narrative which makes the attempt. Several historians have contributed to *The Opening of an Era, 1848* (London, 1948) ed. by Francois Fejtö. This work, though uneven, is the best of the compilations published during the centenary year. There are also many useful specialist contributions published in the *Actes de Congrès Historique du Centenaire de la Revolutions de 1848* (Paris, 1948). A short work by an eminent historian, stimulating, idiosyncratic, and whose argument is not always easy to follow is Lewis B. Namier's *1848: the Revolution of the Intellectuals* (London, 1944). The more recent general and readable assessment, making some interesting new points is P. N. Stearns', *The Revolutions of 1848* (London, 1974). The revolutions also have to be studied in books devoted to particular countries. The following are of particular value:

FRANCE: Roger Price, *The French Second Republic: A Social History* (London, 1972) and the same author's, *The Revolution of 1848* (London, 1989); F. le Luna, *The French Republic under Cavaignac, 1848* (Princeton, 1969). D. McKay, *The National Workshops* (Cambridge, Mass., 1965) and Georges Duveau, *1848: The Making of a Revolution* (New York, 1966); a revealing contemporary analysis is Karl Marx, *The Class Struggles in France, 1848–50*; for the Communist Manifesto, H. J. Laski, *The Communist Manifesto: Socialist Landmark* (London, 1948); and the most frequently cited contemporary comment is A. de Tocqueville, *The Recollections of Alexis de Tocqueville* (New York, 1949).

PRUSSIA AND THE GERMAN STATES: The monumental two-volume study by V. Valentin, *Geschichte der deutschen Revolution 1848–49* (Berlin, 1930–31) remains the unsurpassed detailed narrative account. Some parts of it were translated in *1848: Chapters of German History* (London, 1940); a good study is J. Droz, *Les Révolutions allemandes de 1848* (Paris, 1957) and the best recent German study is R. Stadelmann, *Soziale und politische Geschichte der Revolution von 1848* (Munich, 1956). F. Eyck's *The Frankfurt Parliament 1848–49* (London, 1968) is an authoritative analysis of the work and composition of this often maligned body.

HABSBURG EMPIRE: The complexity of the situation in the various parts of the Empire has defeated even Austrian historians. Light is thrown on the confusion by C. A. Macartney, *The Habsburg Empire 1790–1918*, see under National Histories. Also, R. J. Rath, *The Viennese Revolution of 1848* (Austin, 1957). R. A. Kann, *The Multinational Empire: Nationalism and National Reform in the Habsburg Monarchy 1848–1918*, 2 vols. (New York, 1964). R. Kiszling, and other contributors, *Die Revolution im Kaisertum Österreich 1848–1849* (Vienna, 2 vols. 1948 and 1952). S. Z. Pech, *The Czech Revolution of 1848* (North Carolina, 1969).

ITALY: There is little new work in English specializing on the '1848' movements in the Italian peninsula. The most detailed treatment is still G. F.-H. Berkeley, *Italy in the Making, June 1846 to January 1848* (Cambridge, 1936) and *Italy in the Making, January 1848 to November 1848* (Cambridge, 1940).

BRITAIN: There is a vast literature on working class and radical movements, see especially: Dorothy Thompson, *The Early Chartists* (London, 1971); F. C. Mather, *Public Order in the Age of the Chartists* (Manchester, 1959). G. D. H. Cole, *Chartist Portraits* (London, 1941); J. T. Ward (ed.) *Popular Movements c.1830–1850* (London, 1970); R. Schoyen, *The Chartist Challenge: A portrait of George J. Harney* (London, 1958); for an older comprehensive, well-written narrative see J. L. and B. Hammond, *The Age of the Chartists* (London, 1930).

France: Louis Napoleon, the Second Republic and the Second Empire

F. A. Simpson's two illuminating volumes remain the best detailed treatment of Napoleon III's rule to 1856, *The Rise of Louis Napoleon* (3rd edition, London, 1950), and *Louis Napoleon and the Recovery of France 1848–1856* (3rd edition, London, 1951). For the Second Republic see also F. de Luna, *The French Republic under Cavaignac, 1848* (Princeton, 1969). There are two good studies of Napoleon III, J. P. T. Bury, *Napoleon III and the Second Empire* (London, 1964) and J. M. Thompson, *Louis Napoleon and the Second Empire* (Oxford, 1954); an earlier work of interest is A. L. Guérard, *Napoleon III* (Cambridge, Mass., 1943), also T. A. B. Corley, *Democratic Despot. A Life of Napoleon III* (London, 1961); G. P. Gooch's, *The Second Empire* (London, 1960) is a readable survey. T. Zeldin's researches have made a substantial contribution to our knowledge of politics and society during the Second Empire, especially in *The Political System of Napoleon III* (London, 1958) and in *Emile Ollivier and the Liberal Empire of Napoleon III* (Oxford, 1963). Two interesting books dealing with special aspects are, C. S. Phillips, *The Church in France 1848–1907* (London, 1936) and I. Collins, *The Government and the Newspaper Press in France 1814–1881* (London, 1959); an excellent brief synthesis, J. F. McMillan, *Napoleon III* (London 1991).

The Italian states in the period of unification

An excellent biography which throws much light on the *Risorgimento* is Jasper Ridley, *Garibaldi* (London, 1974); Christopher Hibbert, *Garibaldi and his enemies* (London, 1965), is also good. The best brief survey is Derek Beales, *The Risorgimento and the Unification of Italy* (London, 1971). D. Mack Smith, *Cavour and Garibaldi 1860* (Cambridge, 1954) was a provocative analysis based on a wealth of archival research which did much to change the direction of *risorgimento* studies; the same author's *Victor Emmanuel, Cavour and the Risorgimento* (Oxford, 1971) is a penetrating collection of interlocking studies. The best narrative life of Cavour in English, though now dated by more recent research, is A. J. Whyte's, *The Early Life and Letters of Cavour 1810–1848* (Oxford, 1925) and *The Political Life and Letters of Cavour, 1848–1861* (Oxford, 1930). H. Hearder's Historical Association pamphlet on *Cavour* (London, 1972) is an excellent introduction to the subject. A. Ramm reviews historiographical trends in another Historical Association pamphlet, the *Risorgimento* (London, 1972). The following books throw valuable light on different aspects of Italian history: Raymond Grew, *A Sterner Plan for Italian Unity: the Italian National Society in the Risorgimento* (Princeton, 1963); H. Acton, *The Last Bourbons of Naples, 1825–1861* (London, 1961); Giorgio Candeloro, *Storia dell' Italia moderna*, vol. 4 (Milan, 1964) is said to be the best Italian survey and S. B. Clough, *Economic History of Modern Italy* (New York, 1964) a good economic history.

Britain at Home and Abroad

Besides K. T. Hoppen with a full bibliography and R. Shannon already cited, H. Perkins, *Origins of Modern English Society* (London, 1967) is a thought provoking analysis, R. Blake, for the classic biography, *Disraeli* (London, 1967) and P. Smith, *Disraeli: A Brief Life* (Cambridge, 1996); P. Magnus, has an older readable biography of *Gladstone* (London, 1954), really superseded by Gladstone's authoritative biographer and editor of his diaries, H. C. G. Matthew, *Gladstone 1809–1898* (Oxford, 1997); on the formation of parties, H. J. Hanham, *Elections and Party Management: Politics in the Time of Disraeli and Gladstone* (London, 1959) and J. Vincent, *The Formation of the Liberal Party, 1857–1868* (London, 1966); still well worth reading for ideas, is G. Kitson Clark, *The Making of Victorian England* (London, 1962); the most detailed analysis of British policy toward continental Europe only in German based on the archives is K. Hildebrand, *No Intervention. Die Pax Britanica und Preussen 1865–1870* (Munich, 1997); K. Bourne, *The Foreign Policy of Victorian England 1830–1902* (Oxford, 1970) for a sound survey; also, C. J. Bartlett, *Defence and Diplomacy: Britain and the Great Powers, 1815–1914* (Manchester, 1993); for the early phases of imperialism, C. C. Eldridge, *England's Mission: The Imperial Idea in the Age of Gladstone and Disraeli, 1868– 1880* (London, 1973).

German unification

The subject is frequently analysed in the context of biographical treatments of Bismarck. The classic modern biography in German is Erich Eyck's *Bismarck*, 3 vols. (Zürich, 1941–44); some of the arguments of that magisterial study can be obtained from the briefer *Bismarck and the German Empire* (London, 1950). A sound and readable biography is Werner Richter's *Bismarck*, available in an English translation (London, 1964); an older readable biography is A. J. P. Taylor's, *Bismarck: The Man and the Statesman* (London, 1955). The best brief study, with more emphasis and analysis on policy is W. N. Medlicott's *Bismarck and Modern Germany* (London, 1965). E. N. Anderson, *The Social and Political Conflict in Prussia 1858– 1864* (Lincoln, Neb., 1954) is a good monograph. For an authoritative full study of domestic and foreign policies, O. Pflanze, *Bismarck and the Development of Germany, 1815–71* (Princeton, 1965). Bismarck's diplomacy in a short collection of documents translated into English with commentary can be studied in W. N. Medlicott and D. K. Coveney, *Bismarck and Europe* (London, 1971). An important treatment of European diplomacy during the years of unification is W. E. Mosse, *The European Powers and the German Question, 1848–1878* (Cambridge, 1958). An attempt to get away from an entirely Bismarck-centred view of German history in this period is H. Böhme's *Deutschland Weg zur Grossmacht* (Berlin, 1966); Böhme's major arguments can be usefully studied in a brief collection of documents translated into English with a number of introductions entitled, *The Foundation of the German Empire* (Oxford, 1971).

More specialized topics are dealt with in the following books: L. Bergsträsser, *Geschichte der politischen Parteien in Deutschland* (7th edition, Munich, 1952); W. Carr, *Schleswig-Holstein, 1815–1848* (Manchester, 1963); W. O. Henderson, *The Zollverein* (2nd edition, London, 1959); L. D. Steefel, *Bismarck, the Hohenzollern Candidacy and the Origins of the Franco-German War of 1870* (Cambridge, Mass., 1962); for the documents on the Hohenzollern candidacy translated into English, G. Bonnin, *Bismarck and the Hohenzollern Candidature for the Throne of Spain* (London, 1957). Prussia's and Germany's social history and political ideas are brilliantly discussed in two volumes by Theodore S. Hamerow, entitled *The Social Foundations of German Unification: Ideas and Institutions 1858–1871* (Princeton, 1969) and *Struggles and Accomplishments* (Princeton, 1972). For one penetrating contemporary view, F. Engels, *The Rôle of Force in History. A study of Bismarck's policy of blood and iron*, introduction by E. Wangermann (London, 1968). A biography translated from the German, is, L. Gall, *Bismarck: The White Revolutionary* (2 vols, London, 1990); a perspicacious brief account, is, W. Carr, *The Origins of the Wars of German Unification* (London, 1996).

We are not nearly as well served when it comes to an analysis of the policies of the other German states and of the Habsburg Empire. But for Bavaria, M. Doeberl, *Entwicklungsgeschichte Bayerns*, volume 3 (Munich, 1931) is especially useful. This period is dealt with in the general histories of the Habsburg Empire already cited. The classic analysis of the Austro-Prussian conflict is H. Friedjung's, *Der Kampf um die Vorherrschaft in Deutschland* (Stuttgart, 1897), translated into English and abridged as *The Struggle for Supremacy in Germany* (London, 1935); of value is C. W. Halberg, *Franz Joseph and Napoleon III 1852–64* (New York, 1955); the later years of Austrian foreign policy can be studied in a detailed analysis by H. Potthof, *Die deutsche Politik Beust (1866–1871)* (Bonn, 1968). An authoritative treatment of the history of the Habsburg Empire in German during this period was undertaken by Josef Redlich in his biography, *Kaiser Franz Joseph von Österreich* (Berlin, 1928) and in his two-volume *Das österreichische Staats – und Reichsproblem* (Leipzig, 1926).

Diplomacy: mainly the Eastern Question, 1848–1878

M. S. Anderson's, *The Eastern Question 1774–1923* (London, 1966) is a reliable synthesis of recent work. On the origins of the Crimean War the best study remains, H. W. V. Temperley, *England and the Near East: The Crimea* (London, 1936); also G. B. Henderson, *Crimean War Diplomacy and other Historical Essays* (Glasgow, 1947).

The diplomatic consequences are analysed by W. E. Mosse, *The Rise and Fall of the Crimean System, 1855–1871: the Story of a Peace Settlement* (London, 1963); also see, T. W. Riker, *The Making of Roumania: a Study of an International Problem, 1856–1866* (Oxford, 1931). For the later phases,

B. H. Sumner, *Russia and the Balkans, 1870–1880* (Oxford, 1937); R. H. Davison, *Reform in the Ottoman Empire, 1856–1876* (Princeton, 1963); R. T. Shannon's excellent *Gladstone and the Bulgarian Agitation, 1876* (London, 1963) is an original study. The standard work on the Congress of Berlin is W. N. Medlicott's, *The Congress of Berlin and After* (London, 1938). For an important sound reassessment of the early years of Bismarck's diplomacy after 1870 see Bruce Waller's *Bismarck at the Crossroads* (London, 1974). The most comprehensive and best general treatment of European diplomacy is still W. L. Langer's, *European Alliances and Alignments, 1871–1890* (2nd edition, New York, 1956). The Crimean War in its military aspects can be studied in Christopher Hibbert, *The Destruction of Lord Raglan* (London, 1961); O. Anderson, *A Liberal State at War: English Politics and Economics during the Crimean War* (London, 1967); J. S. Curtiss, *The Russian Army under Nicholas I* (Durham, N. C., 1965) and B. D. Gooch, *The New Bonapartist Generals in the Crimean War* (Hague, 1959). For Habsburg diplomacy F. R. Bridge's excellent *From Sadowa to Sarajevo* (London, 1972).

Reform in the Russian Empire

Besides the general histories already mentioned, the following books are of particular value. For a good introduction, W. E. Mosse, *Alexander II and the Modernisation of Russia* (London, 1958). The history of rural Russia, the emancipation and its consequences are authoritatively analysed in G. T. Robinson, *Rural Russia under the Old Regime* (New York, 1932); Poland played an important role and may be studied in R. F. Leslie, *Reform and Insurrection in Russian Poland 1856–1865* (London, 1963). For a critical and fascinating contemporary view, *The Memoirs of Alexander Herzen*, parts 1 and 2, translated by J. D. Duff (New Haven, 1923).

The Franco-Prussian War and the early years of the Third Republic

The best detailed history of the war seen in the wider context of war preparations and strategic planning, is Michael Howard, *The Franco-Prussian War* (London, 1968). W. R. Fryer, 'The War of 1870 in the Pattern of Franco-German Relations', *Renaissance and Modern Studies 1974* is an interesting survey and critique. The standard multi-volume history of the Third Republic is that by J. Chastenet, *Histoire de la Troisième République, 1870–1940* in 7 volumes (Paris, 1952–1963). G. Chapman provides a good treatment in English in *The Third Republic of France*, vol. 1, 1871–1894 (London, 1962). A good introduction is D. W. Brogan, *The Development of Modern France, 1870–1939*, new edition (London, 1967); an old work containing much fascinating detail and interesting to read is J. E. C. Bodley, *France*, 2 vols. (London, 1898); another recent individual approach to French politics and society is T. Zeldin's *France 1848–1945. Ambition,*

Love and Politics (Oxford, 1973). J. P. T. Bury has analysed the early years of the republic in *Gambetta and the Making of the Third Republic* (London, 1973); D. B. Ralston, *The Army of the Republic* (Cambridge, Mass, 1967) discusses an important aspect.

There is a large literature on the *Commune*; Eugene Schulkind provides a good introductory essay in an Historical Association pamphlet, *The Paris Commune of 1871* (London, 1971); among histories in English the following three books are recent and useful; A. Horne, *The Fall of Paris: The Siege and the Commune 1870–71* (London, 1965); Stewart Edwards, *The Paris Commune 1871* (London, 1971) and R. L. Williams, *The French Revolution, 1870–1871* (London, 1969).

Index